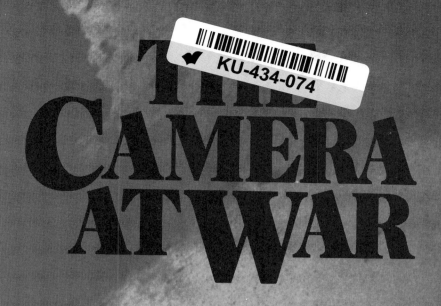

THE
CAMERA
AT WAR

A history of war photography from 1848 to the present day

Jorge Lewinski

BY THE SAME AUTHOR

Photography – A Dictionary of
Photographers, Terms and Techniques

Byron's Greece
Jorge Lewinski with Elizabeth Longford

Colour in Focus
Jorge Lewinski with Bob Clark

Set in 'Monophoto' Ehrhardt

Printed and bound in Great Britain by W & J Mackay Limited, Chatham
for the publishers, W. H. Allen & Co. Ltd
44 Hill Street, London W1X 8LB

ISBN 0 491 02485 1

Contents

Acknowledgements

First I should like to thank Francis Bennett without whose support this book would not have appeared, Sue Hogg for her invaluable help in editing and in checking a thousand and one details, Nancy Hammerman for her encouragement throughout, and especially Gary Woodhouse for his professional and dedicated help with the picture research. The assistance of John Swain and Derrick Knight is also very much appreciated.

I am greatly indebted to Philip Knightley for his generous permission to quote extensively from *The First Casualty*. This book and his personal comments have provided me with innumerable hints and information which I most gratefully acknowledge. I should also like to thank O. D. Gallagher for his reminiscences and recollections.

Above all thanks are due to the many photographers who gave permission for their pictures to be included in this book. I would like to extend specific thanks to some of those who gave generously of their time for the interviews and discussions – William Rider-Rider, Bert Hardy, Bert Curry, Don McCullin, Philip Jones Griffiths, Bela Zola, Terry Fincher, Ian Berry, Romano Cagnoni, Catherine Leroy, Sally Soames, Clive Limpkin, Tony McGrath and Neil Libbert.

It would be impossible to mention all those who have helped me in my attempt to provide as much material on war photography as possible. To all those whose names do not appear, I apologize most profoundly.

Introduction

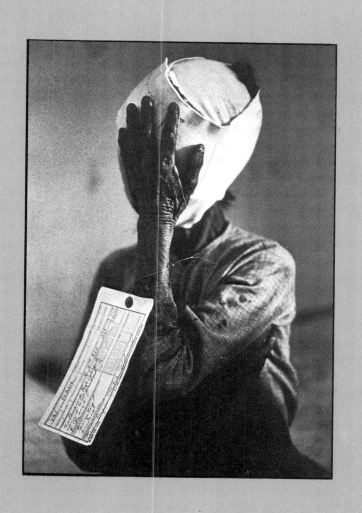

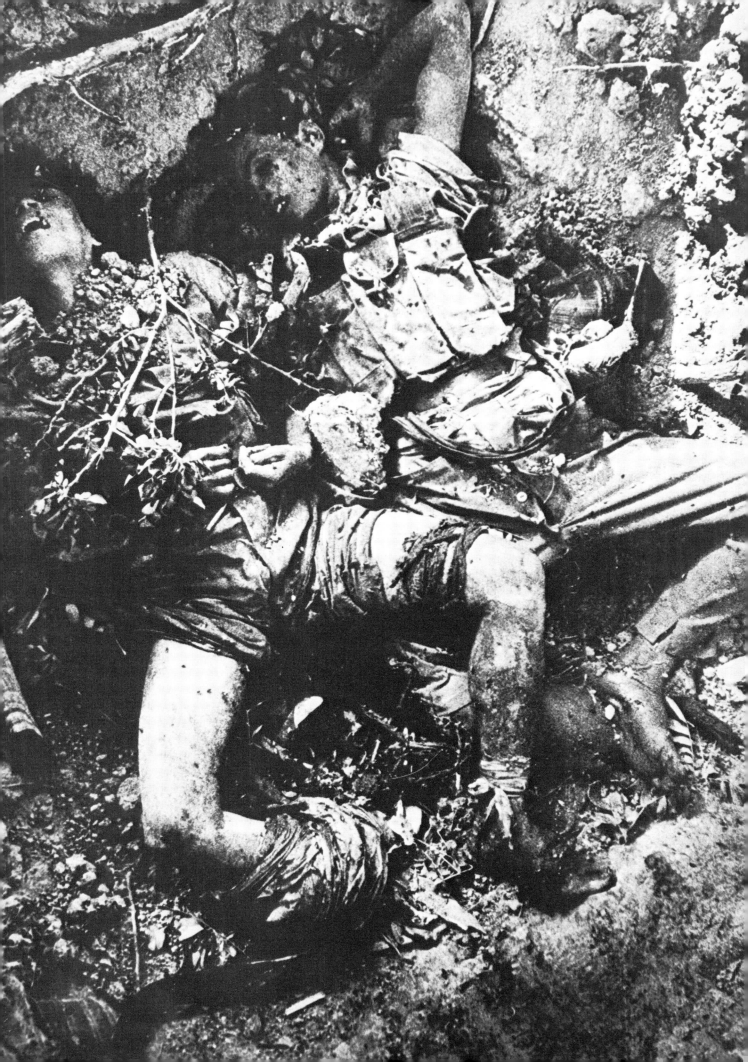

I started off as such a simple, little man once upon a time. I just wanted to walk around and photograph people in the streets with my camera. And I seemed to find myself being arrested, beaten around sometimes by soldiers, being accused in Africa of being a mercenary, and locked up. And I, over and over, ask myself – You are supposed to be a photographer, why are you in jail in Africa, why are you afraid, why are you saying a prayer with some other men in prison, and why is the man next to you sliding down a wall with dried blood on his head? And, at the end of the day, you have lived more in one day than some people would live in their whole lives.

Those are Don McCullin's words, at the start of a BBC television interview in 1977. Not all war photographers would think and speak in such terms about their profession; nevertheless, as we shall find, McCullin's statement is a fair representation of the attitude of many of them.

In the last thirty years war photography has come of age. It has acquired authority, skill, and vision, and, in the process, has made its mark on how we see and think about war in a way in which the first exponents in the nineteenth century could never have dreamed possible. War photographs have become a staple diet of many people throughout the world. Certainly since the Second World War there has been an abundance of subject matter for the war photographers, but at the same time people have become increasingly intrigued, and also perhaps fascinated, by the activity of warfare itself. The men and women who provide food to satisfy this constant hunger for war images have thereby attained, in some cases, a measure of star status and acclaim. But many have suffered, indeed died, in their pursuit of fame and riches in this dangerous and exhilarating profession. Seeing and recording pain and death inevitably affect a human being. Some photographers have become callous and unfeeling; others, like McCullin, disenchanted and unhappy. Photographing war changes the photographer, for better or for worse, just as war itself has changed the face of the world.

The twentieth century has done little to preserve man's traditional concepts and beliefs. The last seventy years has wrought great changes, not only in our way of life, but also in our basic attitudes and our understanding of life itself. Our fundamental assumptions about the nature of matter and energy were thoroughly shaken by the theory of relativity and by the emergence of new theories of genetics and the origins of life. New insights into man's psyche and behaviour have overturned previously held ideas. The explosion in communications has shrunk the world from a vague infinity to a pebble, bringing us closer to one another. The quintessential constructs of human existence – the family, religious beliefs, art, morality, sex – are being subjected to a profound reappraisal.

It is not surprising, therefore, that in this process of reassessment, our attitude to war, one of life's seemingly integral parts, intermittently but inexorably present throughout history, has also undergone a change. War was seen by many as 'a part of man's fate, part of animal heritage and biological development', the oldest phenomenon in recorded history. Not only was it considered part of our fate, it was invariably and readily regarded as justifiable, even indispensable. 'The war that is necessary is just, and hallowed are the arms where no hope exists but for them,' wrote Livy. The idea that war might be unjust, for aggressive rather than for defensive purposes, is a relatively new one. Throughout history, 'the strong did what they could while the weak suffered what they must.' Wars were fought for many, various reasons, but rarely for the ideal of freedom. To question their morality or justification was a futile exercise.

The paradox is that while history records one long bloodbath, many writers and thinkers have found much that is beneficial and positive in war. For Theodore Roosevelt and Oliver Wendell Holmes, war represented 'a moral tonic for citizens of healthy nations'. Both William James and William McDougall maintained that war brought out the best traits in man – heroism, selflessness, courage, friendship. They provided optimum stimulation, made the blood run quicker, while satisfying that craving for excitement which is so much a part of human need. As the psychologist Abraham Maslow suggests, war brings to men's humdrum existence a 'peak experience', a red-letter day.

If this were the end of the story, there would be little hope for the human race. Sooner or later, with individual aggression being constantly translated into major confrontation, the time would come when the war to end all wars would blow our planet apart. This may yet happen, but in our changing attitudes we can find one ray of hope. Some anthropologists, among them Margaret Mead, believe that although there is no denying the existence of man's aggressive instincts, these do not have inevitably to be formalized, in the higher-order civilizations, into communally aggressive acts of war. In her essay, 'Warfare is only an invention, not a biological necessity', Mead argues just that. According to her, warfare is only 'an invention like any other invention in terms of which we order our lives, such as writing, marriage, cooking our food instead of eating it raw, trial by jury or burial of the dead and so on.'

We may not yet be ready or sophisticated enough to accept a new invention to obviate warfare, but there are signs at least that our attitudes to the inevitability and acceptability of war are changing. If we look back no more than sixty years to 1915, and consider the response to Field Marshal Kitchener's famous appeal for volunteers after the initial severe reverses of the Allies on the Western Front, should we expect a similar response to such an appeal today? A response that takes the form of half a million men rushing to enlist in the

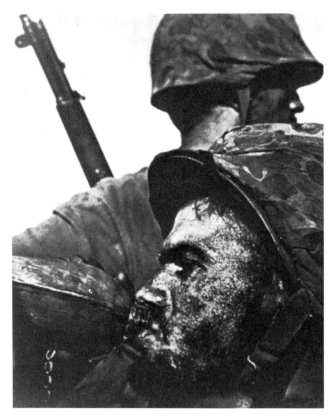

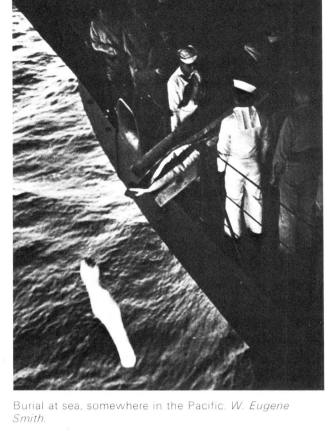

Two American marines, Saipan, Pacific, 1944.
W. Eugene Smith.

Burial at sea, somewhere in the Pacific. *W. Eugene
Smith.*

first three weeks, with the total number of those willing
to die for their country eventually swelling to two
million? It is more likely to be the response of the draft-
dodgers in the USA, and of the drug-addicted army
in Vietnam, which culminated in the almost nation-
wide rejection of America's involvement in the East; or
the response of French youth demonstrating in the
streets of Paris against the war in Algeria. Even in the
thirties, the Chamberlain government, prompted by
strong public feeling, vacillated about the need for war
with Germany. In the Second World War itself, a
lengthy period of propaganda was required to drum up
the necessary hatred of the 'Hun'. Today the call
'Better dead than red', or more likely 'Better dead than
a slave', sounds positively hollow. In any case, the
nature of war has been totally transformed. It is no
longer a matter of personal sacrifice for a cause. There
seems to be no cause big enough or important enough
to draw men together. Modern war is not so much a
flexing of individual muscle; it is the probability of
total annihilation. In such a war, there would not be the
attraction of the 'peak experience'.

Today the average man in the street in New York or
Paris, Buenos Aires or Sydney, looks at war from a
diametrically opposed view to that of his counterpart in
the 1920s. There are indeed exceptions, such as Israel
or South Africa, where young men are conditioned,
morally and psychologically, to accept the idea of

waging war in defence of their possessions or beliefs.
But they are the odd men out, out of tune with the rest
of the world. For most of us, the face of war has become
totally repellent. The aspect that it wears is un-
equivocally odious, suffused with cruelty, evil, hatred,
and degenerate indifference to suffering. It no longer
shines as something heroic, adventurous, uplifting,
worthwhile for a cause, or even something to be
stoically endured because it is unavoidable. The face of
war has become too dreadful to contemplate. It has
simply to be avoided, to be fought against. Many are
fighting now to prevent another war.

How much this drastic change of attitude has been
influenced by the flood of war images in the media, we
cannot tell. But they have played a significant part. The
first signs of a change of attitude can be traced to the
First World War, in which the unprecedented scale of
the death toll, although it was appallingly misrep-
resented both in print and in pictures at the time, was
finally understood. However late, however much dis-
guised, the facts of nine million dead and twenty-one
million injured were eventually made public. So too
were countless horror stories, used as propaganda by
the ruling classes, to awaken the public to the beastliness
of the enemy. Reports of the sinking of passenger liners
like the *Lusitania* by German U-boats, summary
shootings of prisoners, rape of women in occupied
territories, executions of civilians like Nurse Edith

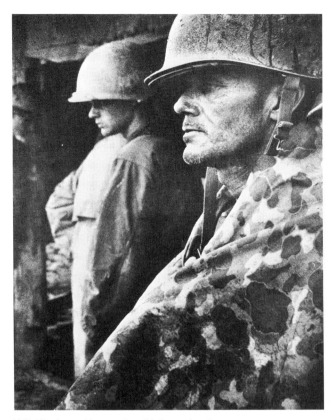

U S Marines, Korea. *David Douglas Duncan.*

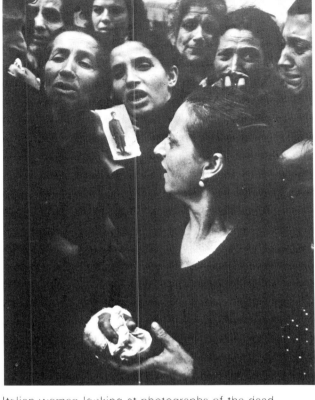

Italian women looking at photographs of the dead, Naples, 1943. *Robert Capa.*

Cavell, usually greatly exaggerated and sometimes completely unfounded, created in the public mind a picture of the Germans as fiends, monsters and barbarians. At the same time, they served to give a composite image of war as evil beyond belief. Photographs of war activities, though scant and uninformative during the war, finally started to surface after the armistice. A comprehensive book of war photographs, published by the *Daily Express*, did not appear until 1933, but some smaller collections were published or exhibited earlier. For all these reasons, the Great War was the first war to have its justification and necessity questioned.

The photographic medium has a quality that is pervasive and convincing. Photography has a validity which is, for most of us, synonymous with truth. 'Photography cannot lie' was a well-known and much-quoted maxim right from the time of the discovery of the process. Even now this belief still lingers, although we know that photography can lie and lie very convincingly. Yet we still have a tendency, even a compulsion, to trust the veracity of a photographic image when first we see it, even though we may later come to question its message. This inherent property of the photographic medium makes photographs of war automatically credible, whereas a written description may be doubted or only half-believed. Unaltered, untampered-with reality is the raw material of photography, something that each

of us has proof of each time we take an unposed snapshot of the family on the beach. It is this property that makes it hard to question the evidence of the lens when it relates an image of war.

Even though the authenticity of a photograph of something that has happened in the past is rarely questioned, its immediate impact is reduced by the fact that what it presents to us is over, part of the historical past, no longer relevant to the present moment. The people it shows are not our neighbours, not even our contemporaries; they dressed differently, lived differently. Such pictures evoke nostalgia rather than sympathetic identification. But a photograph that reveals something which has just happened, which may still be going on, calls forth a more vivid, personal, emotional response. It is for this reason that the impact of the photographs of the First World War was cushioned, for they only appeared long after the event. The consciences and emotions of the public were stirred more by the facts about the war than by the pictures. War images began to assert their power much more effectively when they were published concurrently with the events they recorded, as were Robert Capa's pictures of the Spanish Civil War. The photographs of the Second World War, though powerful and dramatic in themselves, were not published immediately they were taken and were heavily censored. It is only in the post-war period, starting with the Korean War, that the

11

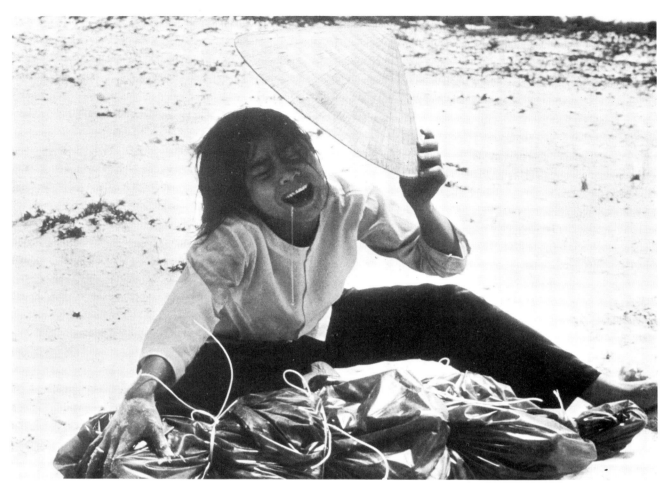

immediacy of war photographs begins to have a significant effect. Since then, a stream of authentic, powerful, terrifying, immediate images has overwhelmed us with a cumulative power. The images from Korea, Cyprus, Israel, the Congo, Biafra and Vietnam have left their indelible mark on our imaginations.

What has been their effect? Has the vivid depiction of warfare in the media managed finally to scotch the strange and snake-like attraction that war holds for men? In 1910 William James wrote: 'Showing war's irrationality and horror is of no effect upon men. The horror makes for fascination. War is a strong life, a life *in extremis*.' Now, seventy years later, with the horror and irrationality laid explicitly before us, and also with the knowledge of the certain annihilation that another world-scale war will bring, has the lure of warfare gone? Philip Knightley, in his book *The First Casualty*, quotes a young English photographer, Tim Page, talking about Vietnam: 'No one wants to admit it, but there is a lot of sex appeal and a lot of fun in weapons.' It was by such 'sexy' weapons that Page was wounded on several occasions, twice coming close to death. And yet, while he was recovering, on being asked to write a book which was to be entitled *Through With War*, the purpose of which was to help kill the glamour of war, Page replied: 'Jesus, take the glamour out of war? How the hell can you do that? You can't take the glamour out of a tank

above: Woman mourning her husband, Hue, Vietnam, 1968. *Larry Burrows.*

opposite top: Phantom planes dropping high explosive bombs, Vietnam. *Larry Burrows.*

opposite bottom: Father carrying his son wounded by Americans, Vietnam. *Philip Jones Griffiths.*

burning or a helicopter blowing up. It's like trying to take the glamour out of sex. War is good for you. . . . War has always been glamorous. I don't care who he is, if you put a gun into a man's hands then he feels bigger.' Honesty – or the excesses of an immature youngster? Page himself found his 'peak experience', as well as money and sudden recognition, through his war photography. Yet although he may be an exception in the extremity of his views, he is certainly not unique. After all, returning soldiers, who have been licensed to kill, always were and often still are treated as heroes. By and large they are respected and sometimes envied by a section of young people. This attitude may be less prevalent today when war tribunals such as the one on the My Lai massacre have revealed the soldier as less than heroic, but the lure of war still persists. Men are still willing to don the status symbol of a uniform and to get their hands on a gun – a sign of power. There seems to be no lack of mercenaries for whom money is only part of the attraction of their profession. War

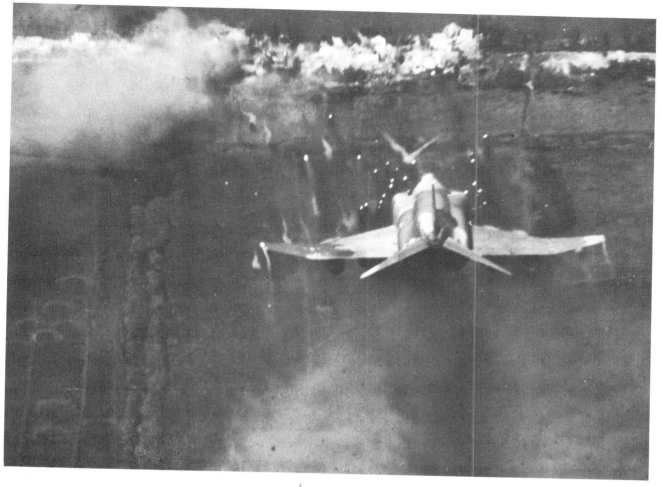

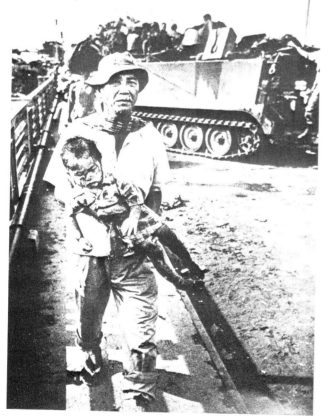

continues to speak loudly and invitingly to a certain kind of person.

War photographers are among that special breed attracted by war. They have something in the nature of mercenaries – the whores of war – but in a more positive sense. They may not be prepared to kill and maim for sheer excitement and adventure, but is the camera not a substitute for a gun? We do not have to look any further for the incentives of a war photographer. On the one hand, he is able to experience the supreme stimulation and intensity of the war adventure, with its attendant dangers; on the other hand, he has the opportunity to perform a seemingly noble deed – to fight the evil and outrage of war by depicting its horror in his photographs. Who could ask for more?

To these two incentives we can add two more. The first of them possibly base, but no less enticing. With the immense and enduring interest that war arouses in the public, photographing war often brings quick rewards – both fame and money. How else can a photographer (and to a lesser extent a reporter), one of a multitude jostling for survival and recognition in the world of the modern media, get such a lucrative return? Page hitch-hiked to Vietnam at the age of twenty-four and made both a name for himself and some $30 000 in the first few months. Some of the reputed earnings of war photographers are greatly exaggerated, but the

13

top-flight photographers are extremely well rewarded. For example, Philip Jones Griffiths was paid in the region of £500 a day by a rich American magazine, regardless of what he shot for them during the civil war in Lebanon. There were rich pickings to be made in Vietnam. But this is true of a small minority only. If we take the Bangladesh war as an example, it was attended by 700 war correspondents from all over the world. Of these only one third perhaps were photographers, and of these over 90 per cent were staff photographers working for various newspapers and magazines. As such most were paid no more than the normal rates. Outstanding photographers like Penny Tweedy of the *Sunday Times* and Tony McGrath of the *Observer* would be paid exactly the same amount for a day at the front in East Pakistan as they would get for a two-hour stint on a portrait assignment in the office of a business executive in the City of London. They do not receive danger money, just straight day rates. When we take into consideration the fact that McGrath was paid less than £20 per day for risking his life, we begin to see how crazy the profession of war photography can be at times.

The final incentive is much more positive. A true photographer is both an avid observer and a compulsive recorder. One of the greatest fascinations of the camera is the opportunity it affords an individual to externalize his impressions and feelings instantly and accurately as an image. Many photographers choose their profession because they are deeply interested in their fellow human beings and their environment. Through the camera they can scrutinize people, learn something about the world and its inhabitants, and record their findings both for themselves and for others. They are able to witness the flow of life, gauge public opinion, participate in momentous occasions, and all the time observe how humans react to different situations – from the ridiculous to the sublime. War is the greatest of motivators, a catalyst, and provider of extreme emotions – joy and elation as well as grief and despair. In war a sensitive photographer–explorer can reap a rich harvest of human responses. Rarely will he find a better chance to learn more about how people behave than by watching them encountering their 'peak experience'. But also there is a quality of obsession in a photographer. Many develop a craving, an inner compulsion, to explore the world and translate what they see into visual images. They feel it is part of their duty to show to others what they themselves discover in the course of their wanderings. They have a missionary spirit. With a camera there is a constant and close correlationship between the photographer, the reality he sees and the image realized through the lens. A photographer is often very conscious of the importance of his role as mediator between reality, often ugly and reprehensible as in war, and the general public. He feels he is the only true link between one and the other, just as a priest is the link between god and the faithful.

These, then, are the motivating forces which prompt a photographer to abandon, temporarily or permanently, the safe, steady course of his career and embark on the adventure of photographing war.

War photography as a specialist job is a fairly new phenomenon. Many photographers throughout the history of photography went to war, but for the majority war was only one out of a variety of subjects. During the Second World War many professional and part-time photojournalists recorded war activities, either as freelances or as members of the forces. Most returned to normal peacetime photography as soon as the war ended as a matter of course. Some, like George Rodger, became so totally disillusioned, disgusted even with the activity that they resolved to take no more war pictures. Rodger is reputed to be the first war photographer to enter Belsen in April 1945. Before him lay the emaciated bodies of the inmates, walking skeletons huddling in little groups – a scene from Dante's *Inferno*. The artist-photographer in him immediately became inspired by this terrible spectacle. Without thinking, he started to shoot, subconsciously arranging groups and bodies on the ground into artistic compositions in his viewfinder. He suddenly realized that he was treating this pitiful human flotsam as if it were some gigantic still-life. This revelation of his own, momentary insensitivity appalled him so much that he promised himself never again to photograph a war. But a handful of those who gained their experience photographing the Second World War – Bert Hardy, Robert Capa, Carl Mydans and David Douglas Duncan among them – went on to make a career out of what was to become recognized as the specialist profession of war photography.

The process of the emancipation of the war photographer was partly the result of the post-war climate. The 1950s and 1960s brought a new awareness of the importance of photography in general. The public showed greater interest in, and grew more informed about, world happenings than they had before the war. This is reflected in the development of the illustrated magazines which reached the height of their popularity at this time. A new kind of photojournalism, with the emphasis placed on the picture essay rather than on single photographs, had already emerged before the war. This trend had originated in Germany with the appearance of the *Berliner Illustrierte Zeitung*, the *Münchener Illustrierte Presse*, and the Communist-sponsored *Arbeiter Illustrierte Zeitung* in the early twenties. Stefan Laurent, the editor of the *Münchener Illustrierte Presse* from 1928, was especially responsible for the development of the picture essay. With the onset of Hitler's régime, this trend was halted. Laurent and a

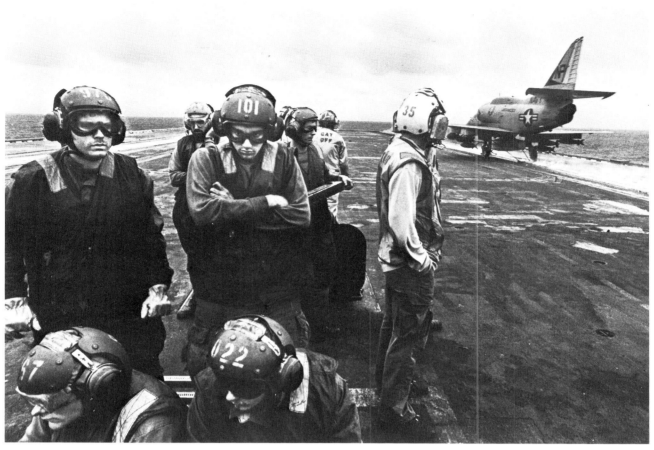

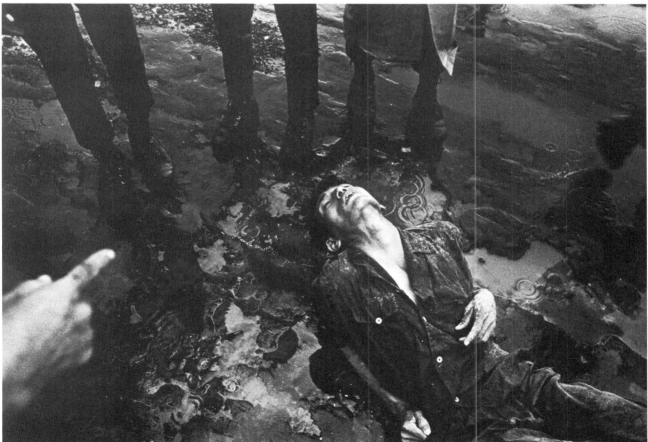

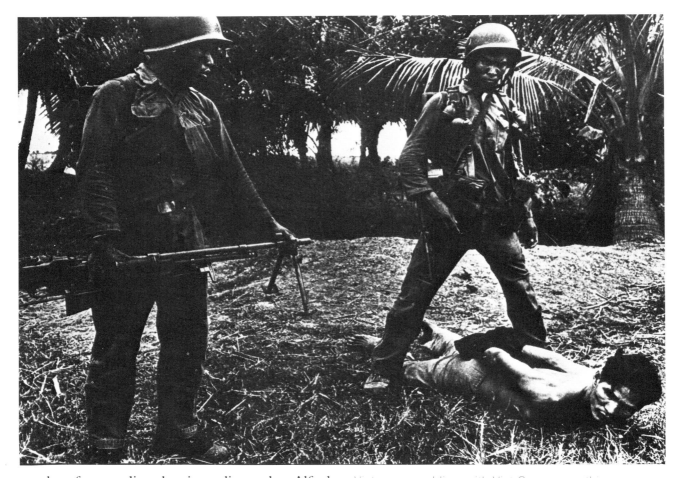

Vietnamese soldiers with Viet Cong sympathizer. Vietnam. *Don McCullin.*

number of outstanding photojournalists such as Alfred Eisenstaedt and Felix H. Man left Germany for the free world. As a result, a number of new illustrated magazines began to appear in the rest of Europe and the USA in the thirties. Laurent himself founded *Picture Post* in Britain, and this was followed by *Weekly Illustrated* and *Queen*. At about the same time *Réalités* and *Paris Match* first appeared in France, and in the USA *Life*, *Look*, *McCall's* and *Collier's* all came into being in the pre-war period. With the proliferation of the illustrated magazines, which relied to a large extent on photographic material, the status of the photographer received its greatest boost. The careers of Robert Capa, Henri Cartier-Bresson, W. Eugene Smith, Bert Hardy and David Seymour all date from this period. The war itself curtailed the expansion temporarily, because of publishing difficulties and censorship, but with the cessation of military activities, the illustrated magazines were given a new lease of life and they all developed very rapidly.

At the same time there was a growing public interest in warfare, reflected in the number of books and films on the subject in this period. Furthermore, the peace itself was of the knife-edge variety. The cold war replaced the recently concluded hot war, and it was not long until new conflicts broke out. The first of these, the Korean War, provided the opportunity for the first of the great post-war photographers – David Douglas Duncan. His picture stories in *Life* and his subsequent book, *This Is War*, were prototypes of a new genre.

Duncan himself would probably reject the label 'war photographer'. In the Second World War he became celebrated as the 'Legendary Lensman of the Marines' for his service as 2nd Lieutenant both with a gun and with his Leicas, although his range of interests in photography is much wider. He specializes in travel, art and architectural photography as well as warfare. However, in the Korean campaign he rejoined his old unit of the 1st Marine Division as a photographer and perfected his individualistic style of close identification with the fighting soldier. He recorded their faces in victory and more often in defeat for the best of his pictures were taken during the American retreat from the border with communist China to the sea – a heroic action which the commanding officer, General Olivier, vividly described: 'Retreat! Hell, we are just fighting in another direction.' Duncan left *Life* in 1955 and devoted part of his time to photographing his close friend, Picasso. He returned to photographing war when the Marines were sent to Vietnam, producing another book on the American soldier, *War Without Heroes*.

It was the Vietnam War which brought a new dimension to war reportage, and brought a new status to war photography. The war itself was protracted, and some photographers were permanently based in Vietnam, fully employed in reporting the war over a number of years. They had unlimited freedom of movement to explore the war in depth and reveal the rich variety of visual imagery it provided: East versus West, communist versus capitalist, sophisticated war technology versus free-roaming guerilla forces. Fought in an exotic terrain among a photogenic native population, the Vietnam War afforded a seemingly unending supply of photographic material, and out of it there came a new breed – the war photographer par excellence.

Of these, Larry Burrows spent ten years of his life in Vietnam, and died there in 1971. Philip Jones Griffiths, after two years of painstaking reportage, produced *Vietnam Inc.*, possibly the finest and most shattering book ever to appear on war. Don McCullin went to Vietnam many times for extended visits between covering other conflicts. For McCullin, war came to be, at this period at least, his natural element. He said of himself in 1967: 'I used to be a war-a-year man, but now it is not enough. I need two a year now. When it gets to be three or four, then I will get worried.' Now, ten years later, McCullin looks back at this time with a certain amont of detachment and amazement. He is an excep-

tionally gentle and sensitive person, yet his name, to his own horror, became for many people almost synonymous with war. His greatest joy is to contemplate a cloud formation and photograph the dawn light over an English coastline, but he is considered by some, totally unjustly, to symbolize a certain kind of parasite who fattened himself on human misery. Nothing could be further from the truth.

Burrows, Griffiths and McCullin probed deeply the totality of war. But Vietnam lured many other photojournalists at one time or another and, in the hot-house environment it offered, their activities were intensified for all to see. The art of war photography reached its peak and the photographers appeared to be consumed by their concern to produce the most striking, vivid, violent pictures of killing, torture and distress. Sean Flynn and Tim Page experimented with a camera that could be attached to a soldier's rifle so that when the gun was fired the camera automatically recorded the death of the victim. Vietnam became the stage on which the photographers revealed themselves.

Among the photographers themselves it is possible to discern three broad categories based on their expressed attitude to their own activities and manifest in their pictures. A small group callously exploit war for all it is worth, producing the hottest, most salable material for their own advancement and profit. They show violence and death in its sensational and titillating aspects, evaluating their pictures in terms of their shock value.

Attack of Russian infantry. *Dmitri Baltermants.*

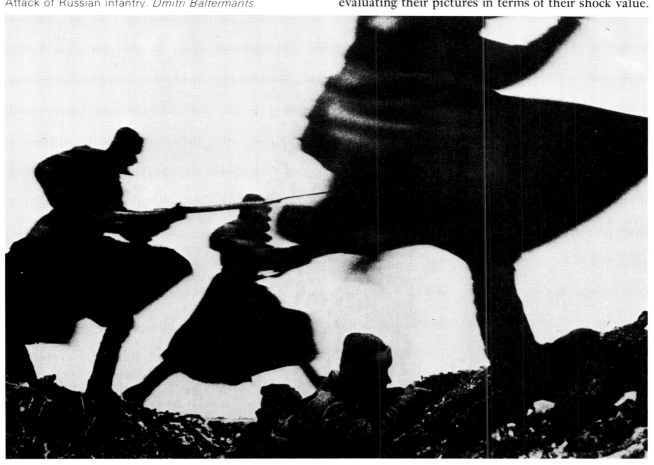

Some photographers were known to have plastered the walls of their rooms in Saigon with horror pictures – those that were too extreme to be published. *Town* magazine in December 1964 described the pictures which decorated Horst Faas's office, pictures which his agency, Associated Press, had refused to handle. They showed heads floating in the water with gouged eyes, hands swinging on pieces of string, and various stages of torture sometimes wittily subtitled with comic-strip balloons: 'That'll teach you to talk to the press.' Fortunately there are few who descend to this level. Most of the outstanding photographers whose work appears in this book are characterized by their humanity, and can be divided according to the degree of ambivalence they display towards warfare itself. There are those who clearly hate war and all it stands for, who see nothing good or uplifting in it, and who avoid any heroic or romantic connotations in their pictures. Both Philip Jones Griffiths and W. Eugene Smith fall into this category. There is another group who, consciously or unconsciously, succumb to the excitement and fascination of war. They enjoy participating in warfare, although maybe vicariously, and therefore find many positive and worthwhile elements in it which emerge in their pictures. David Douglas Duncan is representative of this group. For him war is always a supreme spectacle and all the soldiers, particularly the US Marines, are heroes. Larry Burrows also belongs to this category, although in his last two years, his attitude to war was changing. Don McCullin is a borderline case: he clearly hates war itself, and yet enjoys the idea of going to war with its inherent excitement.

The underlying attitudes of the photographers themselves determine the individual style and emotional content of their pictures. Some remain detached; others reveal a deep emotional response; others express their own aggression through their pictures. Thus there are many dissimilarities between the work of the top war photographers; each of them stands distinct from the others. It is fairly easy to distinguish a picture by McCullin, for example, from one by Duncan or Griffiths.

W. Eugene Smith displays a revulsion for war itself and compassion for its victims in his pictures, however full of power and drama they may be. There is a certain restraint in his images – he rarely shows gruesome detail – but not to hide brutality or atrocity. Rather he reveals the sad and tragic elements, prompted by his concern with the effects of war on the civilian population. Through his images he points to the fundamental implications: a bloody body is an immediate and painful fact, but the aftermath is far more crucial.

Smith, one of the most respected and revered figures among photojournalists, was the creator of some of the finest picture stories ever to appear in *Life*. He took many powerful photographs during the Second World War, but later he wanted to forget and even destroy them, considering them to be total failures. Lincoln

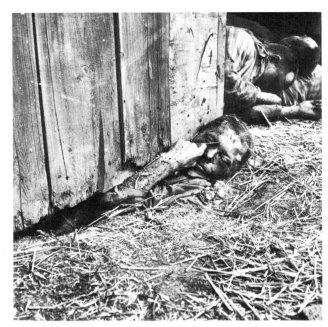

above: Political prisoner who died while attempting to escape, Berlin, 1945. *William Vandivert.*

opposite: Victim of napalm bomb, Vietnam, 1967. *Philip Jones Griffiths.*

Kirstein writes of Smith: '. . . he could not show on a plain paper surface coated with chemicals, in a snapped shot, the plumb immediacy, savor of fright, grief, sadism, fun and luck of war.' Smith indeed, more than perhaps any other photographer, set for himself an impossible target. 'I would,' he says, 'that my photographs might be, not the coverage of a news event, but an indictment of war – the brutal corrupting viciousness of its doings to the minds and bodies of men – and that my photographs might be a powerful emotional catalyst to the reasoning which would help this vile and stupid criminality from beginning again.'

Philip Jones Griffiths stands side by side with Smith. Griffiths's pictures are an emphatic condemnation of war. It has no redeeming features whatsoever. War is shown as the destroyer, the corruptor of the soul. His pictures attest this. He does indeed depict at times the hideousness of violence, but he never attempts to shock with his picture content. What he shows functions as a record. There is a difference between an image of war horror shot for exploitation alone and an image of a similar event taken out of compassion. In the former one can sense the resentment of the victim for the intruder with his lens. Compare this with Griffiths's own story about a picture that he took of a South Vietnamese farmer carrying in his arms a little boy who had been badly hurt, the man's own son. 'We walked about 50 yards like that, with me walking backwards. He fell into step with me – he knew damn well what I was doing! He held his son out, and if you think about it, that's quite an unusual way to carry your son. He is holding him out. That man was angry, there were tears in his eyes.'

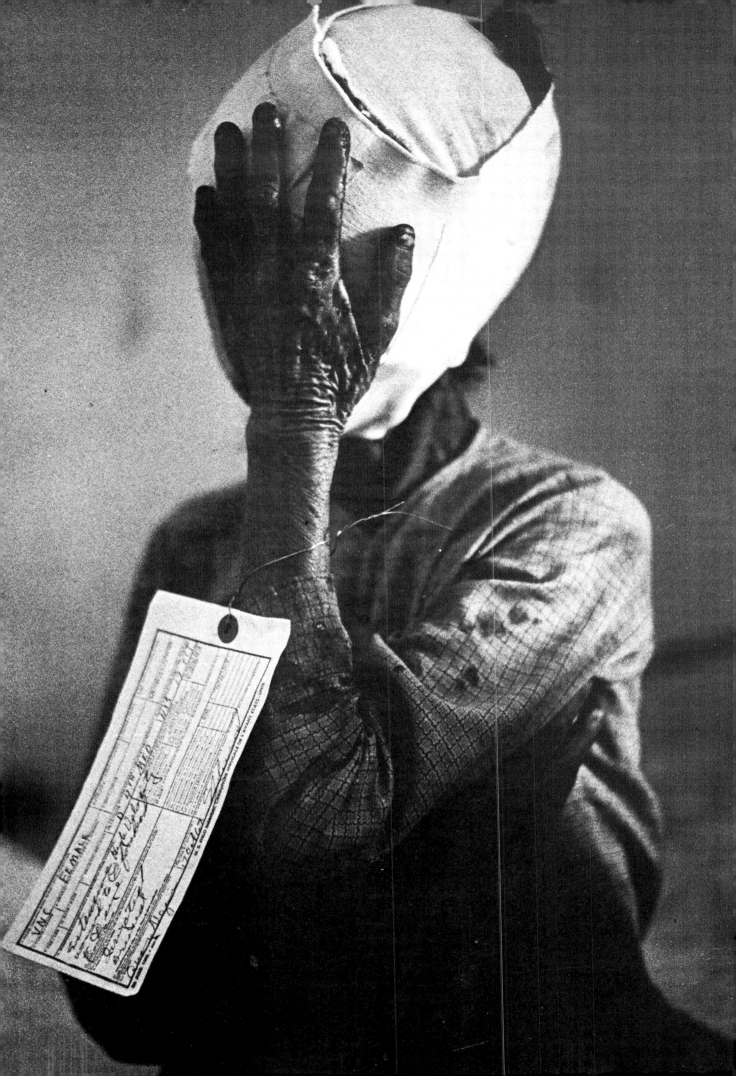

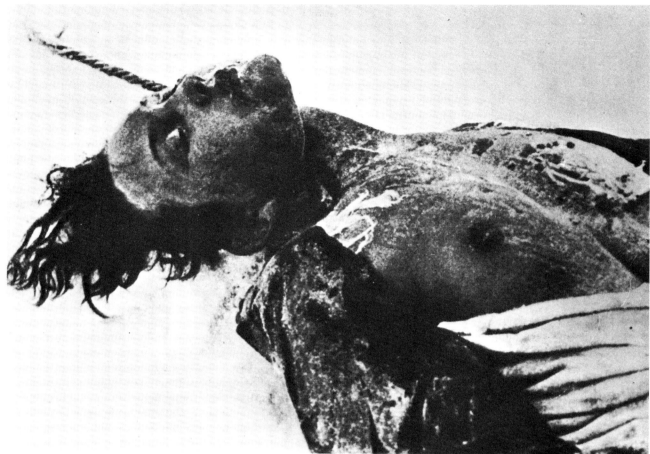

above: 'Tania' — a partisan tortured by Fascists. *S. Strunnikov.*

right: Belsen, 1945. *George Rodger.*

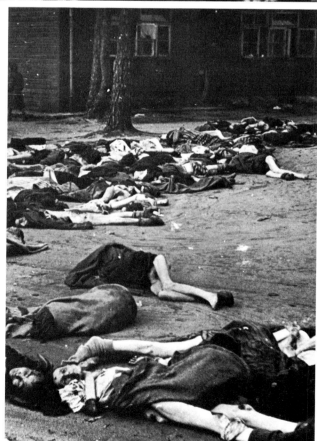

Griffiths is a pessimist. He has gradually lost his faith in the goodness of human nature as it is revealed by war, and simply divides humanity into two sections: the victims and their tormentors. The strong and powerful are there to assert their power; the weak are there to suffer, and perish.

Those photographers who respond to the excitement of war Griffiths characterizes as 'hawks'. 'Even now,' he says, 'you find people who don't question their own purpose. Someone like Horst Faas is still basically a hawk. Larry Burrows, for instance, was a confirmed hawk . . . and David Douglas Duncan, of course, is still a supreme hawk.'

In Duncan's imagery war is elevated to a supreme pedestal, and the participants in this ritual are similar in stature. The American soldier-hero is the chief subject of his lens. Selflessness, courage, fortitude, warmth of comradeship, superhuman resolve and patriotism are the characteristic qualities shown in his pictures. If his soldiers cry, their tears are of frustration or sorrow for their fellow soldiers, never tears of defeat or despair. Duncan remained a hawk to the end. His book on the Vietnam War, *War Without Heroes*, is an extension of his earlier book on Korea, *This Is War*. Politically,

20

Duncan believed that American intervention in Vietnam was justified and necessary, and this forced him to discount the uglier aspects of the war that Griffiths saw so clearly. For example, Duncan vehemently rejected the authenticity of the pictures of the My Lai massacre, despite the fact that their veracity was proven beyond doubt.

Larry Burrows seems to have been caught by an ambivalence that Duncan refused to admit. At one time Burrows used to undertake lecture tours of the USA, using his pictures of Vietnam as illustration. The ostensible purpose was to prove the necessity of the American involvement, but through his pictures he revealed the qualities of the soldier that Duncan so vividly portrays. Burrows's early pictures from Vietnam show bravery, daring and gallantry; at times they seem to glory in fighting, but in them lies a deeper element which gradually comes to the surface as Burrows's work progressed. Tom Hopkinson, editor of *Picture Post* for a number of years, calls Burrows the 'greatest war photographer there has ever been', and indeed there is no other photographer to match his professionalism, his complete mastery of the craft, or his sense of composition and visual beauty.

Burrows was born in London, and started his career as a laboratory technician in *Life*'s London office. He first specialized in art photography – paintings, sculpture and architecture – and it is probably this involvement which led to his sense of classical composition and a feeling for balance which is found in his later war pictures. At first he adopted a straightforward stance of a professional photographer making the most of the opportunity to further his career through war photography. He did not at first question the underlying ethic of such work; this was a later development. 'I was torn between being a photographer and the normal human feelings. I didn't know what to do. Was I simply capitalizing on someone else's grief?' He made these comments about his magnificent picture story for *Life* entitled 'Yankee Papa 13' which shows the last moments of a helicopter pilot in Vietnam. They were taken in 1965, and in the following years of the war, Burrows's dilemma became more acute as the scale of the American military involvement grew and the human suffering increased. He himself admitted that he began to hide excessive horror and suffering, in an attempt to shield the public from making too deep an assessment of the truth. His death in 1971 prevented him reaching a final resolution.

The pioneer of modern war photography was Robert Capa, and for this reason it is difficult to make an evaluation of his work. If Griffiths is judge and prosecutor, Duncan counsel for defence, Burrows a sensitive craftsman, Capa is the carefree buccaneer. His book, *Slightly Out of Focus*, gives the impression of a zestful enjoyment in participating in war, with Capa constantly eager to be as close to the action as possible. The sheer exuberance of his photography suggests that Griffiths

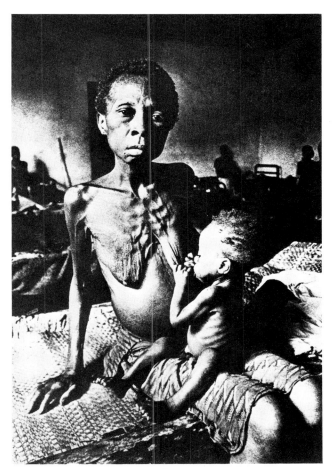

Biafran mother. *Don McCullin.*

would most likely include Capa in his list of hawks. Capa was born in Budapest in 1913 and named Andre Friedman. Having fled from the Nazis in Berlin in 1933, he arrived in Paris and assumed the name of 'famous American photographer' Robert Capa as no one would buy pictures taken by a young, skinny, Jewish Hungarian refugee. He rose to prominence with his pictures of the Spanish Civil War in 1936 – during which he took the famous 'Death of a Loyalist Soldier'. He covered the Second World War for *Life*; his pictures of the Normandy landings are classics. His last assignment was the Indochina War in 1954 where he was killed by a landmine. He was thus spared the ugliness and brutality of Vietnam which challenged the assumptions of so many others.

I have left Don McCullin to the end of this discussion of modern war photographers quite deliberately, for it seems to me that he cannot readily be fitted into any one category. In one sense he is a hawk; he returned to the battleground time and time again, openly confessing his desire for constant action. But there is another side to McCullin which has emerged since those early (1967) pronouncements. There is a growing ambivalence in his attitude to war; he has repeated many times how much he hates it for what it does to humans. I cannot

21

doubt his sincerity. Cecil Beaton in his book, *Silver Image*, expresses this duality in the following terms: 'Hate of war, and wish for danger.'

Of all the war photographers we have so far mentioned, with the possible exception of Horst Faas, McCullin's pictures are most conscious of death, of mutilation, and of the deprivation brought about by war. His book, *Is Anyone Taking Notice?*, is full of the horror war brings, but at the same time, the pictures have a curious dramatic beauty. As he himself said: '. . . photographing a war can be beautiful.' As there is a paradox in his attitude to war, so there is a duality in his images. They are often selected and shot to shock by their content, but they become transformed through McCullin's lens into compositions of harmonious tones and highlights. An emaciated woman in a Biafran hospital is transfigured by McCullin into a madonna of suffering.

McCullin was wounded in Cambodia in 1970, and since then he seems to have started to weigh his chances more carefully, and to be asking questions of himself as a recorder of misery and suffering. The longer he photographed fighting, the more conscious he became of the devastation and harvest of death that war reaps. After witnessing the infernal brutality of the civil war in Lebanon, he resolved to photograph no more wars.

The handful of talented, creative photographers we have just considered chose war as their medium and, through their own attributes of sensitivity, understanding, compassion and profound involvement, achieved in their best pictures a body of work worthy to compare with the products of the world's finest artists.

If the act of artistic creation resides in the capacity to externalize pictorially one's innermost thoughts on the world and its people, allied with a special talent to endow these images with an aesthetic beauty, then these photographers are great artists. Not only do they display an idiosyncratic diversity in their personal attitudes to their subject matter, but they also differ in their methods of presentation and style. Duncan works mostly in dark, inky images, often with stark close-ups of bodies or soldiers' faces. Griffiths avoids any aesthetic connotations. He is almost alone in painting war in extreme contrasts of black and white with no intermediary tones, no redeeming features. Burrows and McCullin appear at first sight to have a similar style – both inject their pictures with an action and urgency which make those of Duncan and Griffiths seem almost static. But of the two, McCullin's images are more aggressive, whereas Burrows's warriors glide and dance through their violent rituals. McCullin's figures are jerky, spasmodic, and in consequence, register greater pain and suffering. Capa's most memorable pictures are those which are 'slightly out of focus', as in the title of his book. The blur of bodies in a headlong rush, either engaged in combat or overcome by death or injury, attest to the veracity of the image. But it is W. Eugene Smith who, for many critics, remains the most accomplished of the war photographers. Whether ghostly, as in 'Funeral at Sea', or cataclysmic – an explosion dwarfing soldiers cowering in the foreground

A victim of US bombardment of a town in which 85 per cent of the population was destroyed. *Philip Jones Griffiths.*

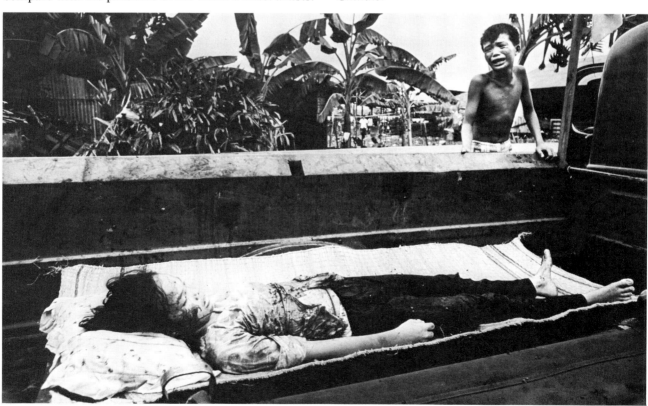

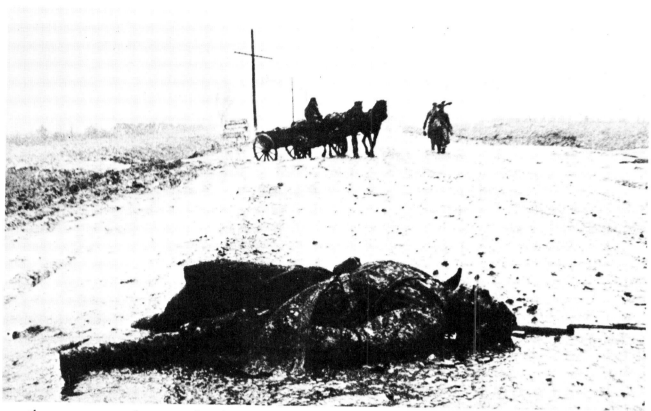

— or the enormous tenderness and pathos of a soldier hugging a wounded baby, each of his pictures wrings a response of recognition from the viewer, and each can be placed next to paintings by Goya or Blake without detriment.

There is an inevitable question which is often voiced about the activities of the war photographer. It usually takes the following form: 'At what point should a war photographer lay down his camera and take direct action?' The assumption behind the question is that the photographer of war feeds off the misery and grief of others and that to refrain from the immediate involvement of picking up a gun or helping the wounded implies a callous indifference to the plight of the humanity that the photographer is recording. The question can be answered in many ways. By now it should be evident that war photographers are among the least indifferent to the suffering of other people. To set the effect of a single act of mercy against the wider effect achieved through a photographer's pictures is a false equation. The question asks the photographer to abandon one role and to assume another, and mistakenly attributes compassion solely to those able to take direct action, rather than to those also whose actions are mediated through the camera's lens and therefore indirect. The question is usually asked by people who are not involved, either directly or indirectly – critics, writers, philosophers, acquaintances or friends – whose experience is vicariously provided by the actions of the photographer himself. Perhaps they have the right to ask such a question – provided they ask a similar question of themselves.

'This way went the war.' Russian front, 1941. *Dmitri Baltermants.*

But for the photographer the question does present a moral dilemma of which he is not altogether unaware. McCullin is one who has debated the dilemma: 'There are many areas of doubt in my mind. Whether the photographer can and should actually interfere in a situation when, in fact, he is merely an observer. And if he does, he can actually start a chain reaction, perhaps make the situation worse. In any case his role becomes confused. When people say to me "Did you do this or the other?" "Did you help or try to prevent something dreadful happening?" – of course I carried wounded men, and bandaged their wounds and gave them water. Once in Vietnam I tried to stop a stream of lorries passing two wounded men. I snatched a rifle and held it up towards the lorries, but no one stopped. In most of the war situations one is like a speck of dust. If men are bent on killing and destruction, one photographer with a Nikon will not really affect their action.'

But it is through the actions of one photographer with a Nikon, one speck of dust, that the rest of us come to see and understand the actions of those who wage and those who suffer war, and thus to understand the nature of warfare itself. The great photographers of war, through their skill, experience, vision and above all compassion awaken us to the need for the same compassion.

overleaf: Ruins of Murmansk, Russia, 1942. *Yevgeni Khaldei.*

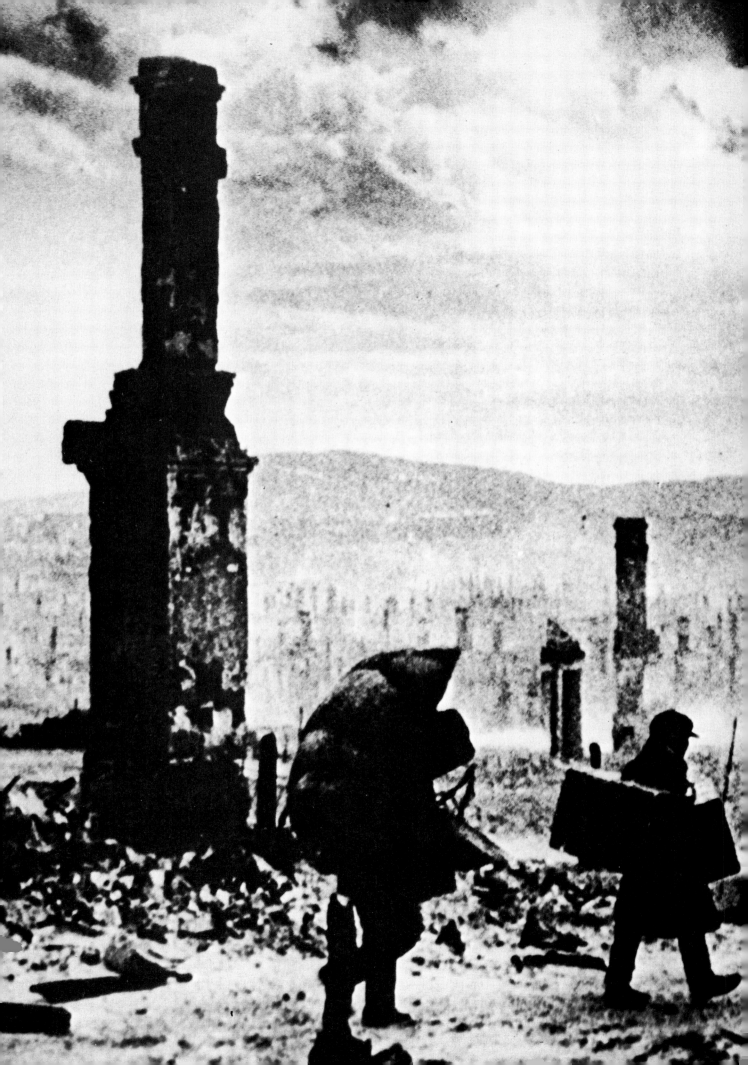

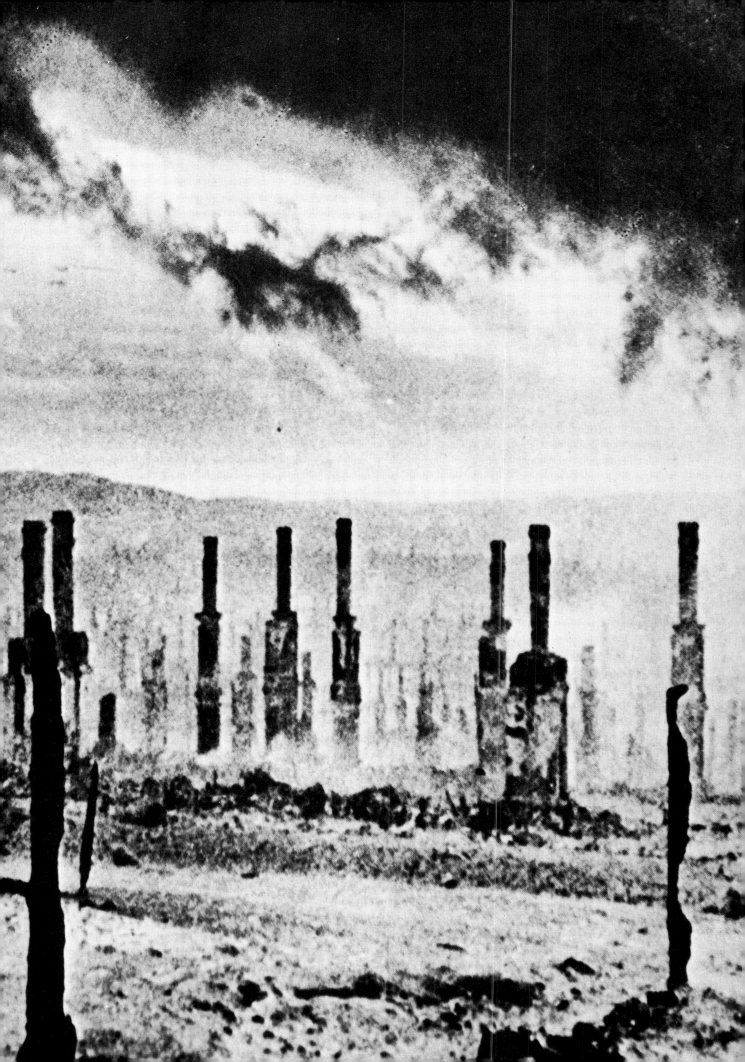

This chapter would be incomplete without a special postscript. In our assessment of war photography, introducing the most distinguished practitioners of the art, hardly a single female name has been mentioned. War, a man's game, seemed destined at the start to be recorded by men alone. The first professional woman photographer to record a war was Margaret Bourke-White who worked for a short time in Russia, and then covered the campaign in Italy and the invasion of Germany during the Second World War. However, the work of this remarkable and exceptionally brave woman does not place her in the ranks of the outstanding photographers of war. For a time she remained an exception; up to 1960 war photography continued to be a men's preserve, but with the onset of the Vietnam War, this ceased to be the case. It is ironic and significant that Capa's death in Indochina at the end of the French involvement in the East was followed by the death of a woman photographer at the beginning of the American intervention there. An American, Dicky Chappell, whose work is now largely forgotten, was killed while photographing in Vietnam in 1965.

The late sixties and the 1970s saw an increase in the number of women photographers covering war. French women led the way; the generation of students who had hurled bricks at French gendarmes from behind the barricades in Paris in 1968 supplied a number of exceptional women photographers. Some travelled to Vietnam with their photographer boyfriends, and started by borrowing a camera; others came alone. They found an outlet for their pictures – Associated Press, United Press International, Reuters and other agencies were willing to buy pictures from all comers, from anyone, in fact, who was able to deliver them. A number of girls became agency 'stringers' and some with talent and determination, like Catherine Leroy, rose to world-wide recognition.

Leroy arrived in Saigon in 1966, having bought herself a one-way ticket. She possessed one Leica, $500, and 'A great desire to become a photographer–journalist.' Horst Faas, picture editor for Associated Press in Vietnam, took her on as a stringer. She still remembers vividly her visits to his office: 'I would come completely exhausted, after a week or so in the field among soldiers. My films would be taken for processing and come back in a short while. Then Faas would scrutinize each of them with a little magnifier and from time to time would clip a neg with his scissors. Each clipping meant $15 for me. Sometimes he would clip a lot and I would come out $200 richer. I felt great then.'

It was not easy being a stringer for AP. At the briefing sessions, when the authorities would reveal in which sectors the greatest military activity was expected to take place, there were usually some thirty or forty photographers present. Leroy had to chose areas to cover where there were no other AP photographers at work, as Faas would not clip her negs if he already had similar pictures from his staffers.

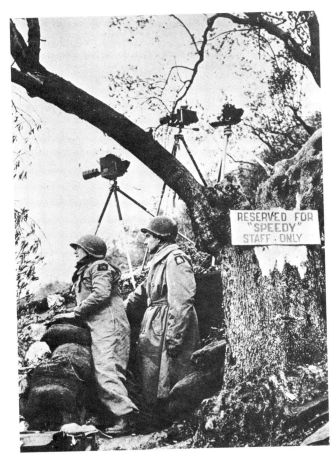

Margaret Bourke-White at an observation post overlooking Monte Cassino, Italy, 1943.

She learned a lot in her first two years in Vietnam, however, and began to build a reputation for herself with stories such as one on a parachute drop with the Marines (she had already become an experienced sky diver in France). Her series taken in May 1967 of the Marine assault on Hill 881 was published throughout the world.

Leroy displays amazing courage and determination in following her profession. She relates the story of how she was seriously wounded in 1967: 'I was with a group of soldiers. All around there was a lot of mortar fire and from time to time I would see one of the advancing Marines fall. I walked behind and would keep three or four of them in my viewfinder, but it would always be that I would see the falling Marine with my left eye and not with the one in the viewfinder. I was still trying to get the shot when I was hit.' She was punctured by some twenty bits of sharpnel and had to spend a month in hospital. As soon as she recovered she returned to Saigon, again making excursions to combat areas. She started to work for CIPA, and won a number of prizes for her pictures, including the Capa award. She covered Cyprus in 1974, and Lebanon in 1975–6 her pictures of the civil war served to confirm her position as one of the leading war photographers.

Two other French women photographers who have specialized in pictures of warfare are Francoise

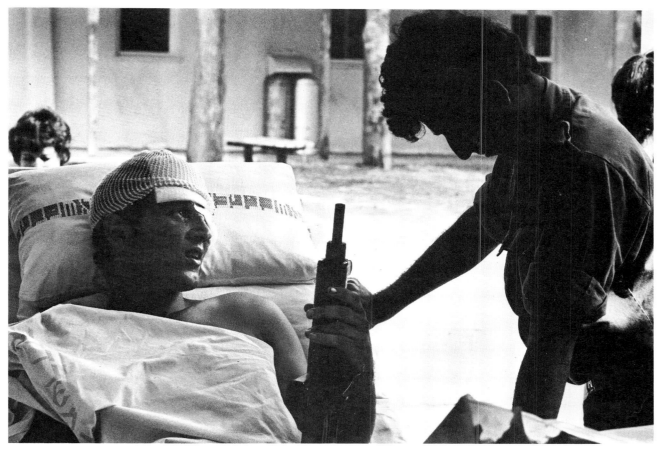

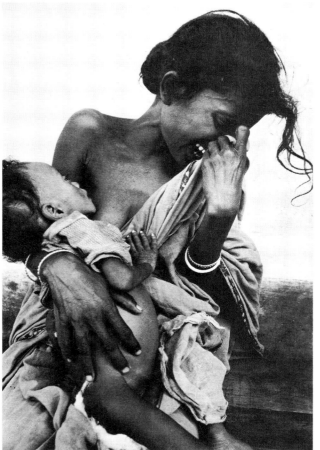

above: A wounded soldier being visited by a comrade, Israel, 1973. *Sally Soames.*

left: 'The first dead person I had ever seen' Bangladesh, 1971. *Penny Tweedy.*

Demulder and Christine Spengler. Francoise first visited Saigon in 1973, travelling with a photographer friend. She started taking pictures herself, and worked in Cambodia until the fall of Phnom Penh. She covered the fall of Saigon, and also visited Lisbon and Angola, photographing the war from the M P L A side. She also covered the Lebanon conflict, winning several awards for her distinctive pictures. Christine Spengler also started her career in Cambodia. Some of the pictures she took there, though tragic and gruesome in content, have a haunting beauty.

Penny Tweedy, whose work appears later in this book, does not really consider herself to be a war photographer. 'It's the innocent victim of the war that is my main concern,' she says. 'Not so much what soldiers do to each other, but what happens to the people caught up in the conflict.' Her best work records the suffering of people on the sidelines of war. She has done extensive work for Shelter, Oxfam and other charities, photographing refugees in Vietnam and Cambodia, Montagnard orphans, and famine victims in India. She did, however, cover the fighting in Bangladesh and the Yom Kippur War in Israel where she worked in the front line. She is fascinated by the problem of a photographer finding himself, or herself,

27

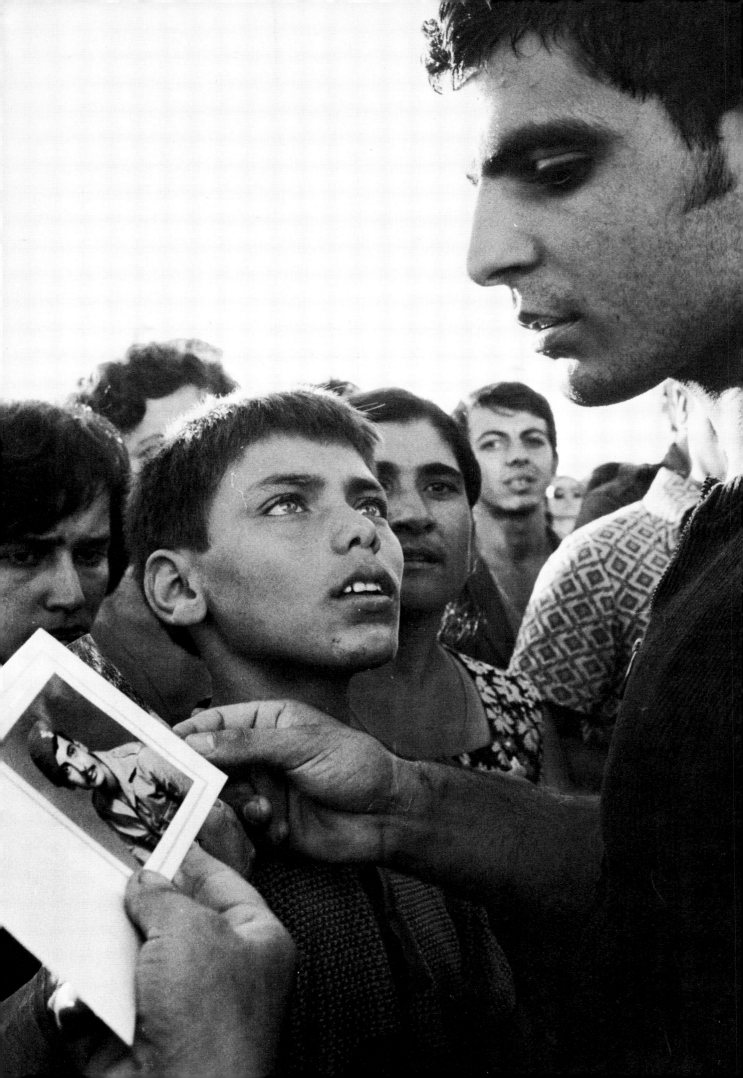

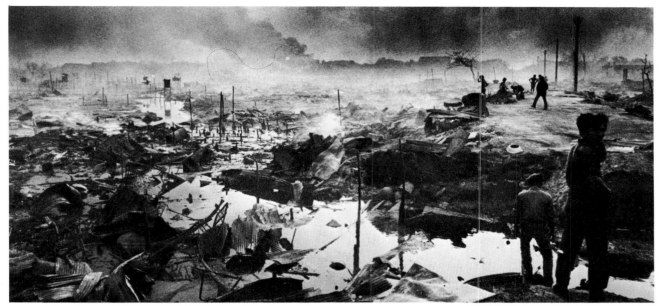

Devastation in Cambodia. *Christine Spengler.*

in the midst of aggression. 'When is a photographer, by taking pictures, not only recording but aggravating the situation?' she asks. She was one of the few who stayed to photograph the disgraceful incident in the Dacca stadium when four prisoners were bayoneted to death in front of an audience. She argues: 'The fine line of responsibility as a recorder-documentarist photographer can be easily overlooked in the heat of the moment.'

For a woman photographer, the fact that she is a woman holds certain advantages when photographing war. Catherine Leroy maintains that soldiers rarely object to a woman being present; on the contrary, they often welcome her. Being the only woman among a large number of men gives her a certain illusion of security. The soldiers respond by being protective, offering assistance which they would not extend to a man in the same circumstances. There were objections raised early in the Vietnam War to women photographers and journalists going into combat situations, but these were overcome. However, an underlying prejudice is revealed from time to time: a woman may be treated as a voyeur, or a sightseer who has no right to be where she is, or she may be considered to be incompetent and unreliable. Catherine Leroy encountered such an attitude when she was planning her trip to Angola. In order to get her accreditation papers, she was asked to produce cuttings to prove that she was indeed a professional photographer. No man was asked to provide similar evidence.

Does war hold a special fascination for a woman, one different to the attraction it holds for men? Perhaps it

News of death, Cyprus. *Catherine Leroy.*

draws those women who are excited by death and danger and who also are drawn to men who live in such a charged environment. Perhaps also wars offer a situation in which an exceptionally ambitious and enterprising woman can test herself, in the most difficult and exacting way, against men. After all, we are living at a time when women are in the midst of a fight for equality and liberation from their traditionally restricted roles in society. Perhaps, in the end, war provides the same kind of excitement for women as it holds for men: the presence of danger, a life which is out of the ordinary, intensely experienced feelings, the possibility of quick recognition, financial gain, and a unique subject matter – these factors, and many more, make war a powerful magnet for all photographers.

'In the beginning every photographer and journalist that goes to war does not go already activated against the inhumanity of war,' says Don McCullin. 'He goes with excitement, almost love for war. He goes to test himself, to see if he has got the courage.' Gradually, the glamour fades as the reality takes over. 'Modern warfare is only glamorous since Hollywood made it so. But when you are there, there is no glamour. There is nowhere to sleep, you are eating tinned food, and seeing dead men next to you, men in tremendous pain, you are seeing the bodies of young men destroyed. Nothing whatever glamorous in that.' These are the words of one who has seen many, too many so he thinks, wars – words of experience and disillusionment. But so long as war exists, there will always be young men and women eager to go and prove themselves in the most exacting school of all.

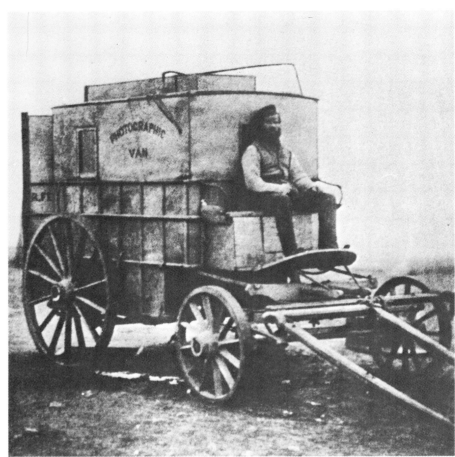

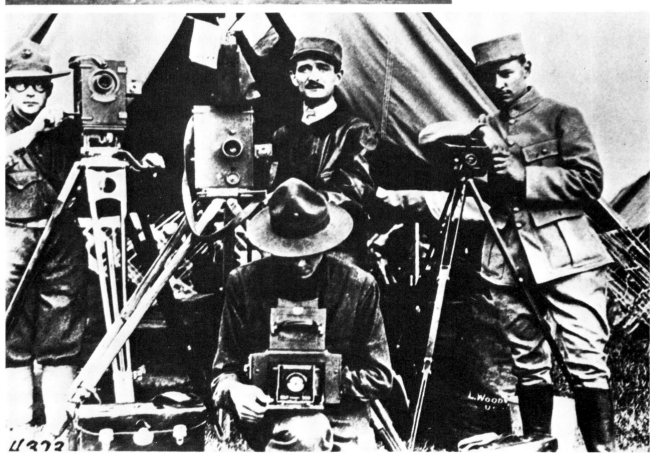

left: Photographic van used by Roger Fenton in Crimean War.

below: A group of still and movie cameramen of the First World War.

opposite top: Military photographer in a trench on the Western front, June 1917.

opposite bottom left: William Rider-Rider, First World War photographer.

opposite bottom right: Robert Capa, the veteran war photographer killed in Vietnam, 1954.

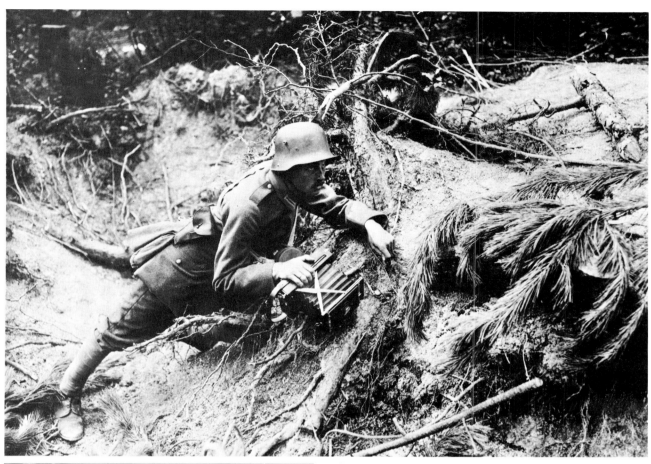

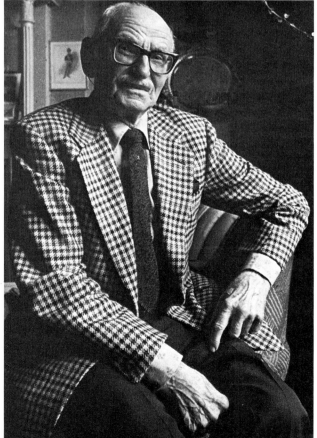

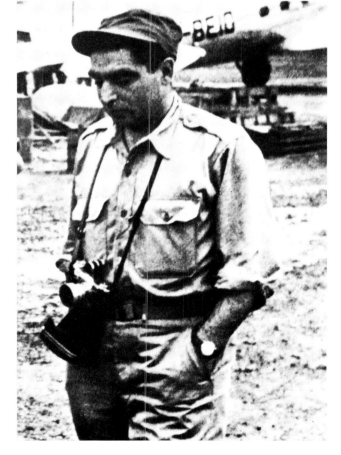

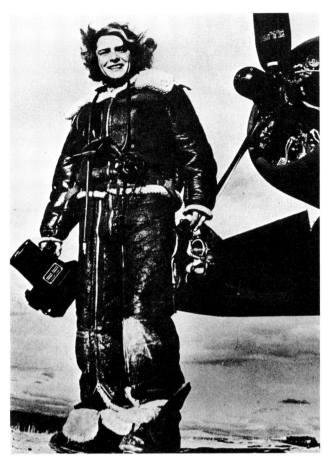

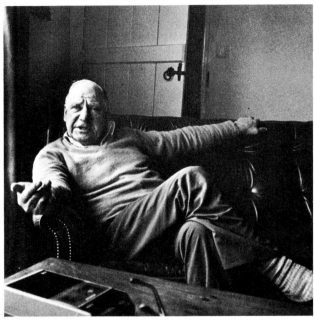

opposite: David Douglas Duncan in a specially built transparent cone for photographing from a flying aircraft.

left: Margaret Bourke-White in high altitude flying outfit, England, 1941.

below: Bert Hardy in an interview with the author.

bottom: 'Chet's Circus' in the Western Desert, 1942.

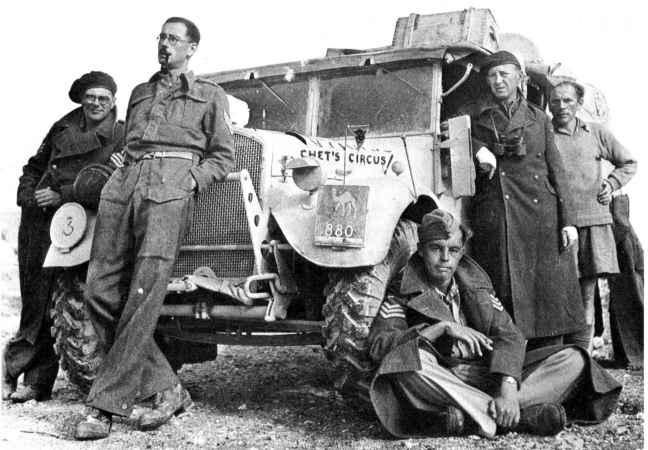

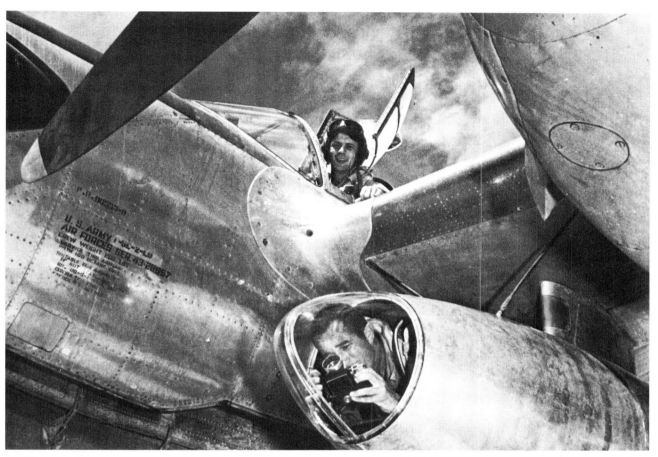

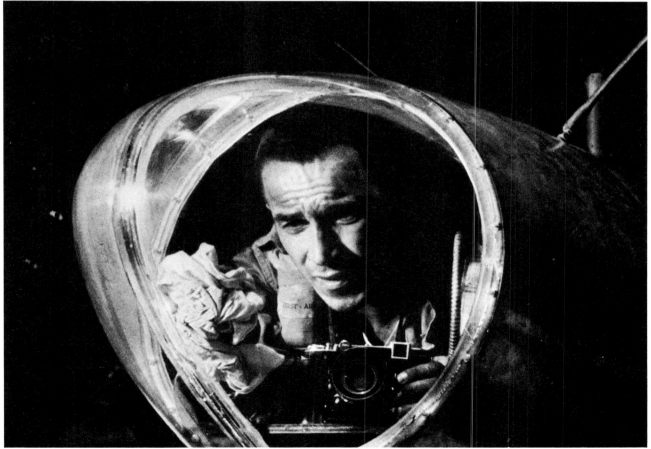

below: Larry Burrows photographed by Mark Godfrey in Vietnam.

right: Don McCullin wounded in Cambodia, 1970.

bottom: Catherine Leroy in action photographed by Larry Burrows.

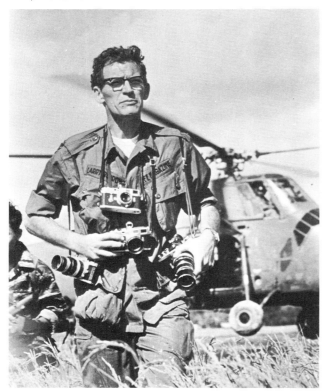

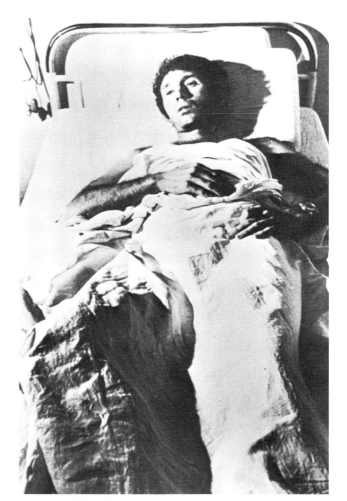

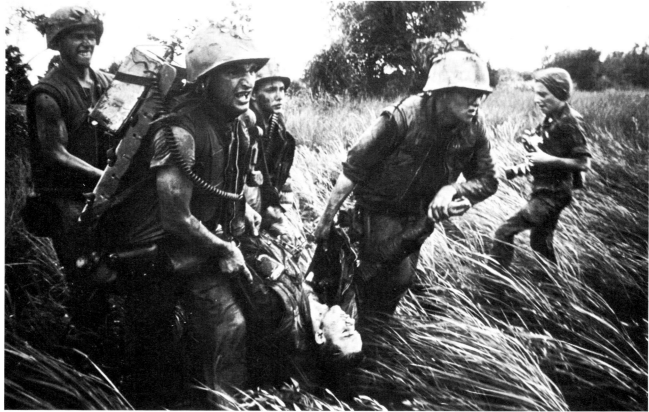

Part One
DISTANT WITNESS
1848–1912

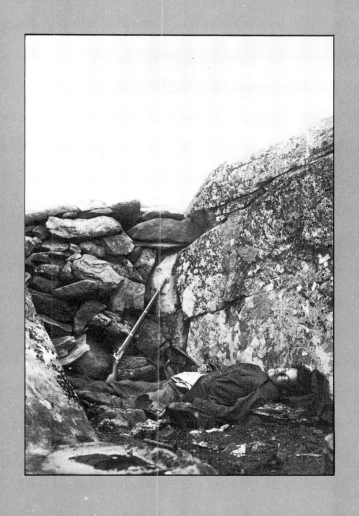

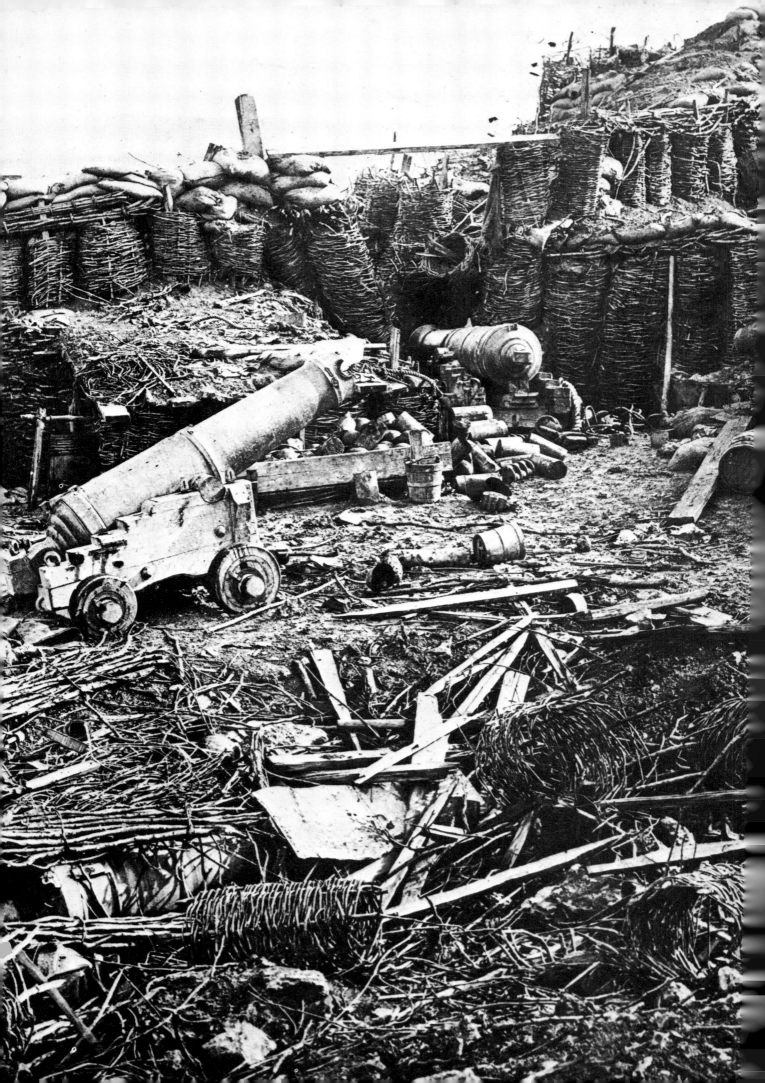

The history of war photography starts with a paradox. Of the two chroniclers of war – the writer-correspondent and the photographer – it should be the writer, with his total freedom of the pen, who can conjure up awesome, flamboyant, romantic and hence not always strictly accurate visions of conflict. By contrast, the photographer can only record what he sees in front of him. Yet these customary functions seem to have been entirely reversed in the first war to be officially recorded by photography – the war in which the Russian troops faced the might of the English, Turkish and French alliance in the Crimean peninsula.

In the spring of 1855, the war, which had started in 1853, was not going well for the allies. This was especially true of the English contingent, which was not so much outfought by the enemy, as ill-supplied, underfed and badly led. Soldiers were dying in their hundreds, not just from enemy bullets, but from hunger, cold and disease. This tragic state of affairs was forcefully reported by the outstanding war correspondent, William Russell, of *The Times*. Russell not only brilliantly described the battles, the suicidal charge of the Light Brigade, the see-sawing encounter of Inkerman; as the severe Russian winter set in, he dwelt on the miseries of the English soldiers, stressing especially the inadequate clothing and medical supplies. Partly as a result of his despatches, the government of Lord Aberdeen tendered its resignation in February 1855. Public disillusionment with the war mounted steadily. The new cabinet faced a crisis: how could they reverse the trend of growing opposition to the war? How to counteract the reports of the pernicious war correspondent and convince the public at home that conditions were not as bad as Russell suggested?

It was possibly Prince Albert himself – an enthusiastic admirer of photography and patron of the newly formed Photographic Society – who suggested sending a photographer to obtain visible evidence to set against Russell's accounts. And soon Roger Fenton was packing his equipment and setting out for the distant Crimea. The choice proved fortunate: Fenton's pictures were so mild, so reassuring, that the damning words of Russell were quickly forgotten.

The Early Exponents

Although Fenton is usually considered to be the first war photographer, strictly speaking he was preceded by a number of others.

The author of the first historically recorded photographs connected with war activities is not known by name. He was, most likely, a street-corner portrait photographer in Saltillo, Mexico. During the Mexican

War of 1846–8 he took some daguerreotypes of groups of soldiers and officers. One scene shows a group of American cavalry in a street; another is possibly the first picture to be taken of a battleground – at Buena Vista. The first war photographer known by name was an amateur: John MacCosh, a British surgeon with the Bengal Infantry. Although the photographs which he took during the Second Sikh War in the Punjab in 1848–9 were confined to portraits of his friends in the British Army, in the following war, the Second Burma War of 1852, he became more ambitious and took a number of pictures of ruined cities and implements of war. His picture (from the collection of the National Army Museum) of artillery guns and soldiers with the splendid Grand Pagoda of the Burmese city of Prome in the background, has a curious, surreal quality, which makes it a fitting opening to the history of the bizarre ritual of war as seen through the camera lens.

There are two other photographers who could claim precedence over Fenton. The first, Karl Baptist von Szatmari, a dilettante painter and photographer, was unable to resist the lure of colourful uniforms and the excitement of a campaign. In Wallachia in 1854 he followed the Russian Army in the war against Turkey. Alas, most of Szatmari's pictures, though apparently successfully shown in the Paris exhibition of 1855, seem to have vanished without trace. Only an engraving made from one of them survives.

A similar fate befell Fenton's immediate predecessor in the Crimea, but on this occasion the photographer, Richard Nicklin, also perished with his work. Nicklin, a civilian professional photographer, was commissioned by the military authorities, at a salary of six shillings a day, to photograph military installations in the early stages of the Crimean War. He was accompanied by two assistants, both soldiers with the Royal Sappers and Mines, who were given a course in photography before embarkation. They thus became the first photographic unit to be attached to the army. Nicklin left for Varna in June 1854 and was heard of no more. It is likely that HMS *Rip van Winkle* on which he sailed was one of some twenty British vessels which sank in Balaclava harbour during a hurricane in November 1854.

Roger Fenton and the Crimea

No such catastrophe awaited Roger Fenton and all of the 360 photographs which he took during his four months' stay in the Crimea survived. Today they are collectors' items.

Roger Fenton, the second son of John Fenton, a wealthy Rochdale industrialist, first studied painting in London and then in Paris which was still the fountainhead of nineteenth-century art. There he became a pupil of the painter, Paul Delaroche, who had taken a keen interest in photography from the moment of the announcement of Daguerre's discovery in 1839.

The interior of Fort Redan, Sebastopol, Crimea, 1854.
James Robertson.

37

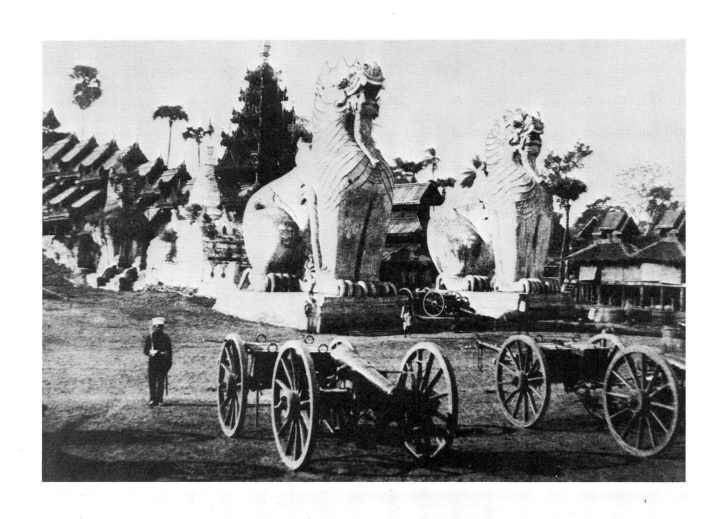

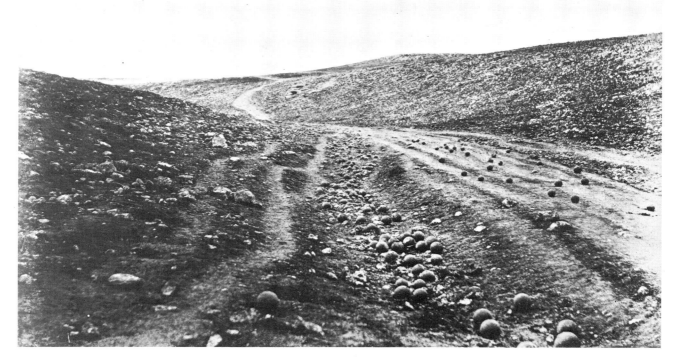

Second Burma War, 1852. *John MacCosh.*

It is likely that Fenton acquired his own interest in the subject from him. At the time, neither painting nor photography seemed to offer a young man a sufficiently secure profession; Fenton therefore turned to law, and in due course became a practising solicitor. His interest in photography persisted, however. He became an active practitioner, and a founder member and first honorary secretary of the Photographic Society (later to become the Royal Photographic Society) formed in 1853.

In 1852 Fenton visited Russia and brought back a number of photographs, including his famous picture of the Kremlin. He decided to devote his entire time to professional photography and by 1854 he had become well known as an artistic, landscape and portrait photographer, taking many pictures of the royal family. Thus, Fenton was the obvious choice for a photographer to go to the Crimea. Although he was almost certainly sent on behalf of the government and with Prince Albert's blessing, he was in fact commissioned and financed by a firm of Manchester publishers, Thomas Agnew and Son, who wanted to exploit his pictures commercially.

Three years before Fenton set out for the Crimea, the wet-collodion process had been invented by Frederick Scott Archer. Wet-plate photography quickly replaced both the daguerreotype and the calotype. The Mexican street photographer in Saltillo took daguerreotypes – which gave a faint, but sharp positive image on a polished metal plate. With the daguerreotype only a single copy could be obtained; it was impossible to reproduce the image. The calotype, invented by Fox Talbot at the same time as Daguerre was working on his discovery, was the first negative–positive process, allowing a number of positives to be printed from a single negative. The paper negatives had a rough surface, which reduced definition, giving a very soft image, and were extremely slow, requiring long exposures, as did the daguerreotype. MacCosh's Indian pictures were calotypes. By comparison, the wet-collodion process needed a fraction of the exposure time, yet achieved a clear, sharp, grainless image with no limit to the number of positive copies. However, the wet-plate method had one major inconvenience: the glass plate for the negative had to be sensitized immediately before exposure and developed immediately after. For optimum quality the plate had to be damp during exposure and if it dried before development had taken place the clarity was also

The Valley of the Shadow of Death, Crimea, 1854. *Roger Fenton.*

impaired. This meant that a photographer had to transport a complete darkroom whenever he went out to take pictures.

So, before he left England, Fenton prepared a special photographic van for use in the field. It was converted from a wine merchant's vehicle and fitted with yellow window panes, shutters, a cistern for fresh water, and racks for gutta-percha dishes and chemical bottles. It also contained a bed and washing facilities.

After an operational 'dry-run' in the Yorkshire Dales, Fenton embarked at the end of February in the *Hecla*, arriving in Balaclava on 8 March 1855. Besides the van, he took with him two assistants, William and Marcus Spalding, five cameras, the largest for 16×20 inch plates, thirty-six cases of equipment, 700 glass plates, and three horses, which he acquired in Gibraltar, to draw the van.

Fenton's photographs of military encampments, harbours, trenches and general views are an extremely valuable record of the period. At the same time, it is possible to describe Fenton's coverage of the war as a series of harmless, mild, drawing-room pictures. They mainly comprised photographs such as 'Lt Col Hallewell, his day's work over', 'L'Entente Cordiale' with French and English officers regailing one another with drinks, or 'Cantinière tending a wounded man' – all spick and span, not a drop of blood to be seen. Nevertheless, in Fenton's defence, it must be realized that with his equipment action pictures were out of the question. His exposures had to last between 3 and 20 seconds, even in the best summer light – long enough to blur the slightest movement. Thus, Fenton had to pose virtually every shot. In fact, apart from a few chance snapshots, real coverage of battle scenes does not begin until the First World War. In addition the wretched conditions which Russell had described had improved considerably by the time of Fenton's arrival. Supplies and medical care (Florence Nightingale was by then at work in the Crimea) were better, and the worst of the winter weather was over. But even when all this is taken into account, it is clear that a more conscientious man, mindful of his duty as a recorder-photographer, would have done better than Fenton.

Even in his own letters to his family and his employer, William Agnew, Fenton often described vividly the horrors of war – the ravages of the Valley of Death, the pillage and plunder by the soldiers of the civilian population, the sight of the dead and maimed. In his letter of 2 June 1853 he writes: 'We came upon many skeletons half buried, one was lying as if he had raised himself upon his elbow, the bare skull sticking up with still enough flesh left in the muscles to prevent it from falling from the shoulders.' And again, on 8 June: 'Meanwhile wounded men were going past, some carried, others staggering along to their own quarters, groaning and asking for water or faintly asking the way.' But Fenton did not set up his camera to record such

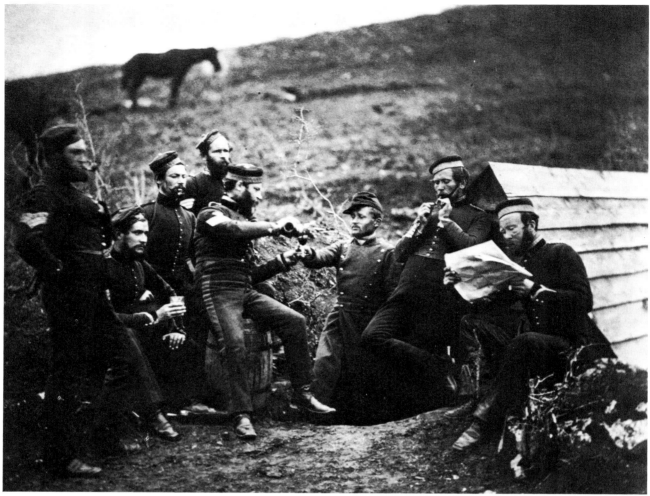

L'Entente Cordiale, Crimea, 1854. *Roger Fenton*.

images; perhaps he knew they would not be welcome. His task, after all, was to reassure and placate the public, not to shock. War was a necessary part of affairs of state, and Fenton an official servant, not a crusading reporter. He chose to remain a distant witness, not just through the limitations of his equipment, not just through his role as propagandist for the government. Rather, he remained the fashionable artistic photographer of Victorian upper-class society, concerned more with the technical and aesthetic qualities of the new medium than with the outwardly directed possibilities it opened up – the social, humanitarian impulse to drive forcibly home a message about the nature of war and the horror, decay and corruption it metes out to the common man – the message that this is what war is.

By the beginning of June the temperature had risen to such an extent that working in the darkroom van became an unendurable ordeal. '. . . the plague of flies commenced. Before preparing a plate, the first thing to be done was to battle with them [the flies] for possession of the plate,' Fenton later related to an audience at the Photographic Society. 'The necessary buffeting with handkerchiefs and towels having taken place, the intruders been expelled, the moment the last one was out, the door had to be rapidly closed for fear of a fresh invasion and then some time allowed to pass for the dust to settle before coating a plate. . . . As soon as the door was closed to commence preparation of the plate, perspiration started from every pore; . . . the van at this period, though painted a light colour, grew so hot towards noon as to burn the hand when touched.' The high temperature made it impossible to dry the collodion; it simply flowed off the plate.

In addition, Fenton became ill and, harrassed by constant demands from his sponsors in England for new pictures, he decided to return home in June 1855. He met with general acclaim, visited his royal patrons, the Queen and Prince Albert. Napoleon III expressed a wish to meet the celebrated photographer, and Fenton travelled to France. His pictures themselves, however, were not so well feted. They were exhibited and then, mounted in albums, they sold rather sluggishly. Later they had to be auctioned. The Victorian public were not interested in images of war, however mild.

Fenton's early departure from the Crimea prevented him from witnessing and recording the main objective of the conflict there – the recapture from the Russians of the port and fortress of Sebastopol, which finally fell on 8 September 1855.

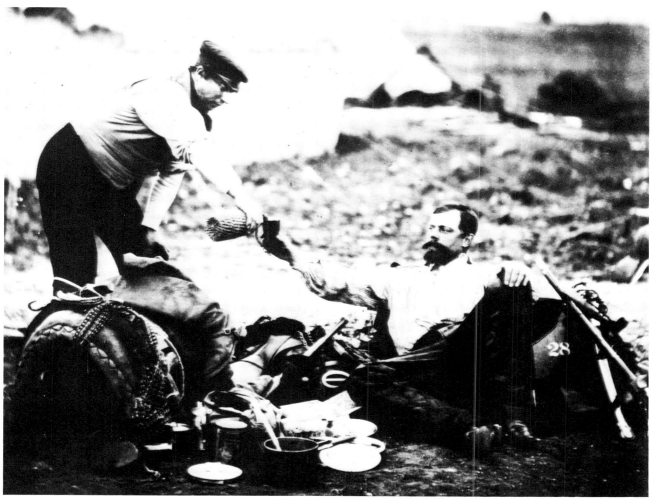

James Robertson and Felice A. Beato

The privilege of photographing the last stages of the war fell to another Englishman, James Robertson, who in the 1850s exhibited views of Athens, Malta and Constantinople. Robertson, superintendent and chief engraver of the Imperial Mint at Constantinople, arrived in the Crimea in the early days of September 1855, just before the final successful assault on Redan and Malakoff. He took some fine pictures of the preparation for the attack and of the scenes of destruction and death after the surrender. Like Fenton, he experienced difficulty selling his pictures, of which there are some sixty in all.

A third set of Crimean photographs were taken by Captain Charles Langlois, a French officer stationed there from November 1855. Compared to Fenton and Robertson, Langlois' work is virtually unknown.

Between 1853 and 1857 Robertson worked with another photographer, an Italian, Felice A. Beato, and after the Crimea they travelled together to India. By the late 1850s there were many photographers in India, both amateur – mostly officers in the Indian Army, such as Captain Robert Gill – and professional, including Samuel Bourne and John Burke. Soon after his arrival, Beato opened a studio in Calcutta, but

Lt Col Hallewell: his day's work over, Crimea, 1854. *Roger Fenton.*

seems to have been less interested in making portraits of English residents than in following the British Army and recording its activities, in particular the suppression of the Indian Mutiny in 1858. Although Robertson also photographed the Mutiny, it is Beato who left the most impressive series of pictures.

The Mutiny, which broke out at Meerut in 1857 over the issue of the new Enfield rifle to the sepoys, spread quickly through most of Upper and Central India. Its major incidents were the massacre of women and children in Cawnpore, the annihilation of the white population of Delhi and the siege and subsequent relief of the fortified town of Lucknow. Beato's pictures of the ravaged Cawnpore, of the ruined temples of Secondra Bagh on the outskirts of Lucknow with whitened skulls and bones of the rebels represent a shattering record. But in spite of their fine quality and grandeur of composition, they somehow lack the vividness and emotion of even Robertson's static photographs of the Crimea.

Beato must have enjoyed army life and the excitement of conflict because we find him soon after, in 1860, busily arranging his classical compositions in the final stages of the Franco–British war against China.

41

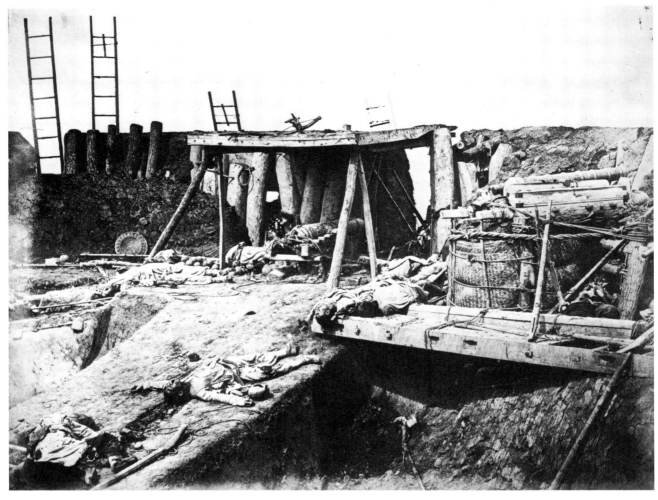

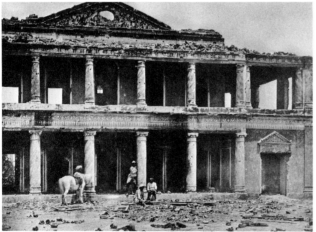

Secondra Bagh after the slaughter of 2000 rebels,
India, 1858. *Felice Beato*.

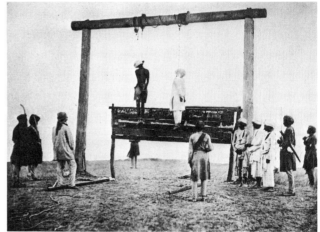

Hanging of mutineers, India, 1858. *Felice Beato*.

The main cause of the Second Opium War was the
blatant aggression by the Western powers in 1856 to
preserve the profitable opium-importing trade in
China. As in India, Beato photographed the closing
stages of the war, the capture, after fierce fighting, of
the forts of Pehtang and Taku guarding the route to
Peking, with the bodies of defenders, broken guns and

scaling ladders. They are a grim record, but also a little
theatrical in Beato's studious treatment.

Fenton, Robertson and Beato – perhaps the photographer officers and gentlemen of an imperial power,
only briefly engaged in an alien, sometimes exotic far-
flung corner; their expeditions were in the nature of a
photographic grand tour to record spectacular land-

scapes and vistas. They show us the topography of a certain kind of war – remote, far from home, a record to be exhibited for the curious in London or Paris. Thus, Beato's grand scenes of horror remain distant and detached; Fenton's elegant compositions cool and uninvolved.

Not so the photographers of the American Civil War, recording over four years their ravaged country. From the pictures of private soldiers in the field to the studio studies of Abraham Lincoln and Jefferson Davis, they portrayed their own people – Union and Confederate. They still remained largely recorders after the event for they worked under the same practical limitations as Fenton, but from the first battle of Bull Run in 1861 photographers were under fire with soldiers on the battlefield; they ate out of the same cooking pot, were soaked by the same rain.

Mathew B. Brady and the American Civil War

The American Civil War was the first war to receive full photographic coverage, due by and large to the efforts of one man – Mathew B. Brady.

Brady was born near New York, of a poor Irish family, in 1823 and came to photography by the unusual occupation of itinerant portrait painter. His art teacher introduced him to Samuel F. B. Morse, inventor of the telegraph and an early exponent of daguerreotype photography. In 1844 Brady opened his first studio in New York, and soon became a celebrated portrait photographer. His daguerreotype portraits won him many medals in American and European exhibitions and he gradually assembled a remarkable collection of pictures of the most notable personalities of the time. He began to use the wet-plate process in 1854, and when Alexander Gardner joined him in 1856, he started to specialize in life-size portraits. It was Gardner, a Scot experienced in wet-plate photography, who introduced Brady to the techniques of enlarging. Gardner became manager of Brady's Washington studio.

In 1860 Brady photographed Abraham Lincoln for the first time. (In all he made some thirty-five portraits of the President.) Lincoln attributed his election in part to Brady's picture: 'Brady and the Cooper Union Speech made me President.' At the outbreak of the Civil War, Lincoln gave Brady his personal authorization to follow the Union armies.

Brady saw himself as a pictorial historian, and this is perhaps what prompted him to embark on the costly and dangerous undertaking of photographing the war. 'I felt I had to go. A spirit in my feet said "go", and I went.' He hoped to pay for the venture out of the sale of stereographs of war scenes, but the demand fell far short of his expectation. The North anticipated a short, victorious campaign and Brady initially had no difficulty in financing his operation himself.

On the morning of 16 July 1861 Brady, wearing his habitual linen duster and straw hat, left Washington with General Irving McDowell's columns on the way to Centreville, Virginia, where the Confederate army was grouping. Despite Lincoln's authorization he encountered difficulty in obtaining permission from McDowell to go to the front:

I did have trouble; many objections were raised. However, I went to the first battle of Bull Run with two wagons from Washington. My personal companions were Dick McCormick, then a newspaper writer, Ned Hause and Al Waud, the sketch artist. We stayed all night at Centreville; we got as far as Blackburne's Ford; we made pictures and expected to be in Richmond next day, but it was not so, and so our apparatus was a good deal damaged on the way back to Washington; yet we reached the city.

Bull Run was a disaster for the Union Army, and a near disaster for Brady, according to a contemporary report:

[Brady's party] got so far as the smoke of Bull's Run, and was aiming the never-failing tube at friends and foes alike, when with the rest of our Grand Army they were completely routed and took to their heels, leaving their photographic accoutrements on the ground, which the rebels, no doubt, pounced upon as trophies of victory. Perhaps they considered the camera an infernal machine. The soldiers live to fight another day, our special friends to make again their photographs.

Another contemporary account gives a description of Brady at work at Bull Run:

Brady has shown more pluck than many of the officers and soldiers who were in the fight. He went – not exactly like the 'Sixty-ninth', stripped to the pants – but with his sleeves tucked up and his big camera directed upon every point of interest on the field. Some pretend, indeed, that it was the mysterious and formidable looking instrument that produced the panic! The runaways, it is said, mistook it for the great steam gun discharging 500 balls a minute, and immediately took to their heels when they got within its focus! However this may be, it is certain that they did not get away from Brady as easily as they did from the enemy. He has fixed the cowards beyond the possibility of a doubt.

It was now evident that the war would not be a brief campaign. Brady set about extending the photographic coverage, paying at times up to as many as twenty photographers in the field. 'I had men in all parts of the army, like a rich newspaper,' he claimed. Initially all the photographs taken by his camera men carried the by-line 'From a photograph by Brady', but only a relatively small proportion were taken by Brady himself, for he spent part of his time in Washington, organizing the photographic operations. However, he continued to make regular visits to the front, photographing the aftermath of Antietam and Gettysburg and coming under fire at Fredericksburg and

Petersburg. His eyesight was already deteriorating by this time.

GARDNER AND O'SULLIVAN

The two most important photographers in Brady's team were Alexander Gardner and Timothy H. O'Sullivan. In the initial stages of the war Gardner covered the battle of Antietam and the Army of the Potomac in Virginia. He left Brady's employment early in 1863, however, and opened his own portrait establishment in Washington, advertising a set of 'Photographic Incidents of the War', which he described as 'The largest and finest collection of War Views ever made. Apart from the interest appertaining to them, they stand unequalled as works of art. Amongst the contributors will be found the names of the most distinguished Photographers in the country.' Gardner claimed to have 'A corps of artists constantly in the field, who are adding to the collection every day.' It is probable that Gardner took with him some of the negatives taken for Brady, perhaps in lieu of payment, as Brady was beginning to encounter financial difficulties.

In the final years of the war, Gardner and his son James were employed by the Army of the Potomac making maps, but they continued to photograph the progress of the war, deploying photographic teams in the same way as Brady.

In 1866, after the South's defeat, Gardner published a *Sketch Book of the War*, a collection of 100 original photographs. It is an important source of identification as the names of individual photographers appear alongside each picture. Of half of these photographs were taken by Timothy H. O'Sullivan, who also left Brady to join Gardner, and who, with T. C. Roche, another of Brady's team, was perhaps the most continuously active in the field. He was at Fredericksburg and Gettysburg in 1863 and with Grant's army in the Richmond campaign in the closing stages of the war. It is O'Sullivan who took perhaps the finest pictures of the war: 'Harvest of Death, Gettysburg' (1863) and 'Death of a Rebel Sniper at the foot of Little Round Top', near Gettysburg.

There were a number of Civil War photographers who were not connected with Brady. Little is known of many of them, apart from their names. The Union Army had its own official photographers, including G. M. Barnard who accompanied General Sherman on his bloody march through Georgia to the sea. There were fewer photographers on the Confederate side. They had to rely on supplies of equipment and materials smuggled in from the North. A. D. Lytle worked on reconnaissance, photographing Union installations and troops for the Confederates, an incredible and hazardous task given the cumbersome equipment he must have used. Another Southern photographer was George Cook, a former employee of Brady.

On the Antietam battlefield, American Civil War, 1862. *Alexander Gardner.*

In all Brady's team exposed some 7000 negatives, taking many risks and often under fire. It is perhaps because of this constant proximity to the fighting that their pictures seem so poignant today. Brady and his men photographed everything – bridges, bivouacs, dead and wounded, guns and fortifications, ruined cities, hospitals and prisoner-of-war camps, as well as many portraits of soldiers and generals alike. The leader writer in the *New York Times* wrote on 20 October 1862:

Mr Brady has done something to bring home to us the terrible reality and earnestness of war. If he has not brought bodies and laid them on our dooryard and along the streets, he has done something very like it. . . . It seems somewhat singular that the same sun that looked down on the faces of the slain, blistering them, blotting out from the bodies all the semblance to humanity, and hastening corruption, should have thus caught their features upon canvas, and given them perpetuity for ever. But it is so.

Richmond fell in 1865, and Lee surrendered. Carpetbaggers invaded the South. In the post-war recession the American public showed little interest in stereoscopic views of battle scenes; they wanted to forget. Brady was unable to pay E. and H. T. Anthony for materials; instead he gave them one complete set of negatives of the Civil War. A second set he tried to sell without success and then, in 1871, he offered 2000 of the portraits to Congress, which failed to take any action. So Brady put his collection into storage. In 1873 in the general financial crisis he was forced to sell his New York gallery. He could no longer pay for storing the negatives, and they were auctioned by the storage company to meet the unpaid rent. The War Department bought the lot for $2840. Belatedly, due to the efforts of General Butler and James Garfield, Brady was paid $25 000 by the government for the collection which was worth $150 000.

After the war O'Sullivan and Gardner went west, to photograph the frontier; Brady, remaining in the east, died – virtually a pauper and almost blind – in 1896.

The Illustrated Press

Both Brady and Gardner produced stereoscopic views of battle scenes to sell to the general public. This was the means by which their photographs were most widely circulated. So far as the mass media were concerned, the use of illustration was only in its infancy. The first journal to carry illustrations was the *London Illustrated News* in 1842, followed in 1843 by *L'Illustration* in Paris and *Illustrierte Zeitung* in Leipzig. In America *Leslie's*

Dead boy in the road at Fredricksburg, 1863. *Timothy O'Sullivan.*

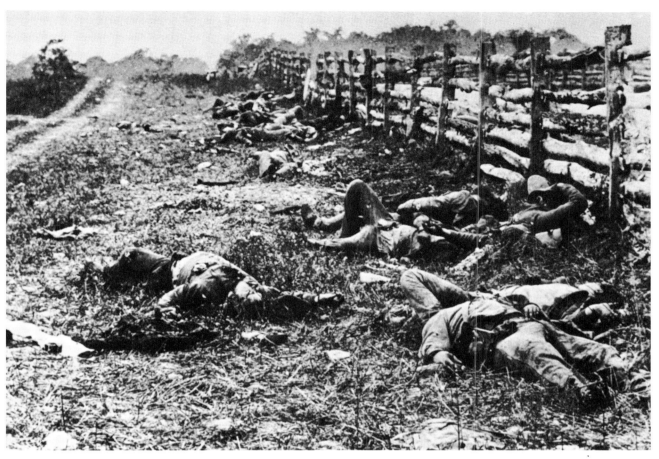

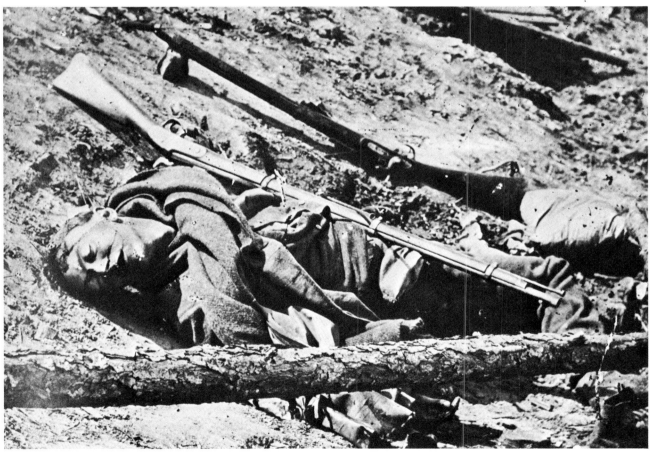

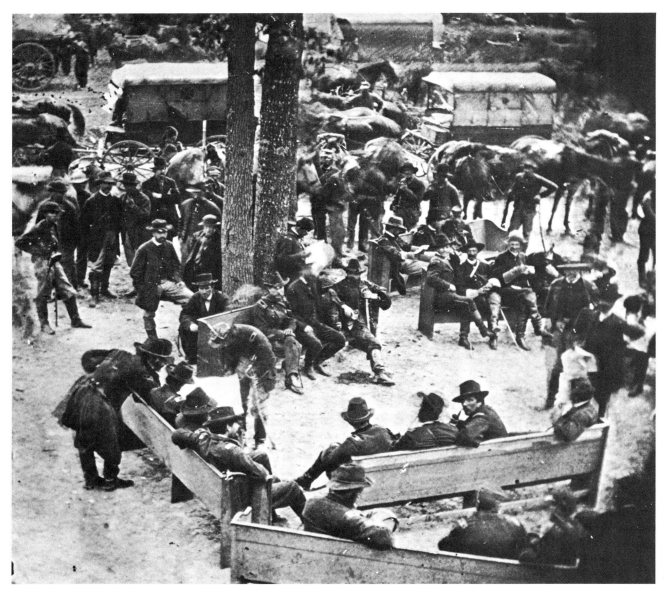

General Grant's council of war, American Civil War, 1864. *Alexander Gardner.*

Illustrated News and *Harper's Weekly* started publishing in the 1850s. Photographs were not used for illustration. Instead, periodicals used line engravings of artists' illustrations. These were usually woodblock engravings, or, for mass reproduction, metal casts (stereotypes) were made of the engraved block. Photography was used in the reproduction process for, with the advent of wet-collodion, it was possible to photograph the artist's sketch directly onto the wooden block which was then engraved. As yet, however, there was no method for reproducing the half-tones of a photograph directly on a printing plate.

The first newspaper to use illustration was the New York *Daily Graphic* in 1873, but not until the New York *World* in 1883 do we find the first example of a modern illustrated newspaper. As with the periodicals, this was illustrated by artists' sketches made from photographs, the line drawings being photographically reproduced on zinc blocks.

Thus, many of the photographs taken by Brady and his staff, as well as those of Fenton, Robertson, Beato and others, were copied by artists and published as line engravings. Photographers sometimes complained bitterly about the incompetence of engravers who altered and impaired the impact and quality of their prints, but by and large these pictorial 'translations' were quite adequate, judging from the comments of the *New York Times* reviewer of Brady's photographs.

Although reproduction of continuous-tone photographs was invented as early as 1866, with the Woodburytype, and the collotype a little later, these were only suitable for book illustration. Mass reproduction of photographs was not technically possible until the invention of the half-tone screen in 1880. In this process, essentially the same as that used today, a screen is used to break up the continuous tones of a photograph into a series of tiny lines and dots, varying in size according to the gradation in tone. When

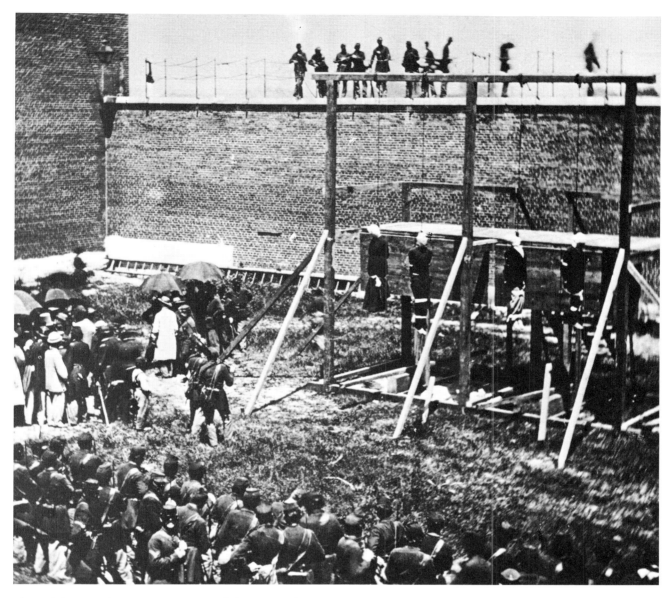

viewed from a distance, the grain of the image fuses, giving the appearance of continous tone. The first half-tone photograph was published in the New York *Daily Graphic* in 1890, but the majority of newspapers continued to use engravings of artists' impressions, partly because of the difficulty of finding a half-tone block suitable for use with a high-speed press. In 1897 the New York *Tribune* began using half-tone photographs regularly and other newspapers followed. By 1900 it was a common practice.

The developments in newspaper illustration did not lead to a demand for war photographs, however. The general public was interested in reading about wars and newspapers constantly carried war reports, but editors still preferred highly dramatized renderings of battle scenes by artists on the spot rather than static images taken after the event by wet-plate photographers. Even in the months leading to the Spanish–American War in 1898, when the faster dry plates and cut film were already in use, the notorious 'hawk' and press lord,

Hanging of rebels in American Civil War, 1864.
Alexander Gardner.

William Randolph Hearst, still preferred to send an artist to Cuba to provide pictures for his warmongering *New York Journal*. When the poor man telegraphed that all was quiet and requested to return, Hearst sent a cable: 'Please remain. You furnish pictures. I will furnish war.'

Competition between photographer and war artist continued well into the twentieth century. The *London Illustrated News* certainly used many more artists' pictures of the Boer War than original photographs, and this practice persisted, though to a lesser extent, even during the First World War. Looking at issues of magazines and journals of that period, one finds that the photographs indeed look tame and dull, even lifeless, in comparison with the artists' versions. Only in the Second World War did the photographer start to produce sufficiently powerful and dramatic pictures to make the artist-illustrator obsolete.

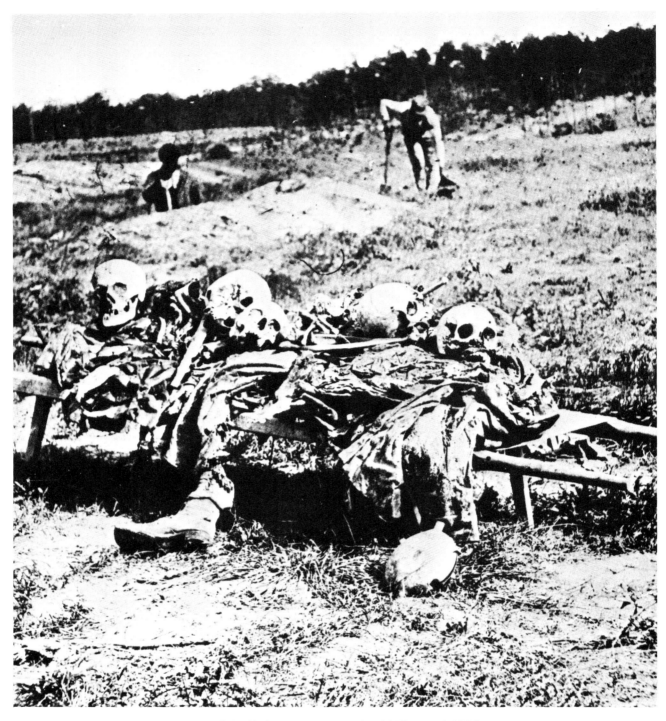

Collecting the remains of the dead at Cold Harbor, American Civil War. *Mathew B. Brady.*

The war photographer was still working under considerable practical difficulties which in part account for the relatively late appearance of war photographs in the popular press. To be able to compete with the artist he had to produce pictures with visual impact, in other words, pictures of action, but at the same time with good definition so that the half-tone reproduced in the newspaper – with low quality ink and paper – was clear.

The 1870s and 1880s
The years between the end of the American Civil War and the turn of the century were liberally punctuated by wars, often of a local nature, enormously varied in character, and fought in diverse arenas. With a few exceptions, most were poorly recorded. As we have seen, there was little demand for views of devastated battlefields and no outlet for them as press illustrations. In addition, their military value had not yet been realized.

Beato continued his activities, photographing the Franco–British venture against Japanese batteries in

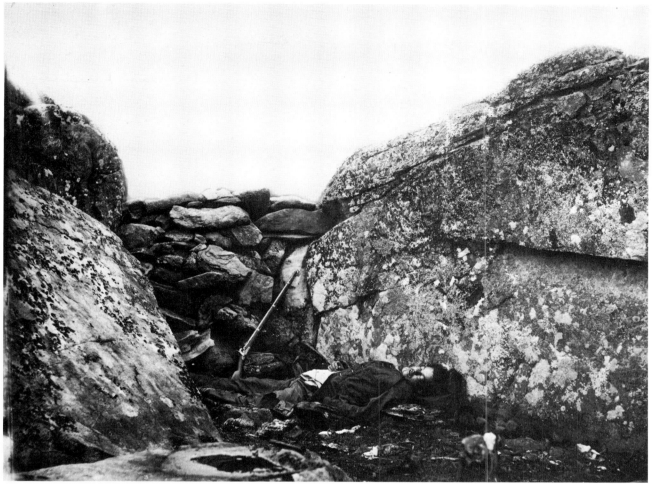

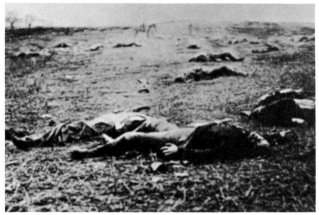

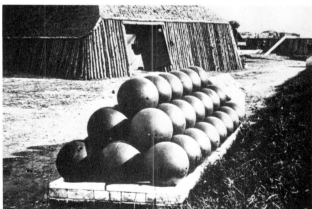

the Simonaki Straits in September 1864, but none of his pictures are of great interest. Of Bismark's three European wars, that against Schleswig-Holstein was recorded by various cameramen; they show little but views of corpses and hills levelled by bombardment. There are no photographs of war activities in the Seven Weeks' War against Austria in 1866. The Franco–Prussian War of 1870 was more extensive, but, although it involved two world powers, it did not receive the photographic coverage that might have been expected. The speed of the proceedings did not help would-be photographers; the war started in July and was virtually

top: Death of a rebel sniper, Gettysburg, 1863. *Timothy O'Sullivan.*

above left: Harvest of death, Gettysburg, American Civil War, 1863. *Timothy O'Sullivan.*

above right: Cannon balls, Arlington, Virginia, 1863. *Mathew B. Brady.*

over in three months when the French armies surrendered in Metz and Sedan. Paris, however, withstood a German siege of four months, finally surrendering in January 1871. Though some pictures of the German advance do exist, the best are those taken during the siege.

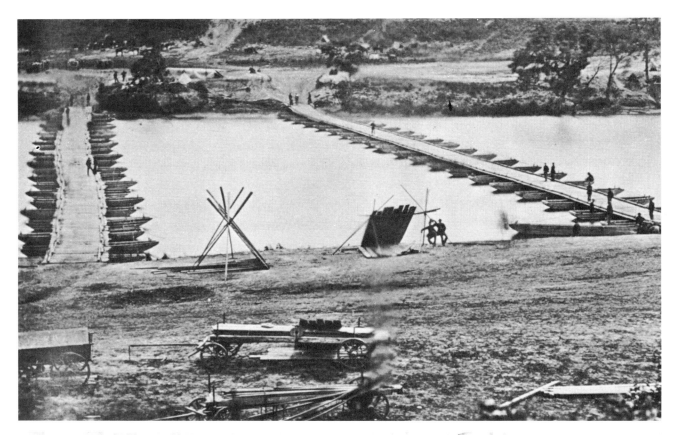

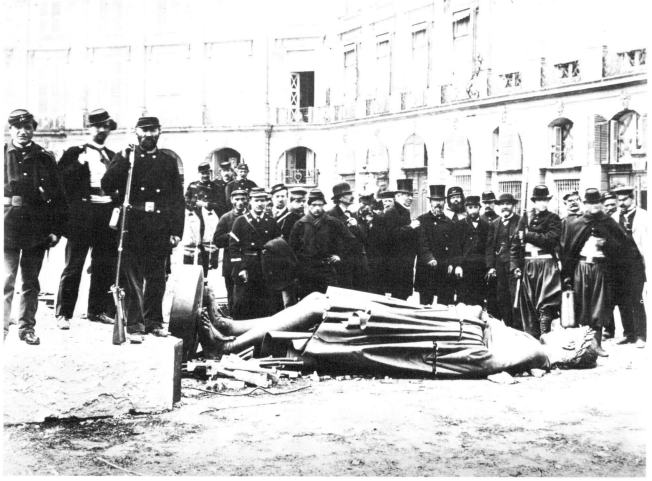

Pontoon bridge across the Rappahannock, American Civil War, 1863. *Timothy O'Sullivan.*

It is the subsequent pictures, by anonymous photographers, during the Commune of Paris in 1871 that are of greater interest. Some of the photographs, particularly those of the ruined column in the Place Vendome – which the Communards demolished because it symbolized Napoleonic repression – and of street barricades, proved ill-starred for the revolutionaries who posed so proudly for them. The resurgents were later identified from the pictures and punished by the Bonapartist government. Some, including the painter Courbet, were made to pay for the re-erection of the column. Charles Soulier photographed the ruined city after the Commune had been suppressed.

In 1872 a series of propaganda photographs was issued by the French government. They purported to show Communard atrocities, including the execution of hostages by firing squad. They were blatant fakes: the faces of the victims were superimposed on actors; the scene itself is hardly credible – the firing squad is three ranks deep.

The Russo–Turkish War of 1877–8, in which the Turkish forces were pushed back across the Balkan peninsula to the Dardanelles while committing dreadful atrocities, was largely unrecorded despite the involvement of large numbers of troops and protracted campaigns. In contrast, the small-scale war fought in southern Oregon and northern California in 1872–3 between the Modoc Indians and the American Cavalry was beautifully recorded by a great photographer. Eadweard Muybridge took some splendid pictures of this tiny conflict caused by the Indians' refusal to be moved to a new reservation. In the end most of them were summarily hanged. Muybridge, an Englishman, later achieved fame with his photographs of a galloping horse – the first pictures to reveal a horse's action – and for his studies of human and animal locomotion – a collection of some 100 000 negatives.

The British, with their far-reaching Empire, were the most frequently engaged in warfare during the second half of the nineteenth century. Between 1860 and 1900 British soldiers fought in Japan, China, Abyssinia, the Sudan, South Africa, Afghanistan, Burma and, of course, India. In India alone they fought well over thirty little wars during the reign of Queen Victoria. Possibly the first purely military photographic unit under Sergeant Harrold of the Royal Engineers recorded the British expedition to Zula in Abyssinia. The purpose was to chastise the rebel king Theodore, who had the temerity to imprison the whole British mission there. Some of Harrold's pictures taken during the march through the mountains to Magdala can be found in the collection of the Institute of the Royal Engineers.

Vendôme column overturned in Paris Commune, 1871. *Photographer unknown.*

JOHN BURKE

Of all the early photographs of warfare, John Burke's images of the Second Afghan War in 1879 are possibly the most impressive. Burke had worked in the Punjab as a professional photographer since 1860, covering most of the 'vicious little wars of retribution' as well as 'pig-sticking', tiger shoots and military reviews from about 1870 to 1900. Though he never photographed an actual battle, in one incident in the Afghan War he came near to a photographic scoop. He was with the British forces in the Sherpur Cantonement where they were to spend the winter months after re-taking Kabul. Burke took some pictures only a day before the British contingent of 5000 men was stormed by 100 000 Afghans. The attack was decisively repelled with the loss of eleven men, possibly the finest achievement of British arms in Asia. Burke's pictures were reproduced in the *London Graphic* as engravings.

Burke remains a distant recorder: his camera never comes near the action, never gets involved. Nevertheless, few of the nineteenth-century photographers can match him for his imagery and the splendour of his views of flowing formations of British cavalry deployed against the Afghan scenery.

The existing pictures of the Zulu War, at best a few odd descriptive shots of places where battles were won and lost, one or two of dead Zulu warriors – these may even be fakes – have none of the quality and interest of Burke's Afghan pictures taken at roughly the same time. Only cinema now can attempt to recreate the splendour of the Zulu attack on Rouke's Drift.

One series of pictures was taken in 1880 specifically as newspaper illustration, although the circulation was necessarily limited. In the First Boer War during the siege of the British garrison in Pretoria, one of the officers, Charles Du Val, started a camp newspaper to relieve boredom and raise the spirits of the officers. A photographer in the camp, H. F. Gros, provided a number of pictures, mainly of camp life, to illustrate it. After the siege, bound copies of the paper were published together with Gros's pictures. One of these albums is in the possession of the Royal Commonwealth Society.

After 1880 the transition to dry plates gradually took place. The gelatin dry-plate process was invented by Maddox in 1871, but the early plates were slower than collodion plates, however. It was George Eastman who was responsible for the popularization of the dry-plate process. He experimented with the materials, improved the speed, and began marketing his own mechanically coated plates in England in 1879 and in America in 1880. With the invention of the roll film (initially with a paper backing, subsequently replaced by celluloid) and the Kodak box camera in 1888, Eastman paved the way for the era of the 'instantaneous' photograph.

But even with Eastman's improvements, the quality

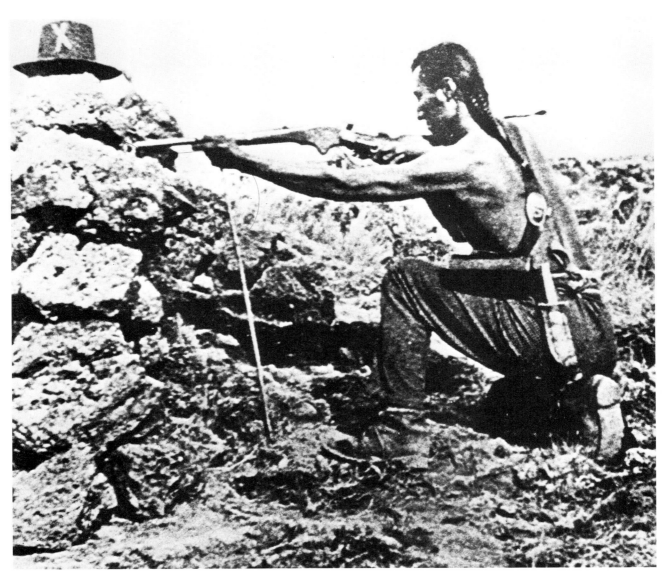

A Modoc warrior on the war path, 1872–3. *Eadweard Muybridge.*

of the dry plate was still inferior to wet collodion in the 1880s, and many photographers continued to put up with the difficulties of transporting darkroom equipment – sometimes carried by native porters – rather than use the slower, harsher materials. By the time of the Second Boer War and the Spanish–American War, however, photographers were finally able to dispense with a travelling darkroom, though to produce a really fine-quality negative, a large plate, and therefore a large camera on a tripod, was still necessary. Most of the photographers in the Boer War, for example, employed the reliable 8 × 10 view camera, with the inevitable loss of immediacy and action.

The enormous popularity of photography in the nineteenth century had prompted the appearance of a great variety of cameras. Even in the wet-plate era, many models and sizes were marketed, including a self-contained wet-plate camera; the processes of sensitizing and development took place inside the camera in a primitive semi-automatic manner. It is unlikely that this ingenious contraption was ever used by a war photographer, however. The advent of the dry-plate allowed manufacturers to run riot and a profusion of cameras was produced after 1880. It is difficult to establish what type of camera was used by a specific photographer. A picture of Jimmy Hare in the Spanish–American War shows him carrying only a medium-sized camera. He managed to produce some almost snapshot-like images of action, but only just of acceptable quality.

The dry-plate pictures taken in 1886–7 by Colonel R. B. Graham of the 7th Bengal Cavalry during the Third Burma War are markedly inferior to earlier Asian pictures; only a few of them are of a military nature. They are in the collection of the Royal Commonwealth Society. Another early set (now in the National Army Museum) were taken during the North West Frontier Wars in India in 1890 and 1895.

The difficulties of transport, the technical limitations and the lack of recognition of photography as a tool of press-coverage made for some lost opportunities in the last decades of the nineteenth century. What a splendid spectacle and subject matter the Sudanese Wars would have been for a contemporary McCullin or Burrows armed with a Nikon and a fast film to record the death of a national hero – 'Chinese' Gordon – and the annihilation of the Anglo–Egyptian garrison at Khartoum by Mahdi warriors in 1885. The photographic unit of the 10th Company of Royal Engineers, trained at the School of Military Engineering in Chatham, arrived in the Sudan only after the action was over. Gordon's death remained unavenged until 1898, when Lord Kitchener gained the victory of Omdurman and reoccupied Khartoum. Again, photography failed to capture the majestic and stirring scenes as recalled by witnesses. One of them described the fallen Khalifa's black flag: 'Round it lay a mass of white-clad bodies, in appearance forming what might have been likened to a large white croquet lawn or tennis court outlined on the yellow sand.' Kitchener hated the press and was unlikely to have allowed professional photographers in the field. All that the photographs in the National Army Museum show is burying the dead, counting, on Kitchener's orders, the fallen dervishes (of whom 10 800 were found), and Gordon's ruined palace. Most of these photographs are attributed to Lieutenant the Hon. F. D. Locke of the Grenadier Guards, but this is uncertain.

It is only at the very end of the nineteenth century that war photographs begin to play a part in press-coverage and photographers to achieve professional status equivalent to war-correspondents. Indeed, it was the press itself which was partly responsible for America's involvement in the Spanish–American War of 1898.

The Spanish-American War

Public support for a war against Spain had been stirred up by the so-called 'yellow press' fighting for increased circulation, with Hearst's papers leading the 'hawk' sentiments. Atrocities of the Spanish occupation forces in Cuba were daily and vividly reported, often with scant regard to authenticity. Thus, when the American battleship *Maine*, on a friendly visit to Havana, blew up killing some 260 men, although there was no evidence of Spanish involvement, President McKinley had no alternative but to declare war.

Because of the long and emotional lead-in to the war, public interest was enormous. Some two hundred reporters were sent to the scene of the action with a whole flotilla of specially hired boats. Reports mostly took the form of written despatches; photographers were hardly prominent – but there are photographs, taken by a variety of people. A number of officers recorded the proceedings: Lieutenant Wide, for example, shot some fine pictures of the landing of American troops in Cuba; several correspondents also carried cameras, among them William Didwiddie reporting for *Harper's Weekly* and J. C. Hemment of Hearst newspapers. It is likely that some of them used the new light cameras and dry plates or film. By now Eastman's Kodak had been on the market for ten years.

JIMMY HARE

The Spanish–American War has its own photographer-hero: Jimmy Hare, a small, energetic American, received his baptism of fire in Cuba.

Infantry men in position, Afghan War, 1879. *John Burke.*

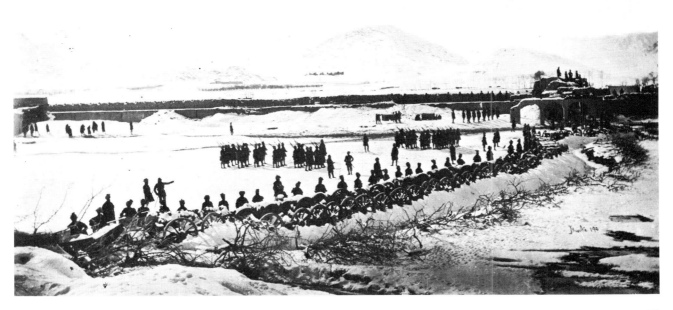

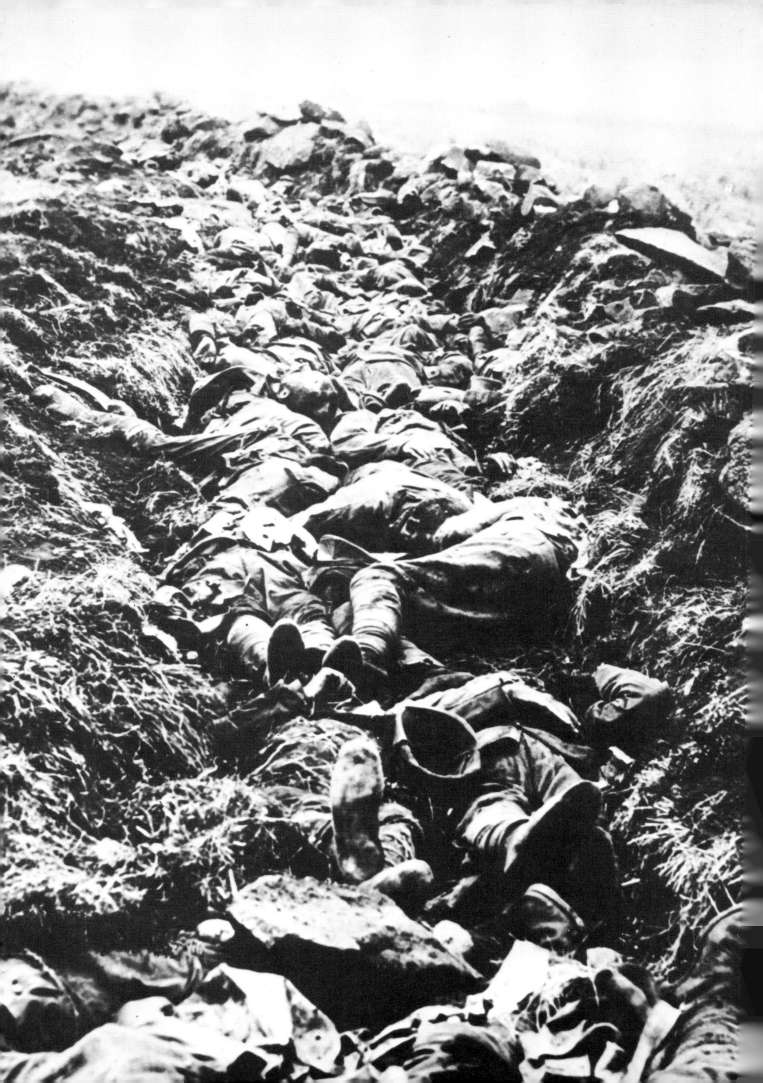

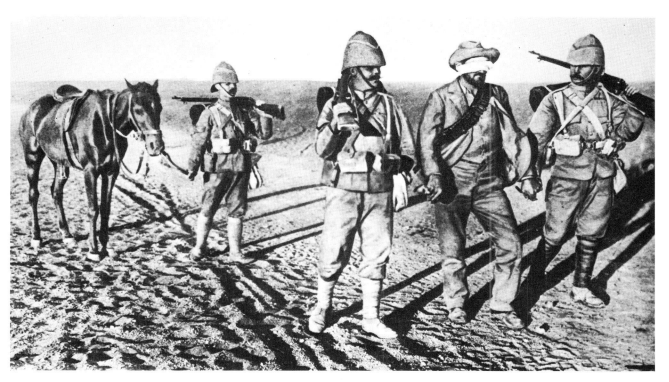

Boer prisoner captured by British. *Reinholt Thiele.*

Hare was the son of an Englishman who settled in America and became one of the early manufacturers of hand-made wooden cameras. He therefore had an early introduction to photography. He left his father's firm and after several years in England, returned to America in about 1889, to work for E. and H. T. Anthony, America's largest photographic firm. He had already started to take photographs himself by this time, and eventually left Anthony's to become a full-time staff photographer for *Illustrated American*.

When the news of the *Maine*'s explosion in Havana arrived, Hare forced himself upon the editor of *Collin's Magazine* and convinced him that he should be their photo-correspondent in Cuba. Thus a remarkable career as a war photographer began.

Hare is, perhaps, the first of the modern war photographers, tempted each time a new conflict erupts somewhere in the world. Soon after his Cuban assignment he was in Manchuria for the Russo–Japanese War of 1905; he covered the Balkan War eight years later; the Mexican Revolution a year after that. At the age of fifty-eight he photographed the First World War – this time for *Leslie's Weekly* – fighting losing battles with censors and officialdom. In spite of this he crossed the Atlantic three times and the English Channel five times, covering several fronts. He even managed to photograph the Polish–Russian War in 1920.

Not many of Hare's pictures have been saved and few

opposite: British dead at Spion Kop, Boer War.
Photographer unknown.

are outstanding. Nevertheless, it is doubtful whether any other photographer could match him for courage, resourcefulness and persistence. There are many remarkable stories about his thirst for news pictures and the lengths to which he was able to push his endurance in order to get them. Many of these, gathered by Cecil Carnes in his biography, *Jimmy Hare – News Photographer*, should perhaps be taken with a pinch of salt; but even if only half are true, war photography finds its first professional photojournalist in Jimmy Hare.

The Second Boer War

There was no equivalent to Hare in South Africa in 1899. Indeed the Second Boer War was fully covered professionally by war correspondents and competent photographers. Yet none of them show the totality of the conflict, not just the battles, but how the war affected the people whose land it was destroying.

By now the camera had begun to face the fact of human suffering, to make clear for all to see the squalors of social deprivation. Captain W. W. Hooper's pictures of the Madras famine in 1876–7 anticipate those by Werner Bischof nearly a century later; and Jacob Riis had already begun to publish his series of pictures showing tenement life and child labour in America in the early 1890s. Photography was beginning to develop a social conscience, but not, it appears, in South Africa.

There is no record of the excruciating effects of hunger and the deplorable conditions of the natives in the besieged garrison towns while officers still ate five-course luncheons, as happened, for example, in Baden-

55

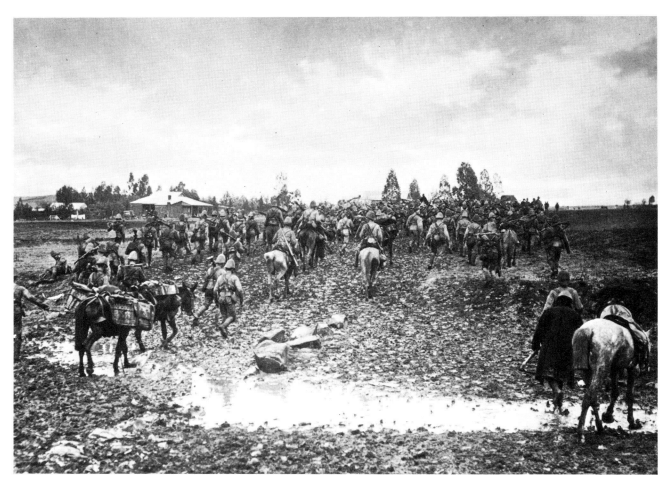

Retreat after a hard day, Ladysmith, Boer War. *Horace H. Nicholls.*

Powell's Mafeking. Some photographers, like H. C. Shelley, complained of boredom, of not being able to photograph anything interesting – meaning action. The most damning omission is the virtual lack of pictures showing Kitchener's drastic methods after the collapse of the main Boer armies, when bands of Boers harassed the British for a further eighteen months. There are no pictures of barbed wire, of the results of the scorched-earth policy, of Boer women and children in prison camps where the mortality rate was nearly 50 per cent and where some 20000 died.

Military censorship may be partly responsible for this; Kitchener was again in command. War correspondents' despatches were checked very carefully and few interesting items got through. But censorship of photographs seems to have been less stringent – perhaps photographs were not considered to be as revealing as written accounts. Indeed, exposed plates were sometimes sent to England for processing as the water in South Africa was dirty and polluted. This being so, photographic censorship could not have been very severe. But no photographer seems to have made a record to be saved for post-war publication, as Philip Jones Griffiths was to do later in Vietnam.

There were some exceptions to the generally low quality of the photographic record. With the Boers under Joubert pressing the British forces, in the first stages of the war, into Natal towards eventual encirclement in Ladysmith, a professional photographer from Johannesburg, Horace H. Nicholls, took a series of impressive pictures of the retreating army, pictures full of mood and drama. Their drama may be their weakness; they are too intentionally artistic, too theatrical. Nicholls said himself: 'I have made it my great aim throughout the campaign to produce a series of large photographs which would appeal to the artistic sense of the most fastidious, knowing that they must as photographs have the enhanced value of being truthful.' They are no doubt truthful, but they seem also consciously preselected for their 'art' and not for their authenticity. However, they still remain an impressive achievement. A set of Nicholls' pictures, 11 × 18 inches in size and printed on carbon paper, is in the collection of the Royal Photographic Society.

Reinholt Thiele, a German photographer living in London, who was working on commission for the *Graphic*, had a rather similar approach. He mainly used an 8 × 10 inch camera and subsequently produced an exhibition of his war photographs. Some of Thiele's pictures occasionally capture the drama of the moment. However, none of them capture the reality as it was experienced by the participants.

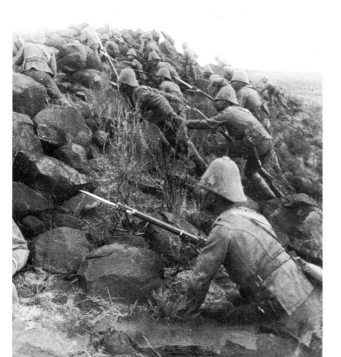

And yet the technical difficulties were far less than in earlier times. One needs only to look at the pictures which Alfred Stieglitz shot at precisely the same time in the streets of New York – in sleet and snow and rain, in generally poor lighting conditions; instantaneous pictures of horses, people and the life of the city. In contrast, many of the South African pictures seem static and often posed. But if we compare the South African photographs with those taken earlier, in Asia, for example, two points are evident. The first is the general deterioration in technical quality. This is no doubt mainly due to the transition from the cumbersome but excellent wet plates to a not yet fully mastered and often much slower dry negative process. And this transition also partly explains the second point, that in South Africa it was mainly the amateur and semiprofessional who seemed to do better than the professional in terms of content and impact.

Luigi Barzini; Herbert Baldwin

The start of hostilities in South Africa in October 1899 drew the attention of the British public as well as the majority of war correspondents to Natal and the sur-

below: American gun position overlooking Manila, Spanish—American War, 1898. *Photographer unknown.*

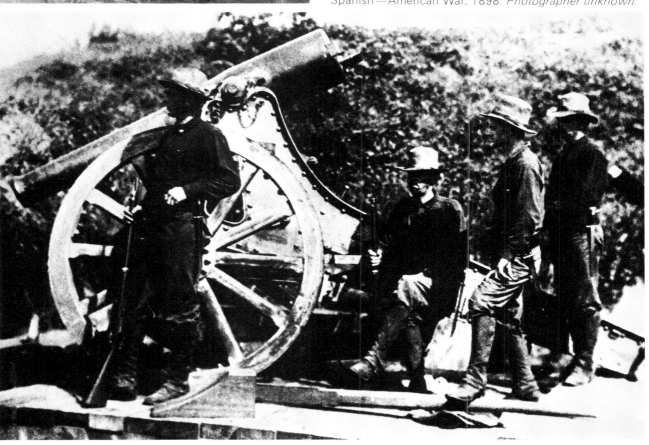

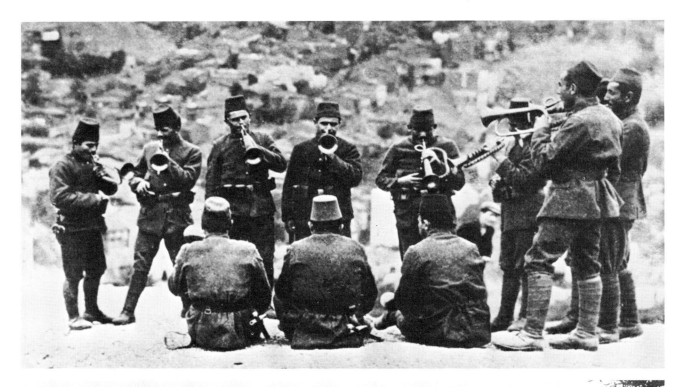

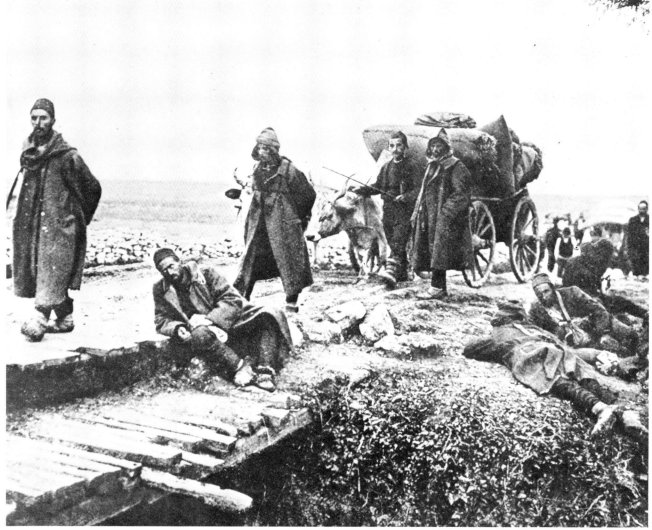

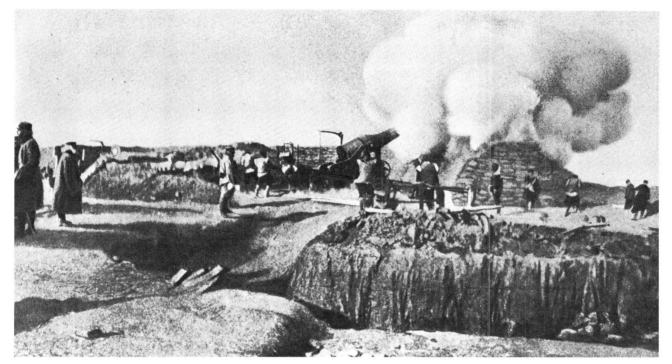

Battle of Mukden, Russo–Japanese War, 1904. *Luigi Barzini.*

rounding area. In consequence, the Boxer Rebellion in China, which an international brigade of western powers quelled in June 1900, passed largely unnoticed. The short but harsh and bloody struggle was almost singlehandedly and brilliantly reported by a young Italian war correspondent, Luigi Barzini. Not only did he write a vivid account of the rebellion for his paper *Corriera della Sera* (later newsboys in the streets of Milan used to call 'Article by Barzini'), but he also took some photographs. In fact, Barzini was as fine a photographer as he was a writer, with a highly developed visual sense, courage, patience, and an ability to find himself in the right spot at the right time.

Four years later Barzini travelled again to the Far East, this time to report the Russo–Japanese War. The Japanese imposed such strict censorship that most of the western correspondents left for home in disgust. But Barzini stayed, and finally was the only correspondent to cover, almost without restriction, the whole forty-mile front, and witness the merciless battle of Mukden in which roughly 80 000 men died on each side.

Two years after the war, Barzini published a book, *The Battle of Mukden*, which is apparently still highly regarded in Japanese schools of military strategy. It is liberally illustrated with his photographs; no longer odd pictorial shots, but a clear and complete visual record of soldiers, battles, the civilian population, and the desolation and tragedy of war. Barzini seems to be the first photographer of war who understood and hated the cruelty and futility of war, and he shows this in his writing and in his photographs.

opposite top: Bugle lessons for recruits, Balkan War, 1912. *Herbert F. Baldwin.*
opposite bottom: Victims of cholera, Balkan War, 1912. *Herbert F. Baldwin.*

Although Barzini's book is illustrated by his own photographs, he was predominantly a writer-correspondent. His son, another Luigi and a distinguished journalist and author in his own right, states that his father took his last war picture in 1911, of Italian cavalry in Tripoli; after that he never carried a camera again, not even in the First World War. Thus his book can hardly be called a photographer's war book. This distinction should be given to an English press photographer – by now the profession has a title – working for the Central News Agency, Herbert F. Baldwin.

Baldwin was sent to Constantinople in the autumn of 1912 to cover the imminent Balkan War between Turkey and a coalition of Balkan peoples – Serbs, Montenegrans, Greeks and mainly Bulgarians – seeking freedom from Turkish rule. The war broke out in October 1912 and Baldwin started his trek in the wake of the Turkish Army. He was at first in what he describes as a 'Press Camp' at Chorlu where there were a number of other war correspondents from British and French papers, as well as another photographer, Bernard Grant, and an unnamed French cameraman. He does not mention Jimmy Hare at all. Baldwin published his book, *A War Photographer in Thrace – An account of personal experience during the Turco–Balkan War, 1912,* in London a year later.

According to Baldwin, 'conditions under which a correspondent to the Ottoman Armies, who aims at securing a pictorial record of modern warfare, has to work are exceptionally and needlessly severe.' Many restrictions were placed on correspondents and especially on photographers; censorship was extremely strict; films had to be developed and shown on the spot; permission to photograph refugees was at first refused and only later reluctantly granted. A photographer had to avoid being seen photographing Turkish women as this was a religious tabu.

Baldwin did not take any action pictures (though he does mention that someone did 'secure under fire' some photographs on the Montenegran side). His only chance for real action, although not in battle, was apparently lost through a broken shutter and a damaged pack of film which failed him at a crucial moment when Turkish troops, in total panic, were streaming through a narrow bridge after the battle of Lula-Burgas. His thirty-six illustrations for the book are confined to the usual scenes of camp life, portraits of generals, some wounded soldiers and refugees.

Nevertheless, his account at first hand of his experiences and especially of technical problems is fascinating for a modern photographer. He offers some sound advice to would-be war photographers: for instance, he says that the side to be on is the one which loses the battle, as retreat gives a better opportunity for authentic pictures while attack always leaves the photographer stranded. He also suggests a bicycle as a better means of transport than a horse, and exhorts the photographer to be as near as possible – twenty-five to thirty yards is an absolute minimum according to Baldwin. Alas, he did not heed his own advice.

The first photographers of war in the nineteenth century had to confine themselves to a passive role of, at best, observers from afar, even if they were able to be present at the moment of action. With their equipment there was no question of active participation, and in fact 90 per cent of their pictures were taken after the guns were silenced – battlegrounds with only a memory of battle, the dead, and the survivors. Their photography may be described as portraiture of the participants and vistas or landscapes of war arenas, rather than records of deeds and action.

Paradoxically, with some exceptions like Nichols and Thiele, in spite of new advances and freedom of movement brought about by faster materials, the quality of war photographs declined quite markedly at the end of the nineteenth and beginning of the twentieth century. Smaller and more portable cameras produced grainier pictures, and the fact that a tripod was rarely used resulted in lack of sharpness and image detail. At the same time the lighter cameras did not bring an immediate revolution in the style of the imagery. Baldwin's pictures in the Balkan War are in no way better than those taken in the Boer War – visually they are just as static and predictable. They are frequently inferior to the pictures by Burke and Beato nearly half a century earlier. And yet Baldwin was able to obtain a small, compact camera, the $2\frac{1}{2} \times 3\frac{1}{2}$ inch Zeiss Palmos, when concealment was necessary. Other photographers in the Balkans, including Jimmy Hare, made better use of the mobility of small cameras.

But by now the era of the instantaneous photograph had arrived. Many examples of action snapshots exist. By 1912, a boy of sixteen, Jacques Henri Lartigue, had taken some remarkable shots of his uncles diving, aunts flying down the stairs, and his father testing a home-made aeroplane. Capturing action was not only possible, it was almost commonplace. Various detective cameras came on to the market, some concealed in a buttonhole, others in the top of a hat. Yet with all these improvements, the only photograph of war action is the shot of Canadian infantry climbing onto a *kopje* in the Second Boer War. It was probably taken by an amateur whose name we no longer know. No photographer seems to have been confident enough, or perhaps sufficiently brave and adventurous, to get involved with war at close quarters. In spite of their equipment, by now quite adequate for the task, they still remained distant witnesses.

Part Two
DISPASSIONATE OBSERVER
First World War – Spanish Civil War

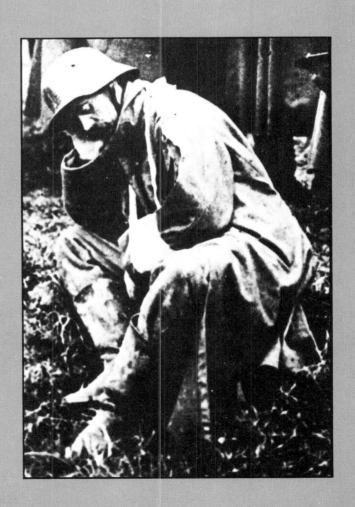

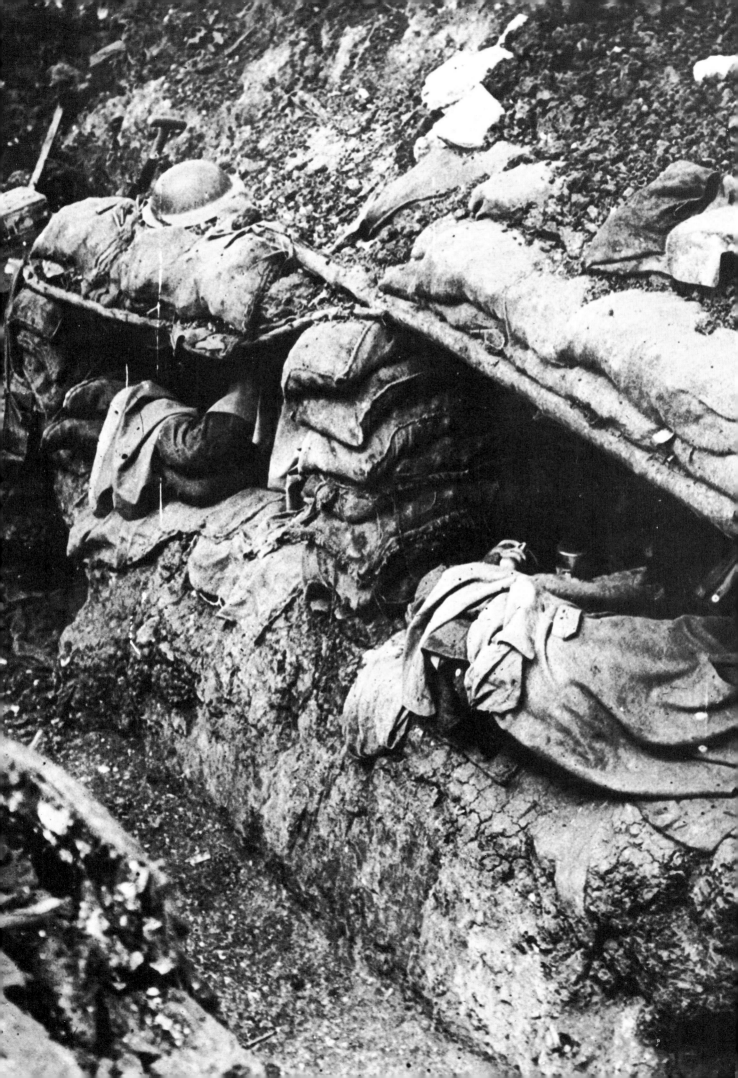

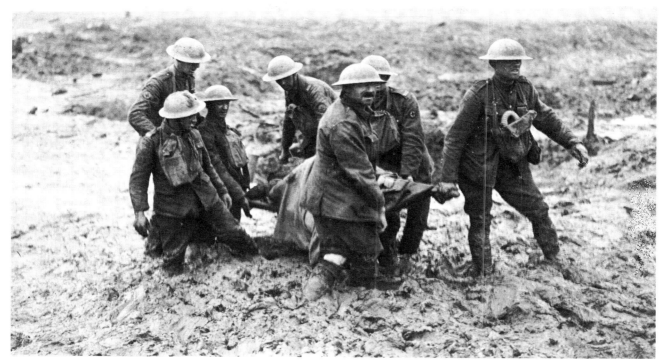

Battle of Pilckem Ridge, First World War, 1917.
Photographer unknown.

The First World War, the Great War with Europe as the battlefield, the war to end all wars, has been described as 'the greatest conspiracy to delude the public'. Indeed, the general public in a mood of naïve optimism rushed to enlist, spurred on by music-hall songs, exhorted by posters urging 'Your country needs you', and by private-enterprise recruiters such as Horatio Bottomley. And so they went, to fight against tanks, U-boats, and aeroplanes, to die in the trenches, bombarded by artillery, entangled by barbed wire, blinded by gas, buried in the mud, at Ypres, Marne, Verdun – 'the anvil upon which French manhood was to be hammered to death' according to Churchill – at Mons, Loos, Cambrai, Passchendaele. The toll of dead and wounded can be scored in millions: Russia seven, Germany six, France five and a half, the British Empire three; in all nine million died.

The delusion which started with the conspiracy of propaganda continued with the deceit of censorship. The public saw very few pictures of the war, only those of the most innocuous kind. No photographs of Passchendaele, perhaps the most horrifying struggle of the whole war, were published until the war had ended.

opposite: British troops resting in their trenches, First World War. *Photographer unknown.*

Right from the outset, no war correspondent was allowed anywhere near the front. Kitchener ordered several reporters to be arrested in France in 1915. Each correspondent was assigned a conducting officer whose one and only function, apart from preventing him from seeing anything, was to waste as much of his time as possible. The usual bland, ironic direction was: 'Say what you like, but don't mention any people or places or facts.'

For photographers the situation was even worse. No civilian photographer was allowed at the front; the penalty for taking pictures was death. Only two photographers, both army officers, were accredited at the very beginning of the war to cover the Western Front. Their instructions were merely to record, not to provide the newspapers with pictures.

In desperation the photographic agencies, deprived of all but officially sanctioned pictures, formed themselves into an organization, the Proprietors' Association of Press Photographic Agencies (PAPPA). This included Alfieri's, Central News, Central Press Photos, London News Agency, News Illustrated, Sport & General Press Agency, Topical, and Barratts. The new association hoped to negotiate with the government for permission to send civilian photographers to the front, but their efforts were to no avail. All they achieved was the introduction of a more efficient rota system for official photographers, a practice which survives today, for example, when photographing royalty.

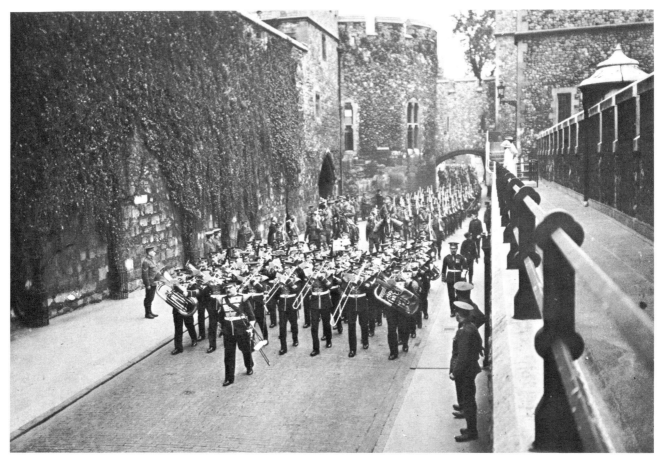

above: 2nd Scots Guards leaving Tower of London, 1914. *Sgt F. Pilkington.*

But there is no lack of pictures of the First World War; rather, there is an overwhelming number of them. The Imperial War Museum alone holds in the region of 100 000. There is another collection in the National War Museum.

There is, however, lack of adequate documentation to the photographs. Little information exists as to who the majority of photographers were – the odd name scrawled on the back of a snapshot, but most of these disappear after the middle of 1915. After that all photographs were pooled, names erased, and complete anonymity became the general rule. We do not know how the photographs were collected or distributed, nor who was accredited as an official photographer, nor whether officers were allowed to carry cameras as a matter of course. According to one source of information, there was a photographic unit in France under the command of Major H. D. Bartholomew (who later became chairman of the *Daily Mirror*). The unit consisted of at least four photographers – Ernest Brook, David McClellan, Tom Aitken and Jack Brooks. However, this information is based on unofficial recollections and is not fully confirmed.

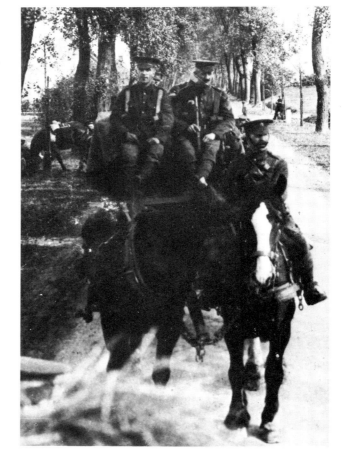

right: 2nd Scots Guards on march in Belgium. *Sgt F. Pilkington.*

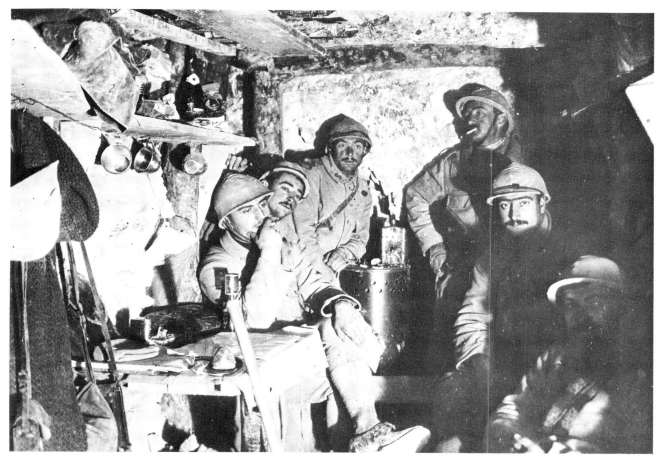

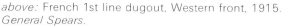

above: French 1st line dugout, Western front, 1915.
General Spears.

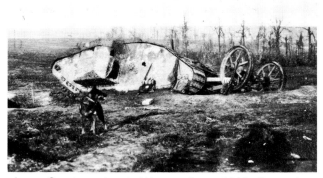

above: Overturned tank, Western front, 1916. *General Spears.*

If one were to classify and sort all available photographic material from a hundred scattered collections, it might be possible to identify individual work more clearly. But this would be a superhuman undertaking. There is no central source of information. The Public Record Office in London holds no documents specifically relating to photographers or photography. A great number of First World War documents relating to propaganda and public relations are known to have been deliberately destroyed; possibly photographic records were also removed.

Leafing through the yellowing records in the Imperial War Museum and the National Army Museum, it is possible to pinpoint various individual photographers in the first year of the war: officers such as Major Money, Lt Col Lanyon, Gen Pitman, Lt Crombie, Col P. S. Haymer, Capt R. J. Clausen, and soldiers from the ranks – R. P. Flack, J. Lightbody, the Hon P. B. Robson. General Spears continued to be credited after the middle of 1915; he took some interesting pictures in the battle of Loos in the October, and even as late as September 1916 his name appears on pictures taken during the battle of the Somme. Some of these, unusually, are of attacks, showing artillery firing; one, curiously captioned 'Coup de Grace', appears to depict a British officer firing at the prone body of the German soldier.

Of the early photographers, Sergeant Pilkington is possibly the best known, not so much for the quality of his work as for the number of pictures that he took in the first six months of the war. Through them, one can trace the history of the 2nd Regiment of Scots Guards, from their mobilization, as they march out from the Tower of London in October 1914, their landing at Zeebrugge and Ostend, to Bruges and Ghent, settling in and camouflaging the trenches, the first battle at Ypres in March 1915, the first dead soldier – Drummer Steer – and then on through Baillen, Neteven,

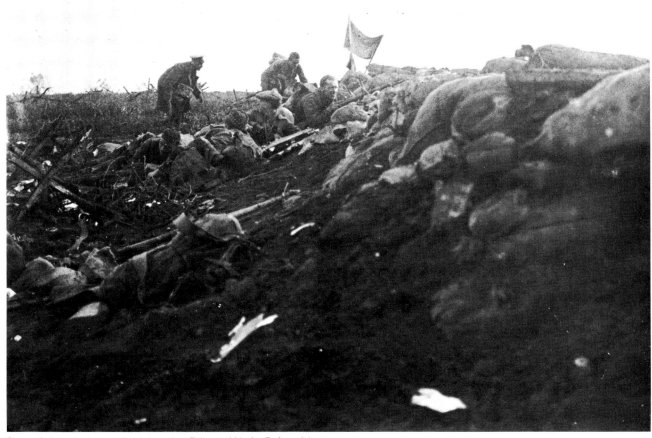

One of the photographs taken by Private W. A. Fyfe with a concealed illegal camera.

Fleurbaix, Sailly-sur-la-Lys. Pilkington snaps them playing football, boxing, attending the funeral of one of their comrades. No other photographer seems to have managed to achieve such a consistent sequence, but most of Pilkington's snaps are mundane, even dull. It is not clear if he was one of the two photographers accredited at the outset of the war and, if not, how he was able to take such a detailed series.

So far as quality of imagery is concerned, Private F. A. Fyfe can be singled out. A press photographer by profession, he enlisted in the army as an ordinary soldier, and in spite of the threat of a court martial and a possible death penalty, he had concealed on him a little camera. He took many pictures of army life, and also – a rarity of the war – pictures of attacks, bombardments, and some photographs immediately after battles. Later, after he was wounded, he took some pictures behind the German lines. It is unlikely that Fyfe continued to take photographs in a clandestine way throughout the first year; he was probably eventually given permission to continue his work in some official capacity.

All record of both Pilkington and Fyfe disappear after the end of 1915.

WILLIAM RIDER-RIDER

William Rider-Rider, now aged eighty-seven, is perhaps the only First World War photographer alive today. He is an exception to the general rule of anonymity which prevailed after 1915 in that he managed to preserve his pictures of the last two years of the war as a complete collection.

He worked for the *Daily Mirror* from 1910 and was conscripted into the army fairly late due to his weak eyesight. He was at first appointed bayonet drill instructor until, in the spring of 1917, on recommendation from Lord Beaverbrook (then Max Aitken and Minister of Information), he was transferred to the Canadian Army and accredited as their chief and only photographer in their French sector. He was soon promoted to Lieutenant and given complete freedom of movement throughout the entire Canadian sector of the front near Vimy Ridge. He covered the successful attack on Hill 70, the Passchendaele torture, and the final campaign of the war. Although he must have worked in appalling conditions, in trenches filled with mud and water, the only inconvenience he admits to is that the chalky terrain near Vimy Ridge made it difficult for him to keep his lenses clean.

In all Rider-Rider shot some 4000 4 × 5 inch glass plates which he and his sergeant developed and contact printed in a little field darkroom. The plates were then sent to General Haig's headquarters to be censored and

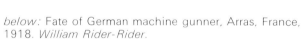

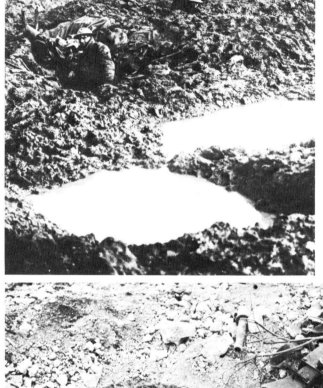

left: Soldiers in shell holes, Battle of Passchendaele, 1917. *William Rider-Rider.*

forwarded to London for distribution by the Central Agency. Payment for their use was donated to the Soldiers' Fund. Rider-Rider was awarded the MBE for his work.

After the war he managed to retrieve most of his plates and took them to Canada where they are now lodged safely in the Public Archives. Several exhibitions of his work were held immediately after the war and again in 1973. Some of his pictures can be found in *Relentless Verity – Canadian Military Photographers since 1885*, published by the Public Archives of Canada in 1973.

Bill Rider-Rider is certainly the best of the known photographers. His pictures are of a fine quality and well composed; they show some spectacular high points. Yet they seem somehow incomplete: they fail to express the real substance of the war. Giving us little from the viewpoint of the participants, they remain on the surface, without letting us see the war from the inside.

The First World War – a conflict of cataclysmic dimensions – did not produce one single war photographer who stands out from the anonymous mass of

below: Fate of German machine gunner, Arras, France, 1918. *William Rider-Rider.*

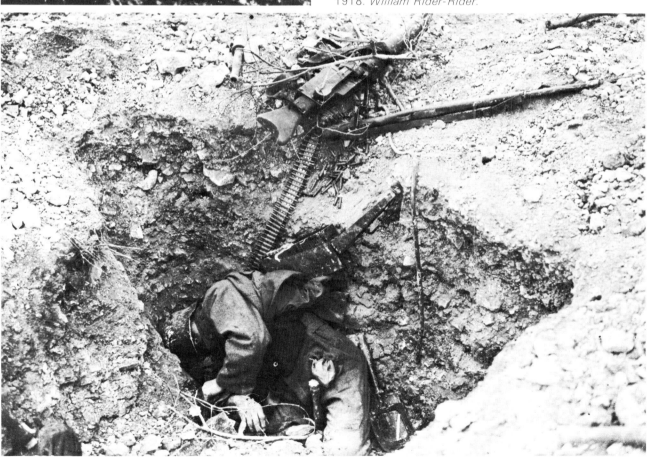

right: Wounded Canadians, Western front, 1917. *William Rider-Rider.*

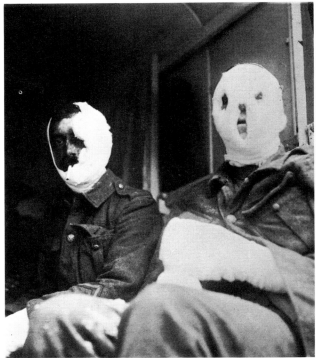

cameramen and shows both the grandeur and the depths of the calamity. In earlier wars it is possible to find individuals who created outstanding images: Fenton in the Crimea, Beato in China, or Burke in Afghanistan. In the Great War all individualism and inspiration were seemingly submerged and drowned in the quagmire of the Western Front.

Most of the early pictures are mundane and un-imaginative. Endless columns of marching men, soldiers eating, cleaning guns, or merely posing for the camera. It is unusual to be able to pick out from the early records a picture that stands out either for its visual beauty or for the sheer poignancy of its subject matter. Perhaps this is too sweeping a condemnation; after all, most of the early photographers were in-experienced and largely amateur.

There is a marked improvement in the overall quality of the photographs by the beginning of 1917.

below: Impromptu operation in a field hospital, Western front. *William Rider-Rider.*

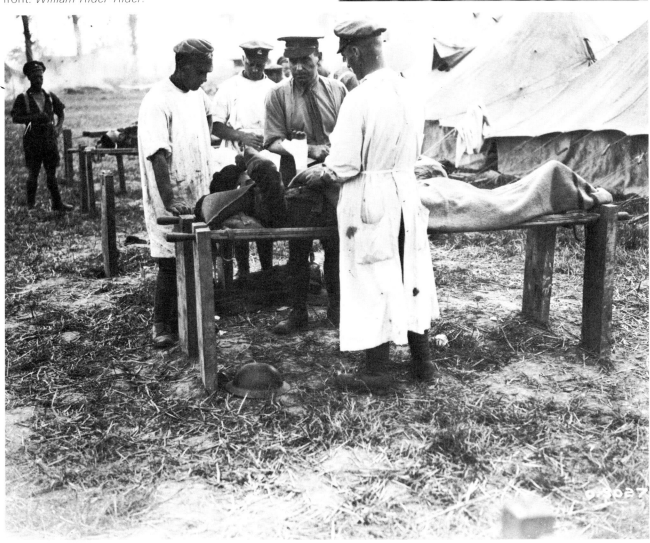

More professional photographers were assigned to front-line duties, partly as a result of the slow realization of the importance of photography both as a record of events and as a propaganda tool. One example of this improvement is the photography of Rider-Rider; no doubt other worthwhile photographers wait to be identified from among the mass of records.

But if we consider any single aspect of the war, there is no one set of pictures which adequately conveys its nature. There is no record which shows the actuality of the war at sea or in the air. Trench warfare, the unique feature of the Great War, is fairly well documented, but no single contemporary photographer produced an extensive record of trench warfare, though many of them must have experienced it. The realities of a war conducted from rat-infested holes in the ground are not vividly expressed in photographic images: the intense cold, the grime, the lice, the mud, the constantly wet clothing, the soaked and swelling feet; the nightmarish unreality of living with the perpetual fear of death from an enemy within earshot; the danger of sentry duty at dawn or dusk with the risk of death from a sniper's bullet; the shuddering periods of bombardment with thousands of shells raining on the trenches, killing, maiming, sending skywards cascades of earth, burying living men in mud; the sky at night crisscrossed with flares, explosions, fire. These sights live in the memory as images – the images in the photographs are inadequate and few.

The concept of the photographic documentary essay was not yet established in the press. The general attitude to the use of photographs as illustrations had not altered since the beginning of the century. Editors continued to show little enthusiasm for photographs. Press photography was treated at best as an information medium of limited scope, further restricted by censorship for the duration of the war. Thus, illustrations were of a routine nature and there was little attempt to use photographic imagery in an imaginative way. The majority of staff photographers were no more than adequate manipulators of the camera.

This general attitude may in part account for the quality of the photographs of the First World War.

Dump of empty shell cases and boxes, Battle of Albert. *Photographer unknown.*

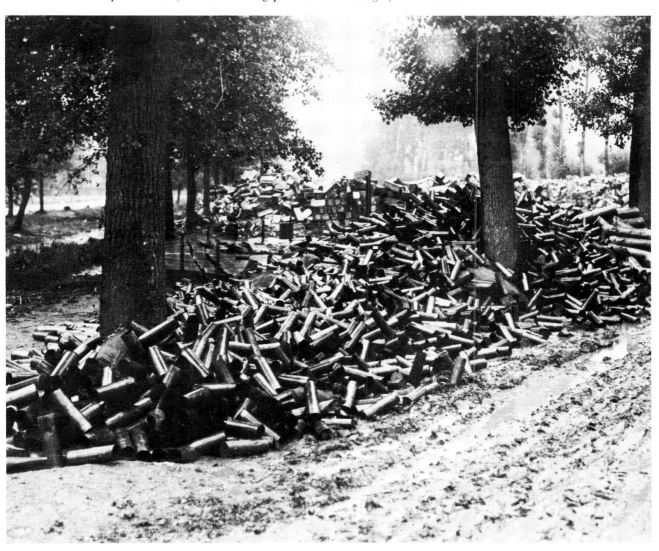

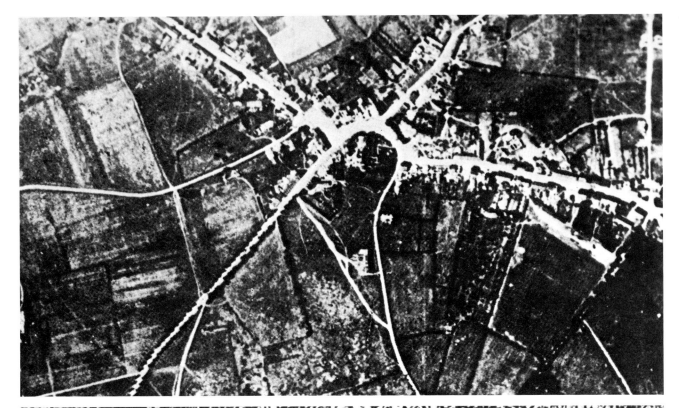

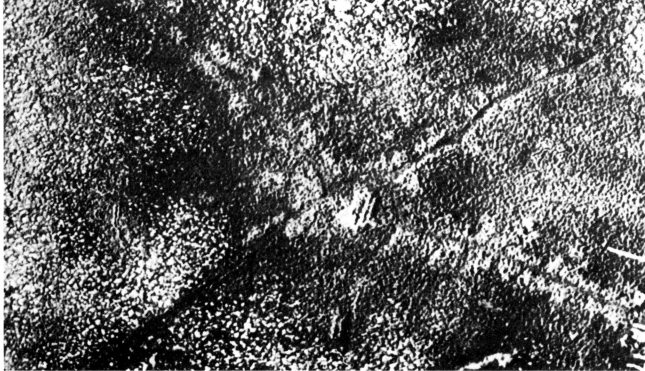

top: Passchendaele, aerial view, June 1917.
bottom: The same view, December, 1917. *Both pictures photographer unknown.*

They have a descriptive clarity but very few show passion or commitment on the part of the photographers. They seem to be describing something of which they are not really a part. Perhaps the war itself had worn away the ability to look too closely at reality. The photographs display a kind of reticence, viewing the dead from middle distance, rarely in close up. The photographers do not attempt to make a point, as if they did not expect that their pictures would be looked at. The power of the photograph to communicate a deeply felt emotion had not yet been realized. The camera had still to achieve the status of witness for the prosecution.

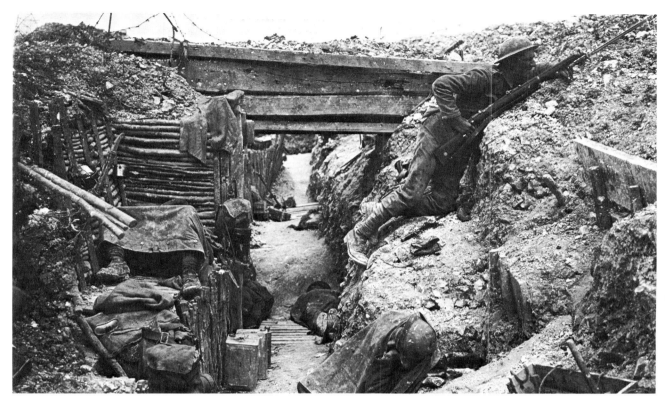

Battle of the Somme, 1916. *Photographer unknown.*

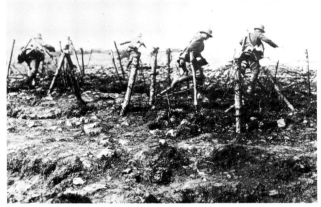

German attack, Western front. *Photographer unknown.*

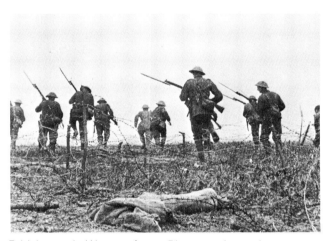

British attack, Western front. *Photographer unknown.*

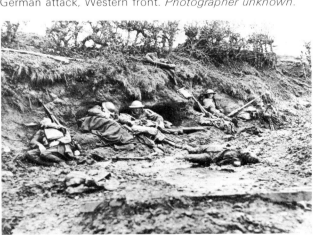

Battle of Passchendaele, 1917. *Photographer unknown.*

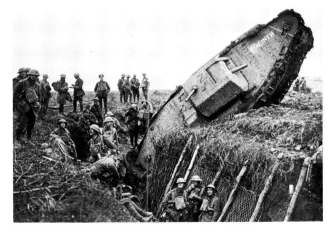

Overturned British tank, 1917. *Photographer unknown.*

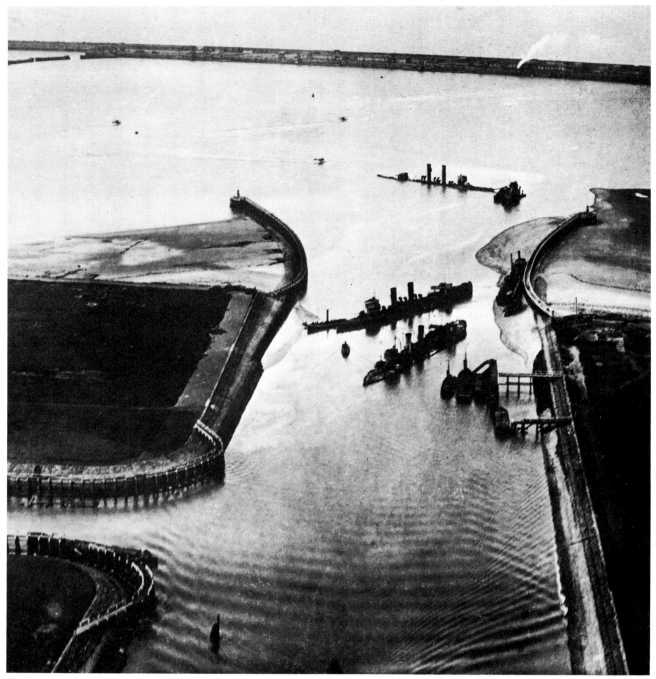

above: Air photo of blocked ships at Zeebrugge, Belgium, 1918. *Photographer unknown.*

German ship at the battle of Dogger Bank sinking. *Photographer unknown.*

opposite top: German air ace, Baron von Richthofen, landing, First World War. *Photographer unknown.*

opposite bottom: Disastrous attempt to land on HMS *Furious*, First World War. *Photographer unknown.*

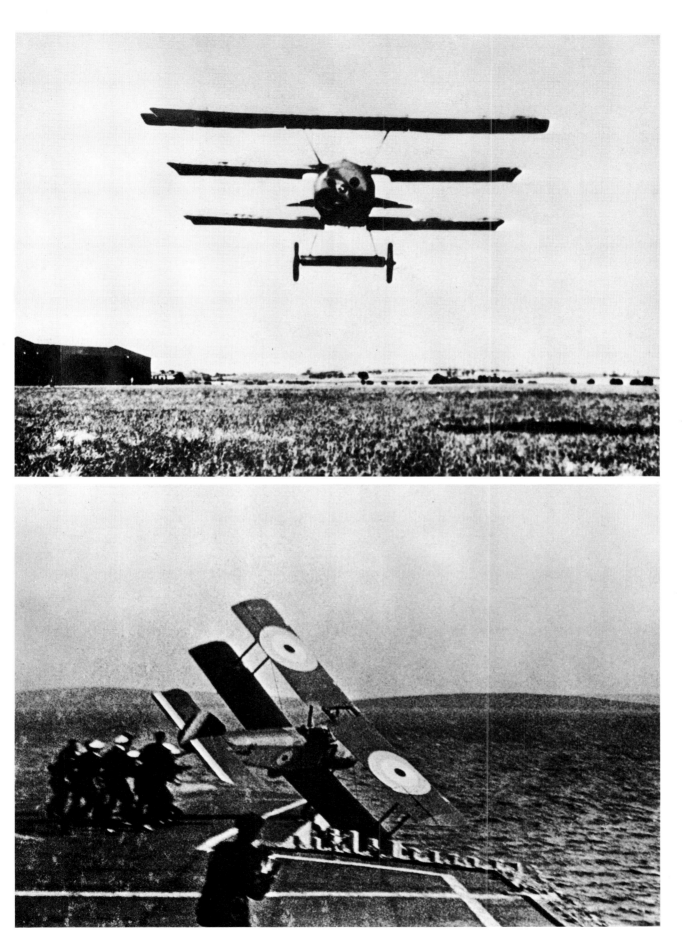

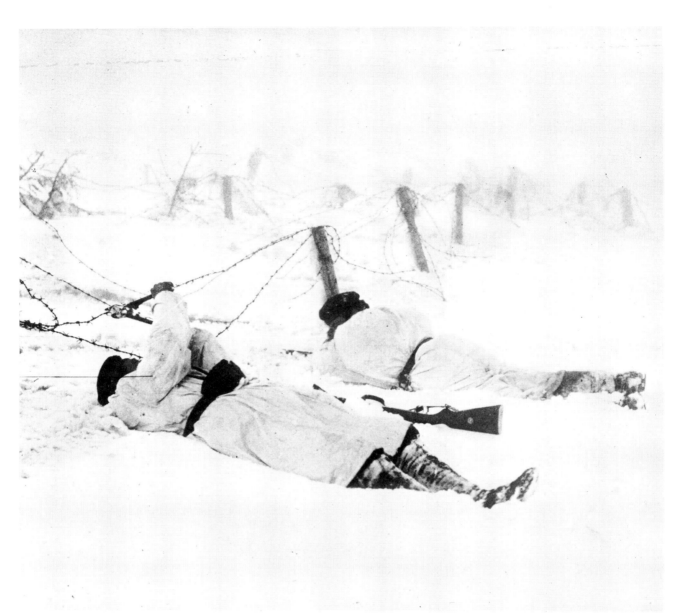

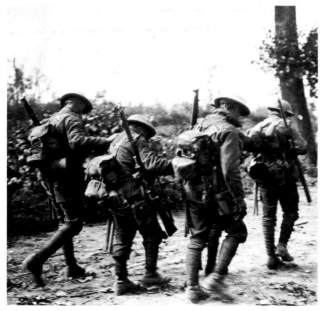

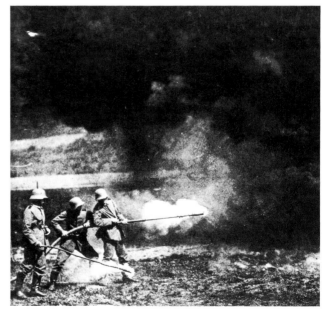

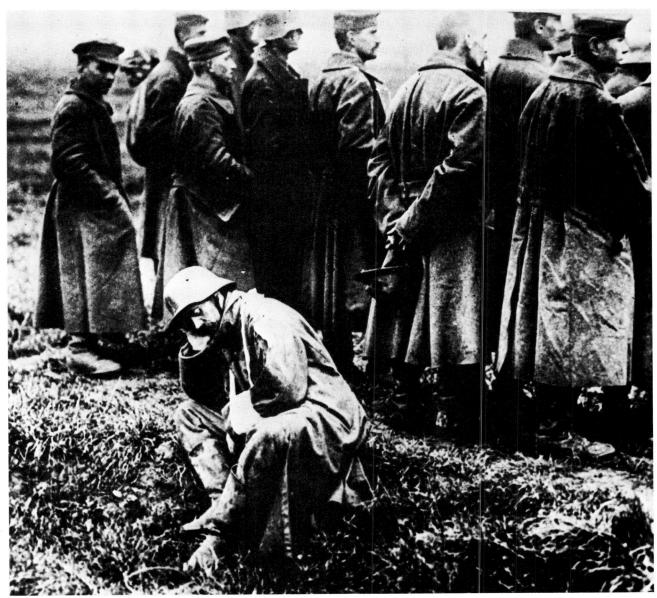

above: German soldier after the surrender. 1918.
Photographer unknown.

right: French refugee in Amiens, France, 1918.
Photographer unknown.

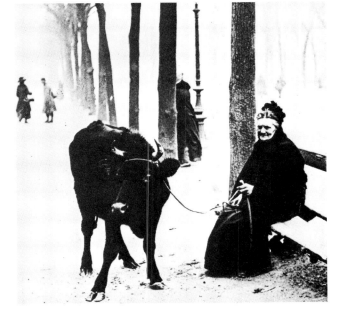

opposite top: German troops in the snow, Western front,
First World War. Photographer unknown.

opposite left: British troops blinded by gas, Western
front, 1918. Photographer unknown.

opposite right: German flame throwers in action on the
Western front. Photographer unknown.

The War in the East and the Russian Revolution

The war in Western Europe was at least recorded; the monumental struggles in the East must remain, as far as pictorial record is concerned, a complete blank. Immediately after the first relative successes of the Russian armies, all Western correspondents were forbidden to go anywhere near the Russian front. However, Robert Liddell, an English journalist working for the illustrated weekly, *Sphere*, and who was fluent in Russian, managed to persuade the Russian authorities to make him an honorary officer with a regiment at the front. He stayed with the Russian forces for nearly two years, but although he was a professional journalist and an amateur photographer, neither his reportage nor his snapshots are of any particular interest. His irregular position prevented him from writing the truth about the disastrous military situation. His photographs, taken with a little Kodak camera which he purchased in England for £4, show general scenes of Russian life and military life in its quiet reposeful moments. His book, *On the Russian Front*, which he published on his return to England in 1916, is illustrated with numerous photographs, none of which shows any action or indeed anything that might reveal conditions in Russia during the war.

With Liddell back in England, the outbreak of the Russian Revolution went unrecorded and hardly commented upon in the West. Rarely was the press so misinformed and misled as during the period from March to November 1917. Thus, possibly the most important event of the twentieth century is represented by a few random snapshots taken by anonymous cameramen.

However, the Russian Revolution, in spite of its tremendous historical importance, was in fact unspectacular and virtually bloodless. The upheavals in March 1917 which led to the eventual abdication of Tsar Nicholas, who was almost permanently away at the front during the crucial period, were accomplished with very little violence. Four-fifths of the city of Petrograd were in the hands of the revolutionary Duma within a day, with few casualties on either side. Most of the foreign diplomats present reported calm and orderly behaviour by the armed insurgents. Lenin's historic journey through Germany and his arrival on Russian soil were also in a low key. Even the unsuccessful *coup d'état* by General Kornilow, who aimed to overthrow the Kerensky government, was suppressed without bloodshed. Certainly the most spectacular, but even then hardly turbulent, event was the final overthrow of Kerensky by the Bolsheviks in October,

Two soldiers bearing the Red Flag, Russian Revolution, 1917. *Photographer unknown.*

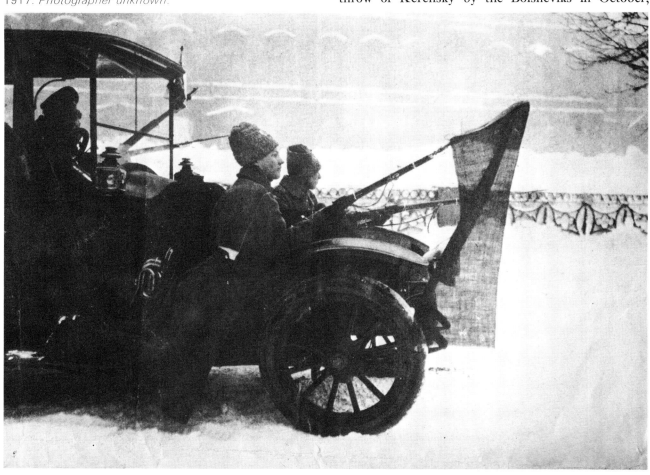

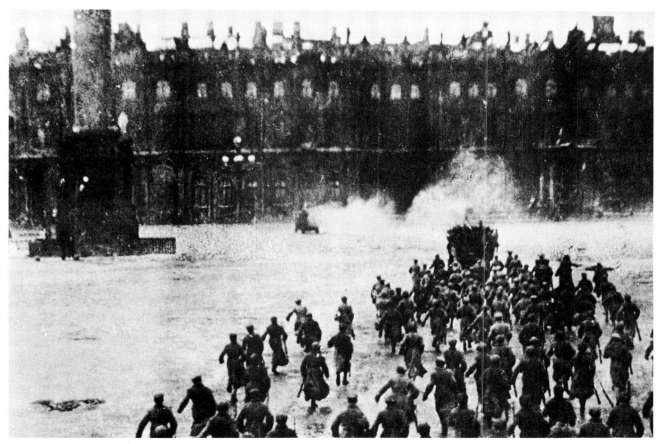

above: Storming the Winter Palace, Russia, 1917 (possible fake). *Photographer unknown.*

left: Troops listening to Lenin in Red Square, Russia. *Photographer unknown.*

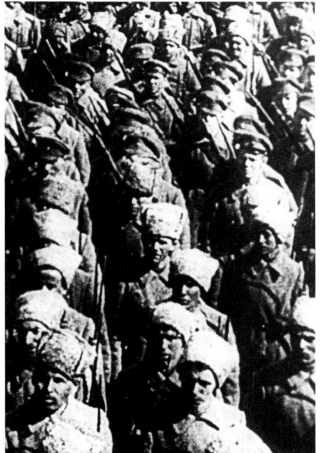

culminating in the famous storming of the Winter Palace. A few snapshots of this event do exist, but their authenticity is doubtful. Most of them seem to be stills from later cinematic reconstructions. All appear to be taken from a high viewpoint, but there was no high building directly opposite the Winter Palace. Nor were high-resolution long-focus lenses easily available at the time.

Nevertheless, a few photographs, though poor in quality, do bring back a little of the drama of those portentous days in Petrograd. The best is 'Street Scene in Petrograd', with frantic figures running in terror in all directions. No one knows exactly when it was taken, or indeed whether it is a genuine photograph of the actual event. A film still might again have crept in as the genuine article, but this particular photograph does possess a reasonable pedigree.

With the Bolsheviks in power determined to pursue a policy of ending the war against Germany and Austria, the West launched a series of interventions against the Soviet communist régime. A number of military expeditions were dispatched to support the White armies already fighting in Russia. There are a great number of photographs of the interventionists –

77

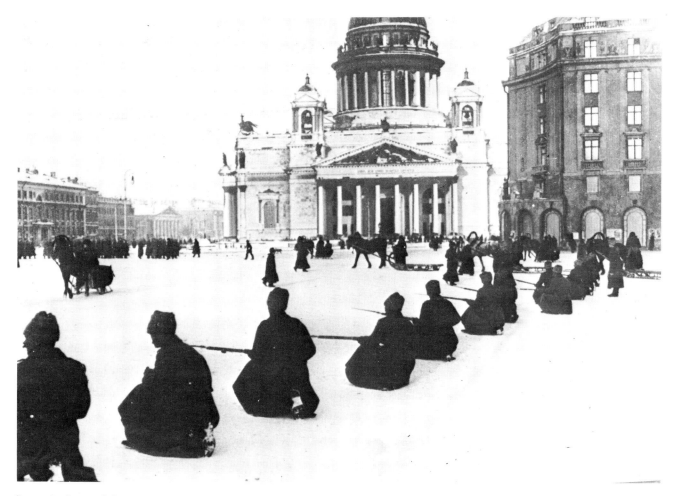

Scene in front of Cathedral, Petrograd, Russia, 1917.
Photographer unknown.

American, British, French and Japanese – operating in Russian territory. Few are of interest in terms of the scope of this book. None show military activities and most are of a very poor quality. Clearly Russian war photography had to wait until the Second World War to show its greatness.

Throughout the First World War and in the years following, professional cameramen continued to use large-size cameras, which partly accounts for the relatively low number of action pictures from that time. William Rider-Rider, for example, used a 4 × 5 inch Gortz with an f 4·5 Zeiss lens. Until the 1920s few, if any, cameras had built-in range-finders. The photographer had therefore to be able to estimate the distance (there would have been little opportunity to measure it), and set the camera manually.

The camera which became almost a standard for press photographers in the early years of the century was the famous Speed Graphic. It was produced in a number of sizes, the most popular being 4 × 5 inch. This model first appeared in 1911. This bulky format continued to be used by newspaper photographers right up to the Second World War and even after. An overwhelming majority of war photographers now came from papers and magazines, so the Speed Graphic, with its wire frame-finder, saw many a war, including Abyssinia and the Spanish Civil War. But by then the 35 mm Leica had made its appearance. It was first on the market in 1925. Its compactness and flexibility appealed to many of the less orthodox photographers, among them Capa and David Seymour, who made use of them in Spain, and Eisenstaedt on his pre-war trip to Abyssinia.

By the 1930s, therefore, with infinitely faster materials and small portable cameras, the war photographer faced few of the technical difficulties which had beset photographers in the First World War. However, the photographs which came from the Spanish Civil War and especially those of Il Duce's Legions during their conquest of Abyssinia were, with a few exceptions, worse technically and visually than those of the Great War fought nearly twenty years before. In addition, the authenticity of many of these photographs is suspect. While the technique of photography was gradually being perfected, so too was the art of subterfuge and faking.

The main reasons for the appearance of a large number of staged war photographs was due to changes in the attitudes and priorities of the press. In the First World War, both the supply of news pictures and to a

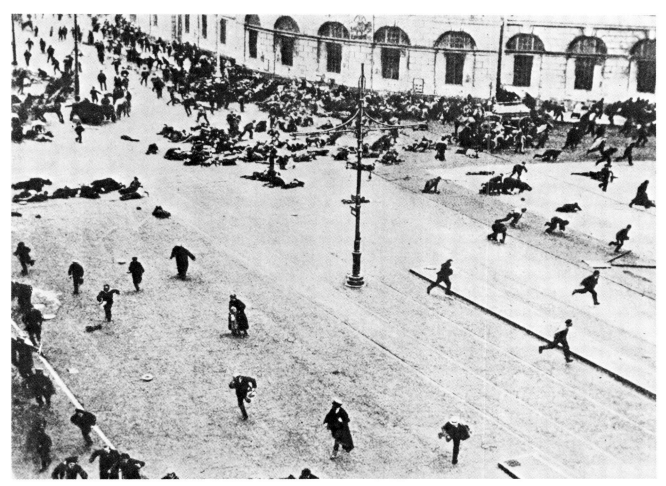

above: Street scene in Petrograd, Russia, 1917.
Photographer unknown.

large extent the editorial policy of newspapers had been controlled; in the 1930s, however, the newspapers of most Western countries were free to use any material available and extremely keen to publish it for their readers. Consequently, war photographers and correspondents on the spot were constantly under pressure to provide suitable pictures and copy for their papers. At the same time, such material proved extremely difficult to obtain. This was especially true of the Italian invasion of Abyssinia which started on 3 October 1935.

The Abyssinian War

The first major conflict for many years had been impending for some time. Consequently it attracted the attention of the international press. Abyssinia, whose identity and geographic location had hardly been known to most of the world's editors, found herself suddenly invaded by a horde of journalists. It was estimated that in the months preceding the outbreak of military activities as many as 150 journalists and

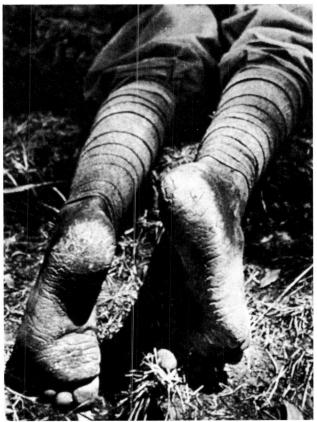

right: Feet of Abyssinian soldier, 1935. *Alfred Eisenstaedt.*

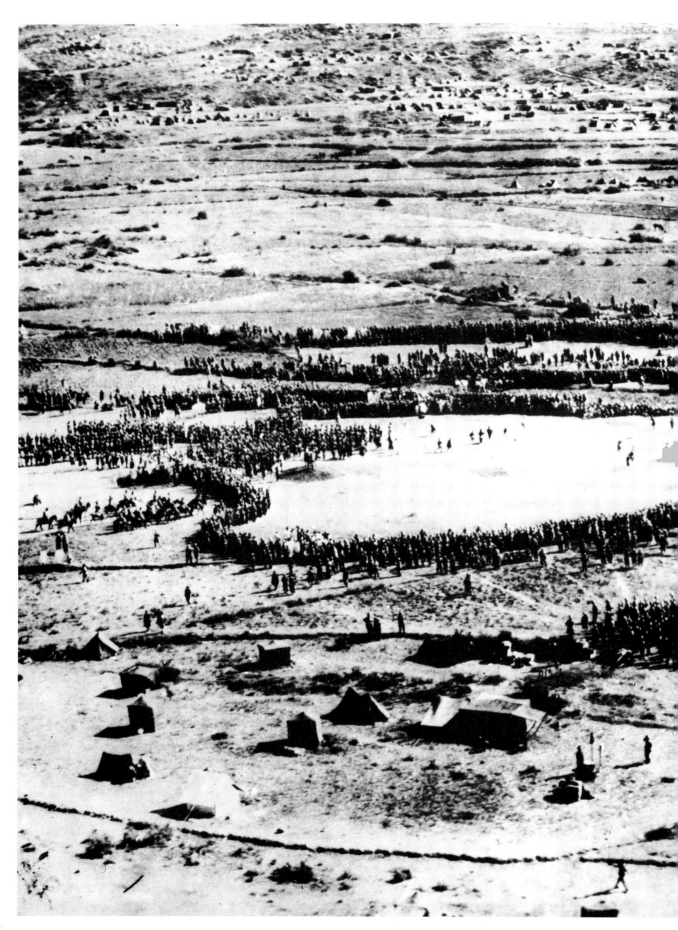

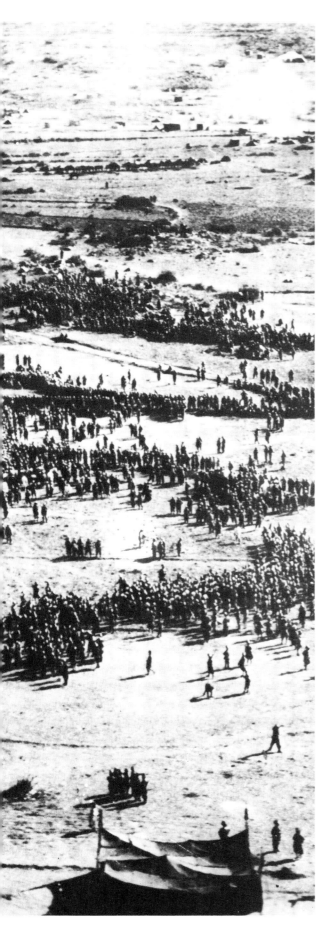

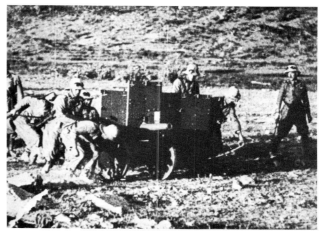

above: Italian advance in Abyssinia, 1935. *Photographer unknown.*

photographers were present in Asmara, the capital of Italian Eritrea. From here the main Italian attack on the Abyssinian border was expected. Similarly no less than 120 newspapermen were living, three or four to a room, in the only 'European' hotel in Addis Ababa, the Abyssinian capital.

Some four months before the outbreak of the war, Alfred Eisenstaedt, one of the finest of the photojournalists who were later to work for *Life*, spent several weeks in Abyssinia shooting one of his best series of pictures – on soldiers and Abyssinian life, including portraits of Emperor Haile Selassie and his court. Sadly, these pictures cannot be matched by any of those shot by the army of photographers working during the war itself. No photographer of the same calibre as Eisenstaedt was engaged during the warfare and the conditions for taking pictures were probably the most difficult ever encountered.

Only during the first three days of the campaign, when Italians under General de Bono penetrated the northern frontier of Abyssinia, swiftly occupying Adowa and Makale, were photographers allowed anywhere near the fighting. Joe Canova of the Associated Press, was first on the scene following the conquering armies on a donkey, with the other cameramen in hot pursuit. But the initial progress of the Italian motorized troops was so rapid that no photographer was able to catch up with the actual fighting. When they finally did arrive, the careful and prudent de Bono – to the rage of Mussolini – prevaricated and consolidated his position for a full month without advancing another yard. The fighting therefore died down. When, finally, de Bono was replaced by the more bellicose General Badoglio, all correspondents (even Italians) were ruthlessly forbidden any participation and in fact were kept, totally inactive, in distant Asmara. Within a month only a handful remained, the majority having either been

left: Concentration of Italian troops at Makale, Abyssinia, 1935. *Photographer unknown.*

81

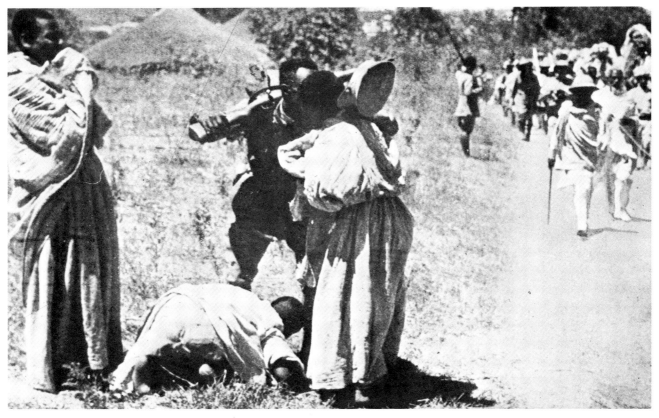

Abyssinian warriors departing to the front, 1935.
P. H. F. Tovey.

recalled owing to the lack of interesting material, or leaving in disgust.

The situation was even worse on the Abyssinian side. There all the correspondents were kept in almost total ignorance of the progress of the war and away from any front. Admittedly there was always the danger that the Abyssinian soldiers might mistake peaceful photographers for their Italian enemies. The watertight censorship and security measures were even more strongly observed after Associated Press had somehow managed to smuggle out the news of the Emperor's projected trip to Dessie, near the front, in preparation for a more active role in conducting the war. While a number of reporters were allowed to accompany him at first, after the bombing of the Emperor's camp by the planes of the Italian Regia Aeronautica – possibly as a result of the newspaper reports – the whole lot was unceremoniously sent back, never to be allowed out of Addis Ababa again. Rapidly, as on the Italian side, the original contingent of 120 soon dwindled to only a persistent few.

One example will convey the frustrations of attempting to cover the war. P. H. F. Tovey, working for the *Daily Express*, spent several months in Abyssinia on the Abyssinian side first in Harar and then in Addis Ababa and only managed to send back a casual portrait of Haile Selassie boarding the plane for Dessie, some pictures of the refugees, one picture of a hilarious incident in which some Abyssinian warriors were riding in a captured Italian mini-tank, and some photographs of the preparations and departure of soldiers for the front. He later published his experiences in a book, *Action with a Clic* [sic]. He tells us that he was allowed to see the front-line fortifications – quite a distance from the actual fighting – only once, and then by accident due to an oversight. However, he was not allowed to photograph them. He writes 'Throughout the Abyssinian war the complaint was the same – nothing to do, hours of unrelieved idleness with always the promise of action postponed until "tomorrow" but never kept, needless to say.'

Every newspaper and agency in every capital of the world, except Rome (and her news was strictly censored), was panting for news and pictures. And here we were, on the spot, and supposed to be attached to the Abyssinian forces in the field but helpless to do anything about it. The situation became farcical, the very purpose for which we had been sent out was being thwarted at every step by the lack of co-operation and sometimes open opposition from the Abyssinian authorities.

Many of the photographers, in sheer desperation and in response to the constant demands and promptings of their editors, resorted to subterfuge and lies. Some correspondents, for example, Herbert Matthews, wrote later that as much as 90 per cent of the Abyssinian war pictures were faked. Philip Knightley writes that Joe Canova had fifty Italian tanks and several companies of soldiers performing complicated war-like manoeuvres for his camera and that these photographs were later printed as 'actual tank charges against the Abyssinians'. This kind of faking was no doubt carried out on an extensive scale but it is impossible to ascertain its extent or even to confirm it.

Very few existing pictures of the Abyssinian War show any action at all. Most depict marches, concentrations of troops, tanks in formation, or show close-ups of the Abyssinian soldiers diffidently handling modern equipment. The great majority are fairly routine and largely posed or arranged pictures. It is a great pity that none of the photographers were able to break through the restrictions as the conflict presented a tremendous visual contrast between the two combatants – civilization destroying a primitive people, white against black – in a terrain of outstanding beauty.

The Abyssinian War was the first war in the history of photographic journalism to be fully covered by the world's press. By now a new kind of photojournalism was beginning to appear – the extended picture essay. The first magazines to use picture stories were the *Berliner Illustrierte Zeitung* and the *Münchener Illustrierte Zeitung* in the late 1920s. As we have seen in the introduction, this trend soon spread to other countries – *Paris Match* was founded in 1934, *Life* in 1936. But so far as the Abyssinian campaign was concerned, the coverage resulted in little more than a dismal crop of pictures – swarms of soldiers seen from afar or pre-arranged tableaux. The reporting restrictions were largely responsible, but the inexperience, lack of standards and professional dishonesty of the photographers themselves contributed to the generally mediocre quality. Although cameras were now able to come close to the subject and record fast action, the photographers failed to take advantage of this new freedom. Instead, they remained in the distance, as uncommitted observers.

The Spanish Civil War

Whereas the authenticity of a great many of the Abyssinian pictures is in doubt, a different, but no less disturbing, dilemma surrounds the Spanish Civil War photographs. No war before or since, including Vietnam, resembles the Spanish Civil War. In some aspects it stands unique. What makes it exceptional is not only the unprecedented cruelty exhibited on both sides, a cruelty directed by brother against brother, but also the degree and extent of the partisanship which divided the country. On the one hand there was the largely communist or left-wing devotion to the republican cause; on the other a similarly fervent following for nationalism with its strong fascist tendencies and, more strangely, its ardent and rather morbid attachment to Catholicism. Factionalism embraced even peripheral groups hardly involved in the struggle. It was most clearly seen in the written reports of the war. Philip Knightley quotes many examples of bias in newspapers and magazines by correspondents

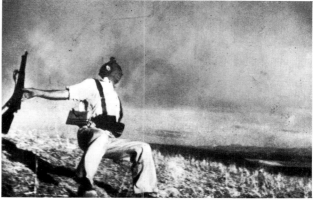

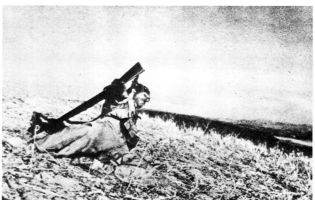

Two photographs taken by Robert Capa, Spain, 1936. The top one is possibly the most famous war photograph ever taken.

committed to one side or the other – including authors such as Hemingway, Koestler, Dos Passos, Spender, Malraux and Orwell.

A similar sort of taking sides can be discerned, if less clearly, among the photographers, thus inducing a certain amount of caution in assessing their work. Whilst it is fairly easy to detect bias in a writer, whose works are usually signed, it is more difficult in photography. There is less respect for authorship, and consequently a great number of photographs have lost their accreditation and remain anonymously on the files of many agencies. Without the name of the photographer it is even more difficult to establish their validity and authenticity. In view of this, and at this distance in time from the event, it is impossible to present an accurate and coherent account of the war photography which took place between 1936 and 1939. Many photographs were taken by ordinary staff photographers on various papers and journals, and were originally printed without a photographer's by-line. Some were shot at the instigation of or as a direct commission for one of the factions – again without acknowledgement. The task is not helped by the fact that the number of internationally known photographers working in Spain was quite small.

The inadequacy of the records is certainly not proportional to the quantity of photographic material.

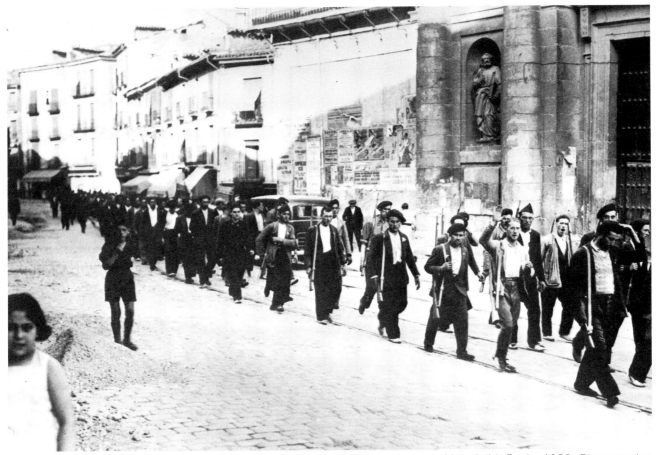

Fascist volunteers, Valladolid, Spain, 1936. *Photographer unknown.*

An enormous number of pictures were taken, both sides actively encouraging the cameramen – provided, of course, that the results were helpful and complimentary to their cause. And herein lies the crux: both the rebel fascist troops under the leadership of General Franco and the loyalist forces of the republican government depended to a significant extent on outside help. Thus, Franco's forces counted on German and Italian military aid and, to a certain degree, on military units, whilst the republicans drew their strength partly from the International Brigade of volunteers, partly from desultory supplies coming across the French border, but mainly from Russian armaments and supplies. In order to preserve and encourage this aid, a considerable amount of propaganda was required. Both sides understood that the photograph is the best kind of publicity if it is of the right sort.

An interesting example of their awareness of the power of an image is a book published by the Franco régime in 1937 – only in the second year of the war – under the title *500 Photos of the War* (*500 Fotos de la Guerra*, Imprenta Castellana, Valladolid). It contains a series of captioned pictures and was obviously designed as an instrument of propaganda for the unaligned portions of the Spanish population as well as for foreign consumption. It shows, predictably, the triumphant progress of the nationalists, and also horror pictures of mutilated bodies, dead children, ruined churches – all this the work, according to the book, of the anti-christian devils of the red republicans. Equally obvious is the fact that many of these photographs are blatantly forged.

In fact, according to those who were present in Spain during the war, faking, as in Abyssinia, was a common occurrence. P. H. F. Tovey, already quoted in connection with the Abyssinian struggle, writes:

It was then [on arrival in Burgos on the Republican side] I learned that the majority of pictures which had decorated the back pages of most of the British and foreign newspapers or the cinema screens of the world had been faked. They had been taken on the rifle range just outside Burgos. Young recruits lucky enough to have uniforms on acted as escorts. I was promised more pictures of this type. Faking was the order of the day, even a tumble down cottage was used as a background and bodies placed in heaps to look like casualties of war. Men carefully rehearsed in their parts would fall as though shot at the blast of a whistle. On comparing these pictures it was possible to recognize the same soldiers escorting prisoners on two fronts, Bilbao and Samosierra, which were at least one hundred miles apart.

opposite top: Republican forces attacking Red Farm, San Sebastian, Spain, 1936. *Photographer unknown.*

opposite bottom: Fascists in action, Spain, 1936. *Photographer unknown.*

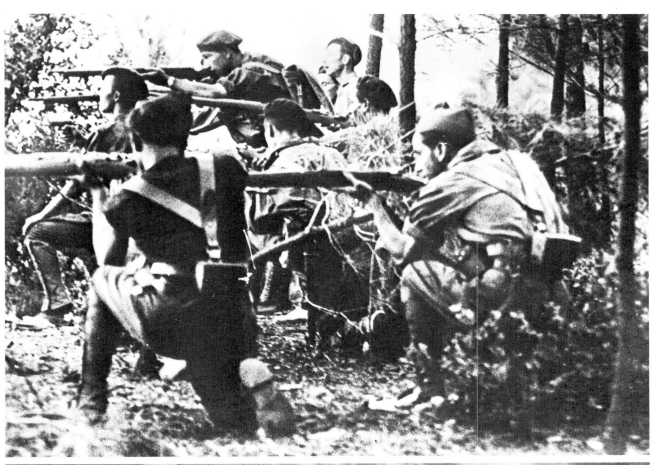

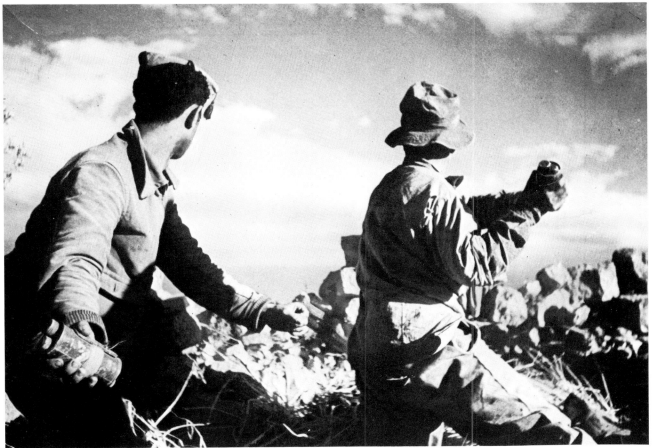

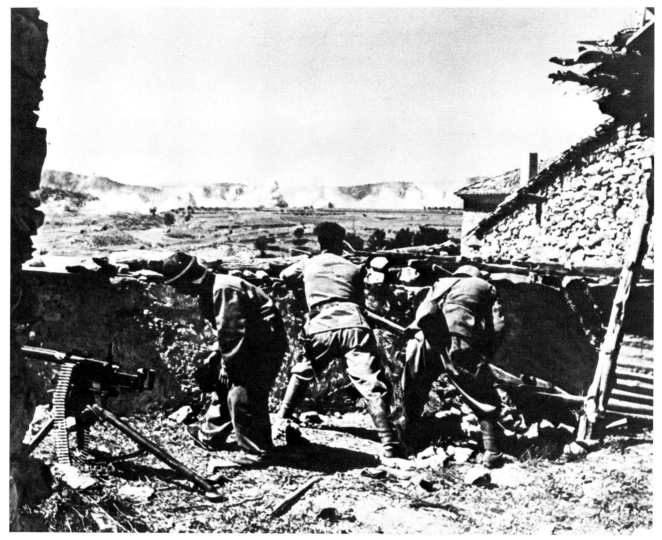

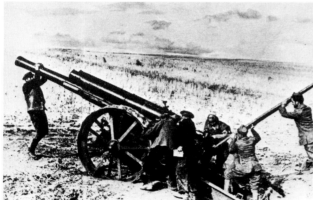

above: Artillery near Madrid, 1936. *Robert Capa.*

Tovey adds that he wanted to take some of these pictures and then expose the whole racket on his return to England. But somehow the promises did not materialize and finally he was recalled, mainly because of total inactivity and inability to take any printable pictures.

As in Abyssinia, the censorship in Spain was very strict. Foreign correspondents and photographers, unless acting on behalf of and in co-operation with one of the sides, were hampered at every step. During his several months' sojourn in Spain, moving through different war-torn regions, Tovey took hardly any action pictures. His best were the bombing of Algeciras by Franco's artillery, weeping Spanish women pleading for the lives of their menfolk, and mopping-up parties as the nationalists entered Constantina. As Tovey was a respected photojournalist of the *Daily Express* for many years, this can hardly be dismissed as incompetence.

The difficulties that photographers encountered were present almost equally on both sides. H. Edward Knoblaugh – a correspondent for Associated Press – confirms this in his book, *Correspondent in Spain*. After describing difficulties with censors who were both strict and at the same time ignorant he adds:

The photographers fared worse than we in attempting to cover the war. Nothing that would indicate the confusion

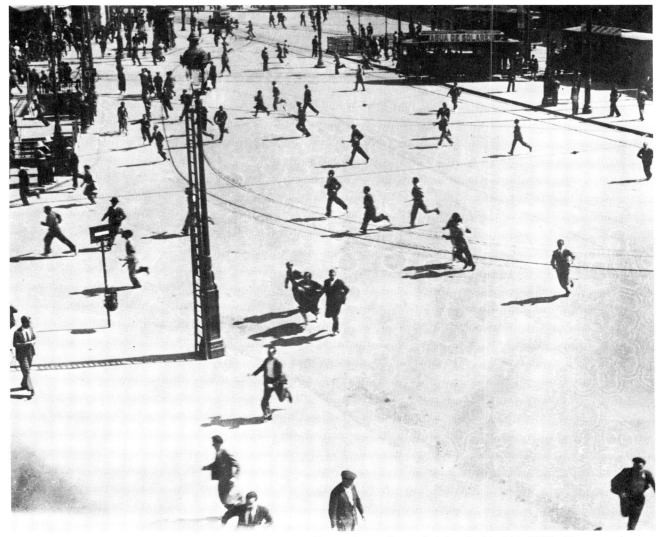

above: Street fighting in Madrid, 1936. *Photographer unknown.*

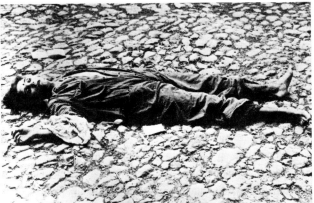

above: A civilian killed by General Franco's troops. *Photographer unknown.*

existing in Loyalist territory, the woeful inefficiency of the army of irregulars, the damage caused by enemy shell fire or the lack of discipline in Loyalist ranks, could be taken. The photographers and newsreel men were given splendid passes authorizing them to take 'anything they saw', but if they happened to snap something the government considered injurious to its cause, the passes were instantly revoked and their cameras impounded. Anarchist militiamen pursued right into my office a visiting photographer who had been seen pointing his camera at enemy planes flying low over Madrid. 'This is serious reflection of the efficiency of our anti-aircraft', they said. 'The pictures must be destroyed.'

Elsewhere Knoblaugh quotes Floyd Gibbons, at the time a well-known news commentator, as saying 'I've worked in many countries and under many a censorship but none so unreasonable as this one.'

Quite apart from these external and internal difficulties, the Spanish Civil War was, by its very nature, quite hard to record visually. In the first place it was fought between members of one nation and largely of one creed. The photographer could not play on any distinguishing features between the contestants as in Abyssinia or even in the First World War. Second, in spite of some larger battles and localized areas of fighting, the war was often fought in a very sporadic and unpredictable manner. Particularly on the loyalist republican side, there was hardly any discipline, leadership or unity, and often only intermittent concerted action. Throughout the war the republicans were constantly torn by antagonism between their own factions – communists, anarchists, Basque separatists, left-wing moderates and a number of others. There were individual outbursts of violence between these groups, often creating open warfare within the war, and especially so between the anarchist peasant groups and communist units. The eventual defeat of the republicans had as much to do with their internal instability and lack of co-operation as it had with the superior might of Franco's forces, helped throughout by German and Italian brigades egged on by Mussolini's thirst for military prowess.

The rebel nationalists were possibly marginally easier to work with, partly because they were more united and partly because they were winning and anxious to show this to the world. The difficulty there was that the insurgents were anxious to hide the numbers of German and Italian helpers, which were considerable. So there too the photographers were hampered in their attempts to gain free coverage.

Thus the difficulties for the war photographers were twofold: first, the lack of freedom to report; second, the inability to be in the right place at the right time. Both of these were almost impossible in Spain. Most of the records consist of the aftermath rather than the action which few photographers were allowed to follow.

Many of the photographers who went to Spain to participate in and cover the Civil War were strongly partisan and professed a passionate involvement in the cause, especially those on the republican side. But the pictures we are left with are not passionate at all. They are not even interesting to an unusual degree. Above all they do not say very much. They do not convey visually the highly charged, emotional mood of the war.

This even applies to the most famous photographer-protagonist of the Civil War – Robert Capa. Capa was sincerely committed to the republican cause; in Spain he shot a number of strong pictures but, on the whole, he was too inexperienced to communicate his feelings in his photographs with any consistency. In the introduction Capa is heralded as a pioneer of the métier. However, in Spain he was just at the beginning of his career.

Robert Capa

Capa came to Spain in the early part of 1936 accompanied by Gerda Taro, a German photographer, possibly his wife, with whom he had fallen in love in France. Together they compiled their Spanish Civil War book, *Death In The Making*. Gerda, whom the republican soldiers affectionately nicknamed 'La Pequena Rubita' (little redhead), never saw it published. She was crushed to death by a loyalist tank in the rush of retreat. Capa later dedicated the book to her.

Both of them were passionately devoted to the loyalist cause. As he later explained in *Images Of War*: 'The issue is clear. It is their [republican] fight to defend their homes, their culture, their very lives, against a General who cannot govern while they live. They grew up together, worked side by side in the shops, laboratories, and now fight side by side to hold what they won.' Capa fought on their side, if only with his camera, throughout the war, in besieged Madrid, in the gallant Teruel, and he saw the territory held by the republicans slowly melt away. Along with segments of defeated loyalists – some 400 000 of them – he crossed the frontier into France.

It was one of the pictures that Capa took in Spain which made his name known internationally almost overnight. With the publication of his 'Death of a Loyalist Soldier' in the French magazine *Vue* in October 1936, he became a celebrity. This picture has recently become the centre of a controversy. Is it a brilliant immortalization of the moment of death – the best picture ever taken in war – or is it a fake?

It was O. D. Gallagher, a well-known war correspondent of the *Daily Express* since the Abyssinian war, who was the first not only to question the authenticity of the picture but to state quite bluntly that it was a deliberate fake. In an interview for this book he writes:

I began in Spain with Hendaye in France, on the Spanish border by San Sebastian. Most of us reporters and photographers were there in a small shabby hotel. We went into Franco's Spain across the Irun River, when allowed by Franco's press officer in Burgos. They sometimes invited us in for special occasions, and once only the photographers were invited. These included Capa and also movie people [Gallagher was mainly a writer correspondent, not a photographer]. Capa and I shared the room in our shabby hotel with a third man whose name I have forgotten for a moment [Roper from the English *Daily Graphic*?]. Capa told me of this occasion. They were given simulated battle scenes. Franco's troops were dressed in 'uniforms' and armed and they simulated attacks and defence. Smoke bombs were used to give atmosphere. Capa told me he got some action pictures of attacking troops being rebuffed. Soon after the newspapers published pictures of this staged action with captions stating categorically that they were action pictures. But, *most oddly* giving not the smallest hint of the locality, front or objective or even the identity of the military units. If a study is made of European papers of this time I believe that Capa's bogus 'instant of death' picture would be identifiable in many. If not the actual single exposure or exposures that made his name when *Life* boomed them up and added their own 'thunk up' captions, then the uniforms and actual acting soldiers could be identified I think in other 'action' pictures. . . .

Gallagher goes on to claim:

. . . Capa told me the way to get lifelike action shots was to have the camera slightly out of focus and to ever so slowly move the camera when making an exposure. This technique is exemplified in Capa's 'instant of death' picture. I believe it was all tied up with the Franco 'battle' series with acting soldiers and smoke bombs.

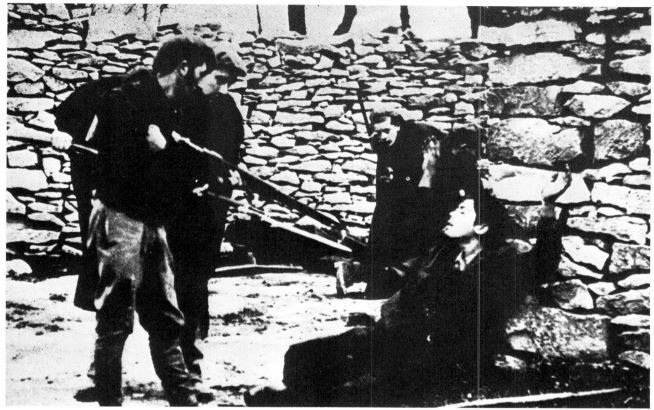

General Franco's men take a prisoner (possible fake).
Photographer unknown.

These disclosures of Gallagher's no doubt prompted Philip Knightley in his book *The First Casualty* to investigate the whole affair most carefully and to check it with many possible witnesses and Capa's friends. Since I certainly could not do any better I have secured his permission to quote his findings in detail.

In the first place it appears that in spite of the most exhaustive search of Robert Capa's own writings he never seems to have mentioned the manner of taking the 'moment of death' picture. Neither Henri Cartier-Bresson, Capa's close collaborator at Magnum, nor Capa's brother Cornell, also a distinguished photographer, nor Stefan Laurent, the first editor of *Picture Post*, could contribute a single piece of information or a clue. But later, Cornell Capa sent to Philip Knightley a review of his brother's book *Slightly Out of Focus* written in a humorous way by John Hersey, author of *Hiroshima*. Here is the relevant passage from Knightley's book:

In this review titled 'The Man who Invented Himself', Hersey gives an account of how Robert Capa took the famous photograph. In reply to our query about sources, Hersey wrote, 'Bob Capa told me the story of the Spanish soldier himself. "The man who invented himself" was based altogether on material I had straight from him. He was a close friend. I had been through the Sicilian campaign with him.' Capa's account to Hersey [continues Philip Knightley] was that he went to Andalusia in 1936 when heavy fighting was taking place. During one battle he was in a trench with a

company of Republican soldiers, fanatical but ignorant fighters, who shouted 'Viva la Republica' and jumped over the parapet and charged the Nationalist machine gun nest. When the machine gun opened fire, killing many of the men, the rest retreated and fired at the machine gun from the trench. They charged and charged again and each time many were killed. Hersey wrote, 'Finally as they charged, the photographer timidly raised his camera over the top of the parapet and, without looking, at the instant of the first machine gun burst, pressed the button. He sent the film to Paris undeveloped. Two months later he (Capa) was notified that he was now in truth a famous photographer, talented and nearly rich, for the random snap turned out to be a clear picture of a brave man in the act of falling dead as he ran and that it had been published all over the world over his name.'

'This is an intriguing account,' Knightley continues in his book.

Some, including Martha Gellhorn, who knew Capa in Spain and later, believed that Capa was pulling Hersey's leg and that this account was not to be taken seriously. Hersey's review gives no indication of this, and there is nothing in his letter to suggest that he took what his close friend told him as other than true and accurate. If this is so, then it shows that Capa's photograph was a million to one chance; a camera aimed blindly and operated on the sound of firing had not only caught a soldier neatly framed, but had caught him at the very moment he was hit.

Further research produced two other strange versions of the picture. It must be stressed immediately that at this distance of time it has so far proved impossible either to confirm or disprove them, and other people who knew Capa in Spain, including Herbert Matthews (a distinguished journalist) and Martha Gellhorn, discount them entirely and firmly believe the photo to be both Capa's and 'without a doubt, authentic'. The first account is from Canadian playwright, Ted Allan. Allan, then only 20, was in Spain with a Canadian blood transfusion unit. He also sent reports for Federal Press, a trade union news agency in North America. He met Capa in Madrid and became firm friends with him and Gerda Taro, Capa's partner and life-long love, and was with Gerda when she was killed at Brunette in July 1937. Allan says that after the 'moment of death' picture was published, he was discussing it one day with 'Chim' Seymour, killed in the Suez invasion in 1956. 'Chim told me that Capa had not taken that photograph. Whether he told me that he, Chim, had taken it or that Gerda had taken it, I cannot now remember.'

Knightley then proceeds to quote the story of O. D. Gallagher, which is substantially the same as that written for me by Gallagher himself. This then is the evidence – if such it is – of the taking of the 'moment of death' photograph. Obviously there are no hard facts either way. Even Gallagher, who vehemently insists that Capa's picture is a fraud, cannot swear 100 per cent that this precise picture is a fake, only that Capa took some pictures which were specially staged for him. But at the same time it is rather strange that whilst most of Capa's other negatives are preserved, this particular one is not. It would have been simple merely to check which frames were shot on either side of the famous picture to establish whether it was a practice session or a real battle. There is nothing else in the picture – part of the trench, other soldiers in the background, part of the foreground – nothing but a man falling. As Knightley sums it up:

It is essentially an ambiguous image. However as captioned in *Life* – 'Robert Capa's camera captures a Spanish soldier the instant he is dropped by a bullet through the head in front of Cordoba' – it does tell us something, something beyond the face meaning of the words. It tells us that the picture was taken by someone who must have put himself at great risk, someone who was perhaps killed as well. With this caption the photograph thus becomes a famous and valuable property in both commercial and political terms. Yet – and there is nothing in the photograph to deny this – if we were to re-write the caption to read 'A militiaman slips and falls while training for action' the photograph would become worthless in both senses.

After the publication of Philip Knightley's book, the *Sunday Times* magazine ran a feature about the picture, printing side by side two of Capa's photographs – the famous one and another very similar, again of a soldier falling with virtually identical background and foreground. It may add another piece of circumstantial evidence, but it does not actually prove the picture to be a fake.

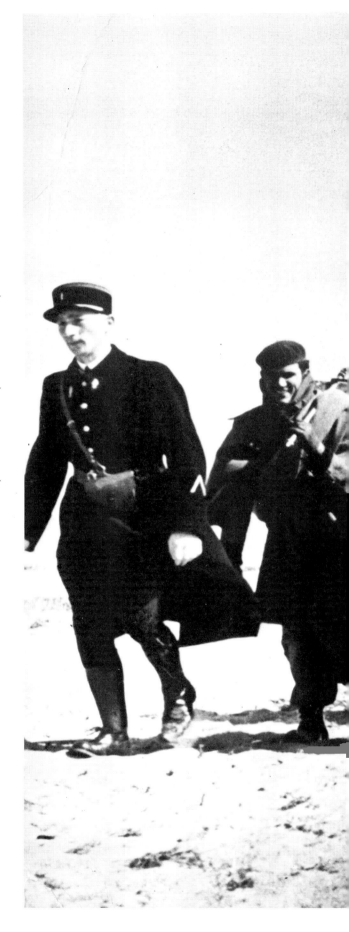

Defeated militia men of the International Brigade cross the French border, Spain, 1939. *Robert Capa.*

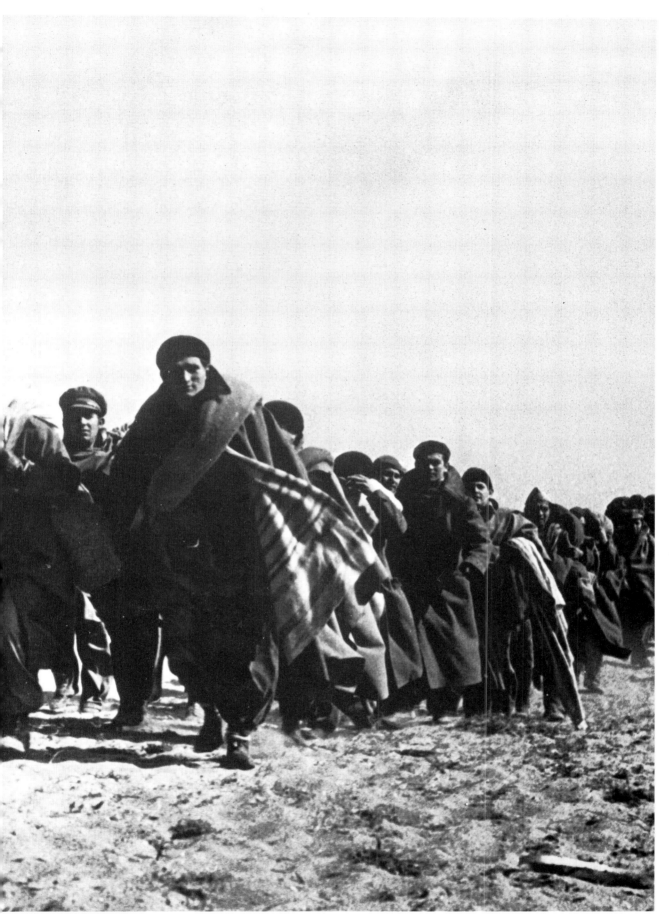

Even if we accept the allegations, and in spite of Knightley's dismissal, there is still little doubt that Capa's picture is a very fine piece of photography – it is an extremely good photograph: if we assume its authenticity, then it becomes great one.

DAVID SEYMOUR

Capa was always a front-line war photographer; his favourite motto was: 'If your pictures aren't good enough, then you aren't close enough.' His future colleague in Magnum Photos, David Seymour ('Chim') spent much of his time away from the front studying the effects of the war on the civilian population. In a way they complement each other: Capa left Spain with many action shots, some taken in haste without time for fine focus and correct exposure, all taken from a position alongside fighting men; Seymour studied the effects of air bombardment and recorded the feeling and atmosphere of a people at war – often those who are the unwilling victims. His picture of Barcelona under siege is especially evocative and powerful. Seymour's love and sympathy for children are clearly shown in his early Spanish pictures. Later, through his images of deprived and distressed children, Chim would produce a lasting monument to the tragedy of war.

On looking at the Spanish pictures of Capa and Seymour thirty years after they were taken, the impression is of amateurishness. As if both they and the majority of other photographers went to Spain to help in a cause – whichever side they were supporting – and also took some pictures along the way. The Spanish pictures, although many were taken by professionals, in so far as they are photographs of war, are pictures taken by non-professional photographers, for covering a war is not just another kind of picture-taking; it is a highly skilled exacting métier. In the Spanish Civil War photographic coverage of war was still very much uncharted territory. But the photographers who gained their first experience in Spain were soon to have a more challenging assignment – the Second World War was just around the corner.

92

Part Three
ENLISTED COMBATANT
Second World War

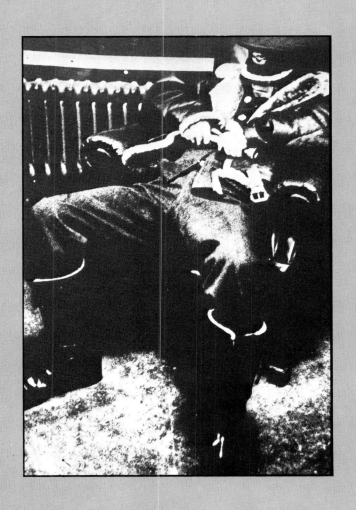

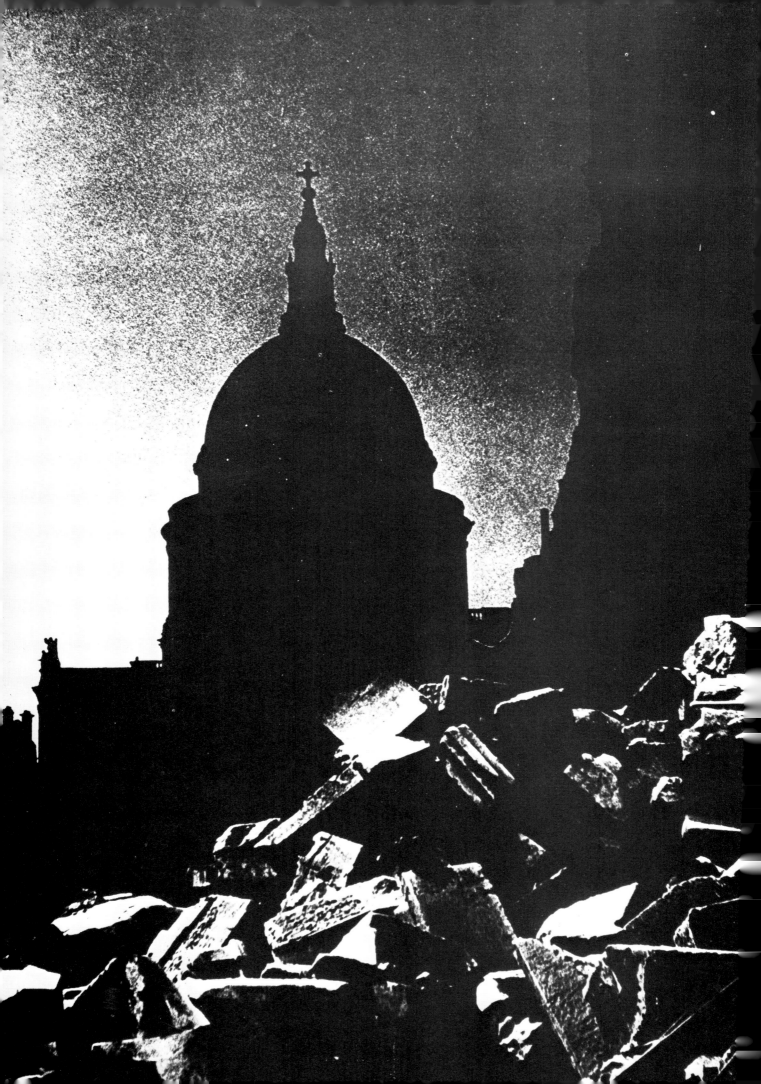

He would be rash indeed who attempts to estimate the number of exposures made during the Second World War, even to the nearest million. The Imperial War Museum in London holds approximately four million negatives in its archives, nearly half of them connected with the Second World War. To enumerate all the institutions, museums, libraries and private collections holding pictures, negatives or transparencies would be a difficult, if not impossible task. The majority of photographs taken between 1939 and 1945, even now over thirty years later, have not seen the light of day. They languish in various regimental stores, headquarters of Military Intelligence and War Ministry departments. Some are inaccessible through bad filing and lack of classification; others have probably already deteriorated in inadequate storage. All these photographs were taken on behalf of the military authorities.

Never before had so many photographers been engaged as at that time – their single mammoth task to record the scale, variety and multiplicity of war activities crowded into the five years between September 1939 and September 1945 when finally the representatives of Japan signed the instrument of surrender on the US battleship *Missouri*. Of Canadian photographers alone, 400 Second World War photographers were present at a reunion in 1971, according to William Rider-Rider.

Never before had the camera been put to such extensive use by the armed forces themselves. Professional photographers were called up for the specific purpose of recording the war and the military authorities trained many non-photographers to serve as cameramen, technicians, laboratory assistants and the like. All German and Russian photographers were part of the armed forces as a matter of course. Every image, every frame they shot was scrutinized by military experts to assess its usefulness, its suitability in the overall purpose of winning the war. Even on the Allied side, which boasted a degree of freedom for the media and hence tolerated a certain number of civilian freelance photojournalists, censorship was very strict indeed. Rarely did a picture slip through which the military had not approved. In the Second World War, for the first and, so far, for the last time, photography was completely harnessed to the war machine itself, an integral part.

The photographers themselves fell into three categories: the first consisted of those trained, equipped and maintained by the armed forces. In the early stages, they were relatively few in number, but as the war dragged on, this group expanded until every unit of the forces – Army, Navy, and Air Force – had a basic team of one stills and one cine photographer. The second group was fairly small in number, freelance photographers working for various magazines and papers. Finally there was an undetermined number of amateur photographers, some civilians who happened to be present, and the soldiers in possession of a camera. During the later stages of the war in Europe, after the Normandy invasion, practically every second Allied soldier managed to get hold of a camera. A Leica or a Contax was virtually a necessity, perhaps a status symbol. It was a different state of affairs to the beginning of the war. Gradually, from initial erratic coverage by *ad hoc* commissioned photographers, the scale and extent of the documentation had grown until, by the end, the Second World War was the best covered of any wars, and the photographers became veterans in the profession of photographing war.

The war itself had so many different facets, so many participants, so many theatres of operations, that we cannot hope to give a comprehensive account of the totality of the photographic record. Instead, we are forced to delimit broad areas which are sufficiently well defined as to have distinctive characteristics, determined by the nature of the fighting and terrain, and within this framework identify the most outstanding photographers, select the most telling images. Our account falls into six sections, overlapping in time, each confined to a single area of operations.

The first corresponds to the initial stages of the war – the invasion of Poland and the occupation of Europe; the second is the war in the desert; the third the Russian front. Fourth comes the Italian campaign; fifth the war in the Pacific; and last the invasion of Normandy. Within each of these areas it is possible to discern an overall similarity of tone and mood in the most representative pictures, the photographers themselves responding, perhaps unconsciously, to the defining characteristics of each arena and revealing them in their pictures.

The first phase, mostly confined to Western and Central Europe, can be imagined as a series of thrust-and-parry lunges, surprise attacks of bewildering rapidity and confusion, one after another: *blitzkrieg* in Poland, the Russian intervention in Finland, the German invasion of Norway, Holland, Belgium, France, the evacuation of Dunkirk, the Battle of Britain. A series of changing slides in a projector, with the underlying pattern of air battles and lightning moves of heavy armour and tanks. The desert war which followed presents a balletic sequence across the expanse of sand – the unending desert the stage, with two companies, one blue-grey, the other khaki-green, performing complicated movements across its vast lengths. The war in Russia appears a heavy Dostoevskian epic of suffering, pain and despair under storm-laden clouds, made darker against the whiteness of the snow. Then the brilliant light of Italy, bright vineyards, sparkling rivers, ripples of light and shade, shine surreal against the struggle for Monte Cassino, the destruction intermingled with moments of laughter and sun-warm wine. The war in the Pacific is full of a different kind of contrasts, a duality of extremes: the openness of the sea, the claustrophobic atmosphere of

St Paul's Cathedral in moonlight, London, 1940. *Bill Brandt.*

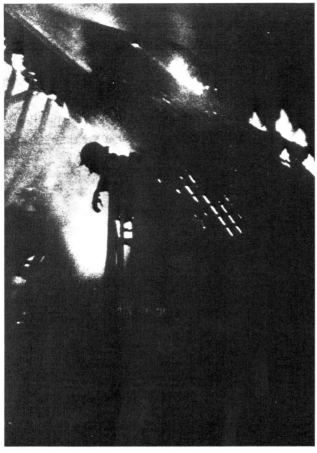

the jungles; the impersonal immensity of war fought between machines on and over the oceans, the personal savagery of hand-to-hand combat on suffocating islands. Finally Normandy D-Day ushers the steamroller of the Allied invasion, a grinding, relentless advance of armour and men pushing deeper and deeper into the ravaged heart of Germany in ruins.

Had the war been shot in colour, each phase would have taken on a distinctive hue – partly symbolic, partly real: steel-blue the first, burned yellow the second; the third shades of grey or stark black and white; the fourth vivid ochre; the fifth dominated by blue-green of ocean and jungle; the last culminating in a dusty red of long summer roads touched with fire and blood. This division into tonalities and colour may be farfetched, but it provides an overall key to the photographs of the different phases, for the photographer's role is to bring visually to life both the vividness of events and their underlying mood and atmosphere. The best of the photographs captures both for us to see.

Phase One The Onslaught

Britain was singularly ill-prepared for the outbreak of war. This unpreparedness extended to the field of photography and film, both as a medium of military record and as an aid to reconnaissance. The British Army had hardly any photographers in its ranks. Recruitment of photographers for the purpose of recording the war quickly became of prime importance. Orders were posted to all units that any soldier, regardless of rank, with film or photographic experience, should report to his superior. From these, forty were selected to form the nucleus of official film-makers and photographers. Among them were some press photographers, but most of the professional newsmen remained with their newspapers, their jobs being considered essential. Even those professionals who were called up were sent on a six-week training course at Pinewood Studios before joining their new units. They were issued with standard equipment – a sturdy Super Ikonta camera $2\frac{1}{4}$ inch square (many of which were bought cheaply in Turkey by the government) and/or a Kodak Medallist mainly used for colour. Some lucky individuals were allowed Rolleiflexes, but 35-mm cameras were not permitted, partly to avoid discriminating between photographers, and partly because 35-mm film stock was more difficult to obtain.

The Ministry of Information – the sole organizer and employer of all the forces' media men – though already planned in 1936, had barely come into being a few days before the outbreak of the war. It soon grew from the

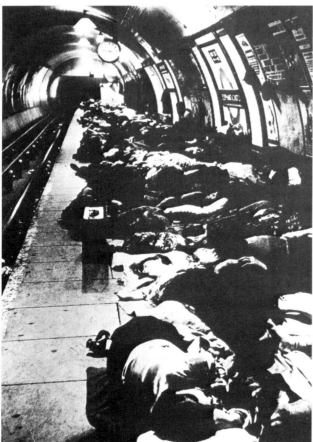

Sheltering in the Elephant and Castle underground station, London, 1940. *Bill Brandt*.

96

original dozen members to a reputed 999 personnel. In the first years of the war it rightly came under considerable criticism both from the public and the press for giving a singularly unimpressive performance compared to Goebbel's efficient Ministry of Propaganda. The quality of the official coverage, which was both sloppy and amateurish, especially at the beginning of the war, resulted from the undeniably rigid attitude of the British military authorities to censorship. Their traditional antagonism towards the press and photography, dating back to Lord Kitchener, continued throughout the duration of the war (it was still prevalent as late as the Suez crisis in 1956). Even the professional photographers who had remained in Fleet Street suffered from the traditional military dislike of the media. In comparison to the Germans, the British attitude was extremely naïve and unprofessional.

The Germans in their thoroughness simply conscripted all their media people into a Propaganda Division under Major General Hasso von Wedel. They became known as the P K (*Propaganda Kompanien*) and their role was to 'influence the course of the war by psychological control of the mood at home, abroad, at the Front, and in enemy territory' ('Der Propaganda-Truppe Ganz und Elend', *Die Welt*, 2 May 1970).

German troops breaking Polish frontier barrier, 1939. *Photographer unknown.*

Thus, the German exploits, often glaringly slanted and pre-fabricated for the glory of Hitler and the Reich, were freely published all over the world and, more importantly still, in the U S A.

The fateful 1 September crossing of the Polish frontier by German motorized units and the simultaneous bombing of Polish cities took everyone by surprise. Photographs of the rapid, merciless conquest of a largely defenceless Poland hardly exist; those that were taken were almost all German. It is alleged that the aggressors even took the precaution of staging a phoney raid on one of their own frontier stations, with German soldiers masquerading in Polish uniforms as would-be invaders to provide the German photographers with the evidence to justify Germany to the world. It has proved impossible to trace these pictures, however, if indeed they were ever taken.

Of the actual *blitzkrieg* in Poland, decisively effective in the first week and virtually complete in three, only odd snapshots are preserved, although the aftermath – the ruins of towns, interminable lines of refugees, homeless people and prisoners of war – was more leisurely recorded. P K Sonderfuhrer Albert Cusian took it on himself to depict the horror of the Warsaw ghetto. He photographed the morning interment of starved Jews, dead from the night before, with their emaciated bodies and vacant eyes. He also photographed the hovels in which they lived and died, as well as the torment, humiliation and tortures that they suffered

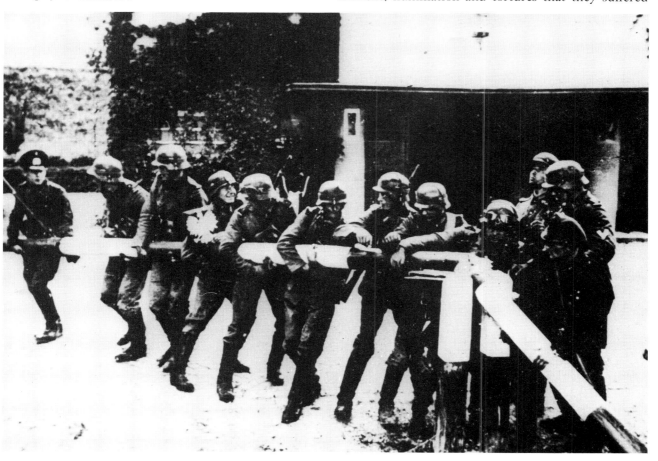

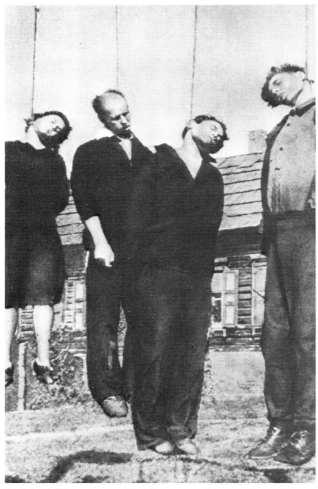

Polish civilians hanged by Germans, Second World War.
Photographer unknown.

from his fellow invaders. One can only speculate on his feelings as he wandered among the victims with his Leica and f3·5 Elmar lens.

With Poland submerged, the 'phoney war' followed. British reporters and photographers had a miserable time during these first months. A few cameramen and photographers were sent with the British Expeditionary Force to France, but, according to many stories related by Philip Knightley, they were chaparoned, encumbered and hindered by 'relics of the vanquished England' – mainly old-Etonian, ex-regular officers who appear to have been drunk most of the time, slow thinking and hopelessly inefficient. In any case, there was little to write about or photograph in the days of the 'phoney war' as George Rodger's weary correspondent and the lonely French sentry at the Maginot line by an anonymous photographer wittily demonstrate.

By now some evidence of the war was to be seen in England. London's precautionary blackout gave Bill Brandt – now the most eminent of British photographers – a chance to create a sensitive series of pictures of London's streets and houses behind the veil of darkness. Later he expanded this series with some wonderful shots taken during the Battle of Britain.

Picture Post and other magazines tried to fill the gap created by lack of war pictures in this calm with series like 'London Getting Ready' or soldiers in training or Home Guard drills. They published some German pictures of London from the air and photographs of the Siegfried Line skilfully taken to make the unfinished, inadequate line of defences on the French frontier look like a chain of impenetrable fortresses. The early war numbers of the British magazines are totally devoid of any real military content. They still clung to the commonplace normalcy of civilian life. They seem to have been singularly inept in building up the morale of a people on the verge of conflict with a ruthless enemy. Their complacency compares sadly with German contemporary magazines, full of jingoistic confidence and pride, pumping out stories of German heroism and superiority illustrated with carefully selected or specially prepared photographic material.

The failings of the British magazines stemmed in part from a general complacency, but the authorities themselves were much to blame. *Picture Post, London Illustrated News* and other publications used German sources in desperation, complaining bitterly and constantly about the inadequate, dull pictures issued by the Ministry of Information. This state of affairs carried on well into the war, and one can search in vain for some good photographs related to the fighting in Europe in the early wartime magazines. Even *Life* rarely contains a vivid picture at this time; when one is found, it is almost invariably German.

The first photographer to break the monotony seems to have been Carl Mydans with his series from the Russo–Finnish war in January 1940. His pictures, taken in the snow after the massacre at Kami River, are strong in their visual contrast – human aggression and death in the midst of an idyllic northern landscape. They are the first notable series by this talented photographer and possibly his best. Mydans himself admits in his autobiography, *More Than Meets the Eye*, that he never quite managed to forget this scene. In the polar temperatures of a Finnish winter, Russian advance troops were surrounded by the swift, ghost-like Finns and, as a result, some 3000 Russians were slaughtered. Mydans came to photograph the evidence left behind of this event. This was the beginning of his six-year wandering from battle to battle, across Africa, Europe, China and the Pacific Ocean. We shall meet him again photographing for *Life*.

A number of official British photographers accompanied the series of ill-timed and tentative commando raids in the north of Norway in early April 1940. Bishop H. Marshall participated in the raid on Narvik, Captain Tennyson d'Eyncourt photographed the attack on the Lofoten Islands, and Lieutenant Malindine the commando raid on Vaagso. The raids came too late to help the Finns, who had capitulated to the Russians; meanwhile the Germans, having over-run Denmark virtually in one day, moved northwards

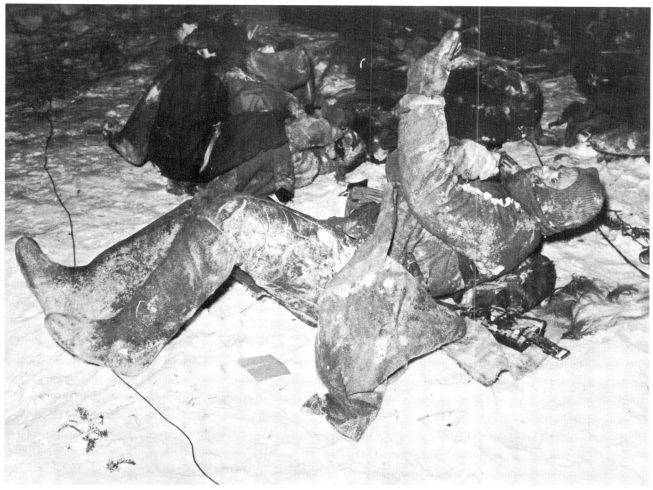

above: Frozen Russian corpses in Finland, 1940. *Carl Mydans.*

into Norway. Five German PK photographers were aboard the heavy cruiser *Blücher* which was torpedoed during the attack on Oslo. Four of them died, but the survivor, Max Ehlert, shot an exciting series showing the sinking of the ship. These pictures were never used, as they depicted the death of a German ship and sailors and were therefore considered unsuitable for distribution. Pictures taken by other PK men in the invasion fleet publicized the triumph of German arms throughout the world.

In May the phoney war ended. German troops bypassed the Maginot Line and attacked neutral Belgium and Holland, then cut through northern France, reaching the sea in seven days. The speed of the advance threw all the photographic units in the field into disarray. The official photographic unit of the British Expeditionary Force was stationed at Arras, not far from the Belgian border. When the Germans occupied the town the unit dispersed and hastily retreated with defeated and bemused portions of the French army.

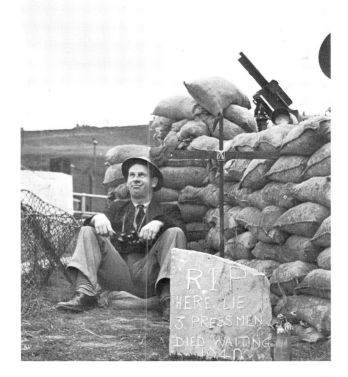

right: Bored pressman on the cliffs of Dover, 1940. *George Rodger.*

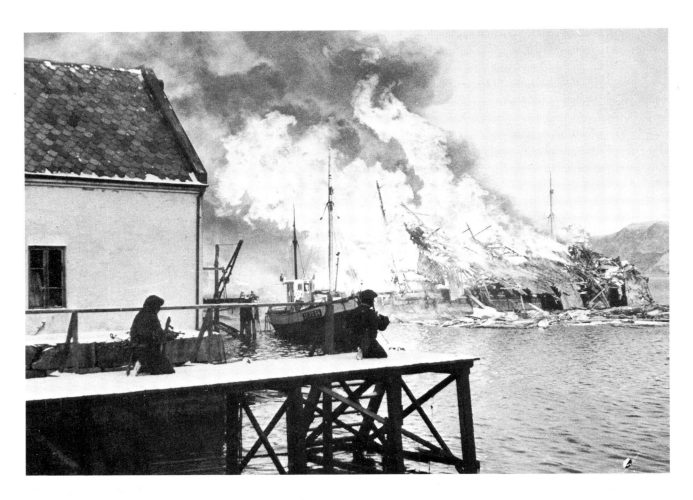

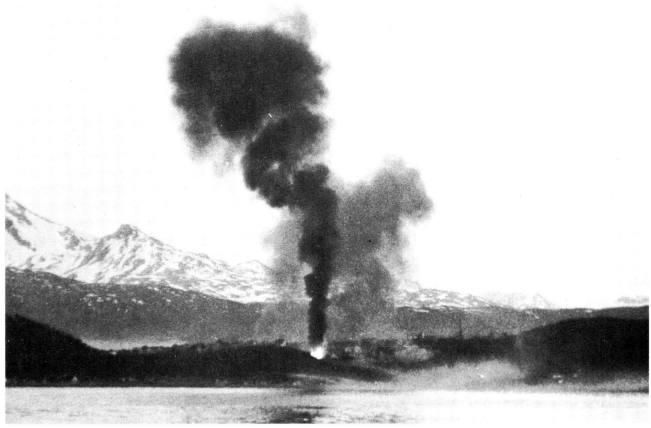

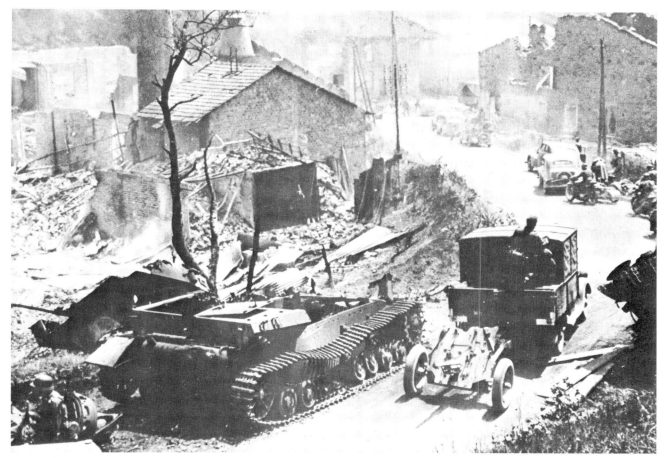

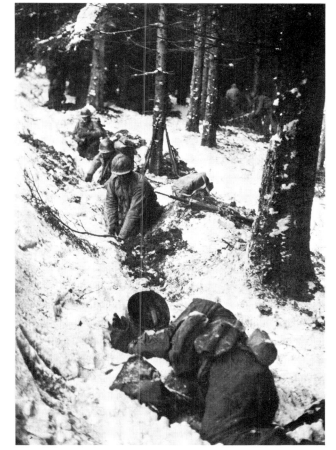

above: German motorized troops advancing on Western front, 1940. *Photographer unknown.*

right: American troops dig fox-holes in Belgium. *Photographer unknown.*

opposite top: Raid on Vaagso, Norway, 1941. *Lieutenant Malindine.*

opposite bottom: Narvic burning during bombardment by HMS *Cairo,* Norway, 1940. *Bishop H. Marshall.*

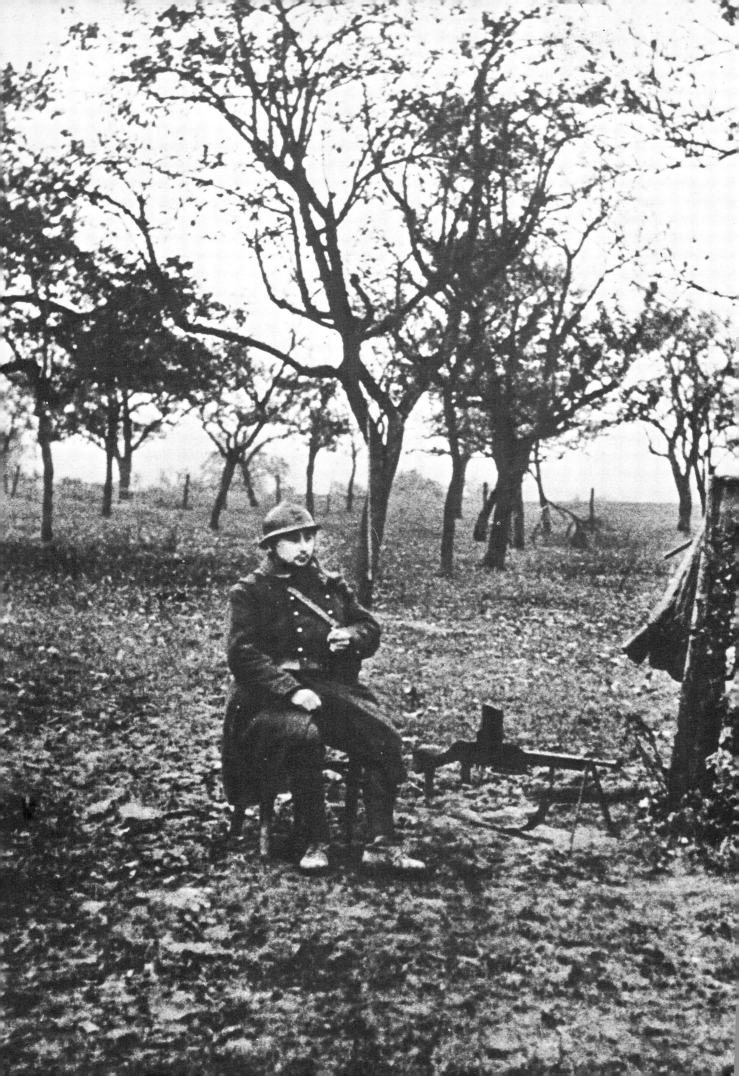

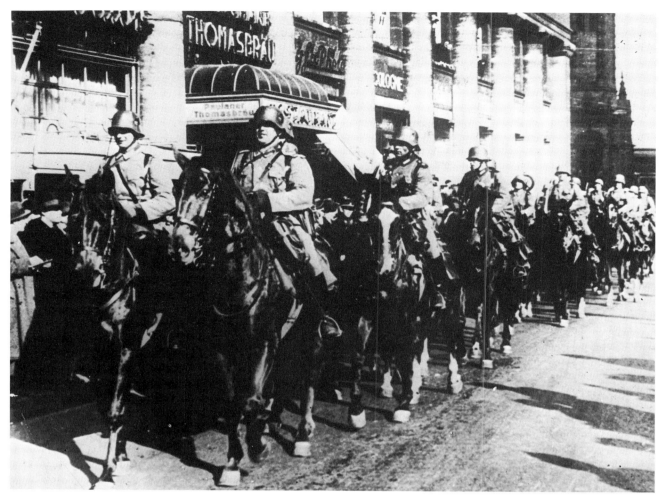

above: German troops enter Rhineland, 1940.
Photographer unknown.

Finally it was evacuated prematurely with hardly any of its recording mission accomplished. The Time/Life Organization had made extensive plans to report the conflict, but their personnel were similarly dispersed and rendered ineffective. There are virtually no official British pictures of the *blitzkreig* in France. It was the German PK correspondents and photographers, riding with the advanced motorized units, who recorded the fall of France. Their forces magazine, *Signal*, carried a constant stream of photographs of the triumphant panzer advance; some of these pictures found their way to the West and were published in a number of magazines. Even the fall of Paris, where two official British photographers were billeted, went almost entirely unrecorded as the Allied correspondents and cameramen retreated with the rest of the forces, leaving the field clear for the Germans.

The evacuation of Dunkirk was the only redeeming feature in the disastrous days of military defeat and humiliation. Again, no Allied photographer was

opposite: French soldier on Western front, 1939.
Photographer unknown.

present, save for one lone film-unit operator, bizarrely left behind, who found himself swept along with the retreating armies towards Dunkirk. We owe our pictures of the evacuation by the flotilla of wildly assorted craft shuttling between the shores of Britain and the Continent to a multitude of anonymous photographers – retreating soldiers and civilians who manned the boats. Thus the heroic defeat was at least recorded.

From July until the end of October the Luftwaffe fighters and bombers attempted to destroy Britain's Air Force and defences. The Battle of Britain was photographed by cameramen from all over the world. *Life* sent William Vandivert, and also used pictures of a German photographer resident in London, Hans Wild. George Rodger was one of the most outstanding of the English photographers to appear in *Life*. He shot a number of stories for them, one of the most powerful series being his set of pictures of the raid on Coventry and the damage it inflicted.

It is Bert Hardy's photographs at this stage of the war that are among the most notable. A Londoner, Hardy started his career with a small plate camera bought for 10 shillings. Later he was one of the first professional photojournalists to use the early Leica. A few random stories shot as a freelance earned him a full-time position with *Picture Post* and he stayed with the

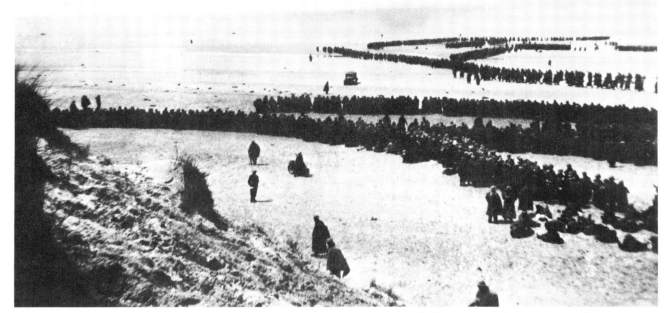

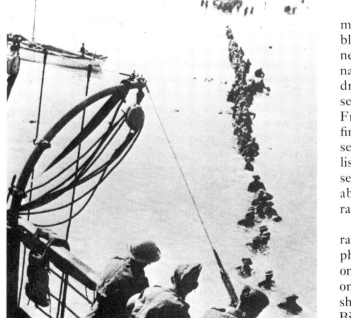

above and left: Two views of the retreat at Dunkirk, 1940. *Photographer unknown.*

magazine until it closed. Hardy's story of the London blitz was so good that, even though photographers were never given credits in the magazine at this time, his name appears as A. Hardy. In June 1942 Hardy was drafted into an army photographic unit. He was not sent overseas until D-Day. He might have gone to France earlier, never to return alive, had he not finished his training course with top marks instead of second place. He was given the first assignment on the list of jobs – to photograph a cadet officer for the service paper; the second assignment was for an abortive raid on Dieppe. Neither the young photographer who went nor his pictures were seen again.

With the war so close to home, even those photographers who cannot, strictly speaking, be termed war photographers tried their hand at recording its effects on Britain. Cecil Beaton shot some very strong images, one or two of them gracing the covers of *Life*; later he shot some fine war pictures in North Africa. But it was Bill Brandt who produced the true masterpieces of ravaged London: St Paul's Cathedral seen through a heap of rubble, pictures of people sleeping in the Underground – these sum up that time of war.

opposite: Tea for two in a bomb shelter, Battle of Britain, 1940. *Robert Capa.*

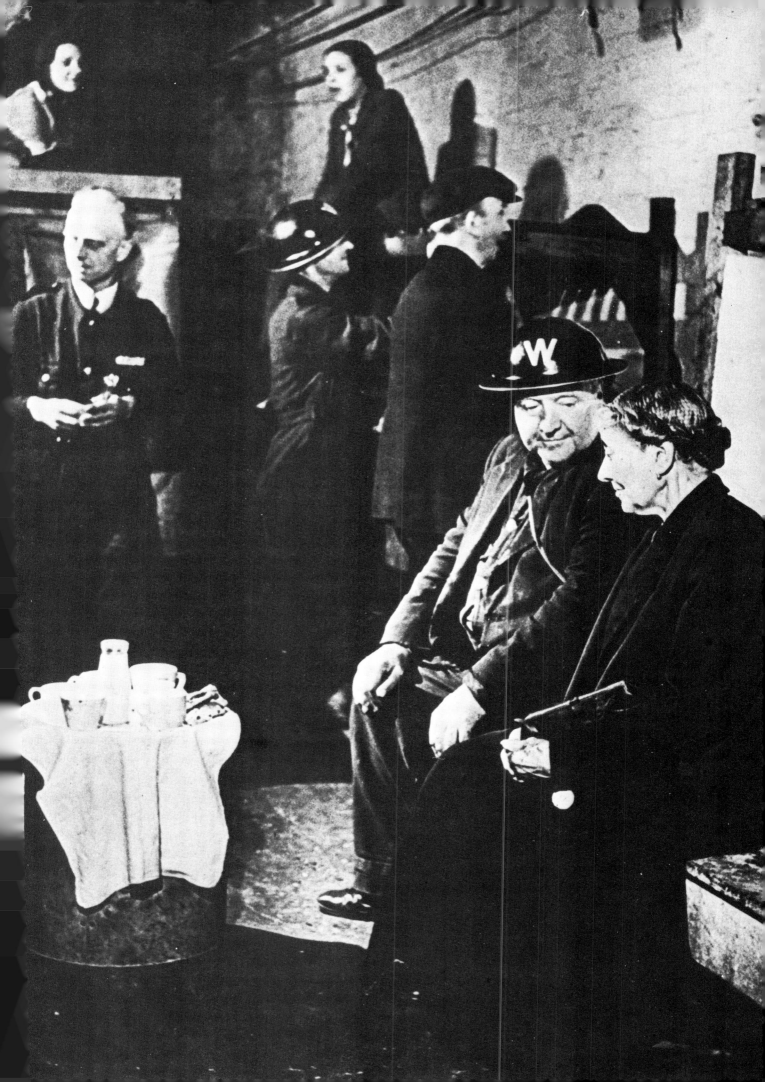

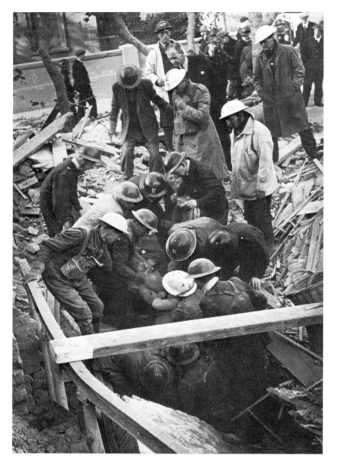

London blitz, 1940. *George Rodger.*

Phase Two War in the Desert

With the war in Europe virtually over by May 1940, there was very little work for the war photographers. Attention shifted to the Middle East as North Africa was the only place where British forces were still fighting. Accordingly, most of the military photographic units were sent to Cairo and it was from there that the main propaganda effort emanated. Cairo became the centre not only of the British photographers in the ranks but also of the many journalists and photographers of the international press. Large processing laboratories were set up to serve photographers as far afield as Iraq, Iran, Palestine, Lebanon, Ethiopia and the whole of North Africa.

It was in Cairo that the most popular forces publication was founded in July 1940. *Parade*, the weekly illustrated magazine of the Army, was started on a grant of £100 by Lieutenant Colonel Harold Ruston, former Cairo correspondent of the *Daily Express*. He remained its editor throughout its life. From the beginning *Parade* was an enormous success. Soon it was no longer confined to the Middle East, but was distributed to all British Armed Forces, printing well over 100 000 copies. It was still being published some three years after the war had ended.

opposite: Desert War photograph, staged 1941. *Sergeant L. Chetwyn.*

The chief photographer with *Parade* from its inception was not an army photographer, nor even a British national, but a Hungarian resident in Cairo. Bela Zola, the son of a professional photographer, was initially a court photographer to King Farouk of Egypt; he eventually became one of the most popular and fearless of *Parade*'s cameramen, covering the second and third desert campaigns, as well as stories in Persia, East Africa and the Congo. Later he followed British forces through Sicily, Salerno and Italy, ending up at the Armistice in Austria. He was aided by other photographers including Tim N. Gidal, and in Italy by an American, George Silk.

It was at the Cairo laboratories that the negative material shot by the various army photographic units in North Africa was processed. It was then transferred to Corps Headquarters to be censored, and then to the public relation unit for captioning. (One of the caption writers was J. Allen Cash, later a well-known travelogue photographer.) The pictures were forwarded to London to the main depot in Curzon Street, and finally to the Central Office for distribution. The Director of the Photography Division was Charles Gibb-Smith. It was in this way that all photographs were pooled and no credits were given to individual photographers.

Few pictures of the war match the best of the shots taken throughout the desert campaign. The expanses of sky and sand, with every soldier darkly, almost tangibly etched out against the infinity of the desert, provided magnificent images for a creative photographer. Many strong, imaginative pictures were taken by photographers who were often unknown and are now forgotten. Only surnames are recorded in the files of the Imperial War Museum. An inquiry as to their fate or present whereabouts is answered with a shrug and a polite reply that no records were ever made or kept. Captain Keating's name appears in the records of the Norway expedition, as well as the desert wars, the Italian invasion, Normandy and France. He was promoted to Major somewhere in Italy. And that is all that we know of him, or of Lieutenant S. McLaren, J. Daakin, Whicker, Slade, or of the sergeants who served under them: Wackett – a wonderful photographer, Bourne, Stubbs, Loughlin, Gunn, Palmer, Dawson, Bowman, Gee, Best, Christie, Travis, Brennan, Walker, Rooke and Gladstone and many more.

Sergeant Bert Curry's name recurs simply because he took more risks than the others. He now runs a photographic shop in Holborn and is an active member of the Army Film and Photographic Units Association.

opposite: Capture of Italian tank, Desert War, 1941. *Sergeant L. Chetwyn.*

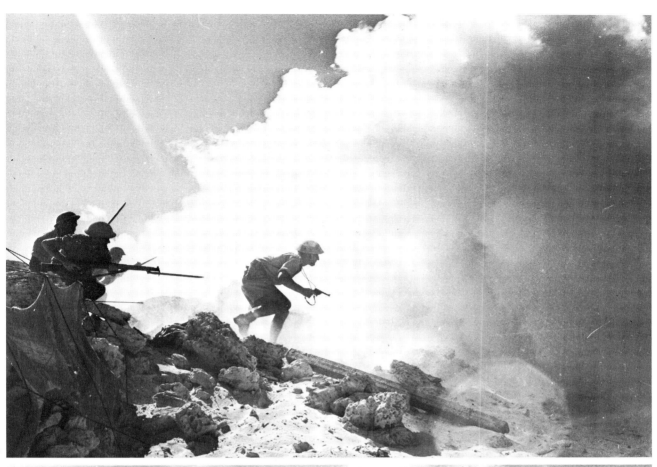

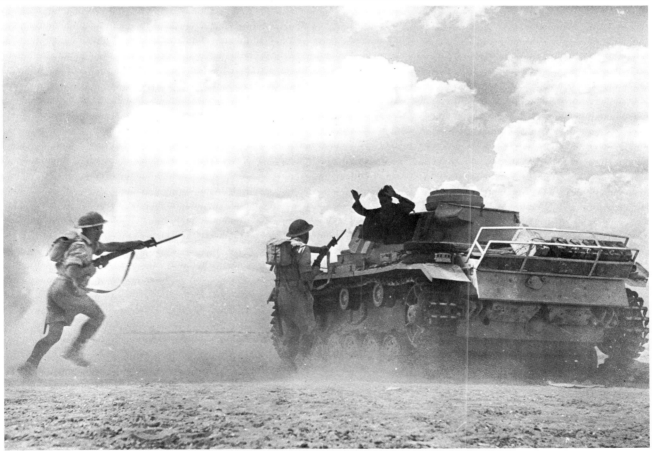

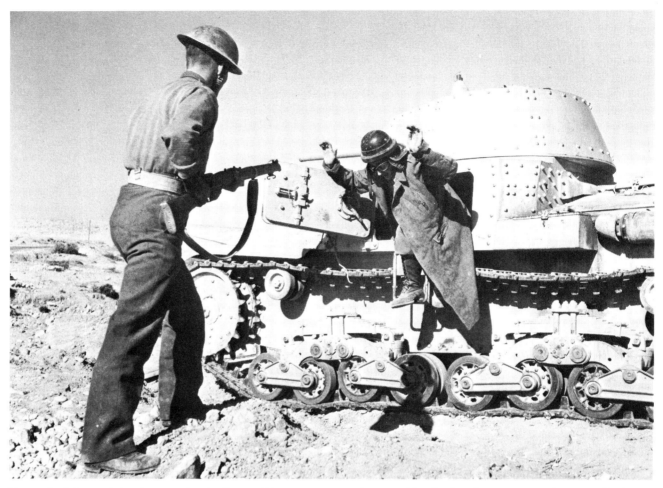

The end of the tank battle near Gazala, Desert War, 1941. *Photographer unknown.*

He was sent to Cairo in December 1940 with the 4th Light Armoured Brigade (part of the 7th Army), and covered their entire progress from Alamein to Benghazi. He was later attached to the Special Air Services under-cover unit, commanded by Colonel Stirling, which worked mostly behind enemy lines. On one of his assignments with the SAS his jeep was blown up and he had to be left behind. He was finally picked up by another famous unit – Popsky's Private Army – but not before he had marched 125 miles in the desert. As it happened, Colonel Stirling, having left Curry behind, was himself captured by one of Rommel's units.

Another name that often appears is Sergeant Lenart Chetwyn, but for a less distinguished reason. In 1977 the *British Journal of Photography* published a series of articles on war photography, based mainly on the collection of the Imperial War Museum. They were by James Clement, who finished the series with an interview with Ian Grant who started his career in the Second World War as one of the desert cameramen and now works for the BBC. In the interview Grant discussed various tricks of the trade, including the 'manufacturing' of pictures. It appears that the desert war was especially suitable for the 'reconstruction' of

action specifically for the camera – cine or still: it was a long, protracted campaign with extensive periods of inactivity; the background was constant and unchanging which made it hard to spot subterfuge. Here is what Grant has to say about the outfit that became well known for their skilful fabrication of dramatic war pictures:

In MacDonald's unit [Maj. David MacDonald in charge of the entire photographic unit] there was an outfit called Chet's Circus which, though it had the approval of the Film Unit, did not meet with the approval of other photographers in the field. This was a team of cameramen whose leader was Sgt Chetwyn – hence the Chet part of their nickname. He got his little group of photographers together, still and cine, and they went into a rear echelon formation of tanks in rest areas, bribing the support of some of the troops who were relaxing with bottles of whisky. Then they created their own little battle sequences. You got things like Chetwyn sitting on the top of a tank with maybe a couple of tanks riding out in echelon in front out of frame of his camera. They would charge forward. In front he would have a box of hand grenades and he would lob the genades in front of him while he was filming. This was approved by the War Office, but a lot of photographers did not like it. In fact there is an official War Office memo about it.

Clement gives the details of the memo in his article. It is dated 10 December 1942 and headed 'W.O.

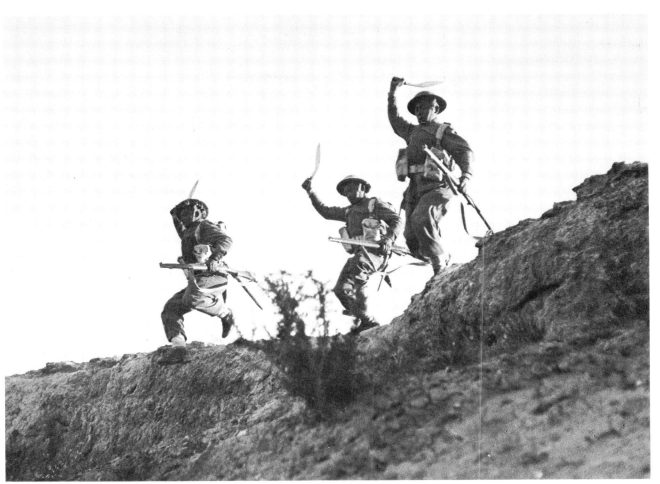

Assignment No. 907. Photographs taken by Sgts. Chetwyn and Mapham'. It is entitled '"Chet's Circus" – a unit of the AFPU in the Western Desert' and reads as follows:

Attack of Gurkhas, Desert War, 1943. *Photographer unknown.*

One of the units of the AFPU is a group of four men and a driver, with a roving commission to go wherever there is action and wherever they think they can get pictures. Their leader is Sgt Chetwyn, a former Fleet St photographer. . . . They have produced some of the finest pictures of this campaign and some of the most striking shots in recent newsreels have come from their cameras. Two of the men take still pictures and the other two use cine cameras. The group consists of Sgt Len Chetwyn, formerly with Keystone; Sgt John Herbert, formerly with Kodak; Sgt Jim Mapham, formerly with the *Leicester Mercury*; and Sgt Chris Windows, formerly with Paramount; driver Dempsey, formerly a Manchester bus driver. They live the life of an ordinary soldier in the front line, with the same rations, often only bully and biscuits – limited water and petrol, and suffer all the hardships and difficulties that go with fighting in the Western Desert. Their weapons are cameras, instead of guns, and they bring back the pictures that illustrate the deeds of the Eighth Army. These pictures show the ordinary life of the men of the 'Circus' when on active service.

Chetwyn, who now lives in Cornwall, does not admit to everything imputed to his outfit, but the majority of the photographers I have talked to have

little doubt that much of his reputation is based on fact.

One of the best-known pictures of the desert war, prominently displayed in the entrance to the Imperial War Museum, of a Desert Rat running into battle with a pistol in his hand is rated by most as a skilful reconstruction of a scene which nevertheless was a common occurrence in the war in North Africa.

Apart from the official photographers, the desert war was covered by many international freelances. George Rodger, the only British representative, spent a considerable time in North Africa. He arrived shortly after the first successful offensive of General Wavell had virtually eliminated the Italian army, and joined the second diversionary expedition to Ethiopia where Count Alba's Italian legions were quickly subdued. There Rodger took some breathtaking shots of the troops dwarfed by the magnificent scenery. He later reappeared in North Africa to photograph the Free French, as well as activities in Libya, before leaving for the North Western Frontier of India and the Burma campaign.

Phase Three The Russian Epic

On 22 June 1941 Germany threw almost three million soldiers in three mighty echelons into battle – north towards Leningrad, in the centre towards Moscow and south in the direction of the Caucasus. In a few months the invaders harvested some million and a half prisoners, killing and maiming many more. The flood of soldiers and guns moved at the incredible speed of up to 50 miles a day, and yet brought little to the aggressors in terms of reward. The enormous area of territory taken, the multitudes of Russian souls disarmed seemed like a small scratch on the giant of Russia. To try to visualize these events is to conceive of the spreading vastness of the conflict. No camera can manage to convey a complete image of this magnitude.

In fact the Russian front was the least photographed of the war; even less was written about it. The only Western photographer to penetrate the Russian barrier was Margaret Bourke-White who, with her writer husband, Erskine Caldwell, was sent by *Life* before the German attack. They were to produce an essay on Russian life, the magazine's editor having a hunch that hostilities were soon to start between Russia and Germany. She was in Moscow when the first air raid took place on the capital, and photographed the bombardment from the balcony of her hotel. She even managed to be conducted briefly to the front near Smolensk. Her movements were severely restricted by the Russians, however; she later had to resort to photographing the German raids at night from the roof of the American Embassy and was forced to leave Russia in the third month of the war.

War photography was very much a male preserve up to the Second World War. Apart from the purely physical dangers, which do not necessarily deter a woman more than a man, the photographer must suffer a great deal of inconvenience and hardship, carry only a minimum of personal effects, and sometimes live in casual and intimate proximity to soldiers, sharing their food and their blankets. Margaret Bourke-White seems to have easily overcome all these strictures and earned for herself a place in the history of war photography. She was a founder member of *Life*'s 'family' and their first full-time photographer.

It is impossible to estimate the number of official Russian photographers working at the beginning of the offensive, but most likely it was quite small. The rapid retreat would have thrown them into total confusion, struggling amongst the harassed Russian troops, and consequently hardly any pictures of local origin appeared during the early part of the war. Later, however, when the Soviet forces were beginning to recover and counter attack, the photographic record becomes more substantial. Until very recently there was no published collection of Russian war pictures in the West

opposite: Fallen German soldiers on Russian front, 1941. *Galina Saṅkova.*

below: German parachute flares over Kremlin, 1941. *Margaret Bourke-White.*

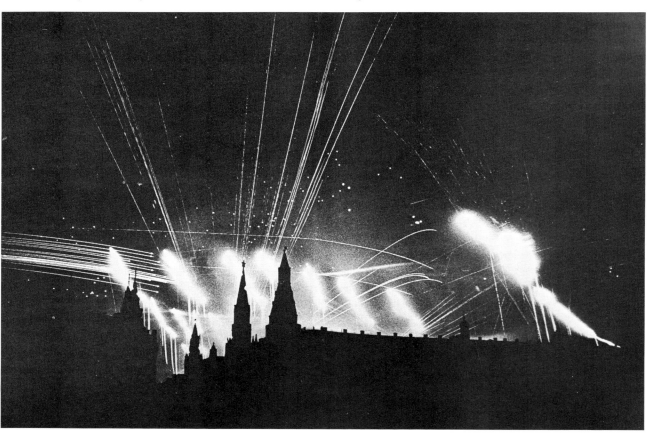

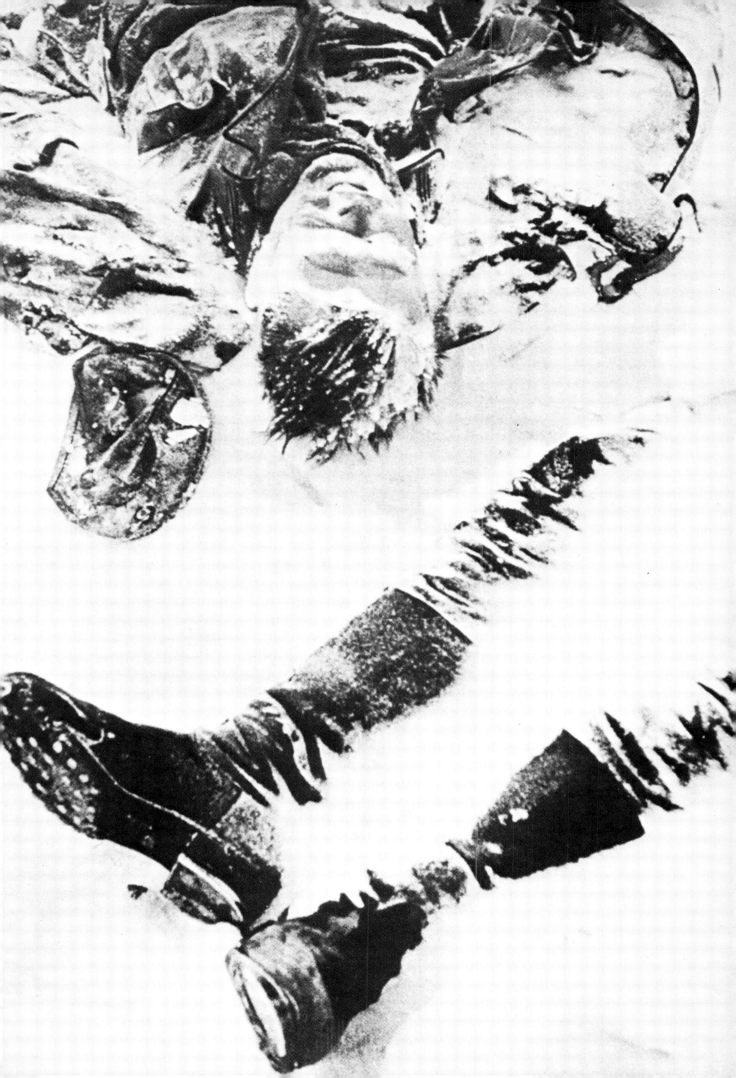

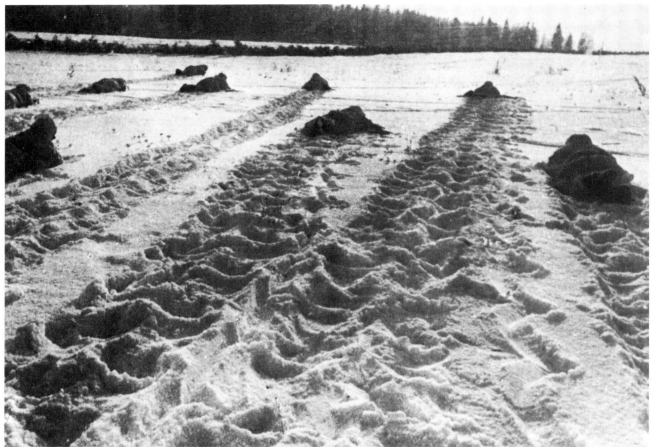

above: Soviet infantry men advancing on Russian front, 1941. *Photographer unknown.*

and, as few magazines had penetrated the Iron Curtain, little was known about the achievements of Soviet war cameramen. In 1975 a Czechoslovakian publication, *They Photographed War*, revealed the excellence of the Russian war photographers (an English edition was published in 1978 by Jonathan Cape, entitled *The Russian War: 1941–1945*). Assembled by Daniela Mrazkova and Vladimir Remes, the book contains many reproductions and lists a number of photographers but still only manages to cover a minute proportion of the work that must have been carried out on the huge Russian front. The selection of photographs in the book is so good that all the photographers included seem of remarkable ability, but the work of Dmitri Baltermants, already known in the West, stands out as the most accomplished and versatile.

Born in Warsaw, Baltermants worked for the daily paper *Isvestia* and covered almost all the important fronts including the defence of Moscow and Sebastopol, the Battle of Stalingrad, the occupation of Poland and the last battles for Berlin. Max Alpert – a photojournalist for *Novosti* and *Pravda* – also worked on

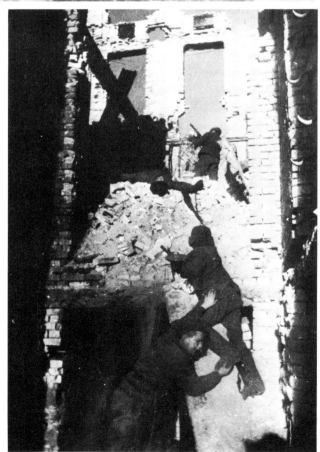

right: Fighting in Stalingrad, 1942. *Photographer unknown.*

112

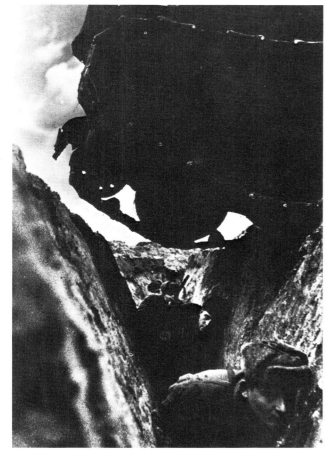

many fronts and his pictures possess great strength and impact. Robert Diament mostly covered the activities of the Navy, while the husband and wife partnership of Alexandra and Michael Ananimov recorded the discovered graves in Katyn, and the Polish campaign. The battles for Berlin and its aftermath were photographed by many Soviet cameramen including Ivan Shagin, Viktor Tomin, Viktor Grebnev, Jakov Rjumkin and Yevgeni Khaldei. Of the other photographers, mention should be made of the excellent work done by Alexander Ustinov, Georgi Lipserov, Anatoli Garanin, and two very fine woman photographers, Galina Sankova and Olga Lander. We can really only manage to single out a few of them, for the Russian campaign was large and filled with such outstanding battles and seemingly superhuman deeds.

In the horrifying 900 days through which Leningrad somehow held out under siege, nearly 1000 people died each day – some from enemy bullets, but the majority from hunger and disease. Boris Kudojarow spent a considerable amount of time with the besieged and produced a remarkable record of heroism, suffering and death. There were other photographers of the epic of Leningrad, among them Mikhail Trakhman. The battle

below: Battle of Stalingrad, 1942. *Georgi Zelma.*

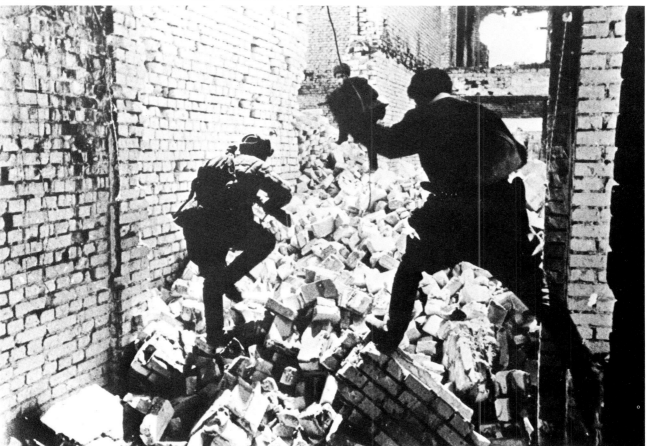

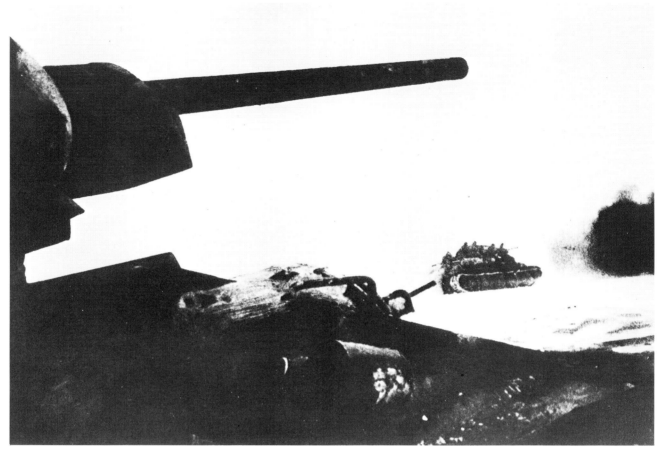

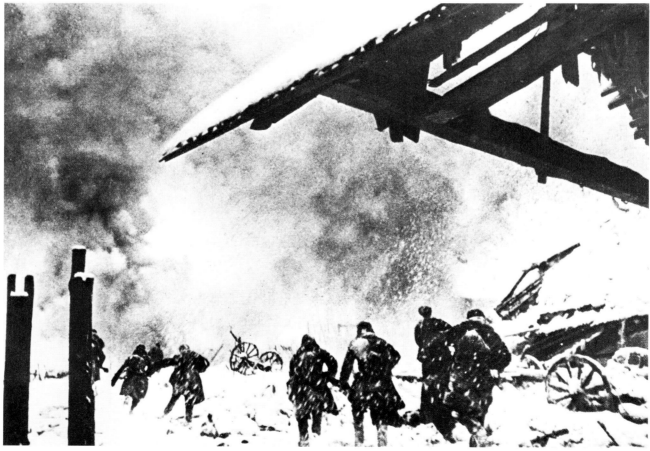

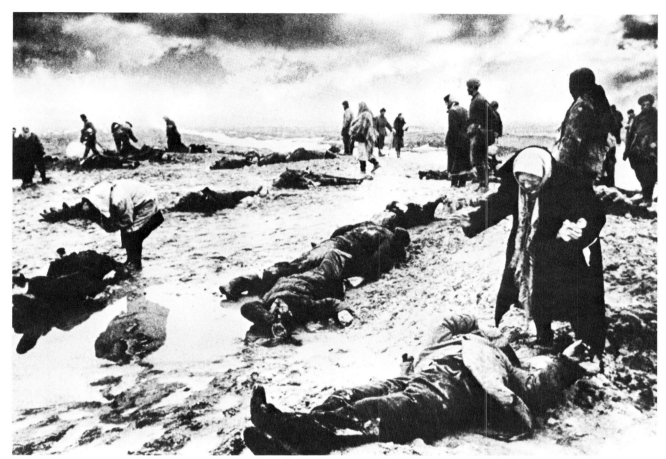

above: Identifying the dead, Russian front, 1942. *Dmitri Baltermants.*

right: Siege of Leningrad, 1942. *Mikhail Trakhman.*

and siege of Stalingrad also presented a fantastic spectacle for the camera lens, but the nature of the struggle made its representation a very difficult task indeed. Jakov Rjumkin and Georgi Zelma met this challenge, visually the most magnificent of the whole war, but sadly did not capture the greatest tank battle of all time – the Kursk confrontation. This meeting of the new German tanks – Ferdinand and Panther – with the Russian giants SU 122 and SU 152 brought together a total number of 6000 machines supported by some 4000 planes. It would have made a superb subject for any war photographer and it is a pity that we are only left with some inept drawings. Apparently a German PK photographer did take some spectacular shots but was captured by the Russians who confiscated his film. His pictures were somehow disinterred and appeared in a television documentary programme shown on British TV in 1972, but I have so far not been able to trace their whereabouts.

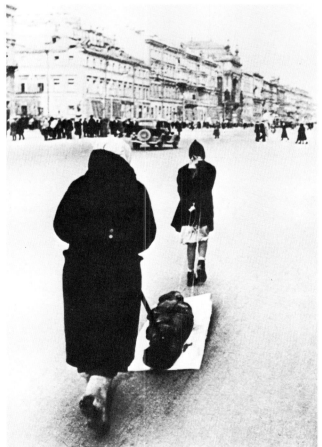

opposite: Two battle scenes on the Russian front.
top: Alexander Ustinov, bottom: Anatoli Garanin.

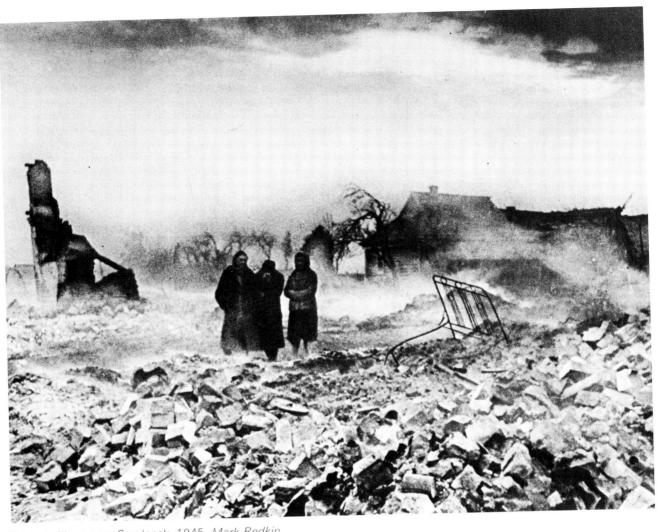

Ruined village near Smolensk, 1945. *Mark Redkin*.

The work of German PK photographers following the army into Russia was extremely good as the many illustrations in *Signal* testify, but the reproductions themselves were very poor and largely unsuitable for copying. The originals unfortunately have disappeared in many cases, most likely during the period of bombing by the Allies and the general disasters which enveloped Germany in the last stages of the war. Many pictures were lost with their authors on the Eastern front, but some names appear in the by-lines of wartime magazines – Krigskorrespondente Waske, Schurer, Frass, Friedrich, Feuchtner, Schlemmer, Geuzler, Hornung, Wiesner, Ritter, Hubmann, Sepp Jager – names without any substance. At the height of the Russian campaign there were as many as 12000 PK war correspondents – photographers and writers – in Russia. How many of them survived no one will ever know. There was Walter Renschl who had the audacity to photograph Stalin's captured son. It is hardly surprising that when the photographer in his turn was captured he promptly disappeared for ever.

If all the best pictures of the Russian photographers could be extracted from the Soviet archives and if the best efforts of the German cameramen assembled, they would make a wonderful collection – possibly the definitive book on war. Unfortunately, this is unlikely, so the problem of sorting the authentic work in these collections from those that were reconstructions will not arise. Even in the Czech book, *They Photographed War*, some of the photographs do have that curious affinity with film stills, and many films were made in the years following the war.

With the two major military victories – Stalingrad and Kursk – the Russian armies started to push the invader back, slowly at first but gradually with increasing speed. By the end of 1943 the German armies in some areas such as the Caucasus found themselves as much as up to 700 miles away from their furthest gains. By this time the Allied troops were halfway through Italy halted by the Gustav–Hitler line of defence with its centre the monastery of Monte Cassino.

Phase Four The Italian Campaign

North Africa, in spite of a certain amount of censorship, was almost a war correspondents' paradise. The space was immense, the terrain picturesque, there was plenty of action, and within reason a photographer could travel anywhere. In Italy the situation was a good deal tighter – censorship was quite strict, accreditation checked more thoroughly, and certain areas were difficult to reach, but in comparison to the Eastern Front, the photographers enjoyed unprecedented freedom. The deluge of media people, which was later to flood France after D-Day, was still to come, but even so a little army of official photographers and a number of well-known freelance photographers were already there. When the Americans landed in North Africa late in 1942, there were twenty-two foreign correspondents and photographers in Algiers; by August 1943 there were no less than 150.

Margaret Bourke-White managed to get herself accredited to the Air Force and arrived in Tunisia for the start of the American invasion of North Africa in November. On her way there she found unlooked-for subject matter when her ship was torpedoed off the coast of Africa. In Africa she was the first woman photographer on bombing missions. She covered the landings in Sicily and the whole of the Italian campaign; she later published a book of her pictures : *They Call It Purple Heart Valley*. All the while she was sending regular picture stories to *Life*, as were Bob Landry, William Vandivert, and Eliot Elisofon, one of the finest technicians in war photography and later a famous colour specialist.

Robert Capa was also there. Having managed to get an accreditation with *Collier's Magazine*, which for a stateless Hungarian living in the USA was quite an achievement, Capa had arrived in England early in 1942. With his makeshift papers he had the greatest difficulty in obtaining permission to enter England and only his stubborness and exuberance saved him. In wartime England he shot many lively stories including one of a trip in a minesweeper in the North Sea and another on Bomber Command. Then, again through sheer persistence, he scraped accreditation with the Scottish Division leaving for North Africa. When the Americans landed, he was jobless and patronless once again as *Collier's* had fired their rather erratic and unpredictable photographer. He managed to eke out his stay and lived through the Tunisian campaign when the remnants of Rommel's army were cleared out, but his big break came with the invasion of Sicily on 10 July 1943. The official photographer who was to accompany Major General Ridgway's 88th Airborne Division on his first mission to Sicily cried off at the last minute, because of illness. Capa immediately offered to take his place although he had never before attempted a parachute jump. His devil-may-care attitude so much appealed to General Ridgway that he agreed. A major scoop was the outcome and Capa suddenly found himself once more with his former employer, *Life*. He covered the Salerno fighting and the liberation of Naples and was one of the first to photograph the bridgehead at Anzio

Landing in Sicily, 1943. *Sergeant Wackett.*

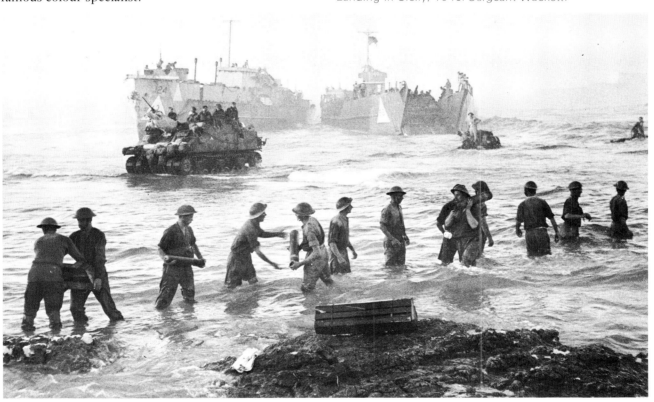

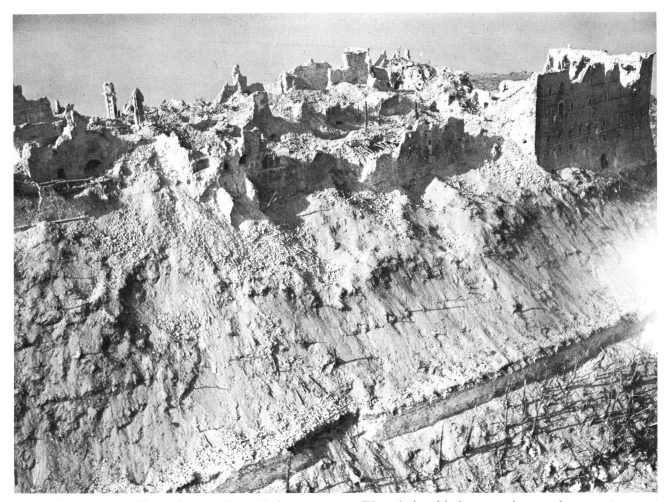

Ruins of monastery of Monte Cassino, Italy, 1943.
Photographer unknown.

where the American 5th Army landed behind the German defensive lines and behind Monte Cassino.

George Rodger returned from his lengthy travels in Burma to participate in the Italian landings. His western desert coverage was published in 1944 as *Desert Journey* and his Burma experiences as *Red Moon Rising*. He photographed the Burmese rearguard fighting by combined British and Chinese forces from the fall of Rangoon in 1942 up to the last battles for Lashio in the north. To escape from Burma, completely over-run by the Japanese, he had to walk across the Pungsao Pass into India. Once back on the European front Rodger followed the victorious Allied forces along the length of Italy with especially fine reportage on the fighting for Monte Cassino which claimed so many Polish and New Zealand lives.

Yet another American photographer who reappeared in time to photograph Monte Cassino, followed by the capture of Rome, was Carl Mydans who had recently been repatriated from a Japanese POW camp. Many other photographers, too numerous to mention, covered the Italian campaign, including the *Parade* team headed by Bela Zola often assisted by George Silk, then at the start of his career.

The relationship between the war photographers and the fighting men was excellent. American generals and soldiers especially liked nothing better than to have their heroics recorded for *Life*.

At this point we can compare the methods and standards of war photography of the nations engaged in the war. Of the four – British, German, American and Russian – the German are the most impressive and certainly of the most consistent standard. Their war machine was excellently prepared, and much thought must have been given to the role that photography had to play in their overall effort. It acquitted itself superbly. A brief look at the German forces magazine *Signal*, which now has gained recognition with several books published about it, is quite conclusive. From the start it was printed in a number of languages. Whereas the British counterpart, *Parade*, was frankly a pleasant forces magazine which carried some war pictures but mostly news from home, *Signal* was conceived as a propaganda force. At all times it presented the German soldier as a superman, and the overall editorial policy was ably supported with very good photographic material.

The illustrations in *Signal* were always far stronger and more effective than almost anything shot or at least

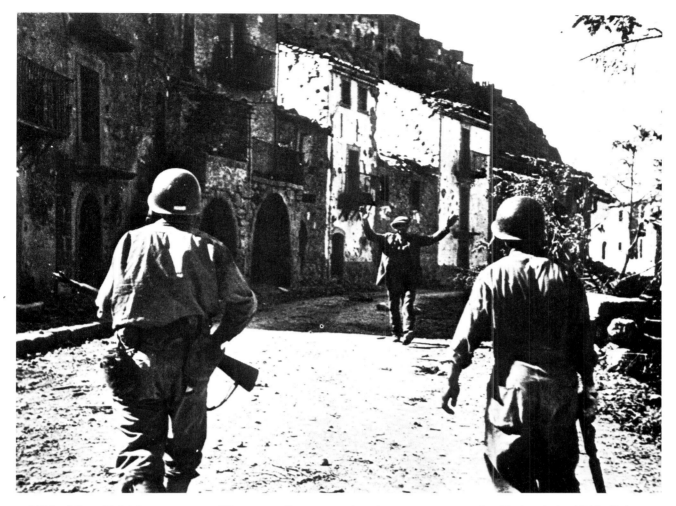

American troops occupying Troina, Italy, 1943. *Robert Capa.*

published from British cameramen. The reason lies not so much, one feels, in the individual ability of the respective photographers, but in the more efficient organization of the propaganda apparatus as a whole, the larger number of photographers, the better equipment and stronger discipline. German war photographers who were found wanting in effort or whose pictures consistently lacked interest, appropriate spirit or excitement were promptly reassigned to the Russian front. No such threat hung over the British propaganda machine. The best talent was entirely at the disposal of the German military, which was not entirely the case for the British.

The most important reason, however, for the discrepancy in quality and content may be attributed to the simple fact that the Germans, in these first years, were winning the war. The best war photographs come from following the attack and advance and not from constant retreat. It is in attack that the photographer can capture the valour of the soldiers, endless columns of prisoners, territory with the unmistakable signs of the passage of the war machine. All that confronts the photographer with the beaten army is virgin territory and dispirited, dejected faces – the last subject on which an editor of a forces magazine wishes to dwell. Consequently German photographic material in the

early days of the war is consistently more interesting and exciting, though there is little doubt that much of it was arranged for the camera. A certain proportion of British photographs had a similar origin – inevitable under the circumstances.

Having said all that in defence of British war photographers, one comes to the inevitable conclusion that the British authorities as a whole were extremely slow to realize the importance of photography and photographers and, in many cases, they were singularly inept in their exploitation of the existing resources. Stanley Devon, a professional photographer with the *Daily Graphic* (and later with the *Daily Sketch*), recounts how badly and unimaginatively photography was utilized by the Royal Air Force. He was the first photographer to be accredited to the RAF – in fact he was called up on the first day of the war mainly due to his knowledge of air photography he had gained with his paper. Yet this experience was hardly put to the test. As far as he remembers, he himself had to suggest possible subjects, otherwise he would find himself totally idle for large tracts of time. The major event of his early service – when he was the only air photographer

119

in the RAF – was a trip to France to cover the visit of King George VI. Later Devon was joined by Henry Heusser from Keystone and John Daventry from the Sport and General News Agency. Soon after Dunkirk, from which they had all been evacuated by sea long before the main evacuation, he joined the rest of the media people in Cairo. The Middle East brought an extension to Devon's activities, however, and, apart from pure reconnaissance photography, he went on some bombing missions and even had a Lockheed Hudson aircraft specially fitted for aerial photography, part of the floor having been removed.

Almost nothing was known of Russian war photography until recently as already noted, but even now it is difficult to evaluate it. The pictures that were finally released by the Soviet authorities for publication are possibly the best of those that were taken. It is a great pity that we cannot find out a little bit more about them. Of all the combatants, the Russians must have worked under the greatest difficulties. Their cameras and materials were far inferior and the conditions often appalling. They are certainly among the many unsung and unknown heroes of the war.

The Americans treated photography, especially aerial photography, in a very professional way. But then they entered the war much later and had more time for preparation than the British who had to improvise at the start. When they landed in North Africa in November 1942, the Americans had been actively engaged in the war for less than one year, but had been planning the western campaign for much longer than that. Consequently, their photographic units were well trained (with at least a four-month course for each cameraman), very well equipped and there were many of them. Immediately after Pearl Harbor, the famous advertising and fashion photographer, Edward Steichen – already a veteran of the First World War in air reconnaissance photography – was promoted to Lieutenant Commander. At the age of sixty-two in 1941, he was put in charge of a very strong photographic unit. Their object was to record all the war activities of the US Navy, especially the air action. The team included photographers from advertising, magazines and science, among them Wayne Miller, Fenner Jacobs and Victor Jorgenson.

By 1942 all the American fighting units, whether on land, sea or air, had a small photographic team attached to them. Therefore, their expeditionary forces in North Africa were amply backed by photographers. Patriotic fervour for the war had attracted a number of prominent Hollywood personalities from the fields of film and photography, adding a glamorous aura to what in the British forces was regarded as merely another job. Most of the American war photographers were of the officer rank while the majority of the British were only NCOs – Bert Hardy, both in Normandy and throughout the European campaign, was drawing a sergeant's pay.

The best American war photography however, was still to come; it reached its zenith with the coverage of their very own war in the Pacific.

Phase Five   The War in the Pacific

The Japanese struck ferociously at Pearl Harbor in the Hawaiian Islands on 7 December 1941. This brought the USA headlong into the struggle. The war in the Pacific was far flung and extensive, fought on the sea, in the air and on the ground. To record reasonably comprehensively the activities of photographers throughout its different phases would require a sizeable document. We can, therefore, attempt to mention only the best-known names and single out only the most significant battles.

With the Americans taken by surprise at Pearl Harbor, there were no freelance photographers present. A number of pictures were taken by mostly anonymous official photographers of the US Navy. Some of these, like the one showing the destruction of the USS *Shaw*, were slightly retouched and partly blocked out before being released for publication. This was done to hide some military installations. Within a day or so a number of photographers had descended on Hawaii, including William C. Shrout, Ralph Morse and Bob Landry, who all obtained permission to photograph the aftermath of the treacherous attack.

After Pearl Harbor, the Japanese captured Guam and the Wake Islands, Hong Kong, and Rangoon in Burma within five months. Singapore fell to them on 15 February, taken unexpectedly from the land. This was followed by the capital of the Dutch West Indies and the Philippine Islands – the most serious blow of all to the Americans. The speed of the Japanese progress in the Pacific made any systematic photographic record impossible. Few of the Japanese conquests were recorded by American cameramen. One exception was the protracted and stubborn defence of Corregidor and Bataan in the Philippines, which was photographed by Melville Jacoby among others.

At the end of March 1942 the Japanese surge was somehow stemmed. The recovery was mainly due to two important naval battles: the first, the so-called battle of the Coral Sea, fought very largely by planes from carriers, took place off the coast of New Guinea. The second and more important, since celebrated by cinematic reconstruction, was the battle of Midway Island. Both were only partially recorded by the official photographers of the US Navy mostly from high flying aircraft. *Life*, for their coverage, had to resort to the services of an excellent model maker and simulator of land and sea battles, Norman Bel Geddes. Some of his photographs of these still-life arrangements are almost uncanny in their realism.

USS *Shaw* exploding, Pearl Harbor, 1941. *Photographer unknown.*

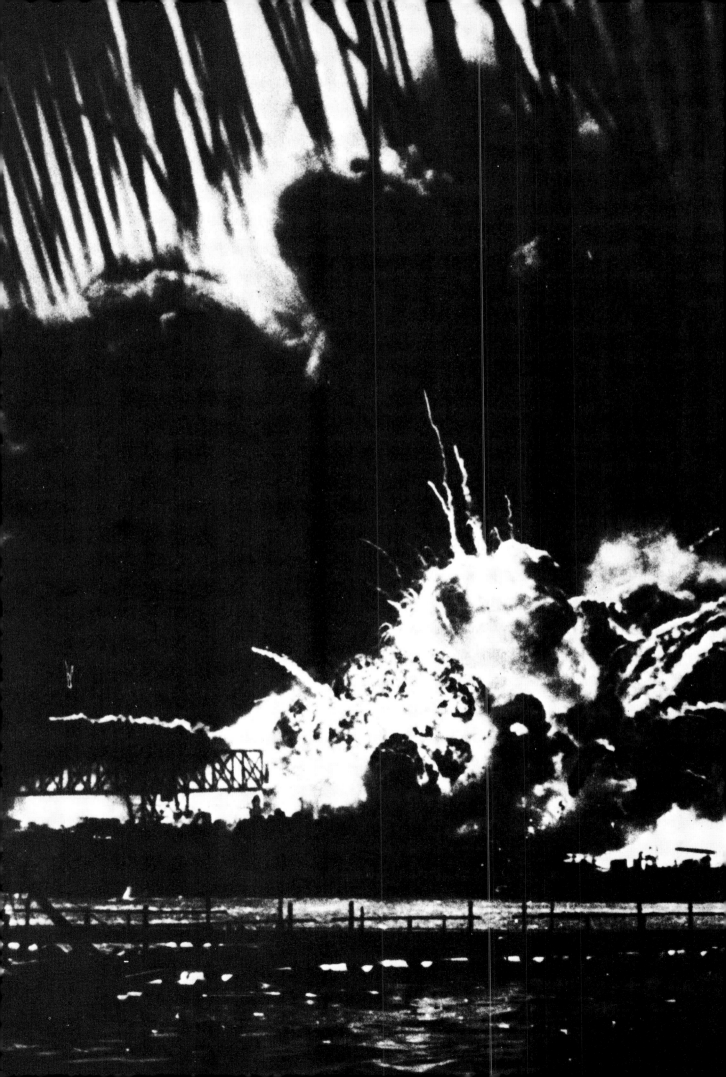

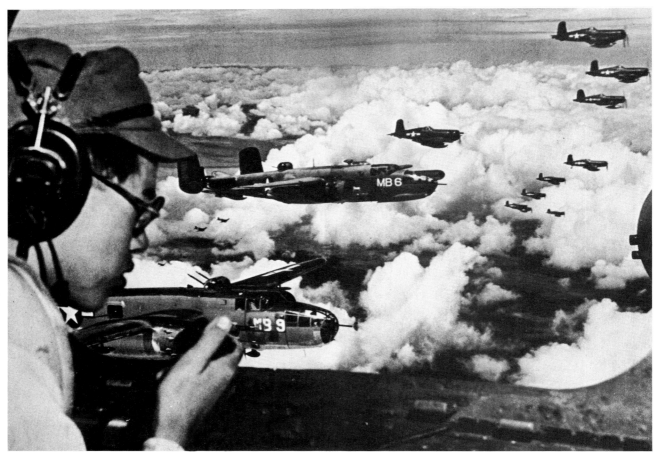

above: American bombers in action over Pacific. *David Douglas Duncan.*

The extent of the Japanese coverage of any of the sea battles is difficult to establish, but it is known that one Japanese cameraman, Teidei Makishima, was on one of the doomed Japanese carriers and managed to record among other things the dramatic sinking of another carrier, *Akagi*.

The end of 1942 and more especially 1943 was the time when the American Navy, its flyers, and the Marine Corps began to fight back in earnest, slowly pushing the invaders back towards Japan. Many names of small Pacific islands now stand as symbols of both the bravery of the Americans and the tenacity of the Japanese. They fought for virtually every foot of each of these islands and each battle was a test of courage and endurance for both sides. The battles for the Pacific islands were photographed by hundreds of photographers. Only a handful can be recalled.

George Strock took some powerful pictures of the fight for New Guinea. His series on the Battle of Buna in the south western promontory of the island, are especially noteworthy. Frank Filan and Johnny Florea photographed Tarava and Myron H. Davis the Lae

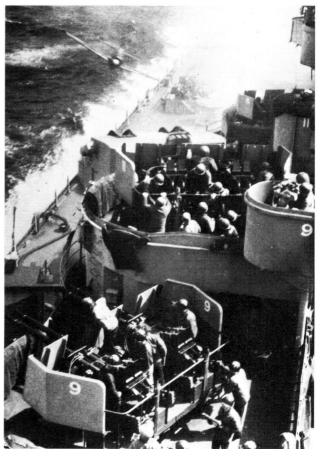

right: Japanese *kamikaze* plane attacking USS *Missouri,* 1945. *Photographer unknown.*

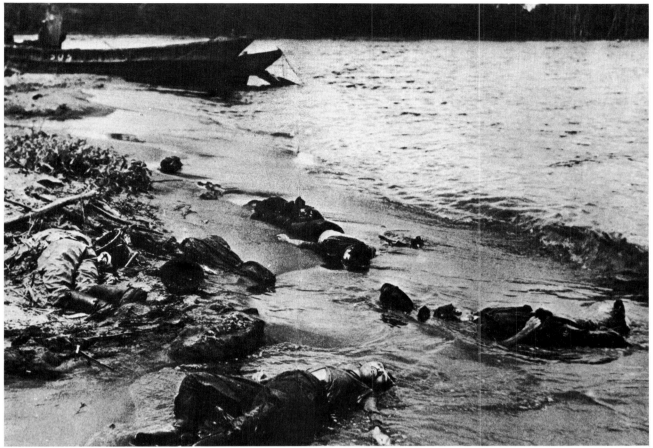

above: Japanese dead, New Guinea, 1943.
Photographer unknown.

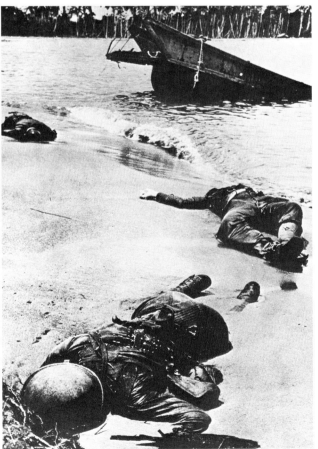

landings, Davis with J. R. Eyerman also photographed the battles of the Marianas. Peter Stackpole, another in the long line of *Life*'s excellent photographers, who up until March 1943 had mainly photographed Hollywood stars, took some remarkable pictures on Saipan. Carl Mydans photographed the battles for Luzon and Tarakan.

Of the many Pacific cameramen, Ralph Morse certainly can claim to be one of the key figures. His pictures of the fighting for the notorious Guadalcanal are outstanding. Morse had a narrow escape when his ship was sunk in the battle of Savo Island; he floated for six and a half hours before being rescued. Many of his films and all his cameras were lost and he had to wait for replacement equipment before being able to continue his brilliant reportage.

The Pacific theatre was also a first baptism for the future great war photographer, David Douglas Duncan. After photographing big game in Canada and Nicaragua and the art treasures of the world, Duncan became one of Edward Steichen's men. He entered the US Marine Corps in February 1943, not only as a trained marine

left: Dead US soldiers during the attack on Buna island, 1943. *George Strock.*

123

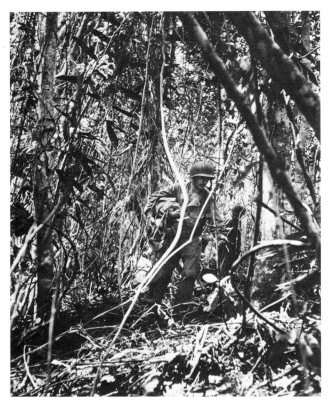

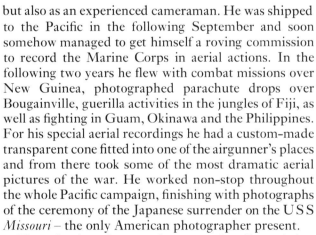

Marines in Pacific jungle, 1943. *Ralph Morse.*

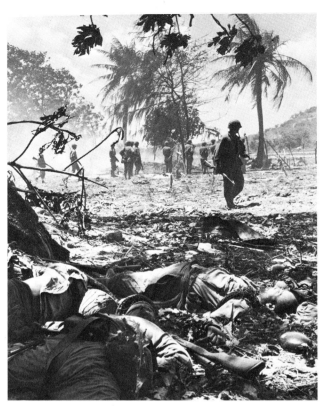

Battle of Saipan, 1944. *Peter Stackpole.*

but also as an experienced cameraman. He was shipped to the Pacific in the following September and soon somehow managed to get himself a roving commission to record the Marine Corps in aerial actions. In the following two years he flew with combat missions over New Guinea, photographed parachute drops over Bougainville, guerilla activities in the jungles of Fiji, as well as fighting in Guam, Okinawa and the Philippines. For his special aerial recordings he had a custom-made transparent cone fitted into one of the airgunner's places and from there took some of the most dramatic aerial pictures of the war. He worked non-stop throughout the whole Pacific campaign, finishing with photographs of the ceremony of the Japanese surrender on the USS *Missouri* – the only American photographer present.

Though other photographers started earlier and shot more missions, W. Eugene Smith emerges from the Pacific wars as the most memorable and profound of all the war recorders. I have tried to summarize his philosophy of war photography in the introduction and there is little doubt that during the short time he filled this role – beginning with the Napang Harbour fighting in March 1944 – he created more moving and unforgettable images than anyone else. Later, in the Mariana Islands, he photographed from a foxhole, alongside the 2nd Marines, virtually in the front line, creating pictures of indelible immediacy and visual beauty. Although serious wounds prevented him from taking part in the last stages of the war, he nevertheless participated in thirteen landings.

Eugene Smith also photographed the capture of Iwo Jima, the scene of a curious incident concerning possibly the most famous and most frequently reproduced picture of the Second World War – 'The Raising of the Flag on Iwo Jima'. After some three months of bitter fighting, Iwo Jima was captured in March 1945. The picture of the raising of the Stars and Stripes on the top of Mount Suribachi was published throughout the world. It was taken by an Associated Press photographer, Joe Rosenthal. Later it was established that this was not a photograph of the original event. The first flag-raising was photographed by S/Sgt Louis R. Lowery, working for the Marines' magazine *Leatherneck*. While the ceremony was taking place, a hidden Japanese survivor threw two grenades at the group on the summit. The first grenade blew up the flag; the second fell at the feet of the photographer. Lowery dived down the steep side of the dormant volcano, rolling some 50 feet before he stopped, having dislocated his side and breaking his cameras. Later the same day a second raising of the flag was arranged, using a larger flag. This time a far more powerful and carefully worked-out picture was shot by Rosenthal.

opposite top: Wounded American, Okinawa, 1945, *W. Eugene Smith.*

opposite left: Japanese skull, Guadalcanal, 1942. *Ralph Morse.*

opposite right: Australian officer about to be beheaded, 1945. *Photographer unknown.*

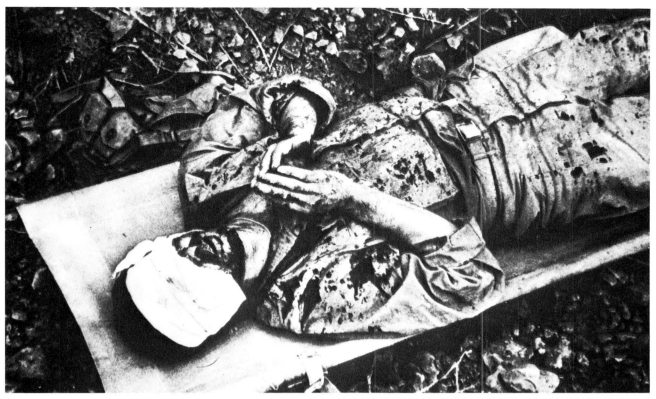

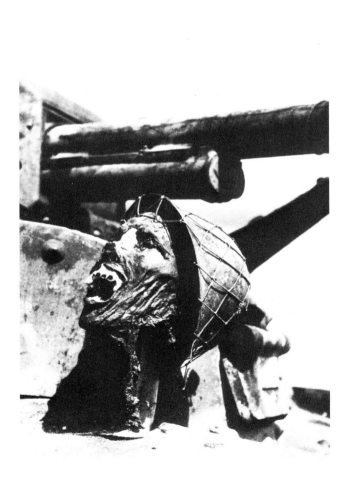

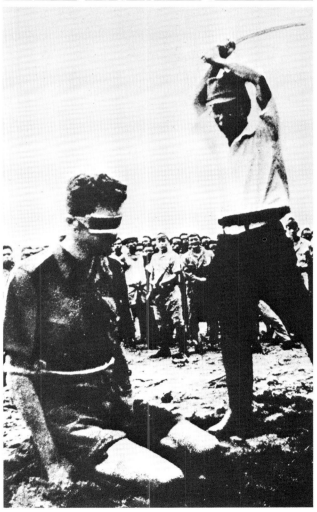

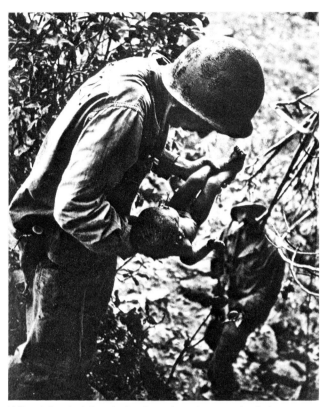

US soldier holding baby found under a rock, Saipan, 1944. *W. Eugene Smith.*

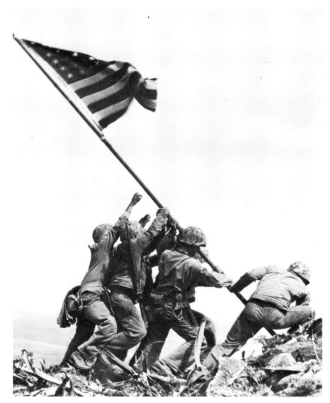

Raising of the flag on Iwo Jima, 1945. *Joe Rosenthal.*

It was this second picture, not the one taken by Lowery – which was also preserved – that gained the fame.

At first no one was aware of the subterfuge. The picture was taken at its face value – as a very good piece of photojournalism. However, when it was disclosed that it was not in fact the picture of the original flag-raising, an argument arose as to its authenticity. If it is considered to be a fake, undoubtedly we are emotionally liable to view the picture with less interest and enthusiasm. But it was not intended to mislead the public, nor, do I think, did the photographer himself perpetrate the myth of the picture in any way. It was a genuine reconstruction of a real event, mainly occasioned by the belief that the original picture had been lost.

Phase Six Normandy Beaches

When on 5 June 1944, W. E. Smith was shooting the invasion of the three islands in the Marianas – Guam, Tinian and Saipan – 130 000 American Marines had been disgorged by a mighty fleet of ships supported by twelve escort carriers, five battleships and eleven cruisers, the invasion of Europe was nine days old. On 6 June an even greater armada of ships started Operation Overlord. Over a thousand warships and as many as 4126 landing vessels, with 1000 other ships held in reserve for supply purposes, were delivering 175 000 men and 1500 tanks, 3000 guns and 5000 assorted trucks, jeeps, etc., to the beaches of Normandy. It is

said that the American contingent itself would have filled 200 large troop trains. Operation Overlord assumed such gigantic dimensions that it can only be absorbed with difficulty by our minds. The amount of organization and preparation required for such an operation must have been incredible – the instructions for various phases took up 700 pages of foolscap paper.

Preparation for coverage of the invasion by the media was equally thorough. Five hundred and fifty-eight correspondents, photographers and film-makers were assembled and, in line with other arrangements to throw German intelligence off the scent, were transported for one week to Scotland only a short while before D-Day. All media people were treated by the military authorities as another branch of the services and, by all accounts, the organization to facilitate the fast delivery of news was extremely impressive. For example, in order to comply with the needs of censorship and security, which were quite strict at all times, and yet at the same time to allow for a rapid flow of despatches, pictures, etc., censorship centres were established on the invasion beaches and even on the landing barges. Later in 1944, when Paris was taken, the army of war correspondents, photographers and

opposite top: First assault, Omaha beach, Normandy, 1944. *Robert Capa.*

opposite bottom: Juno beach, Normandy, 1944. *Sergeant Mapham.*

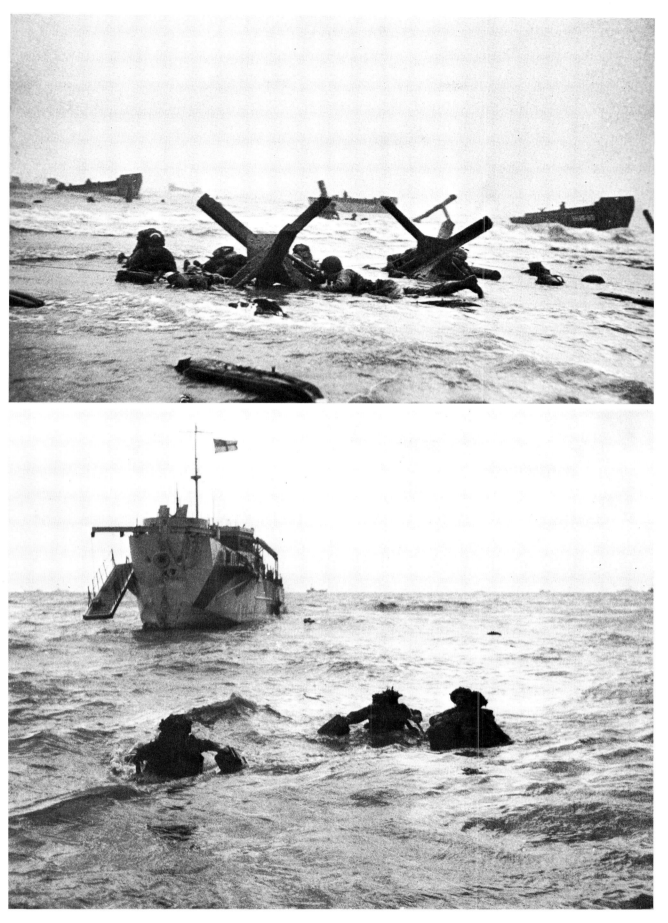

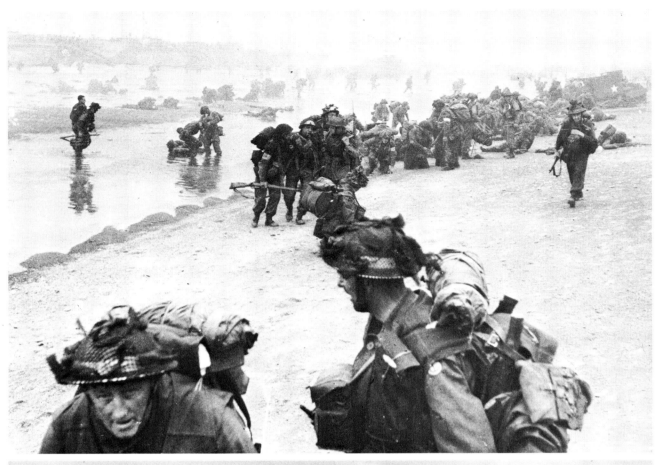

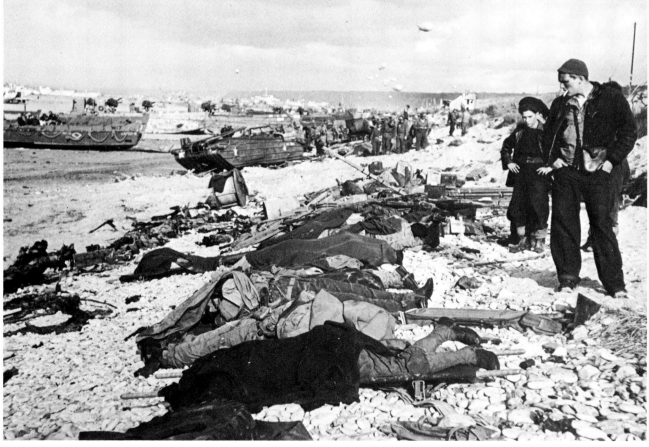

opposite top: Consolidating on Normandy beaches.
Sergeant Mapham.

opposite bottom: Allied dead on the Normandy beaches,
France, 1944. *Robert Capa.*

hangers-on grew to an enormous extent and Public
Relations headquarters in Paris was fully geared to
process, check and despatch up to three million words
and over 30 000 photographs filed by some 1000
individuals each week.

By the time of the invasion, the official photographic
cell of the British army had grown quite considerably.
At the start of the war there had been but one single
unit of twenty-seven men operating in Africa; by
now there were five full units, three of them engaged in
Normandy.

On the night of 6 June the invasion force was divided
into five parts each heading for a separate beachhead
code-named Utah and Omaha – for the Americans –
and Gold, Juno and Sword, where British and Canadian
troops disembarked. Accordingly, the correspondents
were also attached to different groups. It was on the
Omaha sector that the strongest opposition from the
crack German 352 Division was encountered and
where also the landing itself was not as smooth as else-

below: German sniper shooting on French crowd during
General de Gaulle's visit to Notre Dame, Paris, 1944.
Bert Hardy.

where. Many tanks were released too soon in deep
water and some sank with soldiers aboard.

It seems only natural that the most adventurous and
foolhardy of the photographers should find himself in
the middle of the most savage fighting. Capa, back from
Italy, accompanied the US 1st Infantry Division,
Company E, on USS *Chase* in the very first invasion
wave. He describes the occasion vividly in his book,
Slightly Out of Focus: 'After the pre-invasion breakfast
at 3 am with hot cakes, sausages, eggs and coffee,
served on the invasion ship by white-coated waiters,
at 4 am the invasion barges were lowered down into
the rough sea.' The beach was still miles away and
soon most of the soldiers were overcome with seasick-
ness. Half-way there, still far from the beach, they
began to hear sounds of the distant fighting. It slowly
started to get lighter and Capa took one of his Contax
cameras from its waterproof bag in order to take some
pictures. Some barges, having disgorged their cargo
of soldiers on the beach, were passing them on the way
back for the next consignment. Soon their barge hit the
shore with the German machine gun spraying the sea
around them and Capa found himself waist deep in
water. 'The water was cold and the beach still more
than a hundred yards away. The bullets tore holes in
the water around me and I made for the nearest steel
obstacle.' After sharing this cover for a while with a
soldier Capa moved to a half burned out amphibious
tank. With the tide coming in Capa managed to get out

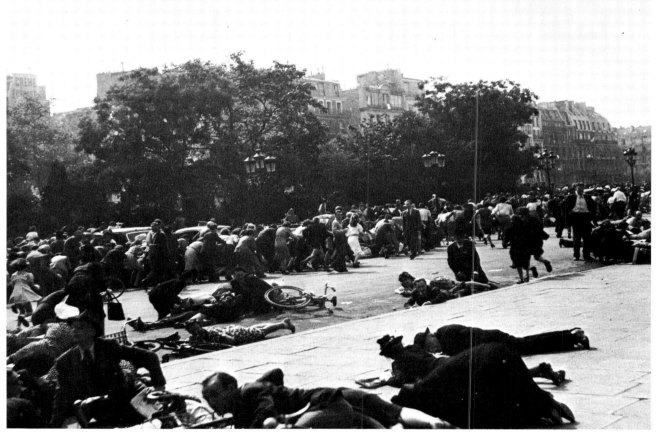

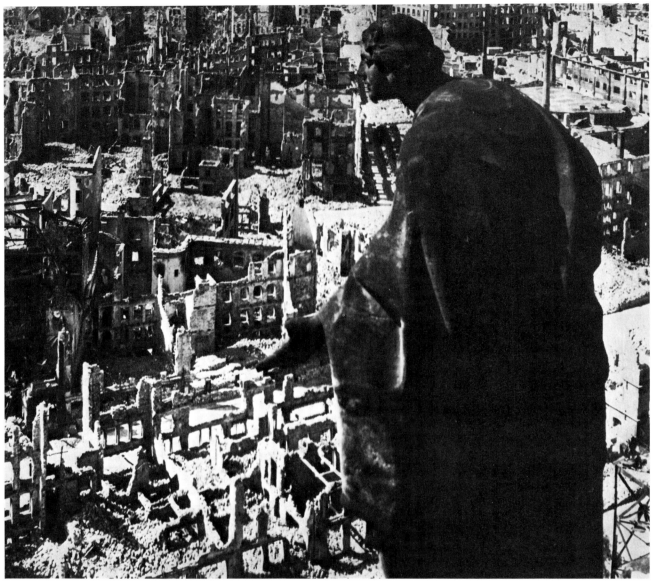

Dresden after the Allied raids, 1945. *Photographer unknown.*

of the water and make contact with French soil – the wet sand of the beach at St Laurent sur Mer.

'From the air "Easy Red" must have looked like an open tin of sardines. Shooting from the sardine's angle, the foreground of my pictures was filled with wet boots and green faces. Above the boots and faces, my picture frames were filled with shrapnel, smoke, burned tanks and sinking barges formed my background.' With mortar shells exploding all around and shaking from both cold and emotion, changing the roll of film in the camera was almost impossible and Capa kept ruining them before being able to insert one properly. With the excuse to himself that he must dry his hands, Capa waded back to the barge. It had been badly damaged, its bridge and most of the sailors blown up by a direct hit, but somehow they managed to get back to the mother ship.

Capa shot three films – 108 shots in all – and did not feel like going back again. A few days later he learned that his were the best pictures of the invasion. Alas, an excited darkroom operator while drying the precious films turned on too much heat. Most of the negatives melted away and only eight exposures were saved. It is surely one of those remarkable twists of fate that the luckless darkroom assistant later took Capa's place as the world's foremost war photographer – his name was Larry Burrows. Two or three of Capa's shots are now classics, having been reproduced many times all over the world.

Having survived the murderous beginning on Omaha beach, Capa followed the American troops right through the whole campaign – through St Lo in Brittany, where he met with his counterpart among war correspondents, Ernest Hemingway. From there on to Bastogne and eventually to the liberation of Paris. In Bastogne, shooting one of the tank battles, Capa prompted an admiring remark from the commanding

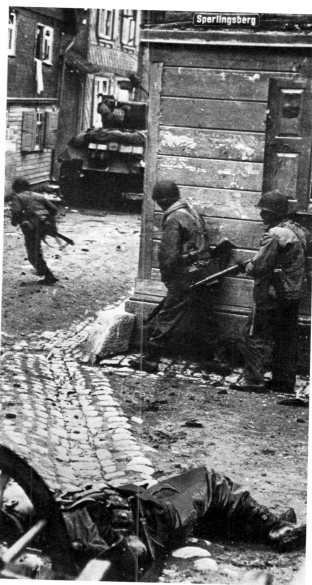

officer: 'He seemed to dart among the tanks like an incongruous, puny ringmaster in a herd of trumpeting and oblivious elephants.'

Other correspondents fared better if less spectacularly. Some followed in the second and third waves, while still others experienced a much easier landing on other beaches. Operation Overlord was photographed by more well-known photographers than any other event in history so we can only mention some of them. On the American team there was David F. Sherman, Bob Landry, Frank Scherschel, and Ralph Morse, with Johnny Florea and George Silk arriving later. Of the English freelances, George Rodger landed in the first wave on Gold sector and found the going fairly smooth. While the freelances were, in the main, able to select their place and time, army photographers had to follow orders. In spite of that some of them produced as fine a record as many of the professionals. Lieutenants Hanford, Flack and Evans led the photographic units and with them were shooting Sergeants Midgley, Wilkes, Johnson, Harrison, Morris and Laing. Sergeant Jimmy Mapham produced perhaps the most vivid pictures on the British sector.

Sergeant Bert Hardy, also a member of the photographic unit, was not in the first wave. In fact he landed in Normandy on D-Day + 6, when most of the action on the beaches was over. Nothing spectacular came his way until the Liberation of Paris on 25 August. This honour was reserved for the French troops of General Leclerc, followed by the Americans, with the British bringing up the rear. However, the French were a little behind and everyone waited for them to catch up. This

below: German prisoners taken by the Canadian troops, 1944. *Photographer unknown.*

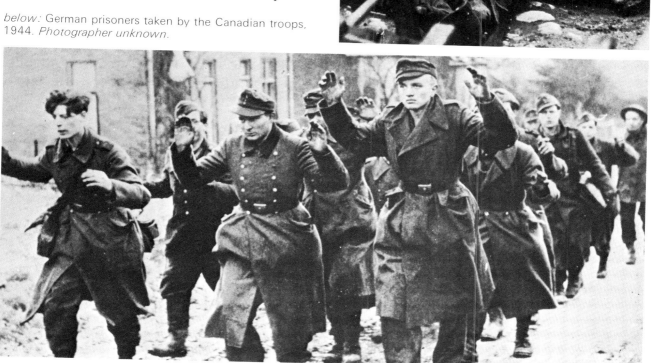

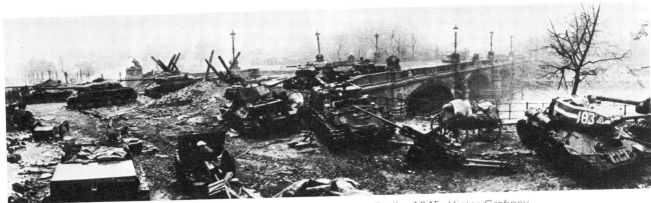

German tanks defeated by the Russians in the battle for Reichstag. Berlin, 1945. *Victor Grebnev.*

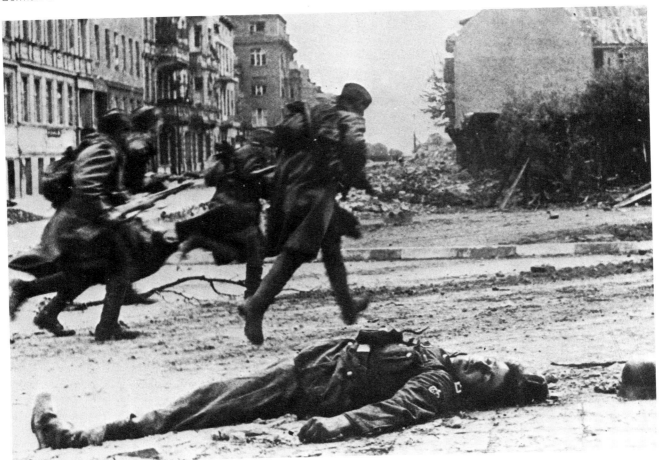

Battle on the streets of Berlin, 1945. *Ivan Sagin.*

was exploited by the British photographic unit who drove their jeep ahead with the Union Jack flying and photographed Paris being liberated by British troops. Hardy's pictures were duly splashed in the British papers and the French were not amused. In Paris too, Hardy's camera recorded a striking incident when the official service of thanksgiving held at Notre Dame was suddenly interrupted by the bullets of two German snipers hiding in the tower. The crowds ducked or fell to the ground and only General de Gaulle walked erect and unconcerned. Hardy's best pictures, however, were taken during the preparations for and the crossing of the Rhine. The biggest smoke screen ever raised, to hide construction and repairs of the bailey bridge from the German's planes, provided him with stunning pictorial subject matter. Later, General Dempsey posed for Hardy's camera, proudly crossing the Rhine at the head of the Allied troops. Altogether most of the leading Allied generals, Montgomery, Patton, Dempsey, delighted in being seen in the papers as often as possible, vying with one another to play the part of Liberator.

opposite: One of the last Allied soldiers to die, 1945. *Robert Capa.*

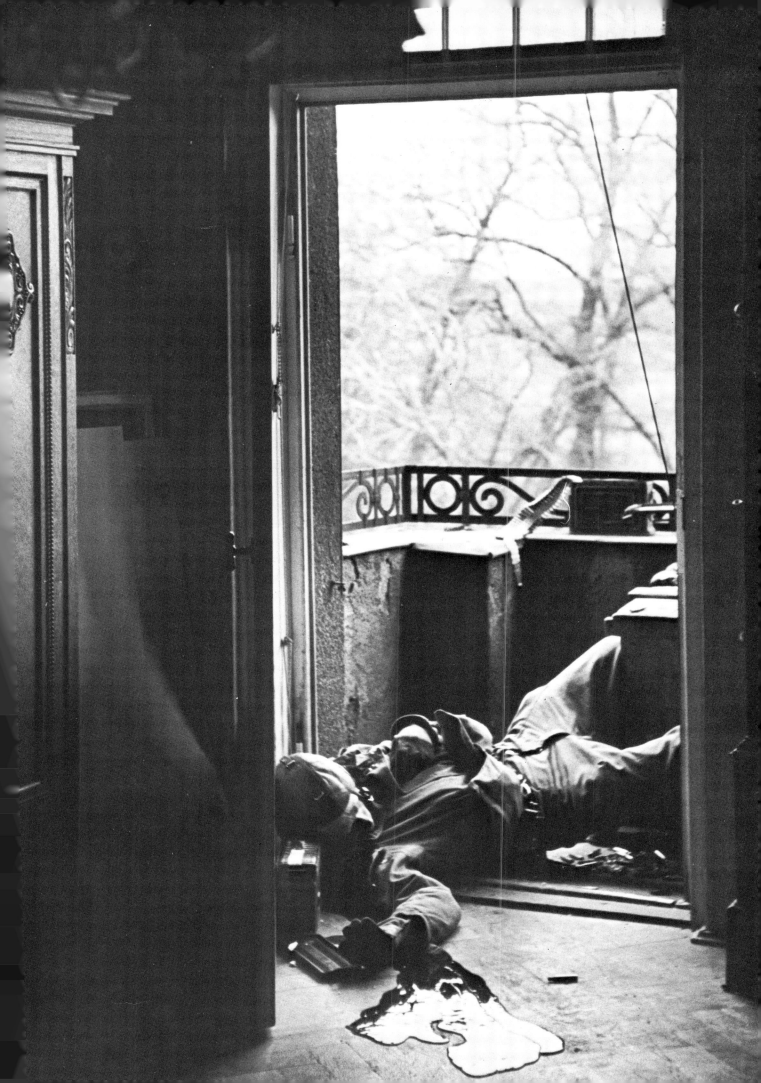

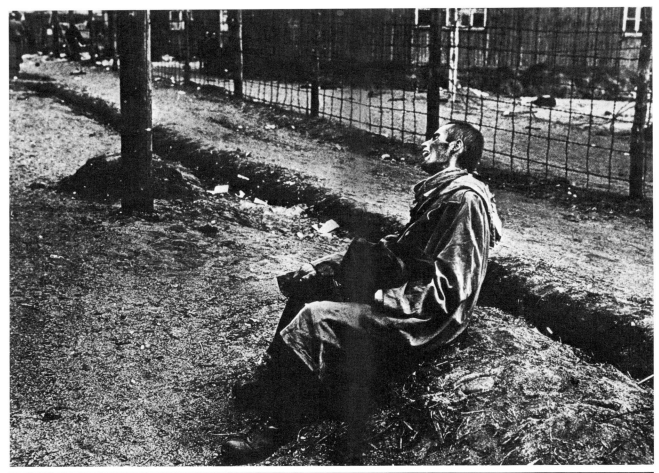

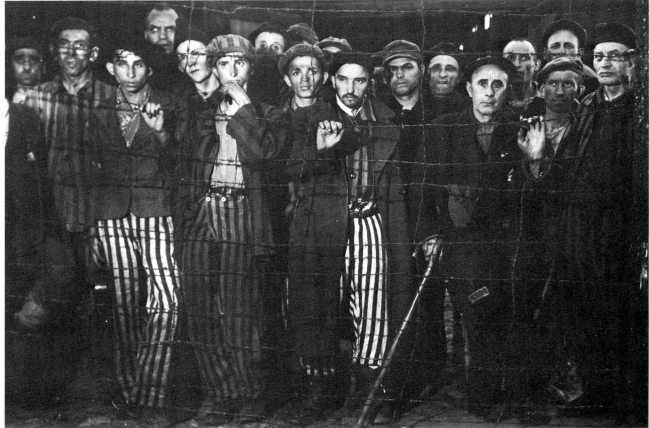

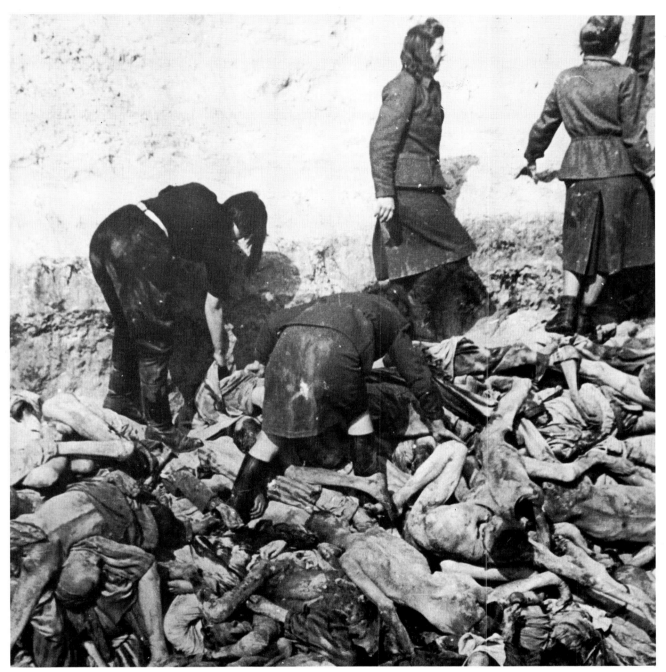

above: SS women guards arranging mass graves of victims, Belsen, 1945. *George Rodger.*

The most harrowing and dramatic coverage came from the liberation of the German concentration camps. Many photographers covered it – William Vandivert, Johnny Florea, Margaret Bourke-White and George Rodger whose experience was so vivid and distressing that he stopped photographing wars and human cruelty.

opposite top: One of the many starving and sick, Belsen concentration camp, 1945. *Photographer unknown.*

opposite bottom: Prisoners at Buchenwald, 1945. *Margaret Bourke-White.*

With the German surrender and Hitler's suicide, ravaged German countryside and the aftermath of the greatest war provided a powerful subject for the camera and many photographers remained in Germany for a considerable time after hostilities had ceased. Margaret Bourke-White's coverage of defeated Germany was subject matter for yet another of her books, *Dear Fatherland, Rest Quietly.*

But possibly the most memorable picture, and a final epitaph of these last days, was Capa's American machine gunner dead in the pool of blood in the window of a balcony, shot a few days before the Armistice.

From the patchy, uneven coverage in the first year of the Second World War, the photographic personnel,

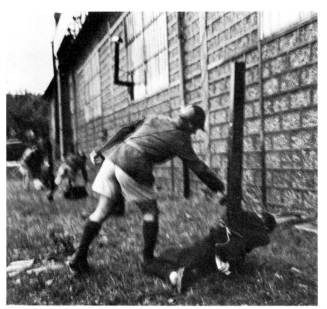

Execution of French collaborators, 1945. *Carl Mydans.*

both official and freelance, had developed into an experienced, highly organized body of recognized status. Although both the military authorities and the media at last realized the importance of making a photographic record of the fighting, and although, by the start of the desert war, official photographic units were actively engaged, the public did not see immediately a great deal of fresh material. On the contrary, only innocuous, fairly mundane pictures were generally released for publication while the war was in progress. Those that were published usually appeared well after they had been taken. At all times the military was in complete charge of what was photographed and what was subsequently used. Right to the end of the war the official military cameramen were shooting and recording far more than the civilian photographers. Up to the time of the Normandy invasion, photographs had to be passed through the long chain of official headquarters and various censors. In this respect, the American sector was always much better served. More freelance photographers were operating and the authorities were more co-operative. Even so, the photographs taken by W. E. Smith on Guam only appeared in *Life* some three or four months after the event. It was only with the invasion of Europe that pictures were processed on the spot and made immediately available to the press. By then, however, the Allies were winning.

However, soon after the war, a great number of photographs were made available for publication. The public at last were able to see reality of the war, the havoc it created. At the time television was in its infancy; it was through photographs that the impact of the war was brought home to the people. How deep an impact, or how lasting, we do not know – but so far another world war has been avoided.

So far as the photographers themselves were concerned, the Second World War produced a generation of war photographers who subsequently trained their lenses on smaller wars – people like Mydans, Duncan, Capa, Silk. And they in turn inspired a new generation – the war photographers par excellence of today.

Part Four

INTIMATE COMPANION

Korea –
Northern Ireland

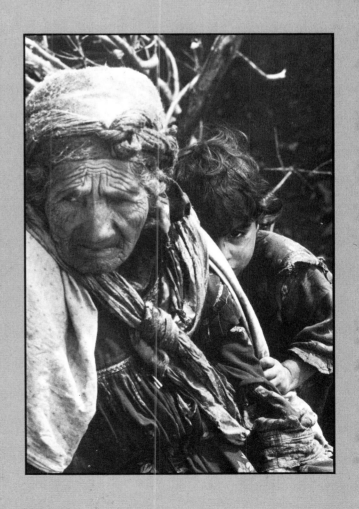

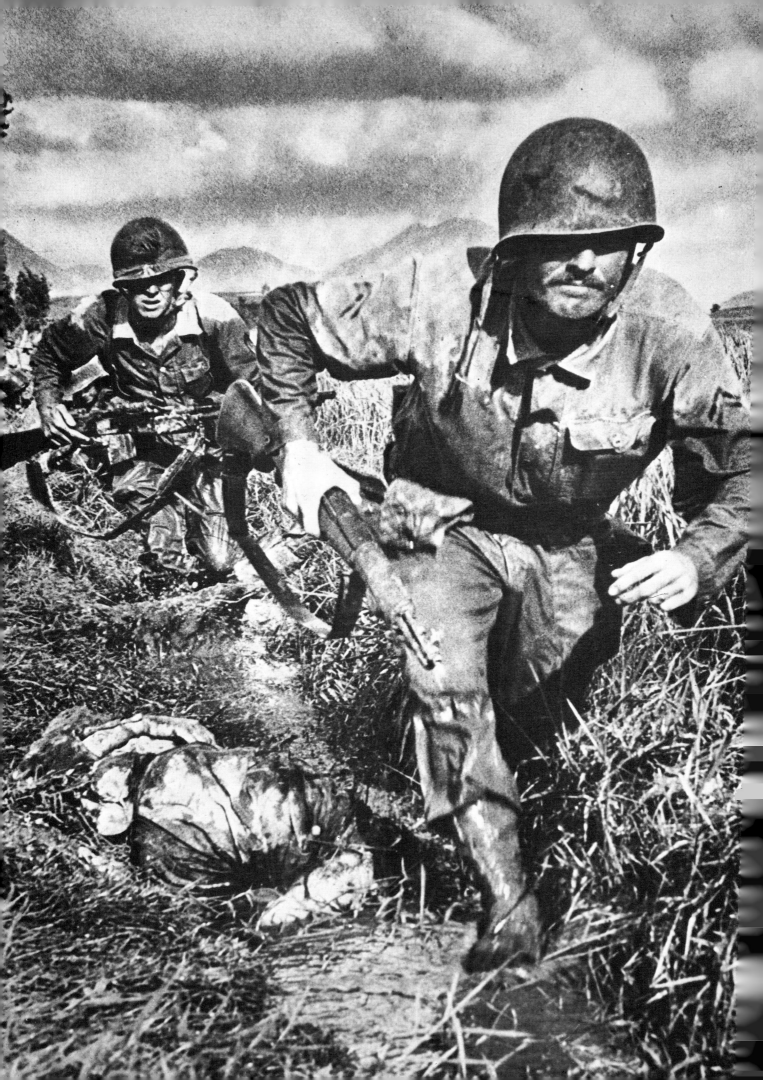

The stakes in the Second World War were high. A defeat for Germany and Japan meant a denial of ambitions, a halt to expansion, and reversion to second-class status; for the Allies, the possibility of total loss of freedom and democracy, a life in the bonds of totalitarian masters. With so much at stake, the authorities on both sides exercised tight control of the media, including photography. But once the war ended, there was a rush to relax all irksome restrictions, a rapid unwinding of military restraints. The call was for freedom of speech, thought and behaviour. In such a climate, the late forties and early fifties saw a great expansion in the media. Newspapers, magazines and periodicals prospered and photography entered a golden age which reached its zenith in the sixties.

The Second World War had provided an excellent training ground for photographers and also a spring-board for recognition. The last years of the war saw the growth in stature and experience of a number of free-lance photographers – Capa, Duncan, Rodger, Mydans, Silk – and even some who were buried in military units, such as Bert Hardy. Photographers began to count, their names to appear with their pictures, and editors began to hire and pay them well because of their proven ability and dependability. They were no longer anonymous button-pushers; they had come to be regarded as individual specialists.

Since 1945 the photography of war has acquired several new features. The number of photographers attached to the peacetime forces has decreased. After the Armistice, most were demobilized and the best joined the band of freelances working for the media. Those who remained in the services were no match for the professional photojournalist: thus the press has no longer to rely on pictures from official sources.

The means by which censorship is imposed has altered. Blanket censorship of the type exercised by the military in the Second World War no longer operates, for overt military censorship is mainly imposed by a country whose territorial integrity is being threatened, as for example in the case of Israel in the Yom Kippur War. Since 1945 no major Western power has had to fight on home ground. On the whole it is the press photographer from the West who goes as an independent observer to relatively small-scale (which is not the same as insignificant), remote conflicts, many of which take place in the Third World. Although attempts at censorship may be made by the authorities of the country in question, these can frequently be circumvented. In the case of a minority fighting against an oppressive régime, the photographer is often welcomed as bringing publicity to their cause. The military themselves have become acutely publicity conscious – an example is the US attitude in Vietnam. The

photographer is no longer regarded as a civilian intruder. Rather he is courted, and given freedom to record at close quarters.

Censorship has moved away from the obvious control by the military and instead is tacitly exerted either through the subjective selectivity of the photographer himself (as in the case of David Douglas Duncan's coverage in Korea) or through discreet manipulation of the press. An extreme example of the latter is the Korean War where a British newspaper suppressed material unfavourable to the Americans.

The very act of selecting which war is to be covered – and in the following account there are some noticeable omissions: the Sudan, Ethiopia, Angola, Aden, Malaya – is in itself a form of censorship. To a certain extent the media controls what is brought to our attention. A long-protracted localized struggle in a remote country can remain unnoticed until, with one atrocity caught as a memorable image of inhumanity, the world's attention is riveted. It would be comfortable to think that the press as a whole was aware of its responsibility to seek out aggression in any form, rather than those acts which are deemed newsworthy in that they involve a world power – such as America in Korea or Vietnam – or threaten world peace – the Middle East – or are distinguished in the scale of their savagery – Bangladesh and Lebanon. What we have here is a record of those conflicts which have hit the headlines. What we lack, there is no means of telling. The picture is not complete.

Not the totality of wars, then, but the totality of war expressed through a series of images by individual photographers. It is here that the role of the photographer is most important: the actuality of a single picture has the power to irrupt upon the public's awareness and remain in the memory as a symbol of a particular war or of a particular kind of violence.

In this respect, the position of the photographer is ambivalent. He is free to choose what he records. His choice may be governed by a variety of attitudes: he may be a detached professional working on yet one more job; he may be motivated by his humanitarian sympathy, identifying with one of two opposing factions in a civil war; he may be ideologically committed to left or right, as happened in the Korean War. But implicit or explicit, whether avowedly political or professedly impartial, his intentions are in one sense irrelevant, for it is by his actions that he brings to the attention of one sector of humanity the plight of another sector in extremis, and in so doing his actions are in the widest sense political. We need seek no further his ultimate justification.

So let us focus on the new style of photography that has evolved from the Korean War onwards: the personal close-up of war; the photographer as intimate companion, not only close to the fighting, but participating in it. He shares the soldiers' fears, desires and sufferings. And through his images we share them too.

Advancing Marines, Korea, 1950. *David Douglas Duncan.*

139

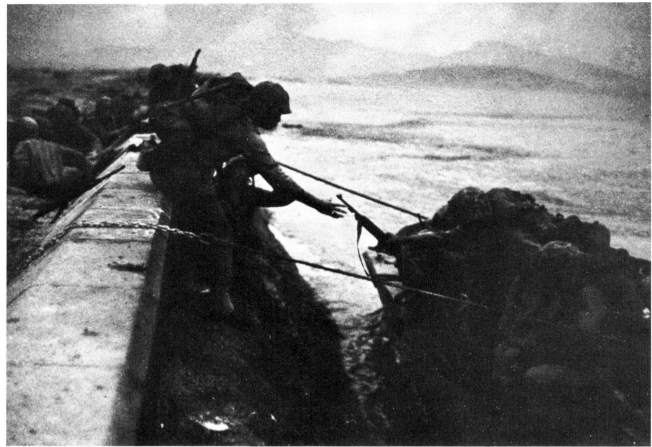

above: Landing in Inchon, Korea, 1950. *Bert Hardy.*

The Korean War

The first of the major post-war conflicts, Korea set the standard for the new-found freedom of war photographers – at least for a time. A war of the United Nations, it was at the outset unencumbered by censorship or restrictions, an open arena for correspondents and photojournalists. The frailty of this freedom was soon to be exposed.

When on 25 June 1950, North Korean troops crossed the 38th Parallel – the frontier between the communist-dominated North and the South supported by the Americans – the first of a number of East–West confrontations began. Korea became what President Truman called 'a testing ground of the ideological conflict between communism and democracy'.

The first few days of the war were reminiscent of the German blitz in the West, when the speed of the advance was so great that there was precious little time to gather thought, let alone analyse or record events. Seoul, the capital of the South, fell in three days, and within a week all that remained of the Republic of South Korea was a small bridgehead in the south-

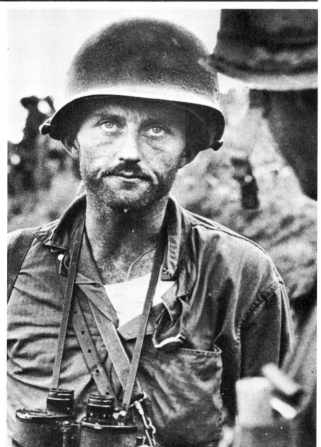

right: Shell-shocked American Marine, Korea, 1950. *David Douglas Duncan.*

140

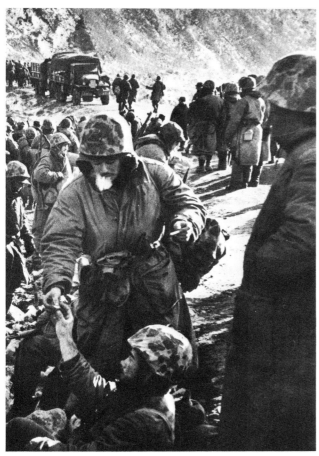

east corner, the Pusan perimeter. But by the second day of the war, the United Nations Assembly had defined the North Korean attack as a 'breach of peace and an action of aggression'. The Korean War had become the United Nations' war and on 4 July the first American contingent arrived from Japan and the advance of the communists was stemmed.

Two of the top Second World War photographers were close at hand. David Douglas Duncan, the 'Lensman of the Marines', had just finished a large photographic assignment for *Life* on the arts of Japan and was relaxing on the beach. He was knocking on the door of General MacArthur's headquarters in Japan within two hours of hearing the news on the radio. It still took him until Tuesday, 27 July, to start for Korea. The first two planes for correspondents had been cancelled; instead, he flew on a special plane to the American base in Korea from which air strikes against the invaders were soon to start.

Carl Mydans had settled in Japan with his wife and children as chief of the Time/Life Bureau in Tokyo. The news of the war caught him in New York, but he was in Korea within a few days and *Life* was soon able to announce that 'Mydans goes back to the fighting'.

below: North Korean prisoners, Korea, 1950. *Bert Hardy.*

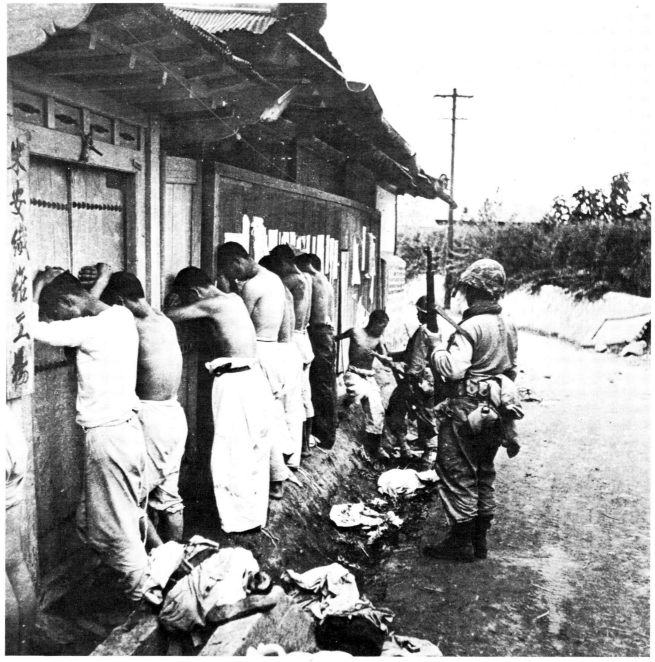

A line-up of suspects, Korea, 1950. This photograph was not accepted for publication by *Picture Post. Bert Hardy.*

By early August, 270 correspondents from nineteen countries were vying with one another for likely scoops. Tom Hopkinson, editor of *Picture Post*, sent the best British team – Bert Hardy, the photographer, and James Cameron, the writer.

In contrast to the strict censorship which many had experienced and suffered in the Second World War, reporting was not at first restricted. But this freedom was soon to prove embarrassing. The first week or two of fighting clearly demonstrated some serious inadequacies in the democratic forces: the newly arrived American soldiers were seen to be raw and unreliable.

Apart from some officers and NCOs who were veterans of the Second World War, most of the disembarking soldiers were young, undertrained and badly disciplined, breaking down all too quickly under pressure. The South Korean troops were simply overwhelmed by the invaders; in addition to their visible lack of fighting spirit, they were also liable to show shocking excesses of savagery and cruelty. Certainly not the kind of standard expected of a United Nations sponsored force. This was seized on by the press and a number of discomfiting stories began to appear in international papers.

One of the most powerful was provided by Hardy and Cameron. It reported the mistreatment of North Korean prisoners at the hands of South Korean troops.

Hopkinson checked the facts painstakingly, and the story was ready for publication in *Picture Post*. At the last minute, Sir Edward Hulton, the owner of the magazine, intervened and suppressed it on the pretext that it would help the enemy. Hopkinson resigned, and the story did not see the light of day until it was shown only recently in a television programme.

The great issue was whether the facts, however painful, should be told or hidden; whether all the pictures should be published or some suppressed. The issue was between truth and convenience. Some correspondents were accused of being traitors to the cause, and strong appeals were made to their patriotism and solidarity in the face of a common enemy. Indeed, certain newspapers and magazines with leftist sympathies did publish a number of very damaging pictures and stories. Execution Hill in Seoul where prisoners were summarily executed was fairly widely written about, and London's *Daily Worker* published a page of photos by I. R. Lorwin of Pix Incorporated of New York (distributed in England by Associated Press) showing a mass execution of North Korean prisoners a few miles from Seoul. Some women were among the prisoners, who, after being shot by the squad, were finished off by an officer with a pistol. Admittedly this airing of wrongs did bring a halt to the worst excesses, but finally convenience won – at the end of December 1950 censorship was imposed.

By then the war had undergone several wide swings. The early North Korean successes led to General MacArthur's brilliant counter-stroke – an amphibious landing behind North Korean lines at Inchon on 15 September, which trapped and pushed back the invaders. Soon they were driven behind the 38th Parallel. By 26 October, helped by additional landings at Wonson and Hungnam on the other side of the peninsula, the United Nations' forces reached the Manchurian border. In November, the Chinese intervened and, outnumbered by five to one, the UN forces were forced to retreat and Seoul was evacuated for a second time by 4 January 1951. By the end of January the UN troops staged yet another counter-offensive and were back at the 38th Parallel or its whereabouts by the end of March. From then on both sides were only able to fight holding actions up to the cease-fire which was agreed on 23 June 1951. The final armistice was signed, after protracted negotiations, more than two years later, on 27 July 1953. Thus for the last two years of the war there was little fighting and most of the media lost interest altogether. The most intense, active period of the war was packed into just one year.

In this short space of time many people came to photograph it. For the American magazines and agencies, Hank Walker, John Dominis, and Joe Scherschel all did a considerable amount of work in Korea. Howard Sochurek covered American parachute drops and Michael Rougier remained there until the end, the last man on the spot. Carl Mydans spent

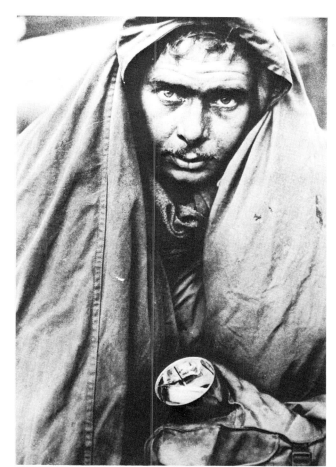

Christmas in Korea for an exhausted Marine. *David Douglas Duncan.*

several intensive periods in the country, covering the landings of the 1st Cavalry at P'chang-dong, the release of the 24th Division at Yondong, and the first re-taking of Seoul. His portfolio of Korean pictures won him first prize in *US Camera*. His photographs, in spite of their inherently gruesome subject matter, possess a special quality of warmth and humanity which is quite rare among war photographers.

Mydans also covered the landing at Inchon, but I do not think that anyone photographed in more vividly and dramatically than Bert Hardy. The landing itself was impeccably planned, but the preparations for the press coverage were much less organized. Most of the correspondents from the daily papers were left behind, some not arriving near the beach until two days later; the magazine correspondents, with far less urgent deadlines, were given a barge in the first wave. Hardy and Cameron were on it. Their landing craft was directed towards a part of the beach bounded by a sea wall.

'When we got to this wall,' Hardy recollects, 'you get no idea what the wall was really like and everything was blowing up, nobody would get over the top because we had no idea what the hell was going on – guns firing, shells falling, rockets landing – and I thought, my god, it's getting dark and I've only got another ten minutes.

143

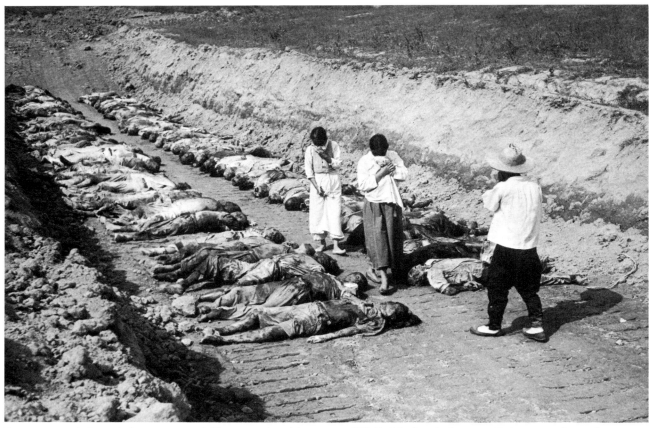

Koreans search for relatives among civilians murdered by North Koreans, 1950. *Carl Mydans.*

You see, these pictures were taken at 1/25th of a second at f1·4 which was nearly at the limit, so I thought, well, we are here and I'd better go ashore. I climbed over this wall – 'cause I realized that the light was going – and then these chaps saw that I didn't get shot so they started to clamber ashore, you see. So I got these pictures and then it got dark. By the way, none of the other photographers got any pictures because they all had 5 × 4 cameras and I was the only one with a thirty-fiver.'

It was only later that they found out that they were put ashore on the wrong beach and that all the visual effects of guns and rockets which fortunately did not hit anybody were provided by courtesy of the American artillery. Wrong beach or not, Hardy's spectacular pictures convey a remarkable impression of an amphibious landing and of impending danger.

Hardy only stayed in Korea for about six or seven weeks but in this time he managed to shoot several features for *Picture Post*. They are all praiseworthy for their individuality, thoroughness and authenticity, as well as being visually beautiful. Hardy and Cameron's first story, 'We follow the road to hell', about general conditions and the appearance of the country and its people in wartime, is a fine example of their skill and courage. Hardy's last story on the Inchon landing won the *Encyclopaedia Britannica* awarded both in Britain and America.

While Mydans' pictures elicit sympathy and compassion and Hardy's bring forth vividly the feel and almost the smell of the place and of the war, those of David Douglas Duncan strike an entirely different note. Undoubtedly he is a conscious artist of war photography – it is not only a record of a specific kind that he is after, but an expressive aesthetic image. But he is also a marine, part of the military unit he photographs, very much on the side of those with whom he fights. Paradoxically, his pictures, when set against the whole canvas of the conflict, appear less authentic and truthful. Of all the photographers in Korea, no one was nearer to nor lived in greater intimacy with fighting men than Duncan. Yet despite this, or perhaps as a direct result of his personal identification with the soldiers and his pride in their courage, he was no longer capable of detachment. He had to slant his images at times to bring them closer to the images he saw in his heart. There was, of course, no question of deception – all his photographs are immediate, instinctive and totally authentic in themselves. But while shooting real people and real happenings, his camera became selective and, partly directed by his feelings, he turned a blind eye to some things of which his soul could not have approved.

Duncan covered the first two weeks of the war, welcoming General MacArthur to Korea and following

opposite: Bewildered civilians fleeing, Korea, 1950. *Bert Hardy.*

144

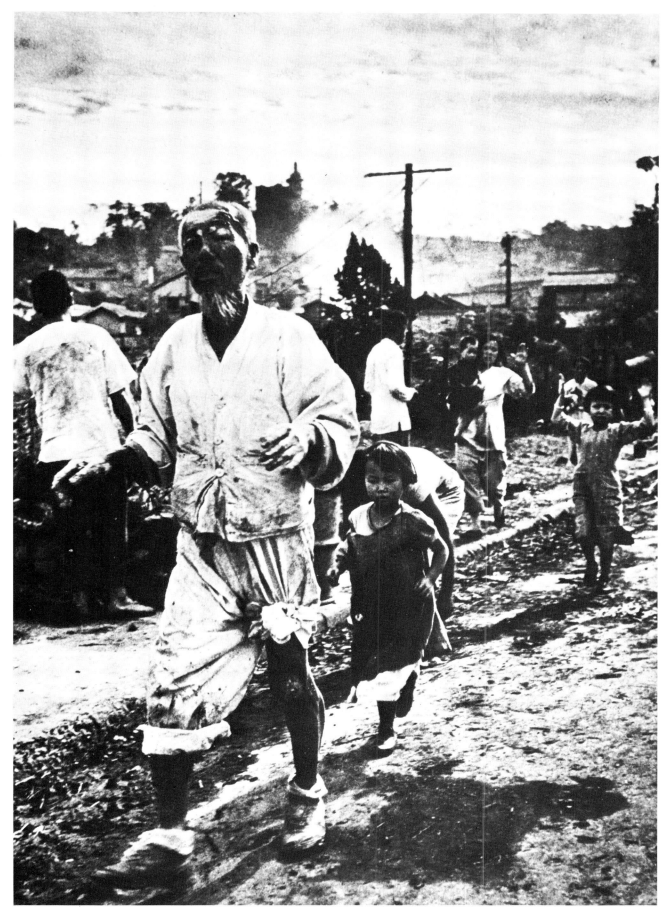

him on his first tour. Then he photographed the out-numbered 24th Division, sent hastily from Japan, holding a delaying action against the enemy advance. During this time also he became the first war photographer to fly in a jet on a strafing and rocket combat flight. He returned later in July to photograph South Korean troops on the slopes of the strategically important Hill 626 and, in August, the largely un-productive attack of the American Infantry. It is in this period that many correspondents reported the atrocious morale and unpreparedness of the young American troops, yet none of this shows even remotely in Duncan's pictures.

It was about this time that Duncan conceived the idea for a book to show 'what war did to a man'. He wrote to *Life* requesting permission to spend an indefinite period in Korea to shoot *This Is War*. The result was a war opera in three acts. In the first, his marines fight a heroic battle for 'The Hill' which came down in history as the battle of 'No Name Ridge'. This was situated in the northern part of the Pusan perimeter near the Nankong River. The second act omits the Inchon landing, which possibly he did not cover, and shows the 1st Marine Division recapturing 'The City' – Seoul.

Duncan's third act covers the fatal retreat of the 8th Army and the 10th Corps, including Duncan's division, with the marines being driven back towards the sea by the Chinese in sub-zero temperatures, eating frozen beans, bent against driving snow, and sharing with the photographer 'the last puff of perhaps the last cigarette'.

This Is War is a great book. It shows the heroic side of war. It depicts how a man is toughened, hardened and in a way bettered by the conditions that war creates. When Duncan asked a marine, during the hardest part of their retreat, what he wanted for the approaching Christmas, the young soldier replied 'Gimme tomorrow'. Duncan's images confirm this kind of truth.

If one is not careful, one can fall under the book's spell and believe it without reservations. And in this lies Duncan's failure – the book does not tell the whole truth but only a small part of it. It shows what war does to a man, but only in the positive sense. It does not also show that the same war corrupts and destroys. The stories about the Korean War and the investigations conducted after the armistice revealed all too clearly the deficiencies of the American war machine. The recording eye of David Douglas Duncan chose not to see these. But that does not alter the knowledge that *This Is War* is a wonderful counterpart to Griffiths's *Vietnam Inc.*, an idealized fable about the greatness of man in war. Both books must be considered master-pieces.

In the history of war photography, the Korean War forms an important chapter. It brought to public notice three important war photographers – Duncan, Hardy, Mydans; Duncan's book emerged as an artist's vision

of a war, a new genre in photography; a new style of war photography begins – intimate images of man's greatest adventure; it ushered in a new breed of photographer – the war photographer par excellence. And what may be even more significant, it laid the corner-stone for McCullin and Griffiths.

Don McCullin's first war picture essay can be seen as a direct descendant of Duncan's *This Is War*. But as thirteen years lie between the two, they are different in mood; McCullin's is less romantic and at the same time more realistic. But both photographers bring a similar balletic quality to their treatment of the human figure in motion, and both are totally intimate in their re-lationship with their subject matter – fighting and suffering people.

Cyprus

When Don McCullin was doing his National Service with the RAF in Limassol, Cyprus, in 1955, he wit-nessed the struggle of General Grivas and EOKA against the British. Nine years later, when he returned to Cyprus as a photographer working for the *Observer*,

Death in a Turkish home, Cyprus, 1963. *Don McCullin.*

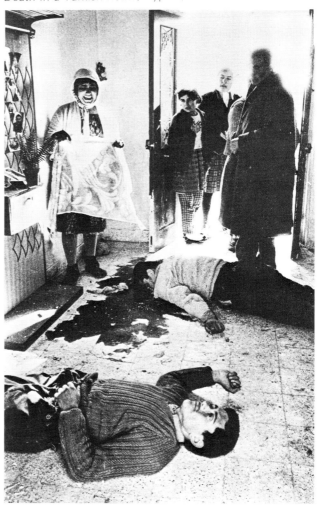

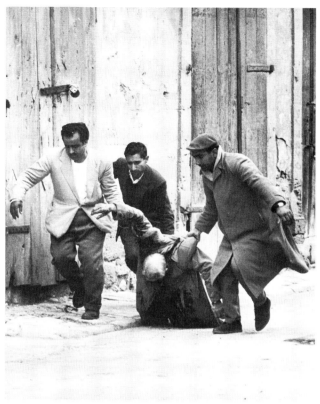

left: Wounded man carried to safety, Cyprus, 1963. *Don McCullin.*

the Greek and Turkish communities were on the verge of hostilities.

The best war photographers are often the lucky ones and McCullin is both: 'It so happens that because I wanted to visit my old RAF camp in Limassol, I was able to be on the spot when the first real battle started. On 11 February the RAF laid on a trip for all the visiting newspaper men to fly over the island, but I didn't want to go and mentioned to my companion, an *Observer* journalist, that I should like to go and see my old camp. Anyway, there was a bit of tension in that part of the island. We were actually driving through Limassol when the battle started. So there I was, on my own (the *Observer* journalist did not stay when he saw the real trouble brewing) in the first battle of my life.'

In this way a distinguished career covering the world's wars began. McCullin shot the finest set of pictures to come out of Cyprus – a spread of ten pages in *Paris Match* – and a top award followed.

below: Two Turkish civilian fighters in Limassol, Cyprus, 1963. *Don McCullin.*

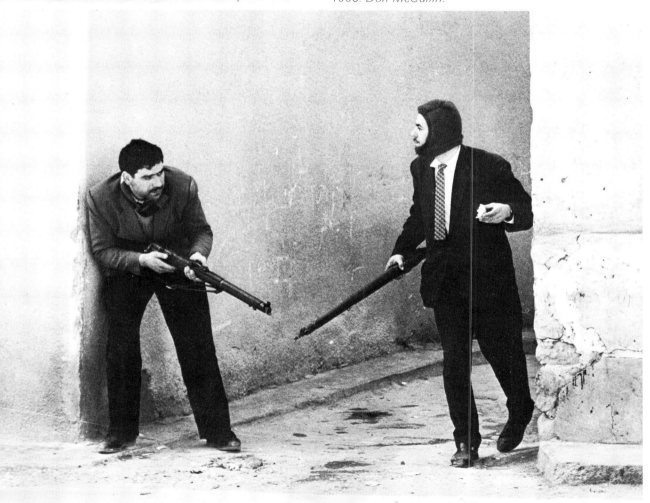

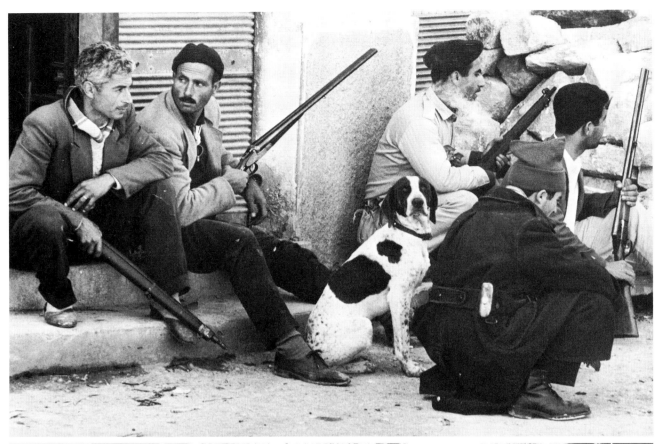

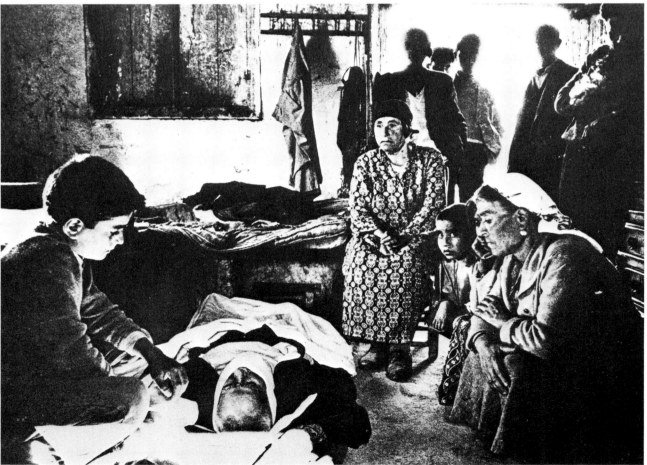

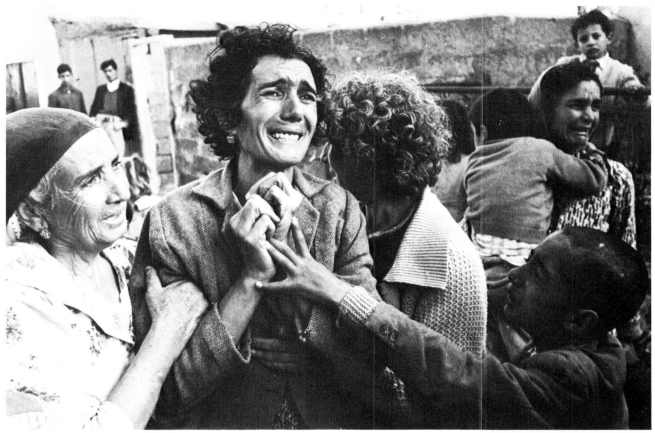

above: Anguish of a Cypriot mother and son for murdered husband and father, Cyprus, 1963. *Don McCullin.*

McCullin's first war involved not soldiers but civilians who took up arms – neighbour fighting neighbour with violence gathering like the downhill momentum of a rock slide. McCullin stayed amid the fighting for several days, sleeping either on the floor in the local hospital or in Turkish houses. He was thus able to take his brilliant, dramatic and intimate pictures of grief and private tragedy inside the home.

Algeria

The war in Algeria spanned a period of nearly eight years, from 1954 to 1962. The French had just been decisively defeated in Indochina at the battle of Dien Bien Phu when, with the start of the revolt in Algeria on 1 November, they were faced yet again with a colonial war.

The Indochinese war provided a model for both sides in Algeria. The Algerians themselves tried to build from small, independent groups of soldiers, operating as guerilla units, to larger formations capable of engaging the French patrols in more open warfare.

opposite top: Street scene in Limassol, Cyprus, 1963. *Don McCullin.*

opposite bottom: Prayers for the dead father, Cyprus, 1963. *Don McCullin.*

They hoped to culminate their efforts in a large-scale battle on the lines of Dien Bien Phu. This proved impossible, however, and by 1957 they reverted to small-scale guerilla encounters. The French for their part were able to exploit much more effectively the lessons they had learned in Indochina. They too used guerilla tactics, but from 1956 they adopted the so-called quadrillage system which consisted of covering inhabited areas – towns and villages – with garrisons of troops. This system tied up a vast number of troops, leaving very few for mobile punitive columns.

The French army retained the initiative throughout, consistently out-manoeuvring and beating the army of the Algerian National Liberation Front (the FLN). The loss of Algeria can be ascribed to the political vacillations of a succession of French governments rather than to Algerian military superiority. When de Gaulle came to power in 1960, he seems to have decided that it would be undesirable and impracticable to keep Algeria French. At the time of the cease-fire in 1962, the French army was in a stronger position than at any other time during the war.

The revolt itself started with a number of isolated terrorist attacks by small groups of insurgents on French military patrols and towns. The French authorities were under the impression that these early raids were unconnected incidents rather than the start of a large-scale insurrection. The press too failed to realize their significance. Only a few photographers were on hand to cover the outbreak of the uprising.

149

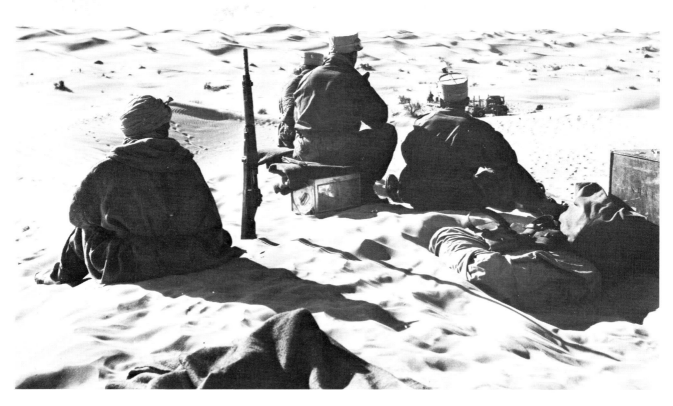

French Foreign Legion outpost in the desert, Algeria,
1957. *Daniel Camus*.

Réné Vital and Gabriel Conessa had lived in Algeria for
several years, and Francois Pages was at the time
resident photographer for *Paris Match* which maintained a regular staff there. Once the French authorities
realized that the Muslim attacks were part of a planned
revolt, they undertook a series of punitive pacification
raids against suspected rebel sympathizers. Pages
covered a number of these, including a large operation
code-named 'Esperance'. In 1956 Pages was recalled
to France, possibly because his contacts with the
military authorities left a lot to be desired. He was
replaced by Jean-Pierre Biot, a former parachutist, who
stayed until the end of the uprising.

As the war progressed, *Paris Match* and other
periodicals built up their contingent of photographers,
including Daniel Camus, who had served as a
photographer with a parchute unit at Dien Bien Phu,
and Charles Courrière, who was perhaps the best
known internationally. By 1961 there were nearly fifty
photographers working for the French magazines,
among them Patrice Habans, Jean Claude Sauer,
Georges Melet, Georges Menager, Claude Azoulay,
André Lefebre and Philip Telier. Most of them had had
some previous connection or contact with the army.

Many had already served in the forces. The nature of
the fighting during the uprising was such that the
photographers had to rely to a great extent on the good
offices of the French army, either to be able to
accompany detachments of troops on raids, or to hear
about encounters on the borders where rebel insurgents were endeavouring to enter Algeria from Morocco
or Tunisia. Consequently most of the photographic
coverage came from the French side and relates to the
activities of the army on retaliatory raids or to coverage
of sites after terrorist attacks. Foreign photographers
experienced considerable difficulties; only a very few
stayed in Algeria for any length of time. Eddie Van Der
Veen and D. Berretty-Ralpho, both working mainly
for *Life*, were almost the only foreign photographers
who took an important number of photographs in
Algeria. Throughout the duration of the conflict, the
Vietnam War was in progress, and many of the top-
line international photographers were fully occupied
there.

By and large, the photographic coverage of the war in
Algeria is rather disappointing. Very few great pictures
can be found among the mass of fairly routine and un-
interesting material. This must in part be due to the
close links between the French photographers and the
army, and the sporadic and unpredictable nature of the
fighting. However, there are certain features of the war

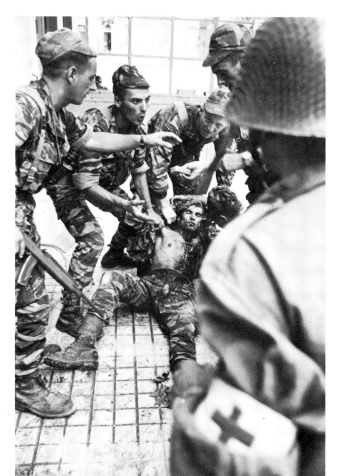

itself which might have a bearing on various aspects of the photographic coverage, and account for some of its omissions.

In the first place, there is little evidence in the extensive archives of *Paris Match* in Paris – the magazine which covered the war most thoroughly – of the numerous atrocities committed during the course of the war. In Algeria itself the hard core of Muslim insurgents – perhaps numbering no more than 400 at the outbreak of the revolt – had to resort to drastic methods of intimidation, including torture, to force their own people, who were unwilling to fight, to give them support. The French paras also, after the disappointment of Dien Bien Phu and the later abortive Suez landing, adopted torture as an almost standard military procedure. The retaliatory measures by the FLN were no less cruel. Although many of these excesses were quoted in various periodicals, not much reliable photographic evidence exists. Perhaps it is not surprising that there are no photographs of French brutality, but the fact that there are few pictures of FLN atrocities suggests that the authorities were anxious to play down the extremism which might have inflamed the opposition in France to the eventual

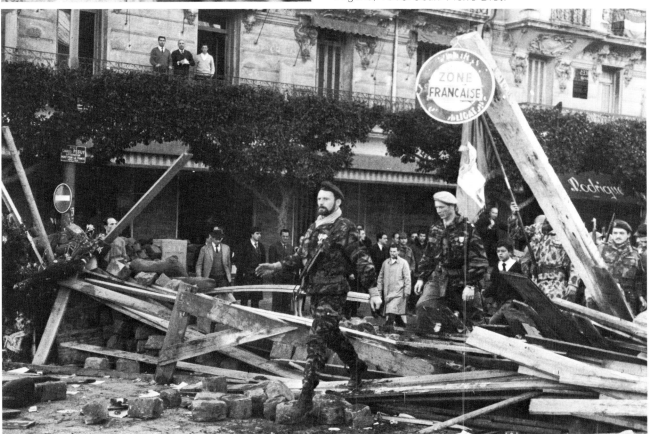

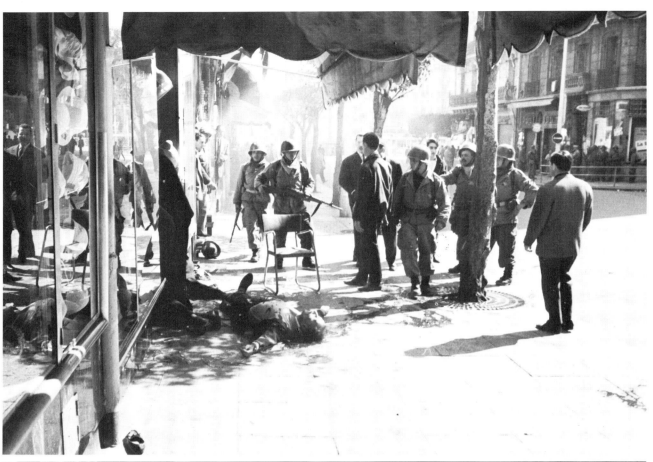

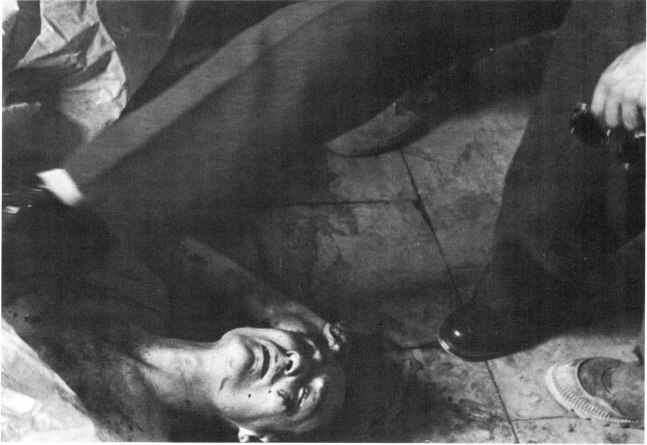

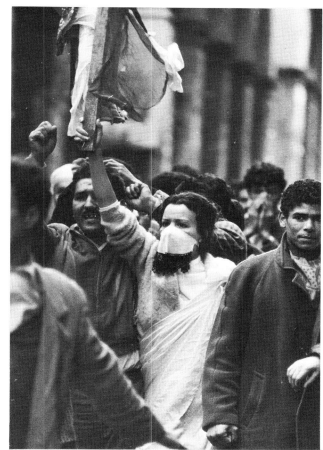

independence of Algeria. In the last two years of the war, de Gaulle set about skilfully manipulating public opinion so that the fate of Algeria became a less emotionally charged issue.

The second important feature of the war was the role played by the resident French population in Algeria. The *Colons* or *Pieds Noirs* were those who clung most tenaciously to the *status quo*, opposing the slightest overtures on the part of the French government to enter into negotiations with the rebels. They had built Algeria from a poor underdeveloped country into a thriving economic colony, which had the additional prospect of rich oil deposits. Thus they fought to keep *Algerie Francaise* by all possible means. The intransigent stand of the French Algerians led to three instances of revolt against the ruling government in Paris. The first revolt occurred on 13 May 1958, when the *Colons* were given assistance by part of the armed forces under

right and below: Muslim women demonstrating against the French, Algeria, 1960. *Patrice Habans.*

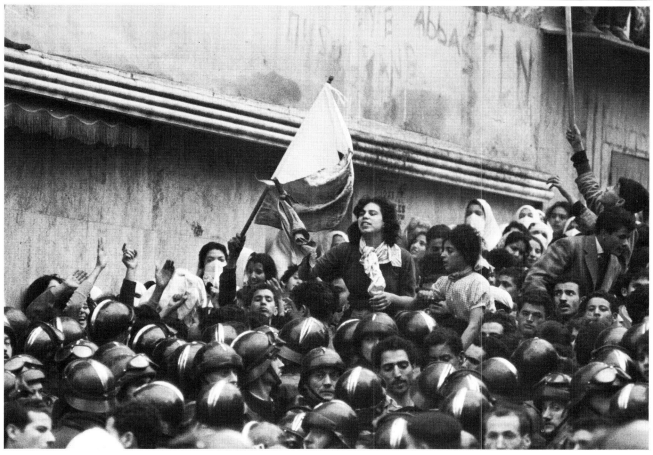

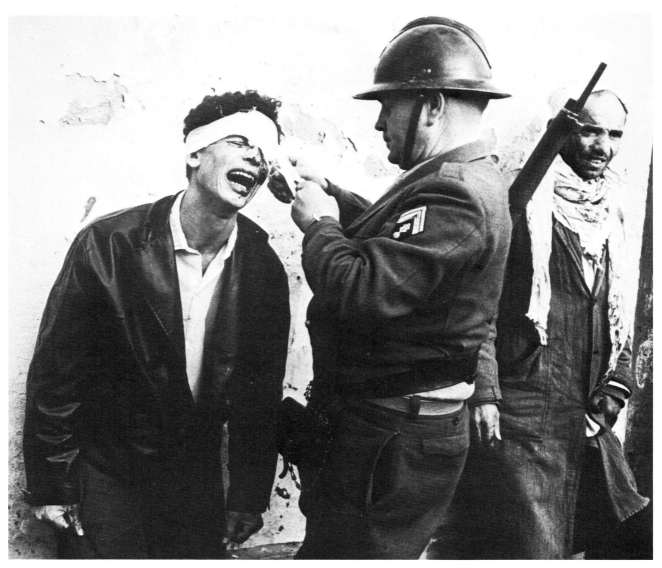

above: Street troubles in Oran, Algeria, 1960. *Jean-Pierre Biot.*

Generals Massu and Salan. In January 1960 they rose again and during the famous 'Barricades Week' were again helped by paras to occupy the headquarters of the Governor-General. The last uprising was in April 1961, the 'generals' putsch', led by Generals Salan, Jouhaud, Gardy and others. This final gesture, abandoned after two days because of scant support, led to the prolonged clandestine terrorist activities of the OAS (the Secret Army Organization) formed by many *Colons* and officers of the paras and the Foreign Legion. All three risings were fully covered by many of the photographers, but none was extensive or dramatic enough to provide outstanding pictures. The attention of the media was thus diverted from the war itself to the OAS activities and the struggle of the French Algerians.

The photographic coverage of the Algerian war cannot be compared, either in the quality of the images or

right: Conclusion of Operation Espérance, Algeria, 1956. *François Pages.*

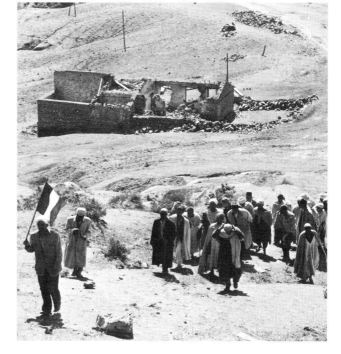

154

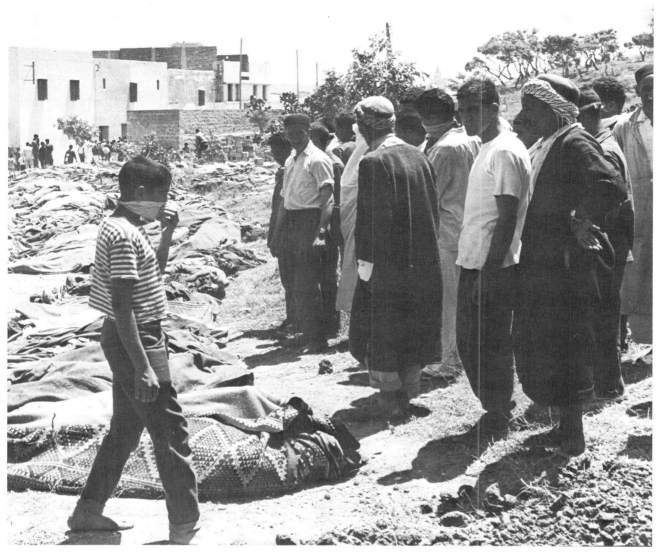

above: Fallen Muslims during the fight for Bizerte, Algeria, 1962. *Eddy van der Veen.*

in dramatic content, to that of the wars in Vietnam or Korea. What character it does possess lies in intimate, personalized incidents, the photographers concentrating on interpreting the conflict through the intensity of expression of the participants.

The Middle East

How does one live and sleep on a volcano? How does one adjust one's life to the constant threat of attack? This is the kind of situation that the Jewish people have learned to live with in the Middle East, even before the state of Israel came into being. Over thirty years of sleeping with a gun under the pillow. On the very day of Israel's independence in 1948, the Arabs launched a determined attack on the new state. The world was

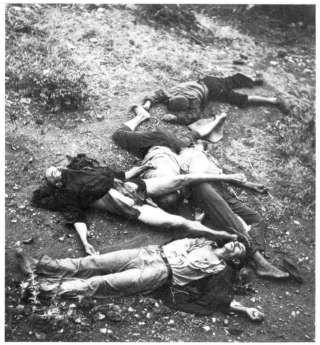

left: Bodies of slain rebels, Algeria, 1958. *Charles Courrière.*

155

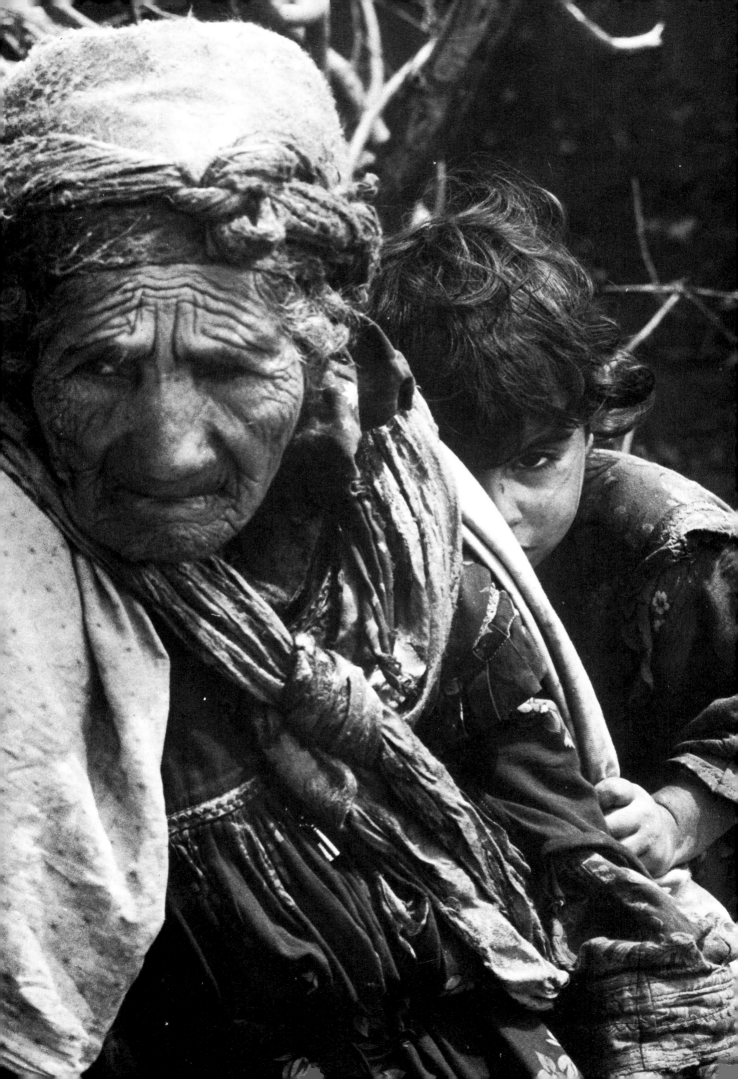

stunned to see that the Jews were not only able to defend themselves but also to counter-attack effectively. Within a few weeks over a million Arabs had fled across the border to Jordan and the Gaza Strip.

Some old hands from the Second World War came to record this historic occasion: David 'Chim' Seymour, Robert Capa, and Bert Hardy. But the world was tired of wars and did not want to look at any more pictures of killing. Besides the confrontation was soon over. Israel started to build a country and new Jewish settlers flooded in from various European countries and from across the sea. The Israeli miracle had begun. But the refugee camps of the displaced Palestinian Arabs remained a constant sore, the threat from across the border was ever present and security comparable to living on a razor's edge. The uneasy peace was to be shattered again and again.

The three major wars in the Middle East – Suez, the Six Day War, and Yom Kippur – were all connected with the existence of the new state. All were highly emotional – wars of survival, watched anxiously by the whole world. Contingents of reporters and photographers from the international press flocked to cover them. They came mainly to the Israeli side, only to meet in each encounter restrictive censorship of one form or another and numerous practical difficulties. An account of the coverage of these wars sums up the range of obstructions that impede full and open reporting, and the ingenuity and determination that have to be exercised in circumventing them, and the risks that photographers in the front line have to take.

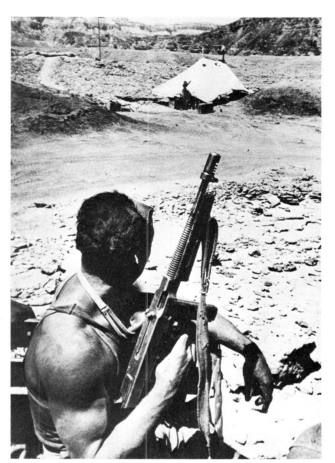

Desert patrol. One of the last pictures to be taken before the photographer's death, Israel, 1956. *David 'Chim' Seymour.*

SUEZ

President Nasser of Egypt precipitated the first full-scale war involving Israel. With his unlimited ambitions, diplomatic skill and appeal as a leader, he was the instigator of a certain degree of concerted action among the Arab states. He was unlikely to suffer the *status quo* without forcing events in the new struggle to oust Israel in some way. When Britain and the USA refused to finance the Aswan Dam, Nasser promptly nationalized the Suez Canal. His action not only provoked Israel, but also two European powers, Britain and France, both deeply involved in Middle Eastern and African affairs.

On 29 October 1956, Israeli forces crossed the Egyptian frontier and attacked through the Sinai desert towards Suez. Two days later both France and Great Britain, in their last attempts at colonial style 'gun boat' diplomacy, joined the fight against Egypt. Anglo-French planes started to bomb Egyptian airfields and paratroopers landed in support of the Israelis shortly after.

opposite: Refugees in the regroupment camp in Kabylie Mountains, Algeria, 1962. *Philip Jones Griffiths.*

Terry Fincher, later one of the most adventurous and consistent of English war photographers, was twenty-one years old at the time of the Suez fiasco. As the trouble had been brewing for three months, there had been ample time to make coherent plans, both for the invasion and for its press coverage. Fincher's agency, Keystone, had been selected as one of the first to take on the job and Fincher, in turn, was appointed their first representative. At the time the system of pooling photographs was still in operation, and so Fincher, along with other journalists, was sworn in at the Ministry of Defence as an official war correspondent. The first party left on 29 October. They spent the night in Naples and the next day in Cyprus where they were issued with uniforms and received a full briefing.

'With all this time we had to plan and prepare,' Fincher recalls, 'the whole operation, as far as the press set up was concerned, was one big mess. We were all taken across Cyprus before it turned out that we had gone to the wrong harbour and had to go all the way back again. Even the terrorist activities in Cyprus, already starting, meant that we had to take some precautions. But finally we were put on a troop ship and proceeded to sail on the Mediterranean for about a week. During this enforced cruise we heard on the

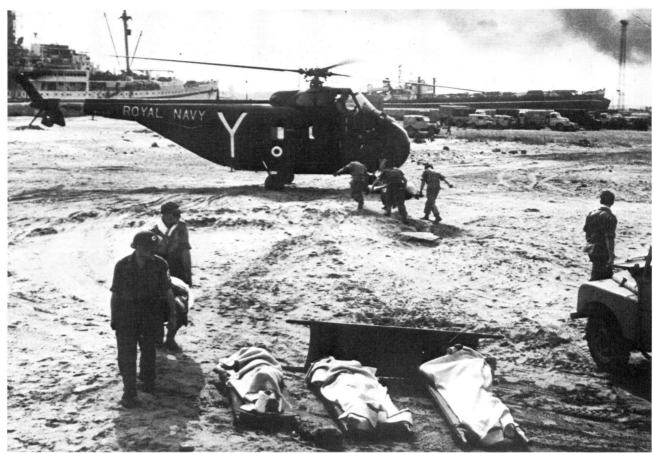

above: Evacuation of wounded, Suez, 1956. *Terry Fincher.*

radio of all the terrible things happening in Hungary and it seemed to us that the next world war was coming. Finally we arrived in Port Said on 6 November with jets already screaming overhead and we went ashore at night. Soon we set up with a press HQ, but we were aware that we were late. The next lot of correspondents was to follow much later, but as it happened they arrived almost immediately after us.

'When we came the action was already in full blast. It was all there happening, the flying out of wounded, shootings in the streets, jets swooping and strafing. I started to shoot immediately and at the time still with a 5 × 4 camera. I had an old MPP with a dozen double Darkslides; I also had a Rollei, but mainly used the MPP as that was what the press were using in those days. I turned to 35 mm two years later, but even then Fleet Street was reluctant to handle small, miniature material. So this was another thing, carrying all this stuff around. Fortunately in the Suez war one had a limited area to cover, only eight miles long and two miles deep. Anything that was likely to happen would be within these boundaries, so I stayed there for about

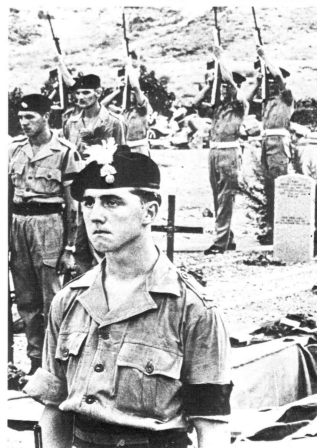

right: Military funeral during the troubles in Aden. *Terry Fincher.*

eight weeks in all and was then relieved by another agency man a little before Christmas.'

But by then it was all over. Strong pressure from the USA throughout the conflict finally forced the hand of the invaders and a cease-fire was signed on 7 November. The most humiliating venture of British arms had come to an end with nothing achieved. Contrary to original expectations, Nasser's and Egypt's position was strengthened and the canal blocked for some time. War in the Middle East came to a halt for a while but the killing went on.

Three days after the cease-fire, on 10 November, a jeep carrying two photographers, Jean Rey of *Paris Match* and David 'Chim' Seymour, president of the Magnum Agency, was approaching the Egyptian lines near El Qantara. The exchange of prisoners was to take place and the two photographers wished to cover it. There seemed no reason to worry or to take precautions; the cease-fire was in operation. But one young Egyptian soldier panicked and suddenly opened fire with a machine gun. The jeep carrying the two men went out of control and plunged into the Sweet Water Canal which runs alongside Suez. Both men died instantly.

Even now there seem to be some unexplained features of the tragedy. William Richardson, who was at Port Said at the time, did not see the incident personally but writes in a monograph on Seymour published in Britain by Studio Vista:

We never got the story exactly straight. He was in a jeep with a French photographer racing down the coast towards the 'end of the line'. A British lieutenant-colonel saw them barrelling down the road flanked by Suez on one side and the Sweet Water Canal on the other. He waved them to halt, but the driver of the jeep gave them the V for Victory sign and roared on. Maybe they never knew that this was the 'end of the line'. About 1000 yards further on, they came to an Egyptian outpost. The Egyptians said later that an officer 'risked his life to halt the jeep', but it did not stop, and a few yards farther on a machine gun opened fire.

Frank White of Time/Life, who came with Seymour from Nicosia in Cyprus to Suez, both of them part of a group of frustrated correspondents not allowed near any of the action, later wrote that they had spent two days in Port Said after they finally received French accreditation. They were driving with Jean Rey in 'liberated' jeeps, signing for petrol 'Pétain, Marechal de France'. Danger lurked everywhere with 'dead bodies, food riots, some sniping, prowling Allied tanks and a seething mass of hostile Egyptians'.

Why did they not stop? Why did an Egyptian soldier fire? And why was a peace-loving photographer like Chim involved in any case? David Seymour, who hated war and preferred to take pictures of beautiful children, not dead soldiers, found his death as a war correspondent.

Street fighting in Aden. *Terry Fincher.*

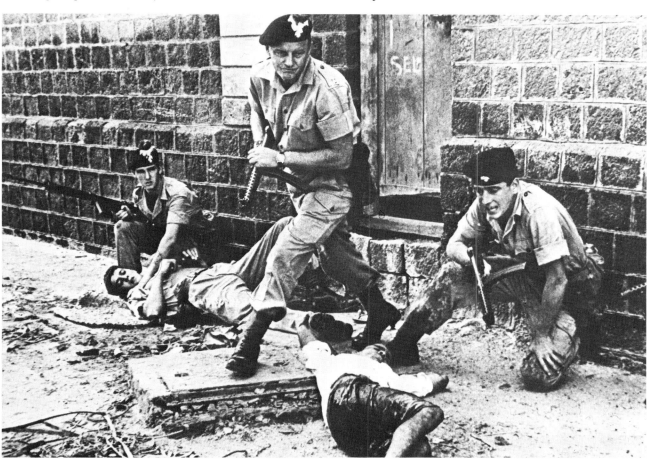

159

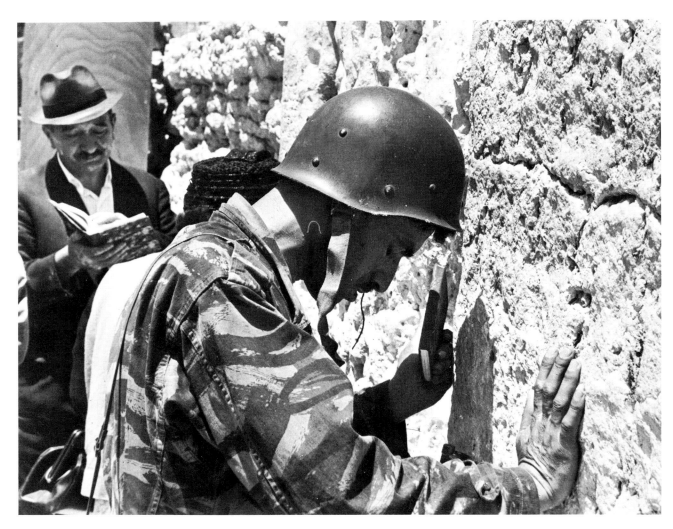

Soldier's prayer at the Wailing Wall, Israel, 1967. *Neil Libbert.*

THE SIX DAY WAR

Precarious, seething with unrest, a warlike peace lasted in the Middle East for some ten years. One side was being constantly strengthened and armed by the Americans, while the other drew support and armaments from the Russians. For most of the time the frontiers were in constant turmoil. Many Jordanian Arabs – some of them refugees from Israel – were organized into commando groups or *fedayeens* ('men of sacrifice') and attacked Israeli settlements over the cease-fire lines. Nasser encouraged similar encroachments from the Gaza Strip. The Palestine Liberation Organization was formed to sponsor undercover guerilla attacks, mostly from Jordan, and Syria intermittently shelled Israel from the Golan Heights poised menacingly over Israeli farming settlements.

In November 1966 these activities escalated considerably and Israeli forces mounted retaliatory raids against Jordanian villages. In April 1967, after a prolonged bombardment from the Golan Heights, Israeli aircraft shot down several Syrian planes in an air battle over Syrian territory. With everyone making threaten-

ing noises, Nasser was pushed into action and troops were ostentatiously moved through Cairo into the Sinai desert. United Nations detachments were asked to make space for them and, strange as it may seem, complied with the request. Now there was, for the first time in eleven years, a direct confrontation between Israeli and Egyptian troops. When in a final defiant move Egypt closed the Straits of Tiran to Israeli shipping on 24 May 1967, the cup ran over for the Israelis. In the early dawn of Monday, 5 June, Israeli aircraft attacked all nineteen Egyptian aerodromes and destroyed over 300 planes on the ground. Later on the same morning they attacked the Jordanian Air Force, with further damage being inflicted on Syrian and Iraqi airfields. Israel had broken the stalemate and declared war in no uncertain manner.

Although the situation in the Middle East had been tense for many months, indeed years, the world (and the Arab military authorities) was stunned by the speed of the Israeli action. Within hours of the news breaking hundreds of editors, in every country, were hastily marshalling their forces and sending their media troops into action. But most of them found that to get to the site of the action was no easy task. Most of the photographers and correspondents did manage to get

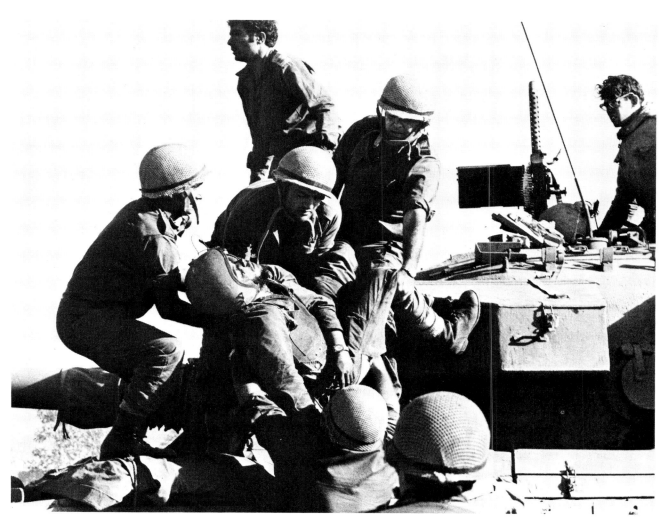

within striking distance of Israel, but only very few succeeded in penetrating the war curtain. The first two days of fighting were covered entirely by Israeli photographers, among them Bar-Am, a prominent journalist and photographer.

The *Sunday Times* team of Don McCullin, Kelvin Brodie (subsequently their Picture Editor but also an active photographer) and Neil Libbert, flew to Cyprus on the Monday morning, where they met a number of other hopefuls all without the immediate means of making the final hop to Tel Aviv. Waiting also was Terry Fincher who attempted to hire a boat to transport the media legions. His negotiations broke down, but the Israelis meanwhile had decided to send a troop-carrier to import the reporting brigade. Neil Libbert remembers that it was an eerie flight, full of tension and anxiety. At one stage two Israeli planes joined the big transporter and followed it as an escort into Tel Aviv. It was strange to land in an entirely darkened city – blacked out against a possible attack which never materialized.

They had arrived on Tuesday night, but by then the war was already well advanced and in some places almost over. The lightning attack on the enemy air-fields had destroyed much of the Arab airpower so that

Wounded gunner being carried from a tank, Israel, 1967. *Terry Fincher.*

Israel had a protective upper hand in the skies and combined their air raids with the advance of heavy armoured brigades on the ground. A two-pronged attack struck north into the Gaza Strip and Sinai, and by the morning of the second day the war was rapidly becoming an Egyptian rout.

All the journalists and photographers who arrived in Tel Aviv on the Tuesday night received immediate accreditation from the Ministry of Information. Neil Libbert and several others decided to make for Gaza in the south-west and set off immediately by taxi without bothering to register at a hotel. They were stopped some two or three hours later, well short of the front line and only just within audible range of the guns. It was not until the Thursday morning, day four of the war, that they were able to make contact with the advanced units. None of them managed to see or photograph the fighting for by then the Egyptian troops were almost completely routed. All that there was left to record was the aftermath of battle – burnt-out tanks, groups of prisoners under escort, the wounded being taken to hospital, the dead bodies left in the dry desert.

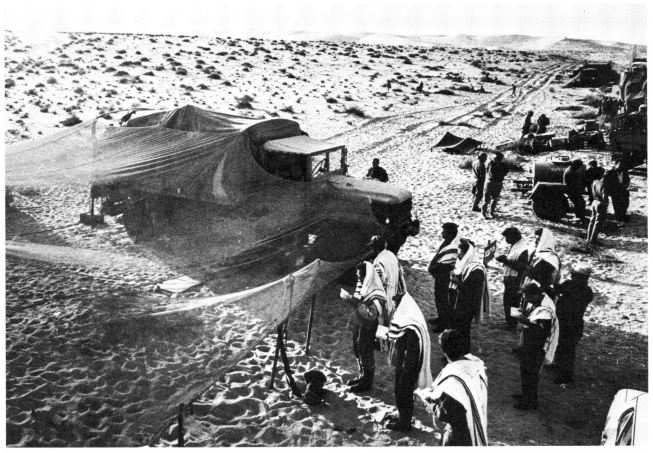

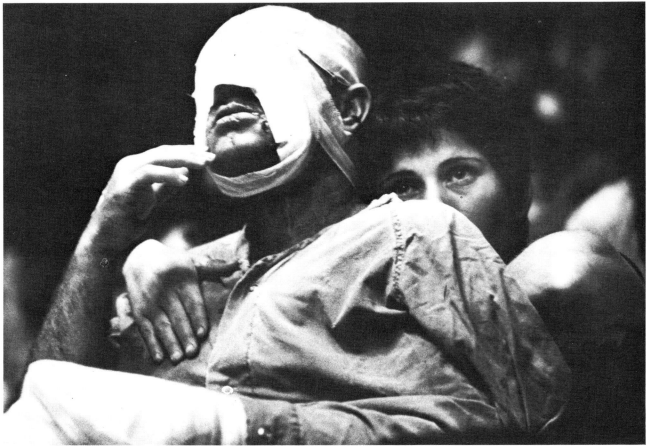

opposite top: Morning prayer in the Sinai desert, Israel, 1967. Neil Libbert.

Don McCullin had headed for the Jordanian front. Here the fighting was fiercer, particularly the battle for Jerusalem. For the Jews the Old City, with its wealth of tradition, and the Wailing Wall were precious symbols of their nation. The Holy City was taken on the Wednesday. The Jews had waited 896 years for this moment, and the joy following the fighting was heady and ecstatic. McCullin was with the first detachment of soldiers through the Dung Gate and shared the privilege of recording the historic occasion with a number of other photographers – David Newell Smith of the *Observer*, Gilles Caron from Gamma, Adriano Mordenti and Paul Ribeaud of Rex Features, and representatives of Associated Press, Central Press and Keystone. Here is part of McCullin's description of the event which he wrote for a commemorative booklet published by the *Sunday Times*:

We came through the gate in a rush. Really spewed through. The minute we got into the city we were hit by light machine guns, heavy machine guns, rifles and sub-machine guns. We all fanned out to escape ricochets. At this point we were in a section lined with little walls about 2 to 3 feet high. If they had used mortars we wouldn't have much chance of getting out of the way. Even without them, things were difficult because there seemed to be snipers everywhere. In the first 100 yards inside the gate we had casualties all the way. The guys had charged in, thinking they would run to the Wailing Wall, and they were being pinned down by this fire. . . . From here we moved just a few yards down the little street when heavy firing broke out. The men were moving quickly, eager to get to the Wall, when the man in the lead was shot dead. Then the next man was shot through the chest and fell. The doctor was screaming at me for a knife to cut the man's vest off, but I couldn't understand because he was speaking in Hebrew. Then someone said 'knife' in English, but before I could find mine, the man had died. And then the man behind me was killed by a sniper firing from a wall about 5 feet high. The men were trying to fight back but they didn't know where to aim. Then they put the last dead man on the stretcher and ran off with him. He had a handkerchief over his face to show that he was dead.

McCullin's account of his on-the-spot coverage of the capture of Jerusalem vividly reveals the closeness of the photographer to those who are in the front line and the extent to which he faces the same kind of dangers. It is this total involvement which characterizes McCullin's work and brought him fast recognition as one of the most courageous of war photographers.

He went on to photograph the occupation of the West Bank of the Jordan on the following day, and the taking of the Golan Heights when the Israelis overcame the remaining Syrian resistance on the Friday,

opposite bottom: Wounded Israeli soldier, Israel, 1967. Romano Cagnoni.

day five of the war. 'By nightfall it was almost over. It was the Sabbath, and Israeli soldiers read prayers beneath the new moon.'

The sixth and last day of the war was spent on mopping-up operations. The humiliation of the Arabs was complete. Nasser resigned, only to be reinstated almost immediately. The day after the war he started to pick up the pieces and prepare for the next chance. Though the main fighting was over, many photographers stayed on to record the sorrow of the defeated and the joy of the victors.

THE YOM KIPPUR WAR

The Six Day War had brought humiliation to the Arabs. Not only had they been defeated by a seemingly weaker opponent, but they had also lost a large section of territory on the West Bank and the Gaza Strip. An enormous gain for Israel, if only from the point of view of making her frontiers more secure and defensible for the next bout.

There was no question of a permanent peace or of a sensible and acceptable solution. The stalemate went on, with disturbances, skirmishes and retaliations as before the war. There were artillery duels across the Suez Canal, *feyadeen* raids over the border with Jordan, Israeli excursions into Egypt, and the occasional air battle. This time the lapse between the major conflicts was shorter. On 6 October 1973 – six years later – the Arab states took the initiative: Egyptian units crossed the Suez Canal while the Syrian Army simultaneously attacked the Golan Heights.

The day of the attack was a Saturday, perhaps deliberately chosen by the Arabs, for it was the Jewish Day of Atonement, a traditional holiday – Yom Kippur, from which the war takes its name. In company with the Israeli leaders and especially Moshe Dayan, the world press found itself caught unawares.

Philip Jones Griffiths, the veteran of Vietnam, heard the news on the radio in London. He immediately put through a call to Paris to Marc Riboud, who was at the time president of the Magnum Agency. Griffiths suggested that one of them should go to Israel, and that he was willing to do so. Riboud agreed, but there was a snag – Griffiths was broke and he would need to find a sponsor. Riboud phoned back within the hour to say that the French *Express* would pay for the first few days. Griffiths was, therefore, first on the scene (freelances can always move faster than staffers on a paper).

Once in Tel Aviv he arranged his accreditation without much delay. It was then that he found out the extent of the change since the Six Day War. No longer was there comparative freedom of movement for the press; they had at all times to be accompanied by an Israeli officer. And on top of that all sorts of difficulties were thrown in the path of correspondents from abroad

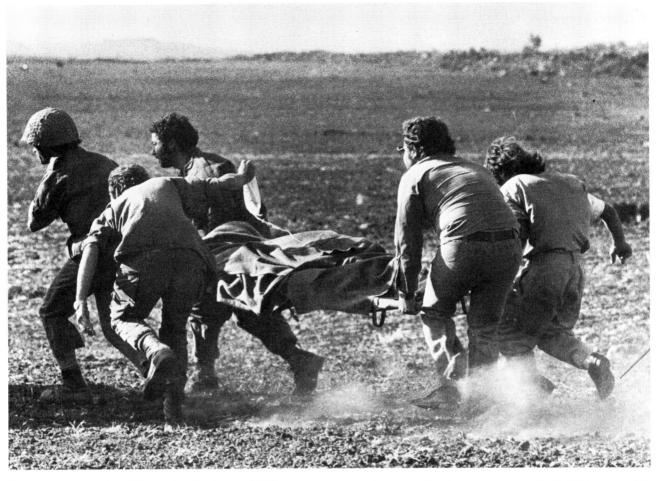

Rescuing wounded soldier under fire, Israel, 1973.
Penny Tweedy.

– a lot of promises, but very little action. The war was not going well for Israel in the beginning and they were not too anxious to let the world know about it. The Golan Heights, where Griffiths particularly wanted to be, was exceptionally tightly sealed off.

It is in such situations that the willingness to gamble, resourcefulness and experience of the good war photographer come to the fore. And Griffiths is one such. He hired a car and teamed up with a young American student who spoke Hebrew and who wanted to be a journalist. Within an hour they were away. They drove to the top of the Lake of Galilee and there found an old tank track used by the Israeli army for training purposes. At all other points their car had been turned back, but no one expected a civilian vehicle on this rough track. They met several military vehicles, but no one paid any attention to them and they managed to by-pass all the major roads leading to the front. On the way they were bombed and strafed by Syrian planes – good material for Griffiths's camera – but fortunately were not hit. After spending the night with an English resident not far from the front, they drove the next morning on to the main road to Syria with all the military check points behind them. Having managed

to arrive near the front unmolested, Griffiths was able to get excellent action pictures. He lost the car, however; it was blown to pieces by a direct hit (one of three which Griffiths lost during his three-week stay in Israel). Finally, and rather inevitably, he and his companion were spotted and escorted back to Tel Aviv.

Griffiths was in possession of some strong pictures, of potentially high value. But his problems were not yet over. Strict censorship had been imposed and every film had to be processed on the spot and inspected. It is likely that a deal had been worked out between the censoring authorities and a nearby laboratory which was charging somewhere in the region of $25 per roll. Griffiths decided to chance his luck once more. He went to the airport and simply boarded the first flight out. He was soon in Athens with all his film smuggled in an overnight case and from there he despatched his valuable cargo to the New York offices of Magnum.

The American magazine *Newsweek* had negotiated with a couple of leading French photographic agencies, which had five photographers in Israel, for exclusive use of their pictures, but at the last moment *Time* had stepped in and offered better terms. *Newsweek* were looking for alternative pictures and Magnum were able to name their own price for Griffiths's splendid photographs. One appeared immediately on the front cover of the magazine.

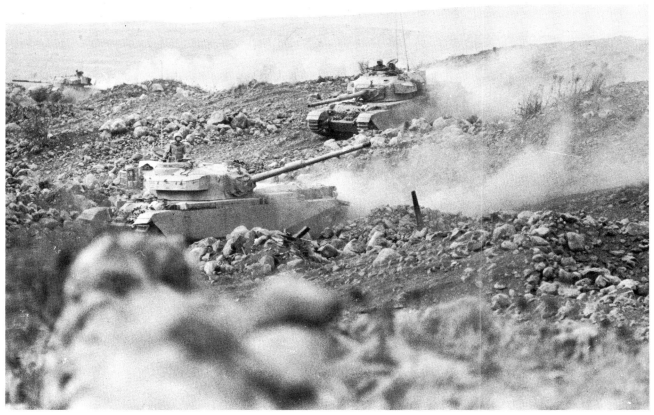

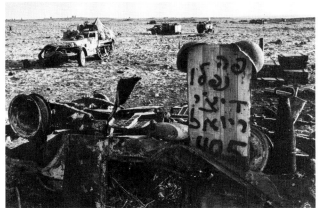

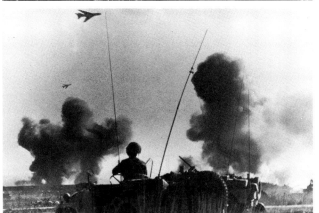

above: Tank battle in the desert, Israel, 1973. *Tony McGrath.*

left: Home-made memorial, Israel, 1973. *Sally Soames.*

bottom left: Aerial battle over Golan Heights, Israel, 1973. *Henri Laurent.*

Griffiths flew back to Israel on the next plane and was met at the airport by his former companion with another car. They drove at full speed down towards the Sinai desert, again managing to dodge the check points, and gathered some more excellent material. This time Cornell Capa, who was in Israel on an assignment not connected with the war, was able to help Griffiths ship his film out of the country in Capa's V I P bag.

Griffiths's exploits read like an adventure story: the photographer-hero leading a charmed life, evading capture, dodging bombs and bullets, challenging death to get his pictures, and emerging victorious. There is an unreality about it which ignores the actuality of the risks and the emotional pressures which are not always apparent in the heat of battle, but surface later. There is a tendency for media people in exposed situations to accept the possibility of death, but not in personal terms – 'After all, why me?' For many war photographers the camera acts as a kind of shield. The scene watched through the viewfinder is never quite real, quite tangible. For the rest of us the death or

165

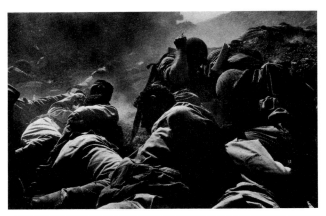

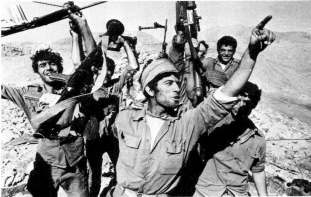

above top: Israelis and Egyptian POWs under fire, Israel, 1973. *Micha Bar-Am.*

above: Israeli soldiers celebrate victory in Golan Heights, Israel, 1973. *Steve Brodie.*

disappearance of a war photographer or correspondent is accepted as a matter of fact, the consequence of following a dangerous profession, a question merely of luck or averages. When the bullets fly, someone in the vicinity is bound to be hit, so why not the voyeur photographer? But the shock of being close to an associate, of working with him one day and attending his funeral the next, brings home to us our own vulnerability in a way that nothing else can. The impact of the death of a person with whom we work, and perhaps indentify, who takes the same risks as we take – whether the risks are obvious or only understood by those similarly engaged – is profound. Such an experience is not unique to war photographers; it cuts across all professions. Not unique, but perhaps more frequent. It was encountered by Sally Soames in the Yom Kippur War.

Sally Soames was part of the *Sunday Times* team which included journalist Nicholas Tomalin and photographer Frank Herrmann. Yom Kippur was the first war that she had covered, but it was not her first visit to Israel, however. She had fallen in love with the country of her ancestors and visited it several times in the previous years. She had only just returned from there to England four days before the outbreak of hostilities. Thus, for her the war had deep personal significance.

It had taken her several days to overcome the resistance of both her employers and her husband to her eagerness to go back to photograph the fighting. When she finally arrived in Tel Aviv on the Wednesday, five days after the onset, she immediately took a taxi to Jerusalem, forgetting in her inexperience to get accreditation. As she approached the front, she saw a platoon of soldiers on a nearby hill outlined against the sun, and on jumping out of the car to take some pictures quickly found herself arrested and marched off to the nearest military police post. Fortunately one of the officers knew her from her previous stay, and the following day brought her accreditation and an offer from Tomalin to accompany him, with an escorting officer, to the front on the Golan Heights.

They arrived at an advanced position exposed to artillery bombardment, constant bombing and the strafing sorties of enemy planes. Tomalin reported in a *Sunday Times* article: 'Sally was acting as if she was shooting at a golf tournament', exposing herself to danger and unable to resist standing up to photograph in the most lethal moments. Reaction set in later, however, and she decided the next day that she would not return to the front. Instead, she would photograph the effects the war was having on the country behind the line of battle.

She was working alone, photographing a supply line to one of the last Israeli outposts, when the news of Tomalin's death reached her. He had died instantly, a shell landing directly on the car that he was driving. Frank Herrmann was following him in another car.

A few days later, Sally returned to London via Vienna, clutching a bag of film. She was totally shattered.

For Griffiths heroics, for Tomalin death, for Soames tragedy – within a short span. War becomes a lens, concentrating and intensifying our experience. A paradox for the photographer; part of the fascination of the profession for us.

The Yom Kippur War lasted sixteen days. On the sixth day the Israeli forces, with reserves already in the front line, began to regain the initiative. On the seventh day the battle against Syria was nearly won. On the tenth day, a great tank battle on the Egyptian front was decisive: 200 Egyptian tanks destroyed and 100 captured in operational order. After that there followed a quieter stage of sporadic fighting. Griffiths describes it in the following terms: 'The war entered a boring phase, of artillery exchanges, air attacks and limited advances.'

It is this stage of a war that, according to Griffiths, is the most dangerous for a war photographer. He

opposite: Aftermath of a tank battle in the desert, Israel, 1973. *Tony McGrath.*

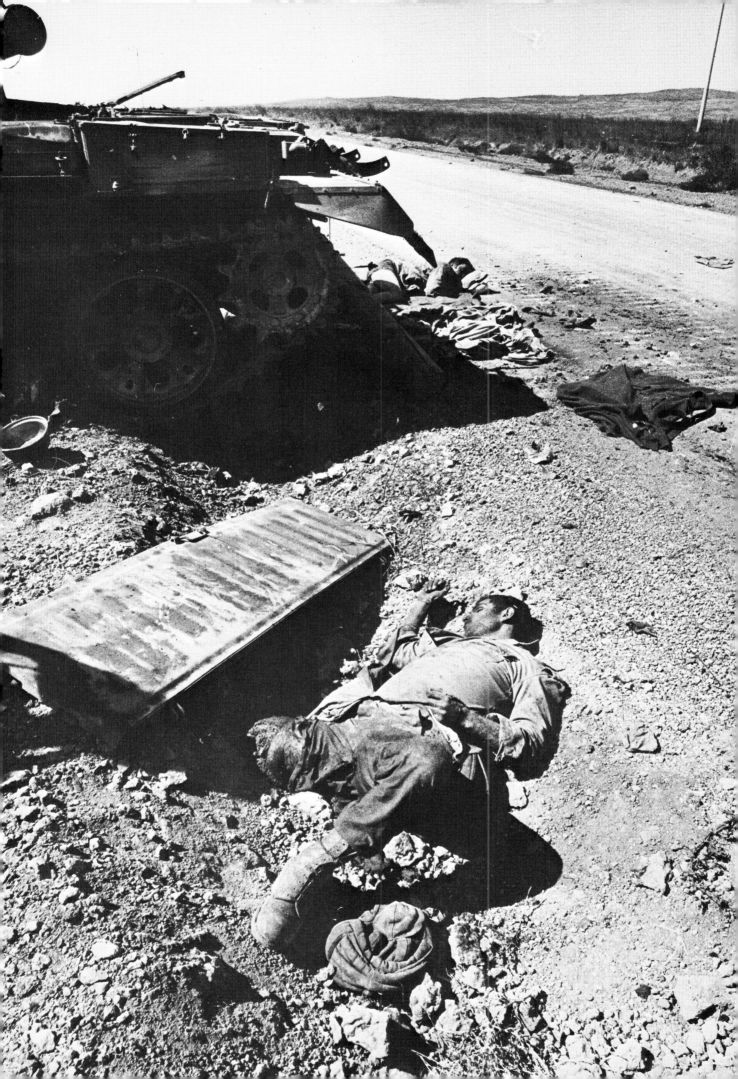

becomes less actively aware of the hazards while at the same time the soldiers, especially the artillery, become more experienced and therefore more accurate. Griffiths vividly recalls an incident from this part of the war, which, despite its frightening aspects, makes him laugh out loud. A coachload of journalists from Tel Aviv arrived in the vicinity of the Syrian front and instead of stopping at a check point the bus continued down the road for several hundred yards.

'It was a very colourful bus, and it must have been visible for at least twenty miles around. So, not surprisingly, the Syrian artillery opened up on the bus. The shells started to fall and explode quite close. Everyone got out in a hurry and tried to run for their lives. . . . It was the only time I saw Horst Faas running at close to 100 mph with his three Leicaflexes, one of them with a protruding 400-mm lens.' Faas is considered to be one of the calmest and most clear thinking of all war photographers.

While this account is being written, yet another disturbance is racking the Middle East. Palestinian terrorists have blown up a bus full of Israeli children. Israeli forces are retaliating with a full-scale attack on Palestinian terrorist camps in south Lebanon. Again strict censorship is in force and few pictures of military activities filter through – a warning that governments are still reluctant for their actions to be open to the world's scrutiny. Photographs are dangerous, it appears; they reveal too much.

Africa

In the Middle East wars there was a bias towards Israel on the part of the press. She could be seen as the underdog, heroically fighting to preserve her existence and displaying a considerable degree of professionalism in the process. For a time she became the exemplar of an aggressive, civilized nation which could be identified with by the rest of the 'civilized' world. This may in part account for the greater number of photographs taken from the Israeli side than from the Arab fronts.

The war photographers helped to create this image of Israel and in so doing they were creating an image which celebrated a modern 'civilized' style of warfare accepted (though not acceptable) in the West. But when warfare was wrenched from its so-called 'civilized' environment and set against the entirely different backdrop of Africa, the photographs could no longer provide a celebration of war. As the documentation took over, so the photographs became a condemnation; the photographer less partisan, making instead a wider identification which recognized a shared humanity, deeper than the skin.

In the 1960s and 1970s, the spectacle of Westernized warfare taking place in Africa is seen as both bizarre and tragic – bizarre because a Western convention is ruthlessly exposed by the new context; tragic because

we in the West are ultimately responsible. The photographs no longer present war as the 'peak' experience. Instead they create a new image – that of the African people reaping the bitter fruits sown long ago when the West first meddled in their affairs. The photographs taken by Romano Cagnoni and others in Biafra both reflect and prompt our understanding.

An uncomfortable symbol of the West's continuing exploitation of Africa appears in the photographs of war in the Congo and Nigeria: the mercenary soldier, the 'defender' of the unprincipled faith of self-interest in the post-colonial free-for-all. In the introduction we make an analogy between the mercenary and the war photographer, freelances both in war. In Ian Berry's account of his Congo coverage, parallels can be seen. The analogy breaks down, however, for it is the impartial but committed photographer who with his camera reveals the involvement of the impartial but uncommitted mercenary with his gun. And therein lies the difference.

THE CONGO

'I had made a tour of the Congo some two years before the trouble started,' recollects Ian Berry, 'and it seemed to me that of all the African states, the Congo had the greatest chance of remaining bloodless. I could not have been more wrong.'

Most of the visitors to the Belgian Congo in the fifties left with a similar impression. Materially the Congolese were far better off than any of their neighbours. Unfortunately they were not being intellectually groomed for their move to self-government. When the Belgians transferred power to a coalition government on 30 June 1960, it was as if a spontaneously combustible bomb had been planted in the middle of the country. The nation itself was an *ad hoc* union of several provinces with little in common with one another. Apart from the government leaders – Lumumba, the Prime Minister, and Kasawubu, the President – most of the high officials of the administration as well as the army officers were Belgian. Within a week of independence the army mutinied against its European officers. Soon afterwards Katanga, the richest province with a well-developed mining industry largely backed by Belgian interests, declared itself independent from the rest of the Congo. The coup was led by the popular Moise Tshombe, who had behind him the resources and support of the Belgian industrial giant, Union Minière. The government of Lumumba and Kasawubu were left no choice but to appeal to the United Nations for help in quelling the revolt. The arrival of the UN troops heralded the start of the four-year Congolese war.

Ian Berry and Tom Hopkinson, previously with *Picture Post* and now editing the African magazine *Drum*, arrived ostensibly for the independence celebrations but stayed on for the fighting. This was the

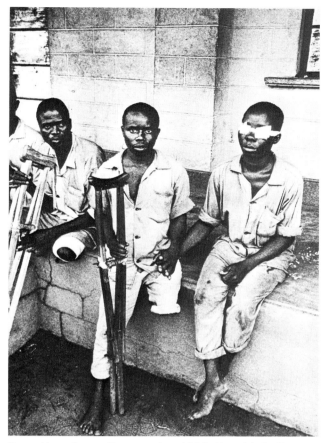

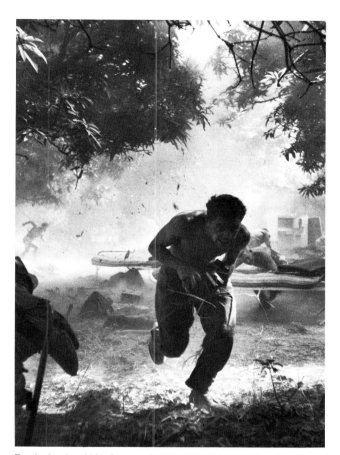

Casualties of war, Congo, *circa* 1963. *Don McCullin.*   Panic in the UN Camp, Congo, *circa* 1961. *Ian Berry.*

first of at least six trips that Berry was to make to the Congo between 1960 and 1964. (At the time he was working with Hopkinson for *Drum*, having recently left the South African paper, *Rand Mail*. As one of his first assignments for *Drum* he had covered the Sharpeville massacre; his pictures were never printed for obvious reasons.)

In the Congo during the early days of the disturbance there was little to photograph except some disjointed clashes and sporadic outbursts of fighting. The UN troops had not yet appeared on the scene, but even so the atmosphere was filled with tension and the possibility of further violence was plain for all to see.

One day during the first week of Berry's stay, he was travelling with Hopkinson and two other photographers in a taxi on the outskirts of Leopoldville in search of subjects to photograph, when suddenly they spotted a large crowd of Africans, armed with clubs, chasing another African. The pursued man, who turned out to be a member of a different tribe to that of his attackers, stumbled not far from the photographers' taxi and fell. The crowd instantly surrounded him and proceeded to try to club and kick him to death. The two other photographers prudently stayed in the car, but Berry jumped out and started to take pictures. To this day he admits to being shocked by his action. Should he have tried to stop the violence? He says that it never occurred

to him that he should. The camera in his hand was a compelling force which blocked all other reasoning. It was Hopkinson who intervened. He left the taxi and approached the crowd, shouting and waving. The crowd halted in their actions and the condemned man managed to stagger up and reel away. Berry describes the incident in detail, not so much for its importance, but partly because it illustrates the general situation and partly because his own attitude to it and doubts about his behaviour are still not resolved.

Berry's second visit was made still some time before the arrival of the UN troops. By then the Belgians were in flight, the central province was in ferment and stories circulated of nuns being raped and civilians killed. Belgian paratroopers were flown into Luluabourg in an attempt to evacuate the white population. They were holding only the airport while the Force Publique, in revolt against the Belgians who had trained them, occupied the rest of the town.

'Together with many other journalists and photographers, Hopkinson and I were also flown into the airport,' continues Berry. 'Soon this incredible man Hopkinson had decided that we were not going to get anywhere very interesting and that we should leave the airport and go into town to photograph the other side. So we walked out and up the road leading to the town and, as we expected, we were immediately grabbed by

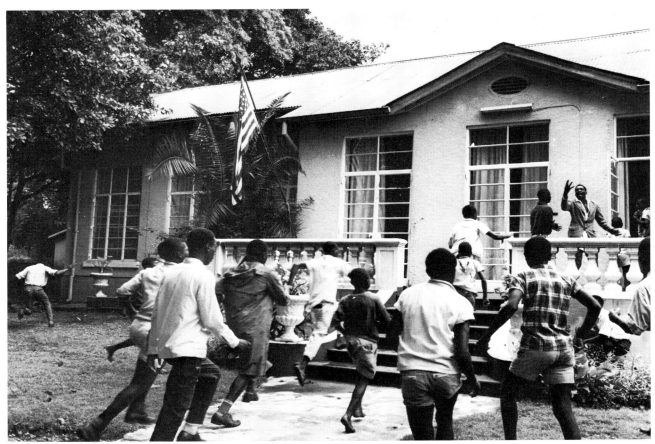

Attack on the American Consulate at Elisabethville, Congo, *circa* 1963. *Terry Spencer.*

the soldiers of the Force Publique and taken where we wanted to go. This was one occasion when speaking French very badly was a great help. Soon the accusations of being spies were dropped as they saw that we didn't know one word of Flemish and very few of French. After that they were quite nice and allowed us to wander around and take photographs. But unfortunately the Belgian paratroopers got worried about our disappearance and sent an ultimatum that they would blast the town unless we were handed back. So our captors escorted us to the other side.'

The UN troops arrived at the end of 1960. The unrest continued until 1964 but the presence of the UN force did, however, prevent a serious outbreak of fighting. The armed removal of the Katangan leader, Tshombe, by UN soldiers finally restored a modicum of calm. Ian Berry remembers this chapter in the Congo conflict as the siege of Elisabethville: Tshombe inside with his mercenaries and the United Nations force outside. The war, for all its horrors and cruelties, had a curious air – like an operetta.

'We all stayed in the best hotel in town (the Leopold Deux) and indeed it was the most extraordinary war to cover. War was going on all around the town and yet one could live a relatively normal life. This phenomenon happened also in Saigon in later years. You could get

up in the morning and have a well-cooked breakfast, try to gauge the situation by putting your nose out of the front door and seeing which way the mortars were falling. Then you could go out to shoot a few pictures and have a leisurely lunch.

'In Elisabethville the mercenaries were all around. They were a motley crew – Belgian, French, and Dutch, with the best of them German Foreign Legion blokes. During lunch a jeepload of them would arrive, they would file into the bar and down a few beers, and out they would go again to fight a bit more. It was a totally grotesque situation and very unreal. We had to cover both sides. Tshombe's and the UN troops' – and that was the most tricky thing to do since one could easily be taken for a mercenary on the way to the United Nations positions and on the way back be fired at as one of the UN Swedish contingent.

'There was one German mercenary who simply ran his own private war. He ran a jeep with four guys and a portable mortar gun on the back and made his own arrangements by attacking some UN outposts without warning or reporting to anyone. One day when we were back from one of the press conferences with the UN forces, we stopped on the way to photograph one of the big Howitzer guns shooting in the general direction of

opposite top: Leopoldville riots after Independence, Congo, *circa* 1960. *Ian Berry.*

opposite bottom: Starvation of the Baruba tribe, Congo, *circa* 1963. *Terry Spencer.*

170

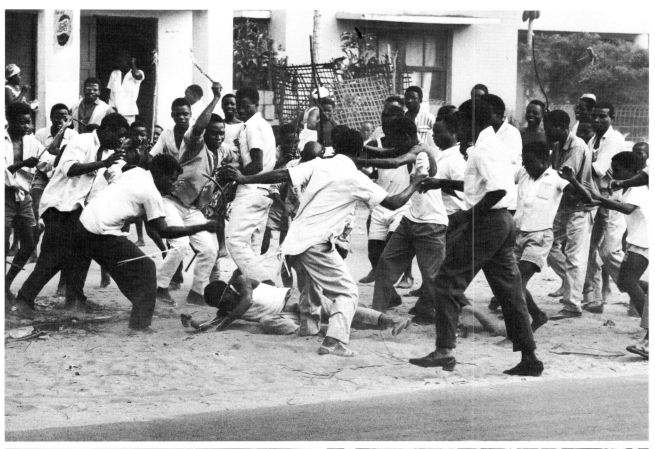

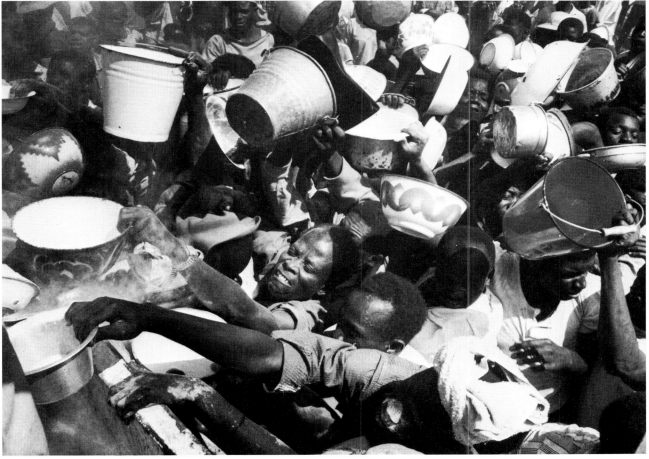

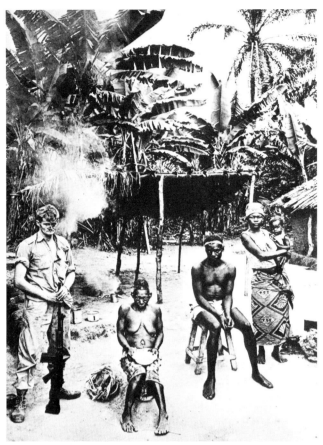

Natives and mercenary, Congo, *circa* 1963. *Don McCullin.*

With Katanga subdued and Tshombe out of the way, for a while at least, some stability settled over the Congo. The United Nations peace-keeping force was withdrawn by mid-1964. This was the signal for a renewal of internal unrest; increasingly strong guerilla units, in opposition to the government, began to threaten even the large towns. Then came the return of Tshombe, accompanied by a large number of white mercenaries and still financed by powerful industrial interests. He took over the government and embarked on a relentless campaign against the guerillas. The last spectacular event of the war, covered by the world press including Ian Berry, was the storming by Belgian paratroopers of the remaining stronghold of the rebels – the Katangan town of Stanleyville – after which the revolt was completely crushed.

The coverage of the Congolese war resembles nothing so much as theatrical photo-call, with a bevy of photographers waiting expectantly for the best moments of the play and shooting them at will. The war itself becomes an incongruous tragedy, enacted by an oddly assorted troupe. McCullin's picture of a mercenary posing proudly with a Congolese family can be seen as a final curtain-call, an ironic conjoining of exploiter and exploited in the vast continent of Africa.

NIGERIA AND BIAFRA

Don McCullin was one of a number of photo-journalists sent to cover the fighting in the civil war in Nigeria in 1966. Until then Nigeria, who had gained her independence in 1960, had been regarded as the model of British-inspired democracy in Africa. But from 1966 to 1970 Nigeria was to provide an alternative to the seemingly never-ending war in Vietnam. Independent Nigeria was a federation of three main tribes – the Christian Ibos in the south east, Muslim Hausas in the north, and the Yorubas of the south western coastal region. In January 1966 the majority of young army officers of Ibo origin staged a coup and overthrew the government of the northerner, Sir Abubakar Tafewa Balewa. They were opposed by the rank-and-file of the army, largely comprising northern Hausas, and the civil war began.

It was then that McCullin suffered one of the most disheartening experiences that a photographer has to face. Having spent three weeks in the Nigerian sun, travelling 1000 miles, exhausted by dust and flies, during which, on his own admission, he shot some of the best pictures of his career, he sent sixty or so rolls of colour film, the result of his gut-busting labours, to the *Life* laboratories for processing. They got no farther, for although *Life* had commissioned them, the editors considered the war too small and insignificant and the coverage too tardy. They simply killed the story. McCullin never saw a single shot of his Nigerian odyssey.

the UN positions. Suddenly this German warrior appeared from the wood, totally drunk, and started to spray us with his machine gun, fortunately completely inaccurately. We ran towards the town and there in turn were shot at somewhat more accurately by the African Tshombe troops. After taking cover in a block of flats, where no one would let us in, we had to go out and face the soldiers who were dying to shoot us on the spot despite our cameras and lack of arms. Somehow we managed to convince them that they should take us first to Tshombe. The whole affair finished fortunately with tea and cakes in the company of the Katangan President, but it could well have finished in a more sinister way.

'A further tricky problem was the despatch of films and texts. These had to be taken to Northern Rhodesia and that meant crossing the United Nations lines. We shipped our film in a pool so that we took the journey in turns. The correspondents' and photographers' contingent was very large, with some twenty photographers from all over the world, among them Horst Faas for AP and at the beginning of his career, Larry Burrows and Terry Spencer from *Life*, Ernie Christie for *Drum*, Don McCullin and a group of guys from *Match* (Dalmas, Leretier) and many others. I worked at the time for *Match* and also *Epoca*.'

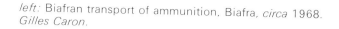

Meanwhile the 'small' and 'insignificant' civil war smouldered on. The Ibos who filled important government posts were either murdered or fled to their native province in the east. Yakubu Gowon, a northerner, managed to re-establish peace and order, but it was only a temporary respite. Many of the most able officers, administrators and businessmen who were of Ibo origin were excluded from the running of the country and, in June 1967, Lieutenant-Colonel Odumegwu Ojukwu declared the eastern region independent and renamed it Biafra. A month later General Gowon's troops crossed the border on a war footing. At first the Biafran troops were fairly successful, but it became obvious that, should they fail to enlist powerful outside help, in the long run they would not be able to withstand the superior government forces. Nigerian troops occupied Okigwi in October 1968, the Biafran capital, Umuahia, in April 1969, and having captured the last stronghold, Owerri, at the beginning of 1970, forced General Ojukwu to flee the country. Surrender terms were signed on 15 January 1970.

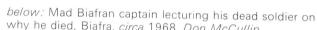

below: Mad Biafran captain lecturing his dead soldier on why he died, Biafra, *circa* 1968. *Don McCullin.*

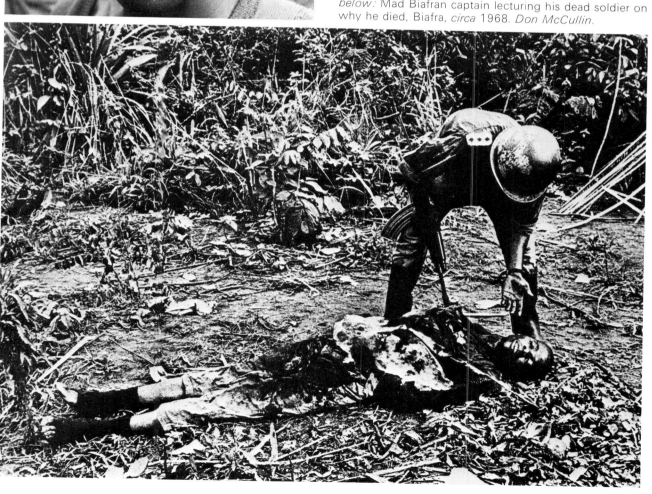

173

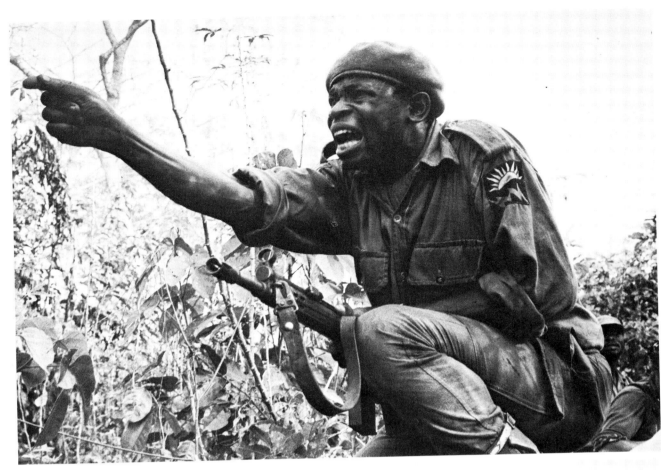

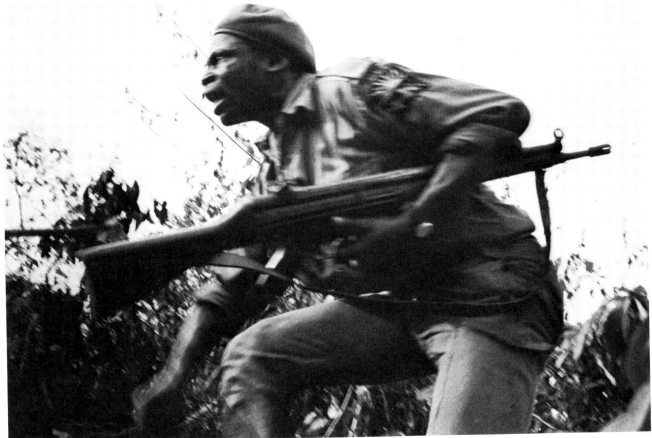

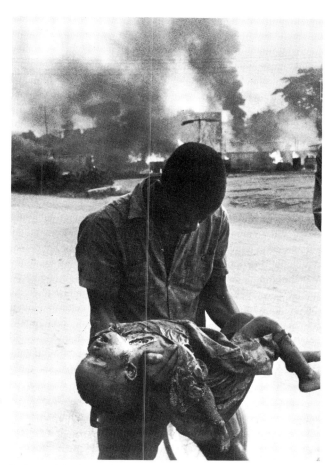

It took a long time for the West to see pictures of Biafra. During the first six months of the fighting, few photographers managed to penetrate anywhere near the front. It appears that only one photographer went to Biafra itself and he died in one of the skirmishes. And so Romano Cagnoni, who arrived with a party of journalists in February 1968, seven months after Biafra's secession, was one of the first on the scene. He had been trying to get permission to enter Biafra for several months, even spending twenty days in Lisbon visiting a Biafran official daily, without success. Suddenly, a planeload of journalists was bound for Biafra with Cagnoni aboard.

One of the first to come, he was one of the last to leave. The other journalists and photographers were ordered out four days later, but Cagnoni stayed over a month, living in a luxury hotel in Port Harcourt, playing cards with General Ojukwu, and making many trips to the front in a Mini Moke. He returned to London convinced that he had a scoop and *Life* bought the first rights to his story. A twelve-page spread was laid out ready for printing. A week before publication, however, Martin Luther King was assassinated. Cagnoni's Biafran story was immediately shelved. It remained in storage for some four months.

Gradually reports began to filter out of Biafra of starving and dying children. The plight of the Biafran people suddenly attracted the imagination of the world. It also attracted a horde of photojournalists who made the war and the airlift of food and medical supplies into a number one story. Cagnoni's pictures were resurrected, the layout reinstated, with the addition of a few pictures of children whom Cagnoni had also happened to photograph to bring it up to date.

He made his second visit to Biafra at the beginning of 1969 after most of the other photographers had departed. This stay of more than two months resulted in his best pictures of the war. Most of the time he lived with the people, sharing their food and their danger. The provisions he had brought with him quickly ran out for he had shared them with others. He came to rely on the assistance, plus the occasional pack of cigarettes, of Irish missionaries and some mercenary soldiers. The little hotel in Humai, with waist-high grass growing around it, was his headquarters, but he moved about a great deal as he was near the front. He usually had to blacken his face; a white face to the Nigerians meant mercenaries – their greatest foe. Often the two adversaries fought so close to each other that Cagnoni was almost able to photograph the Nigerian trenches. There were few other photographers in the country for Vietnam now claimed the major share of the world's press. On his return to England his pictures appeared in most of the leading magazines and an exhibition of

Father with the body of his son, Biafra, *circa* 1970. *Romano Cagnoni.*

his work, organized by a group including Bertrand Russell, was staged in London.

Cagnoni's third and last visit to Biafra came at another crucial point in the war, just before the end. With the impact his pictures had made in the press and in exhibitions, Cagnoni felt himself to be in a strong position. He was anticipating few problems with this third visit. He found that he was wrong. His applications for a visa were met with silence, and in desperation he had to fly to St Thome, a small island off the Biafran coast, before he was allowed in. But he arrived just at the right time. The gallant Biafran resistance was crumbling but, in spite of that, Cagnoni had complete freedom to photograph where he wished. He was able to secure some last pictures of General Ojukwu before his escape and to record the final stages of the war. Again he had a scoop. His pictures were printed non-stop for a week and *Life* gave them a ten-page spread.

Though many other photographers worked in Nigeria and Biafra, among them Don McCullin whose pictures of Biafran children are well known, Cagnoni's commitment to the Biafran cause made it very much his war. Whilst other photographers came, often quite fleetingly, and went, Cagnoni's three extended visits enabled him to come close to the people fighting in the

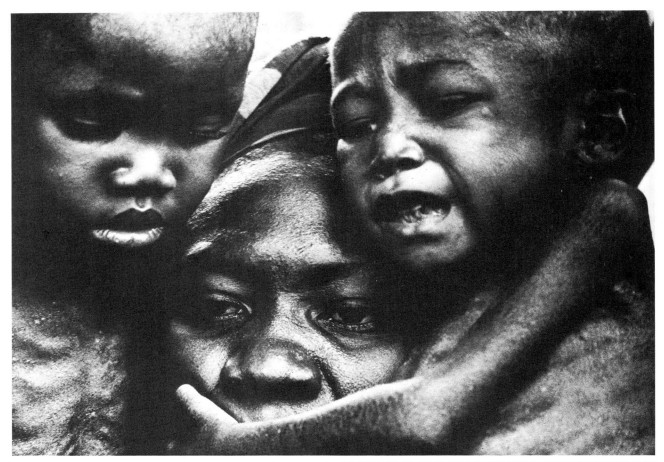

above: Biafran mother with her children, Biafra, *circa* 1968. *Romano Cagnoni.*

war and to understand them better. It was roughly at this time that Philip Jones Griffiths was immersing himself in Vietnam, and a number of other photographers, among them Catherine Leroy, were beginning to cover conflicts at length rather than to pay flying visits. Such attempts at recording a war in depth were a growing feature of modern war coverage. Cagnoni is one of the earliest examples of the photographer's increasing involvement with those he photographs.

In assessing the overall coverage of the Biafran war, Cagnoni feels that the preoccupation with the fate of the starving children, although a valid concern and a highly emotive subject, precluded serious attention to the conflict as a whole. Some of the coverage was too laden with emotion, whilst the more acute cases presented almost a medical record of human suffering and atrocity. For Cagnoni, it was the twenty-year-olds who were fighting and dying who constituted the heart of the conflict and provided the greater interest. The tragedy of these young lives was far more frightening and poignant. His own interest in war photography has always centred on people's reactions to acute stress and

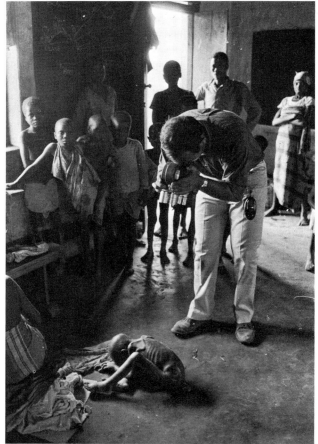

right: Misery and death are always newsworthy, Biafra, *circa* 1968. *Gilles Caron.*

176

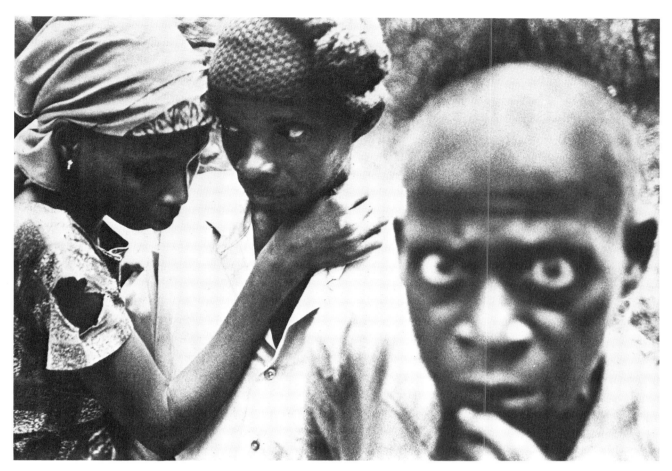

danger. It is these powerful emotions that he wishes to capture in their faces.

The best selection of his photographs can be found in *Presenting Romano Cagnoni*, published by Olivetti.

Terror of war, Biafra, *circa* 1970. *Romano Cagnoni.*

Three Civil Wars

All wars are evil, but we can find, however vaguely, traces of dignity and even logic in wars waged by real warriors – the soldiers. But when soldiers are replaced by ordinary civilians, as happened in Cyprus, Lebanon and Northern Ireland, the conflict assumes a nightmarish quality of savagery, insanity and unreality. Soldiers fight because they are trained to do so; they approach it as an everyday profession. But when civilians fight there is not even this excuse to be offered: the root of war feeds on hatred and pure malice. In civil wars this element of personal enmity between the warring parties is often evident. It is certainly more explicit than in wars between two different nationalities, as Israel and Egypt, for example, where acts of cruelty and outrage brought about by extreme loathing and mutual antagonism were perpetrated far less often. But the three civil wars presented here – in Pakistan, Lebanon and Northern Ireland – provide innumerable examples such as the unnecessary killing of Beharis in Bangladesh or inhuman acts of castration in Lebanon.

Atrocities are featured in many of the photographs from Bangladesh and Lebanon. Northern Ireland is an

exception as the incidents of bombing or murder are so unpredictable and scattered that no war photographer is likely to be able to cover them. In Bangladesh and Lebanon, however, the participants were often quite willing, and at times even eager, to show off their inhumanity in front of a camera.

The personal violence which broke out in the civil wars of the 1970s coincided to a certain extent with a tendency on the part of some war photographers to seek and single out specific violent acts. By the early seventies, both the public and the photographers themselves had become accustomed to seeing and recording explicit war pictures. Indeed, some photographers deemed it necessary to step up the shocking elements in their images in an attempt to produce a 'stronger', more frightening effect. The violent civil wars easily provided this kind of material. The tendency, it must be stated, was by no means general; only a certain proportion of photographers were willing to resort to such excesses. The public, for their part, seemed to want such pictures, or at any rate were prepared to accept them, as though they had been anaesthetized by a constant fare of war images. Thus we have to ask the question – do photographs of war prompt our consciences, or do they merely immunize us to the pain and suffering of others? The answer, I suppose, is that

177

it will depend on each individual's response and on the individual photographs themselves; but only by looking at the photographs and examining our own response to them can we ever make a final judgement.

BANGLADESH

Photographers who covered the various wars in the sixties and seventies invariably remark that each one had its own unmistakable flavour. Some were intense and serious, like the Israeli conflicts; others had an air of theatricality as the war in the Congo. Bangladesh was a curious blend of nineteenth-century British Indian colonial and almost primitive tribal admixtures, with a dash of uneasy modernity thrown in. This variety of elements could be detected in the way in which the media people were treated. At first officialdom conspired to make the life of some 700 international correspondents as difficult as possible; by the end the photographers were almost free to come into very close contact with both sides, with many soldiers childlike in their delight at displaying for the camera their skill in the game of killing and maiming. The situation was always highly unpredictable. At times the photographers were treated with respect and deference; at others they were thrown into jail on the flimsiest of pretexts.

The civil war in East Pakistan started in March 1971, but it was not till later in the year, with the outbreak of more serious hostilities and the crossing of the border by Indian troops in support of Bangladesh against Pakistan, that the majority of correspondents started to arrive. Tony McGrath, the regular staff photographer of the *Observer*, and a multitude of others landed in Bombay in the first days of December. From there they proceeded to Calcutta, only approximately 50 miles from the border with Bangladesh.

It was there that the Indian bureaucracy, with traces of the British Raj still visible, showed all 700 correspondents how unbelievable it could be. Though official accreditation was finally granted in Calcutta, where most of the military authorities resided, every single press representative had to make the lengthy trip from Calcutta to Delhi because it was only there that the initial documents could be stamped. And there was no way round it. With officialdom appeased for the moment, the correspondents were installed in Calcutta's largest hotel, the Oberoy Grand.

They were soon to find out that, even with official accreditation, crossing the frontier was no easy matter. No one was allowed near the frontier for the first six days of the war. Each day a communiqué was issued stating that it was considered too dangerous to permit a trip to the front in view of the fact that the government of India considered themselves responsible for the safety of the correspondents whom they regarded as their guests. In India, it appeared, there was no single authority; every officer seemed to have the right to stop

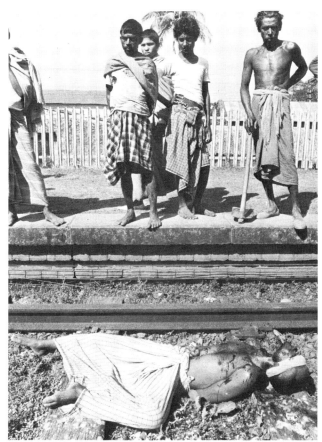

Death on the railway track, Bangladesh, 1971. *Tony McGrath.*

them and prevaricate; even messenger boys would take it upon themselves to censor photographs and messages if, in their opinion, they were detrimental. Sometimes they would refuse to pass them on.

Eventually, with a whole week wasted, permission was suddenly given for the correspondents to visit the frontier. A ludicrous spectacle materialized – a cavalcade of some forty taxicabs, each driven by a Sikh, with a military jeep at either end of the procession, started from the Oberoy Grand to the war some 70 miles distant. There a press conference was held which might have been of some use for the journalists, but was of little help to the photographers. It took them a further two to three days and three more taxi rides into East Bengal to get within camera distance of the war. The military authorities would not allow anyone to stay away overnight, although the correspondents did discover that the nearer to the action they managed to get, the more amenable the officials, and therefore the easier their job, became. The number of correspondent-carrying taxis had fallen dramatically. Only four or five, mainly filled with photographers, actually reached the scene of the fighting.

opposite: The killing of four Beharis in the Dacca stadium, Bangladesh, 1971. *Penny Tweedy.*

178

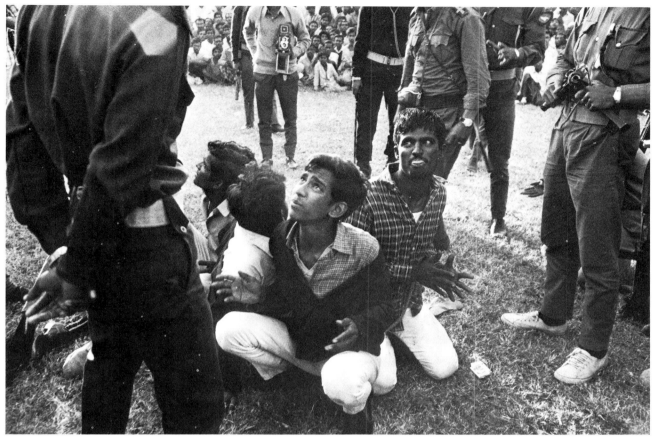

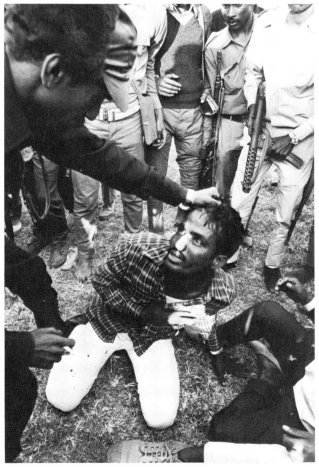

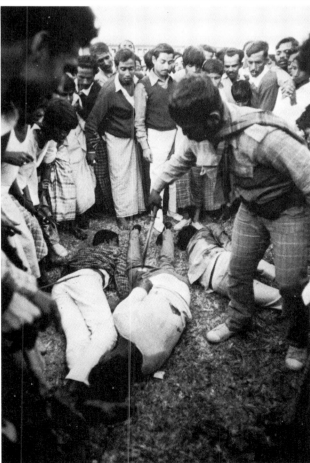

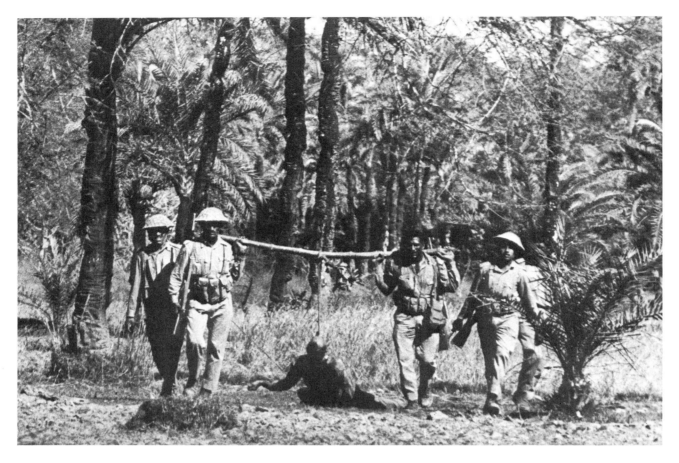

Pakistani soldiers dragging the body of a dead Indian, Bangladesh, 1971. *Abbas.*

But the difficulties were still not over. On one occasion, Penny Tweedy, Bob Whittaker and Simon Drean wanted to cross the frontier by a certain bridge. They were stopped by a sentry. They therefore went further along the river until they were able to cross by another bridge. After a few hours of photographing, they tried to return via the first bridge and were promptly arrested and confined for a day or so as a warning to the others.

The people actually involved in the fighting had far less time for bureaucracy. McGrath found that the officers were quite helpful, preening themselves for the cameras. The soldiers thought the correspondents were completely mad since the front was the last place that they themselves wanted to be. Only once though were McGrath and two other photographers able to shake off their Indian guides. That was on the day of the armistice, and they managed to record the surrender of Khulna, an industrial town in the south.

McGrath stayed in India for about three weeks, most of the time a taxi ride away from the fighting, and waging his own continual war against officialdom and bureaucracy. One of the biggest problems for the photographers was getting the exposed film out of India and on to editors' desks in London and other countries. Officially, all material was supposed to be

processed in Calcutta and approved by the censor, but local processing ruined the quality of the film. All sorts of stratagems were devised to circumvent the restrictions. McGrath's first batch of film, sent with a T.V. shipment, went the wrong way round the world, by way of New York, before finally arriving in London on a Sunday morning – too late for that week's paper. Some Americans had managed to bribe a high-ranking official, and so McGrath combined his packages with those of Penny Tweedy and was able to get them seen quickly by one official only. This was a great improvement on the normal channels, with the long chain of censors. Another method was to send pictures by wire in which case they were censored directly by the operator.

For McGrath personally, the most distressing aspect of the war in Bangladesh – even though this was the third war he had covered – was the amount of casual killing that went on all the time. Killing that was not, he insists, in any way directly related to the war. 'One saw on the side of the roads bodies with slit throats or disembowelled. It was not even Indian killing Pakistani or vice versa, but often Pakistanis murdering their own, mostly Beharis, who belonged to a different caste and religion. But also the victims were various money lenders or adulterers – in other words, a lot of personal scores were settled under the cloak of war. Immediately after the fall of Khulna and with the cease-fire already in force, we came across a line of bound

180

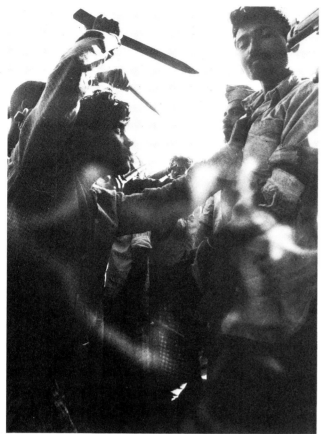

left: Death of a Behari, Bangladesh, 1971. *Tony McGrath.*

Beharis. It is sad now to think that perhaps their captors played up to our cameras and that eventually all these wretches were killed.'

McGrath's pictures of the event were never used by his paper. He returned to England three days after the armistice on 20 December. His editors thought that the pictures were too distressing to be seen over Christmas lunch. Other papers were less squeamish. A set of pictures taken by Penny Tweedy, Bill Lovelace, Horst Faas and Michael Lorent were splashed across the front pages. The terrible event that they recorded took place in Dacca's football stadium after an emotional speech by one of the Bangladeshi leaders about peace and goodwill. After he had finished speaking, he noticed four Behari prisoners as he left the stadium. With a circle of photographers round, for whom a special place had been made, he started to taunt the prisoners, first swearing and spitting, then burning them with a cigarette butt. He then snatched a rifle and bayoneted all four to death. Many cameramen, including Marc Riboud, refused to shoot, but four cameras clicked merrily away, and Lovelace collected

below: East Pakistani family displaced by the war, Bangladesh, 1971. *Abbas.*

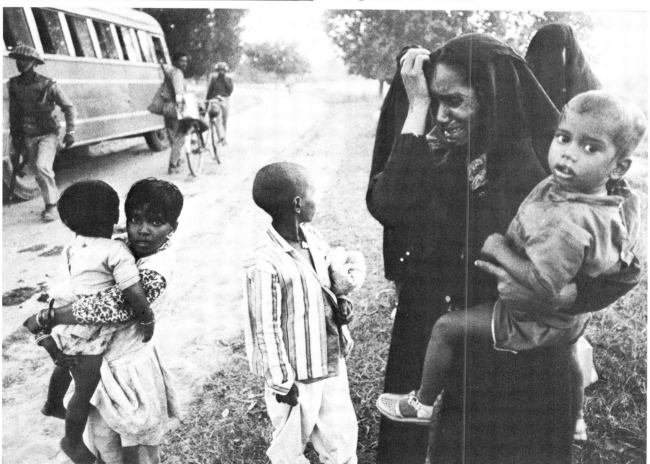

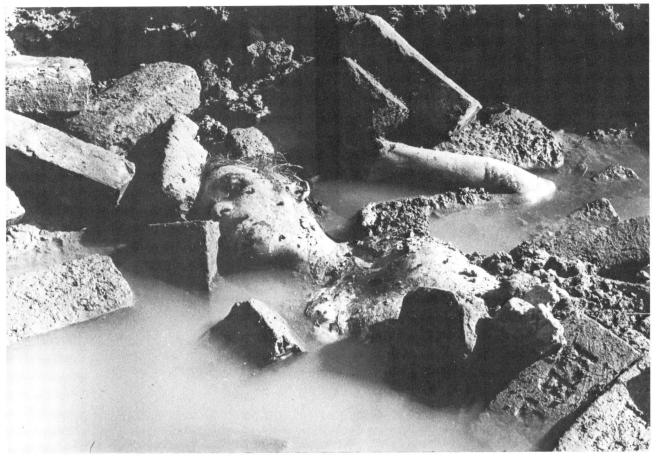

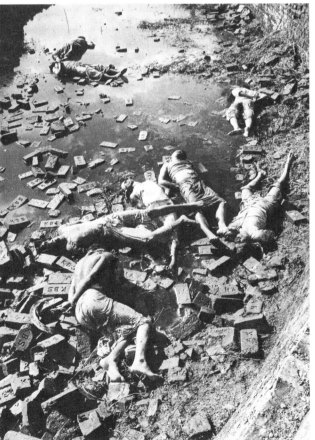

above and left: Bodies of Bengali intellectuals killed by Pakistanis in Dacca brick works, Bangladesh, 1971. *Penny Tweedy.*

a special prize for his photographs. McGrath, who was not present, but heard the event described in detail, is convinced that it was the presence of the cameras that caused this tragic piece of showmanship.

The other most vivid memory, apart from the desultory murders, which McGrath brought back from Bangladesh was the sight ot two high-ranking officers one a losing Pakistani, the other a victorious Indian, exchanging pleasantries after the armistice. Both had been trained at Sandhurst in England, and they greeted each other with British officers' small-talk, comparing notes on the campaign and patting each other on the back for some smart move that had been made. For them it was an exercise with live soldiers – as most wars are, a deadly game to be played by grown-up children. After game, set and match, the two retired for a cup of tea, in the fashion of the English.

LEBANON

There were few contrasts or subtleties about the war in Lebanon. Indeed, it was difficult to tell an enemy from an enemy – they were the same people, spoke the same language. But for pure viciousness, Lebanon's civil war is in a higher league than that of Bangladesh.

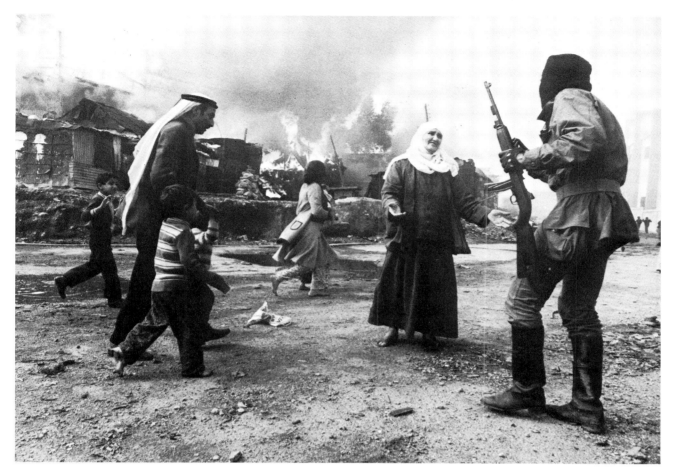

Palestinian woman pleading for her life in Quarantina quarter of Beirut under attack by the Falangists, Lebanon, 1976. *Françoise Demulder.*

'For the few of us who covered the whole course of the civil war,' says Catherine Leroy, 'it was the worst place ever. We compare different conflicts all the time, but this one is definitely the end. This was the war of civilians – entire familes armed with Kalishnikovs. People shooting at each other and children being hit by snipers while playing in the school yards. It was a war of cowards and hostages, with some 200 000 ordinary citizens from both sides dying in the process. Complete madness.'

'Beirut was a nail in my coffin as a war photographer,' comments Don McCullin. 'In one day I saw 100 people machine-gunned, in groups, in various doorways. When I say I saw them, it was not necessarily at the moment of their death but heaps of bodies – both men and women – who had been murdered the previous day, drying in the sun. It was a dreadful war.'

The demarcating line between the two adversaries was tenuous indeed: on the one side, largely Christian and more affluent Falangists; on the other, mainly Muslim and poorer Progressist/Palestinians. But there were rich Palestinians and quite poor Falangists, whilst the religious division did not apply strictly across the board. The religious element ran deep, but the war was about power, as many wars are, and hence political. Two erstwhile partners in a coalition government were unable to work together. To wage a savage war of attrition, killings, torture and maiming, just for the right to conduct a civil government seems ultimate madness. After the fighting stopped, there was still no visible end to the conflict. Even after a United Nations style Arab force, mainly Syrian, had intervened, in a no less savage manner, it did not succeed in taking the cauldron off the boil. The conflict went underground and now crime in Beirut is so rife that few dare go out in the dark in this hapless city.

But to return to the beginning. Of the two photographers already quoted, Don McCullin was the first one on the scene. McCullin started his career with a civil war in Cyprus and now he would like to think that he has finished it with another one in Lebanon. His gradual disillusionment with war and war coverage became more strongly reinforced by his contact with the human bestiality of Beirut. Nearly two years later, it is still his last war, but whether it will remain so even he himself does not know.

With the outbreak of hostilities in Lebanon, the *Sunday Times*, McCullin's employers, rang him on a Saturday and asked him to be prepared to go to the Middle East within ten days. After studying the reports and cuttings, he rang them back with the request that he leave as soon as possible. He was right to move so fast; when he flew into Beirut on the Monday, he was on

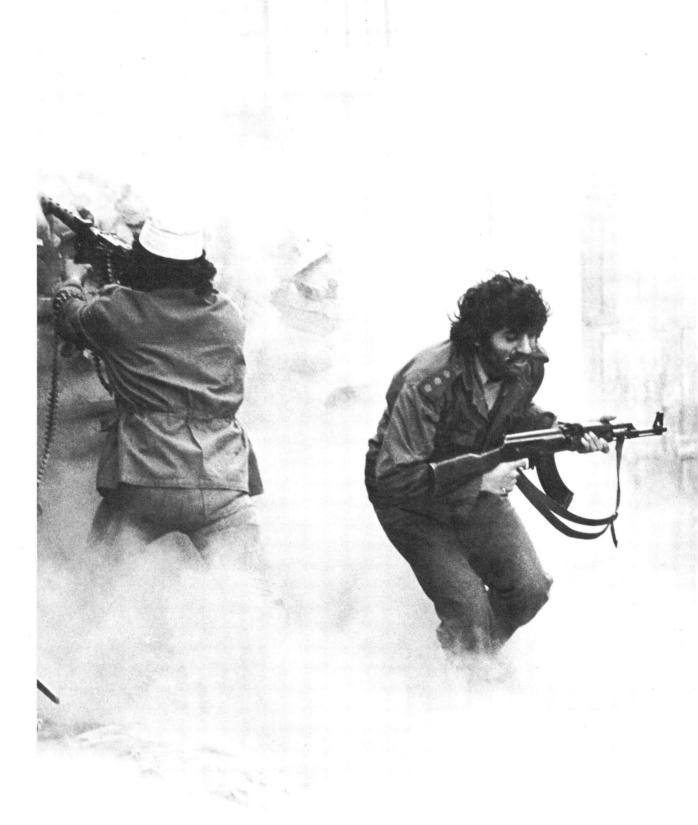

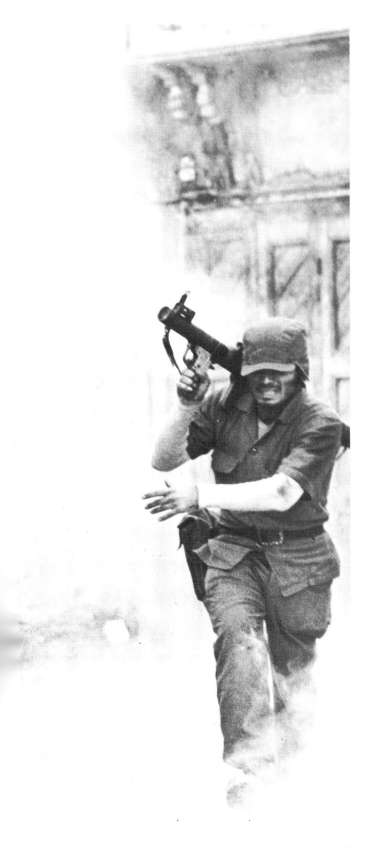

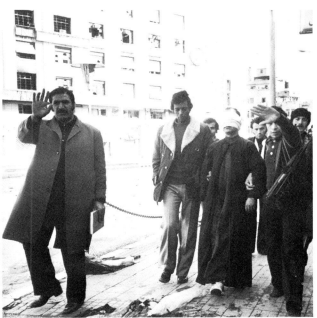

above: Falangist gunmen with a hostage priest, Lebanon, 1976. *Catherine Leroy.*

one of the last civilian planes allowed to land there for weeks.

'As you land in Beirut, you come into the hotel area – you actually fly over hotels. I immediately saw the St George's Hotel already gutted and the Fenitia and the Holiday Inn facing each other and burning on some floors.'

On leaving the airport, McCullin registered in the small Commodore Hotel, a favourite refuge of many journalists, but he slept there only one night. The next day he was already in the area held by the Falangists, in fact on the fourth floor of the Holiday Inn from where the Falangists were fighting their opposite numbers in the Fenitia Hotel across the street. He still remembers a strikingly lovely girl leisurely lobbing sticks of dynamite into the Fenitia.

This was the first of seven dangerous days which he spent exclusively among the Falangists. He reckons that the coverage on their side was easier as the Palestinians were much more wary and restrictive towards photographers, often refusing to allow them a particular vantage point or to photograph certain objectives. He knew that it would be difficult to return once he had crossed the line, so he stayed put for a whole week, 'living mostly like an animal, sleeping under chairs and on tables, and sponging food here and there.' By staying with the Falangists, who did not mind being photographed so long as he did not show their faces – which he did without their knowing – he believes that he was able more conclusively to expose their atrocities towards the Palestinians.

opposite: Palestinians in action in Beirut, Lebanon, 1976. *Catherine Leroy.*

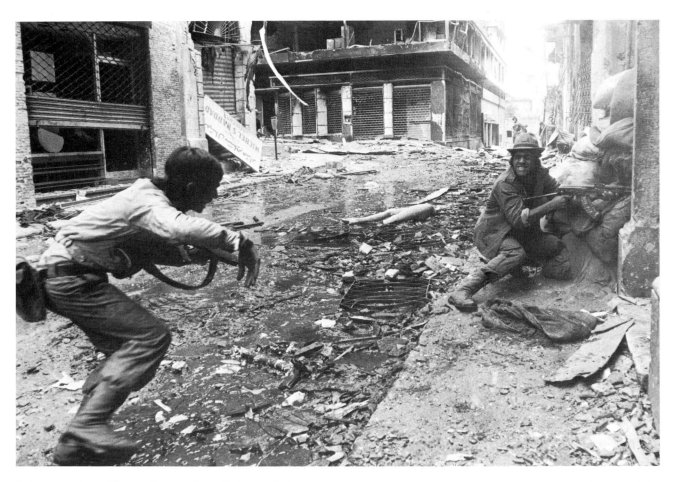

Falangist sniper killing a Progressist militiaman, Lebanon, 1976. *Catherine Leroy.*

But the danger was constant and inescapable. 'On one occasion I saw a group of Falangists occupying a house; the Progressists who defended it had just surrendered, and the next minute the surviving men were summarily shot. The women and children, crying and screaming, were cringing in a doorway and I ran towards them in order to photograph them. The Falangist who was pushing them all into a corner saw me take a picture and the next moment he was beside me, pointing a gun at me, clearly saying: "You shoot another picture and I shoot you." I assured him that I did not take a picture and certainly had no intention of taking any more. Thank god, he believed me, but this was really a close one.

'One of the secrets of my life has been that I am extremely lucky, but also that I have never tried to get involved in the conflicts I photographed. In any case, there is little one can do. I did break my rule on one occasion in Beirut. I tried to intercede and was told merely to mind my own business. They let me stay, they told me, were kind to me and fed me, but their war was their business. I tried to keep it that way.'

McCullin had been in Beirut for nearly a week, photographing the street fighting, when the atrocities in the Quarantina district began to come to light. But

by then he decided that he had had enough and left by taxi for Damascus. It took him nearly four days to get back to London.

McCullin's stay was short, and he concentrated on the Falangist area: Catherine Leroy, who came a little later, stayed nearly eighteen months, during which she worked mainly on the Progressist side. She too saw clearly how dangerous Beirut was to work in. She always had the feeling that she could easily get shot in the back – she was once, fortunately not too accurately.

At first she tried to cover both sides, but soon it became too dangerous to pass from one side to the other. In September she took a picture in front of the Falangist headquarters of a Muslim hostage being brutally beaten on the back at a time when the Falangists were denying that they took hostages. As a result her camera was snatched, but she managed to switch films and gave the soldiers the wrong one. When her pictures were published, the Falangists put a price on her head. From then on she worked with the Palestinians.

Although she carried Palestinian accreditation, on many occasions it was of little use. It was necessary to acquire friends among the leaders. Catherine managed to make a number of contacts in her eighteen-month stay and came to be accepted quite readily. Even so she was nearly killed on a number of occasions. One of these was when a mortar hit a car not far from the Palestinian militia headquarters. She rushed out with some of the

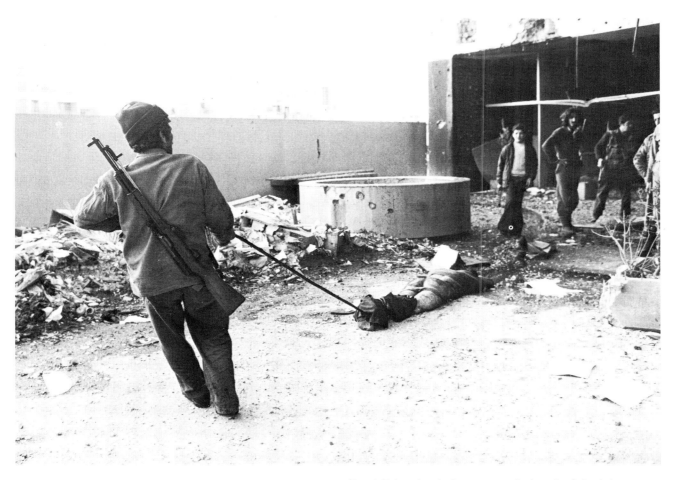

militiamen, and started to photograph it. A crowd of some fifty people gathered. She was suddenly seized from behind by a young Progressist who pressed a 45-mm calibre pistol to her temple and threatened to shoot her. Fortunately a militiaman who knew her managed to distract the attention both of her attacker and the by now hostile crowd, and rescue her.

In spite of her tiny stature, Catherine seems to have an inexhaustible supply of courage. On yet another occasion she found herself with some other photographers in a little street 100 yards from the Hilton Hotel, which had been captured by the Progressists only a few days before. A small tank, snatched by the Palestinians from the Lebanese Army, was parked in front of the hotel and a young man came out and jumped into it. Just at that moment a rocket burst near the top of the tank. The young man, apparently unhurt but rather shaken, began to climb out. Catherine started to shoot, using a 200-mm telephoto lens. Some militiamen immediately order her and the other photographers to stop. The others obeyed and started to walk up the road towards a sandbag barricade, but Catherine disregarded the order and continued shooting until she had finished the sequence. Only then did she begin to walk away quite slowly. It was clear that the militiamen were becoming angry and the other photographers, safe at the top of the street, urged her to run, but she still continued to walk. It was when one of the Palestinians raised his

Dead Falangists being removed after the fall of the Holiday Inn, Lebanon, 1976. *Catherine Leroy.*

Kalishnikov and sent a spurt of bullets towards her that she finally got the message. She says she has never sprinted a faster 100 yards in her life.

All the correspondents and photographers remember Beirut as suffused with a feeling of strangeness, an ominous oppressiveness, as if an evil cloud were hanging over the city. The scene which etched itself most clearly in Catherine Leroy's mind took place a day or so after her narrow escape. The Hilton had just fallen and stood empty and gutted, the streets deserted, the windows of the shops and elegant boutiques gaping and bare after the looting. Dummies from the fashion stores were lying in the street, some shot to pieces, heads torn by bullets, trunks slashed, limbs broken and distorted. Many houses were still smouldering and the manholes of the sewers, often ajar, emitted the odour of rancid food and decaying bodies. The whole scene was bleak and desolate. Catherine was standing outside the skeleton of the Hilton with a journalist, Bernard Estade, when they suddenly noticed in the middle of the road a young man with the inevitable Kalishnikov. A red flower was stuck in its barrel. He created such a contrast to the rest of the scene that Catherine instinctively started to take pictures. The moment he spotted her photographing him, he

187

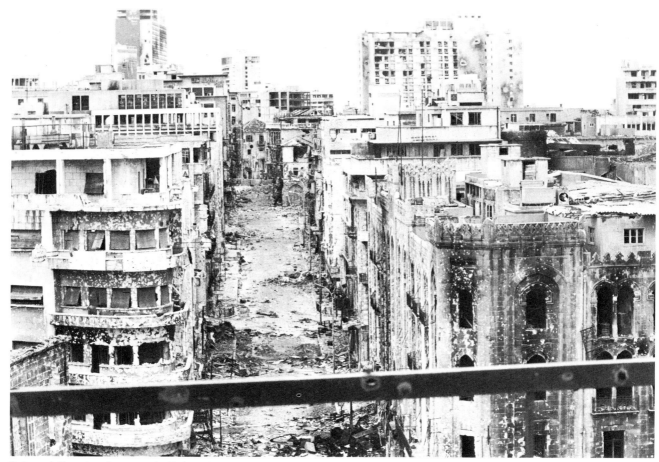

Ruins of Rue des Basques in Beirut, Lebanon, 1976.
A. Mingan.

advanced towards her and lowered the gun to a shooting position with the unmistakable gesture – you shoot, I shoot. In moments like that, Catherine says, one does nothing; one just waits.

'We showed him our accreditation papers and Bernard knew a few words in Arabic while the gunman knew a few in French. Soon the mood of threat visibly relaxed, but he ordered us to follow him. We crossed a few passages and corridors and came to an inner court, normally a parking place. Now there were no cars, but instead five bodies of Falangists. The young Palestinian proudly posed himself in front of the bodies and demanded to have his picture taken. All five bodies, as was quite normal in the Lebanon, had their trousers down and testicles cut off. It was a common thing in this terrible war that people not only killed each other, they had to castrate their opponents as well, often when they were still alive. I had always refused to photograph these mutilated bodies. But here, this proud young killer, his five war trophies, their mutilated bodies and the flower in the barrel of his gun, it seemed like a symbol, or perhaps an epitaph, of this inhuman war.'

NORTHERN IRELAND

If our definition of war be confined only to those major confrontations in which armies face each other along a front line, as in the First World War, or meet in a series of violent headlong clashes, as in the Second World War, then virtually none of the conflicts since 1945, with the possible exception of Korea, would be included in this book. Not even the Vietnam War, for it was fought by guerilla units on the ground, while death rained down from impersonal planes on an anonymous enemy. But if the designation 'war' be given to any encounter between two factions who hate each other sufficiently to kill indiscriminately, then even Northern Ireland is sufficiently qualified for inclusion.

In comparison with the other conflicts, Northern Ireland is no more than a ripple on a pond – in terms of the statistics, it is almost non-existent. But it is seemingly endless. Other wars flare up and subside. In Ireland no truce or meaningful armistice can be signed – there are no real 'armies' to disarm. The Northern Irish armies are the ordinary people, who eat breakfast in their homes and, whatever their sect, go to church to worship on a Sunday. In between, they carry on a campaign of hatred and violence which seems to have no limit, no solution.

opposite: Petrol bomber waiting for RUC charge, Londonderry, *circa* 1970. *Clive Limpkin.*

188

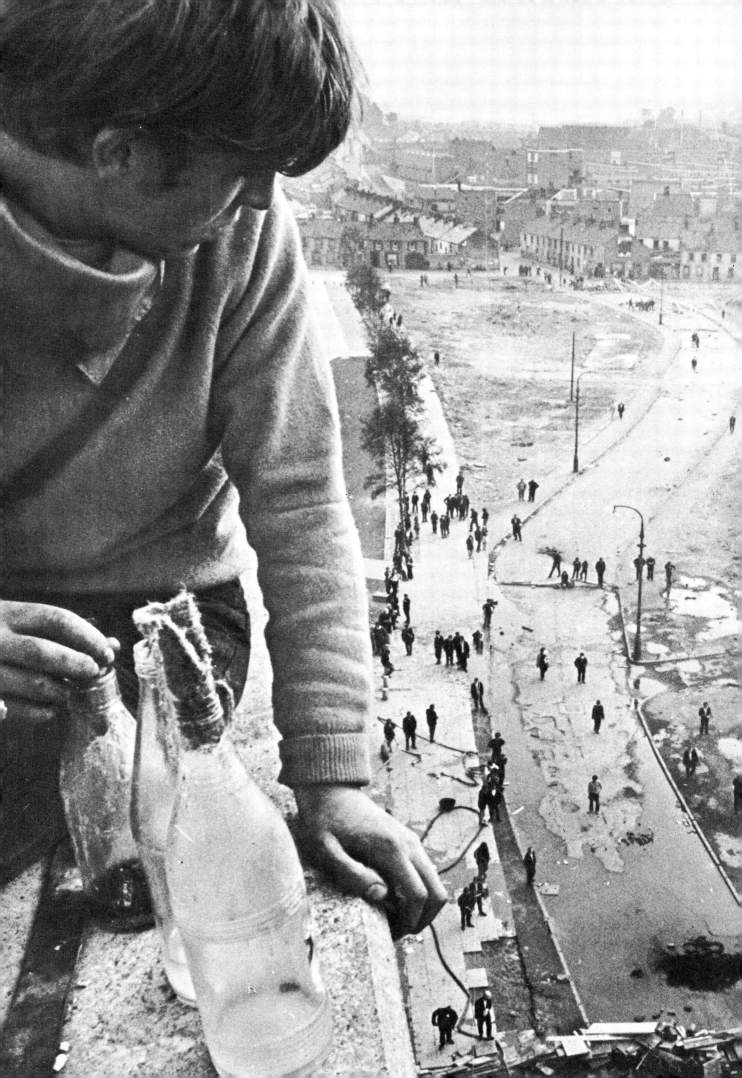

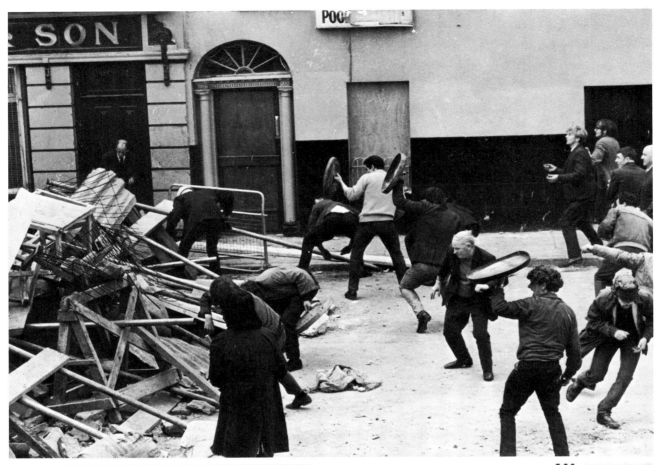

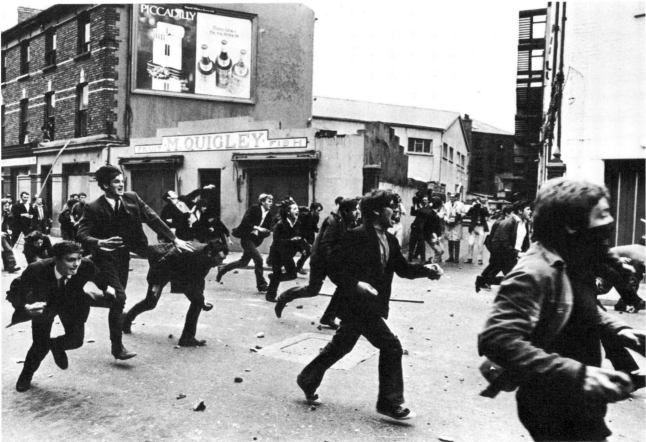

190

Clive Limpkin, one of the most regular photographers of the Northern Ireland disturbances, says that what frightened and perturbed him most during his many years of coverage of the Ulster clashes was not so much the armed skirmishes, petrol bombs or samurai-like charges of helmeted Royal Ulster Constabulary, but rather the matter-of-fact attitude of parents to boys taking part in the fighting. One could often hear mothers and fathers in the Bogside area of Londonderry calling their sons home: 'Why the hell are you not home yet? I told you to be in bed by seven.' Not a word about throwing stones, or swearing, or taunting the other side; not even anxiety about the possible risk of being maimed by a rubber bullet. Just a normal call home, as if the constant fighting did not exist. It was not that they approved their sons' violence, but that they tolerated it, accepted it as normal.

In some sense the Ulster war was, and still is, a war of children and adolescents, condoned and often re-inforced by the grown-ups. The hate has grown so deep that it permeates all age groups, in both the Catholic and Protestant communities, facing one another across a street. As Limpkin tells us: 'Though the problem began centuries ago, it survives today because bigotry, persecution and mistrust have been handed down to each successive generation with the fervour that only religion can create. The children learn to hate before they've learnt to read.'

Bogside is a Catholic ghetto of Derry (as Londonderry is called by the Catholics). Built on a marshy bog, it houses most of the poorer Catholics. Over the years it has been kept under constant surveillance by the Protestant Royal Ulster Constabulary (the R U C) who are renowned for their ruthlessness and brutality towards Catholics. Derry – 'A divided city, in a divided Ulster, in a divided Ireland.' The twelfth of August is a sacred day for all Protestants of Ulster, but particularly in Derry. For it was there that thirteen apprentice boys held out at the Ferryquay Gate on the city's walls against the French and Irish Catholic armies of James II nearly 300 years ago. Each year thousands of Ulstermen commemorate this event by a parade with flags and fifes and drums. On 12 August 1969, after a turbulent spring and summer, the Protestant marchers were met by the long-suffering Catholics of the Bogside and five days of bloody street fighting erupted.

Clive Limpkin was in Derry by chance. The staff photographer on the *Daily Sketch* originally commissioned to cover the march had fallen ill, and Limpkin

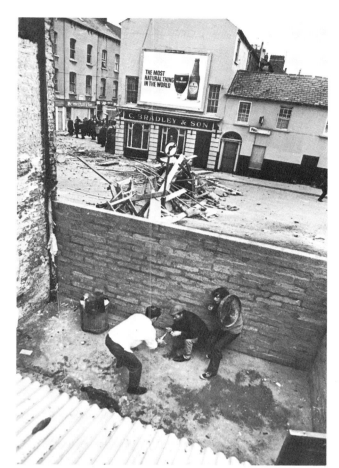

A petrol bomb being lit, Londonderry, *circa* 1969. *Clive Limpkin.*

was chosen to replace him. In the next three years he made no less than twenty trips to Northern Ireland.

It would be hard to find a more testing assignment than the Ulster troubles. To cover Belfast is like trying to be in the right place in London. The bombing and street fighting can break out anywhere and the photographer is invariably on the scene too late. 'All he is left with is a kind of mock-up of the incident – a picture of a dead kid on a mantlepiece or sweeping up rubble in the street. It used to depress me so much,' Limpkin recalls. 'No front lines there where you can go, take a few pictures and come back again later.' Limpkin decided not to waste his time in Belfast. If his paper mentioned that there was to be a protest march or demonstration in the city, he would ask them to hand it to Pacemaker Press, an experienced local agency with many contacts.

Instead, he would hire a car and drive to Derry, in north-western corner of Northern Ireland, a stone's throw from the border with the Republic. He always stayed in Buncrana, just across the border, a beautiful little town on the sea, where 'one could have dinner at night, overlooking a picturesque creek and forget about everything.' But every afternoon he would go to Derry, for in Derry there exists the convenient facility

191

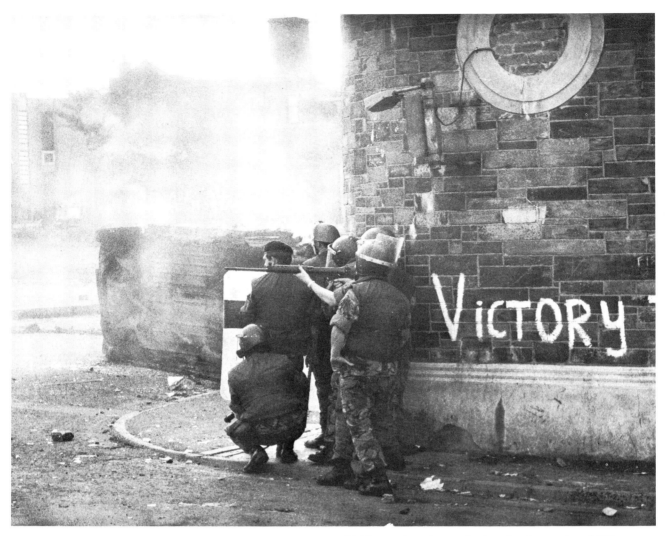

of an 'aggro corner' – where the Catholic Bogside meets the Protestant city – and there it would all start daily. Limpkin would station himself near the aggro-corner, where William Street runs into Roscoe Street, right in the centre of the town. There was never any shortage of action. The sport was regular, for every day after school and every Sunday afternoon, the kids would come out and start swearing at the 'enemy' on the other side. Soon this would be followed by a few stones, then some older men would appear, bigger stones would start sailing over the walls, the swearing would build up to a crescendo, and human nature would do the rest.

Limpkin recalls: 'The pattern was always the same. Some Sunday afternoons, with the soldiers stationed in readiness, it would be a little late in starting if there was a good western on the telly. But once the film was over, the routine procedure would get going as usual.' In spite of the presence of the RUC and soldiers, there were not many casualties.

The toll of constant fighting could be seen in the whole area. 'Slowly the houses and even streets started to disappear, burned down by arson and petrol bombs. On one of my trips I chanced to get chased by a

RUC patrol at the ready, Londonderry, *circa* 1970. *Terry Fincher.*

Protestant mob and a woman helped me to hide. On the next trip over there, a few months later, I wanted to thank her. But when I came to the spot, her house was no more – burned down completely.'

By and large there was little danger in covering the Ulster fighting. In his three years of regular visits to Derry, Limpkin was only once threatened seriously. He remembers the amazement of some of the French photographers (among them Gilles Caron, who later disappeared in Vietnam) who also discovered Derry. It was so easy to walk among the RUC and soldiers photographing at will. All one had to do was keep an eye on the sky – it was from there that the arcing petrol bombs would come.

Limpkin made a deliberate point of never fraternizing with either side, with the result that no one there knew him and he was able to remain anonymous. He also tried to maintain an unbiased, balanced coverage. On the whole he succeeded, but in his book, *The Battle of Bogside*, his heart does appear to be, ever so slightly,

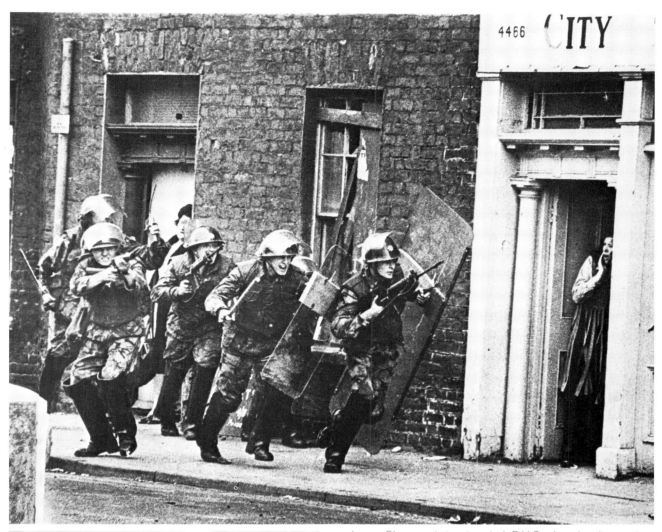

above: Charge of the dreaded RUCs, Londonderry, *circa* 1971. *Don McCullin*.

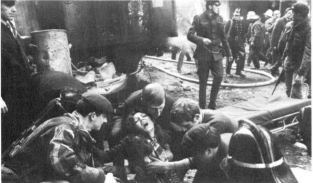

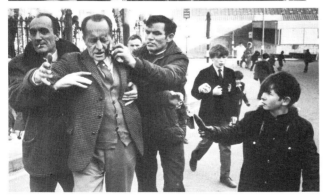

on the side of the poor Catholics. So far as he himself is concerned, he feels that he revealed this bias only once.

'I was among a Catholic crowd, photographing along William Street, when suddenly a voice next to me said, "Move over, we are going to open up with a Thompson on those bastards down there by the swimming pool." I saw instantly that the voice was referring to three soldiers standing in the distance and I moved to one side focusing my long lens on them. Suddenly I realized that I was just waiting for them to be shot. I knew it was my duty to shout to them, "Get out of the way, they're trying to kill you," but I did nothing. It was the only time I felt compromised. I don't think I would have endangered myself had I shouted, but it probably would have made my job more difficult later. Still, there it is and had they been killed, I wonder how I should have felt. The Thompson went off, missed,

left: Two casualties of the civil war; one the result of a bomb, the other a victim of a rubber bullet. Northern Ireland, 1972. *Abbas*.

193

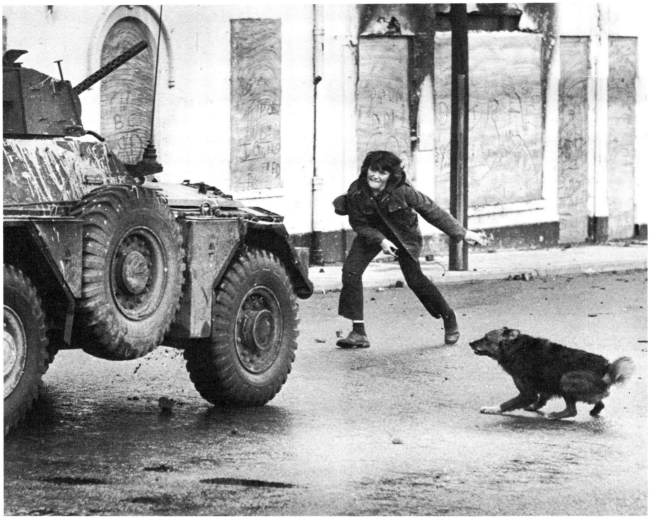

Hatred. Londonderry, *circa* 1972. *Clive Limpkin.*

and the soldiers dived for cover. In a situation like that one does not think straight – all one thinks is, "I may get wonderful pictures" – and that's the tragedy of it.'

Limpkin still occasionally goes to Northern Ireland, when sent by his present employers, the *Sun*. But it is a rare event. The British public have grown tired of Northern Ireland and its troubles; the confrontations in Derry and elsewhere no longer hit the headlines. The last time a soldier was killed there, *The Times* gave three lines to the story. Other wars get settled and a peace treaty is signed – in Northern Ireland no hope of a secure peace exists.

The troubles in Ulster are in the nature of a horrifying family affair. Limpkin's photographs taken over the years in the streets of Londonderry could be mounted in a family album, charting the violent growing-up pains of a boy in his home environment, progressing from mildly aggressive behaviour to stone throwing, to petrol bombs, to guns. The one ray of hope for this family war comes from the families themselves, for it is the women of Ulster, both Protestant and Catholic, who are leading the movement for peace.

The war photographer is now accepted, a recognized figure in modern war. Provision is made for him, facilities are laid at his disposal. He can move quickly, arriving on the spot within a matter of hours. Technically, his freedom to record in depth is virtually unlimited with the advent of lightweight 35-mm cameras, telephoto lenses, and high-speed films. He can shoot in the front line with the soldiers or he can record the impact of war on the non-combatants. What he reveals will be seen by millions. Through his pictures, we see what war is, in all its aspects. By his involvement, we too become involved. The culmination of his art is found in the photographs of the war in Vietnam.

Part Five

INTENSE EXPLORER

Vietnam

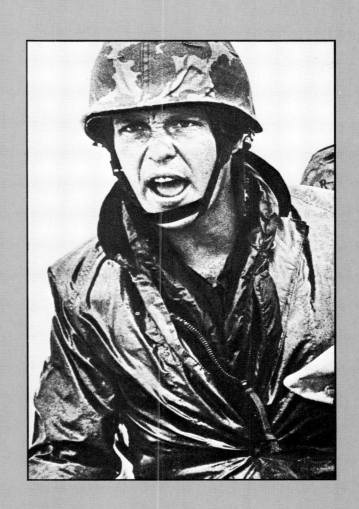

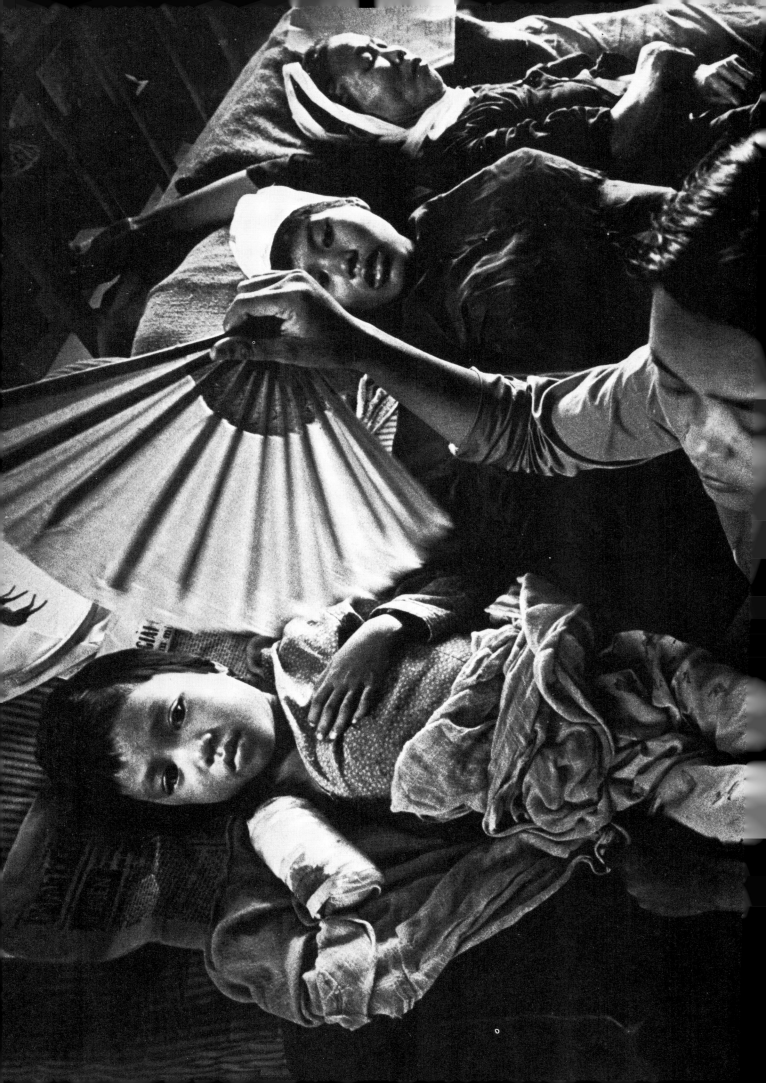

A War in Close-Up

The war in Vietnam started in the early sixties, so from a chronological point of view it should have appeared earlier in this book, as one of the civil wars perhaps. And yet, in the context of the history of war photography, it must be singled out and dealt with on its own.

So far as the photographic coverage is concerned, there never was, and probably never will be, another war like Vietnam. Throughout its long duration not only were photographers and correspondents given absolute freedom but they were actively encouraged. Hotels, transport, and information services were laid on for them by the host warring nation. On occasions even, their fares were paid – just so that they could come, look and report. The Americans argued that in this way their own involvement would be reported world-wide in a favourable light. In effect they were trying to buy good notices, in the same way that a record company will provide free discs and the odd expense-account meal. Vietnam was a big production number, a big sell. This method worked for a while; the good press certainly outweighed the bad at the start, but in the end the whole sordid mess blew up in their faces.

The main point here is, however, that, whatever the reason, Vietnam was the freest war to cover. In other wars, for example the Yom Kippur War in Israel, the tendency was to clamp down, impose censorship, and make the life of a correspondent as difficult as possible; in Vietnam this was never the case. 'You from *Times in Timbuctoo* – have a helicopter and a girl interpreter' could be taken as the slogan of the American public relations' attitude to media people. There were occasional exceptions – some photographers, including Philip Jones Griffiths, were banned from returning to Vietnam after they had published material which

compromised the Americans. But on his first visit, as soon as the correspondent or photographer could produce evidence that he had a platform for his copy or his images – that they would be printed – he was accepted and on the whole was offered a great deal of assistance. For war photographers, Vietnam was in the nature of a 'promised land' which they are unlikely to find again.

There were other aspects of the coverage of the war in Vietnam which made it unique. The growing trend towards more violent images has already been noted in our discussion of the civil wars in Bangladesh and Lebanon. Its gestation period, indeed its birth, took place in Vietnam. Because of the USA's involvement in the war, the American media market – the largest in the world – of magazines, periodicals, newspapers, books and television provided the widest platform ever for the publication of pictures of the war throughout its long duration. The public became satiated on a strong diet of war images, and the press responded by providing a stronger fare of yet more violent imagery to satisfy their audience, seemingly hungry for greater thrills.

The photographer, the maker of the images, found himself in the position of being expected to comply with the demand. There is no intention to suggest here that this stooping to public demand, in effect supplying thrills for the populace in the form of sickening pictures of war, was a deliberate policy of all modern war photographers. It simply is not the case. Many photographers remain idealists. They try to fight violence in the future by showing how horrifying and despicable it is. They may feel, however, that with twenty years of seeing war pictures at the breakfast table, the public needs ever stronger pictures to be shocked out of its complacency. Others, less scrupulous however, do just shovel up dirt and horror because it sells well, because the demand is there. But whatever the intentions behind the trend, whether they be well meant or base, the fact remains that the pictures shot in Vietnam were turned into a means of exploitation. They ceased to be a documentary record of events and

A few hours later this woman, her child and all the inhabitants of this village were killed by the Americans. Vietnam, *circa* 1968. *Philip Jones Griffiths.*

Viet Cong captives in Mecong Delta, Vietnam, 1963. *Larry Burrows.*

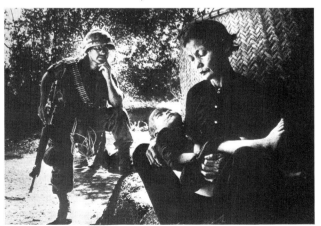

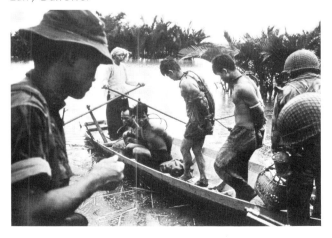

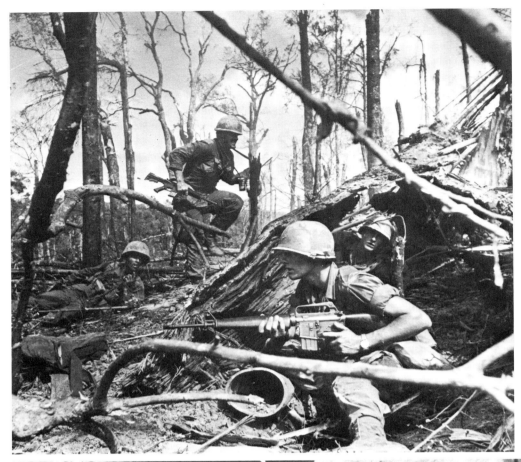

left: A typical example of the photographer's ability to stay close to the action, Vietnam, 1968. *Gilles Caron.*

opposite: Viet Cong prisoner, Vietnam, *circa* 1965. *Paul Schutzer.*

below: Water torture treatment for a Viet Cong suspect, Vietnam, *circa* 1964. *Okamura.*

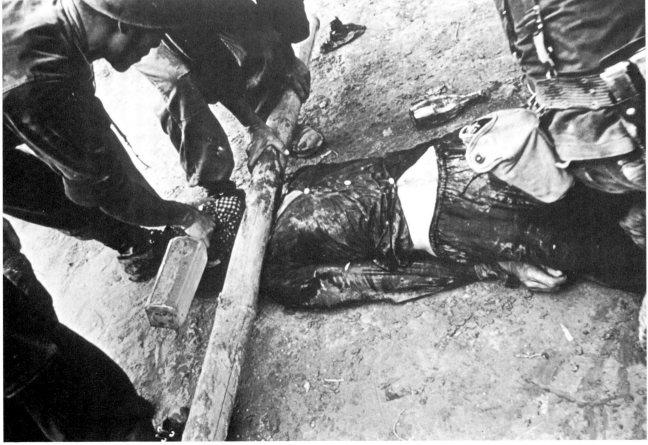

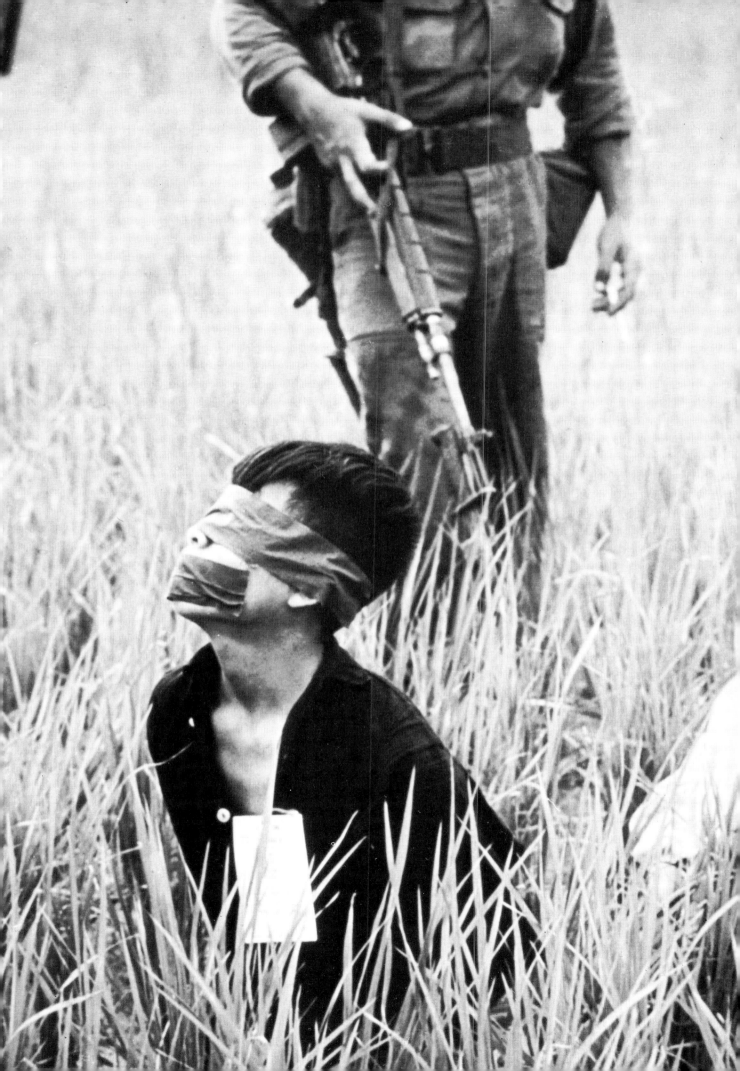

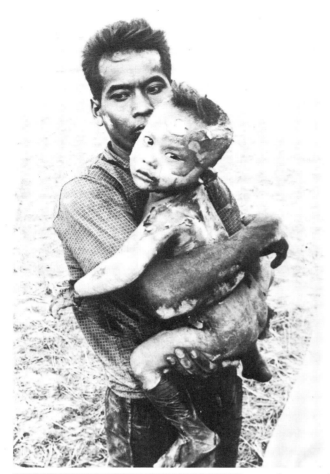

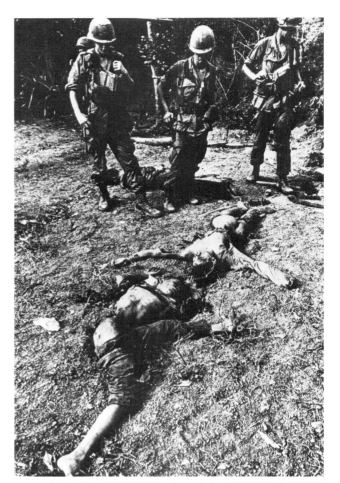

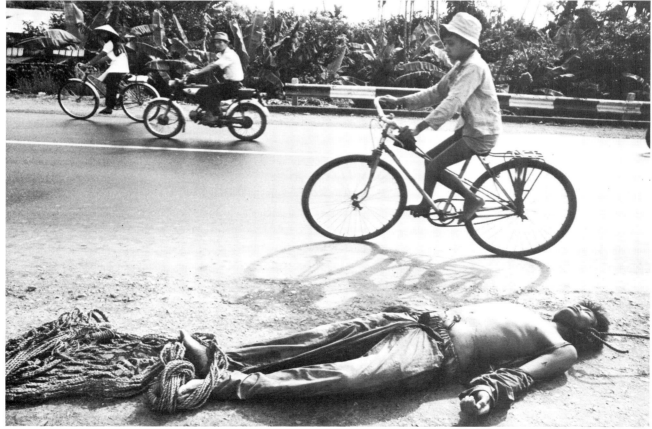

200

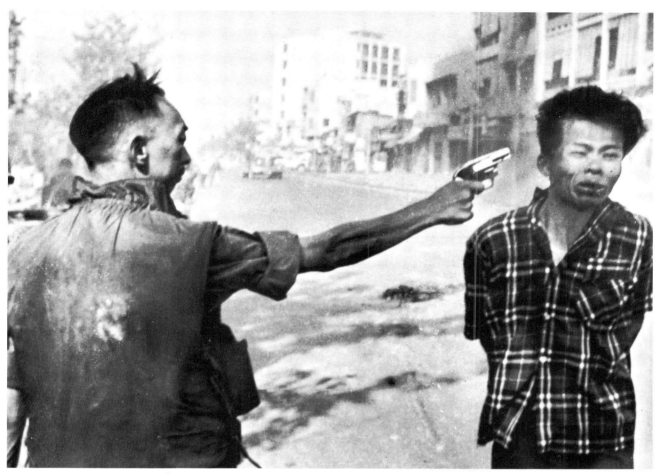

above: Vietnamese general executing a Viet Cong.
Vietnam, 1968. *Eddy Adams.*

became a commodity in themselves – for good or evil
purposes.

This new tendency for war photography to be
undertaken to satisfy extrinsic market demands rather
than for intrinsic reasons – aesthetic or documentary –
is in part a result of the improvement in the quality of
the photographs themselves, for technically the photographer is now capable of achieving more or less
whatever effect he desires. But in the main it is the
inevitable corollary of the omnipresence, the ubiquity
of war in our time. Vietnam contributed to this state
and provided us with more than its share of pictures of
a shocking or atrocious nature.

There is yet another aspect which has to be considered which contributed to the importance of the
Vietnam War in the history of photography. With the

opposite top left: Child covered with napalm burns held
by his father, Vietnam, *circa* 1967. *Horst Faas.*

opposite top right: U S 25th Infantry placed divisional
insignia in the mouths of the victims, Vietnam, *circa*
1967. *Philip Jones Griffiths.*

opposite bottom: Indifference to the dead, Vietnam, *circa*
1973. *Abbas.*

exception of W. Eugene Smith and George Rodger,
both of whom refused to photograph any more wars,
all the greatest living war photographers came to
Vietnam at one time or another. Because of the
importance of the war itself and because of the sheer
volume of images it provided, Vietnam helped to raise
war photography to a new status. We can look back to
the pictures of the war in the Pacific by W. E. Smith and
Duncan's photographs of Korea as the starting point,
but it was in the images of Vietnam that the relatively
new medium of war photography attained the status of a
recognized art form. Vietnam provided for McCullin,
Burrows, Griffiths, Duncan, Leroy and many others
the chance to achieve something more than mere
records of fighting. It helped to create a new style, a
new visual awareness; it helped to produce icons,
symbols of the terrifying essence of war. Many
photographers were given the opportunity to analyse
and dissect, and thereby to understand, the nature of
their work in relation to the war itself, and their depth
of understanding and compassion enabled the public
in general to see the deeper strata of man's emotions as
well as his inhumanity. This introspection and the
insights it engendered led to the Vietnam War being a
stage for intense exploration, for looking at war with
an even more penetrating eye. War photography
started with a cautious glance from a safe distance; it
ends with a keen gaze through a microscope.

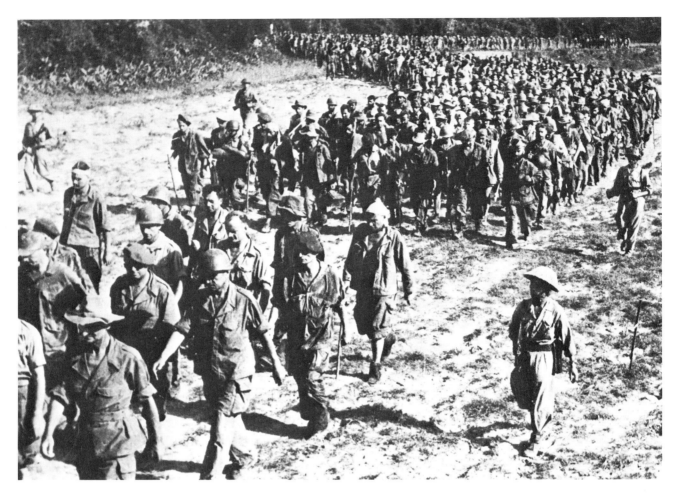

The remains of the French garrison march into captivity, Dien Bien Phu, 1954. *Daniel Camus.*

The Prologue - Indochina

The strange and unreal siege of Dien Bien Phu, which ended with the surrender of the French on 7 May 1954, marked the close of a seven-year struggle in Indochina. It was, to all intents and purposes, a classic confrontation between the colonial power of France, exhausted and not yet fully recovered from the ravages of the Second World War, but anxious to re-establish her lost prestige, and the Vietnamese insurgents with their communist-inspired militant nationalism. The Viet Minh, the League for the Independence of Vietnam, under the leadership of the communist-trained Ho Chi Minh, pitted themselves against French troops in a protracted guerilla campaign. The war dragged on interminably; the flower of the French Military Academy of St Cyr, constantly foiled and outwitted by the tactics of the Vietnamese, liberally soaked the Indochinese soil with their blood.

The battle for Dien Bien Phu, which was supposed to end the war decisively, was a courageous but ill-conceived gamble. A French regiment was parachuted into the centre of enemy-held territory in the north west of Vietnam in an attempt to lure into battle and destroy the guerilla forces of the Viet Minh. Instead, the venture turned into a 169-day siege, until the French were finally blasted out by Vietnamese artillery brought on the backs of peasants all the way from China.

The long struggle which lead up to Dien Bien Phu was hardly reported at all. The attention of the press was focused on the Korean War. But the siege of Dien Bien Phu brought an invasion by the press, although the battle itself was extremely difficult to cover from the outside. It was 100 miles from Hanoi, and with Vietnamese anti-aircraft fire daily gaining strength and accuracy, a flight to the battle area was a very hazardous mission indeed. Only one photographer managed to get through, a French paratrooper, Daniel Camus, but his pictures show little of the dreadful conditions and the final humiliation of the French crack troops.

But the fall of Dien Bien Phu served to bring the war and Indochina to the world's attention, and a number of photographers and correspondents stayed on to record and report the winding up of the French involvement. One of them was Robert Capa.

John Mecklin, a Time/Life correspondent who worked with Capa in Indochina, tells the story of Capa's last assignment. They both came to Indochina during the siege. As no pictures by Capa of the siege exist, presumably neither of them managed to get near the beleaguered garrison. But they stayed on after the

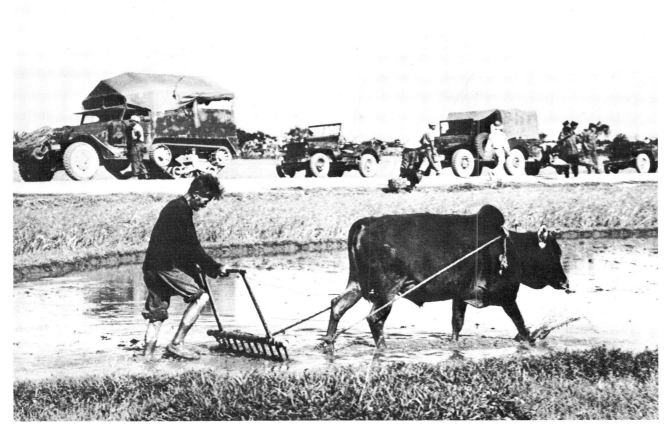

surrender and on 25 May were working together in the Red River delta during the last stages of the French occupation. The cease-fire was to be signed in Geneva seven days later.

Capa was anxious to shoot a story which he had tentatively entitled 'Bitter Rice', a picture essay showing the contrast between the inhuman war machines of the modern army of occupation and the peaceful pursuits of the peasants quietly tending their rice fields – a parable of life and death. The column of French soldiers with which they were travelling was constantly being halted by Viet Minh ambushes and attacks. On one of these enforced stops, about 45 miles from Hanoi, near Thai Binh, Capa, bored with the slow progress and impatient as usual, decided to walk ahead.

Half an hour later a soldier came up to the column and said something in Vietnamese to one of the officers. The officer then approached the jeep in which the correspondents were travelling and said: 'Le photographe est mort.' Capa had stepped on an anti-personnel bomb while walking at the side of the road. He was rushed to a nearby hospital where a Vietnamese doctor, having confirmed that he was dead, asked: 'Is he the first American correspondent killed in Indochina?' When he received the confirmatory answer, he added: 'It is a harsh way for the Americans to learn.' The doctor's words were to prove prophetic. In the

One of the last pictures taken by the photographer before his death by a mine, Indochina, 1954. *Robert Capa.*

years to come, the world and the Americans themselves found that they were to take a long time learning.

The Enactment – Vietnam

The Vietnam war was a war fought 'for the minds of men'. With France, a useful buffer in Indochina, out of the way, China was spreading its communist tentacles even wider. The United States, therefore, decided that a stand should be made, not so much for military bases, but rather to prevent the total spread of communist ideology in Asia and instead to plant the seeds of democratic materialism. Unfortunately, although the Americans never lacked for an abundance of material goods – guns and butter – they were singularly lacking in tact and finesse. The Vietnamese, for their part, were quite willing to accept all that they were given, but they were far less inclined to swallow the ideology and western values that were served along with the abundant goods. The two cultures – brash western and gentle eastern – had no common meeting-point, no way of communicating.

Both ended by disdaining and despising each other. To the Americans, the Vietnamese – whether the

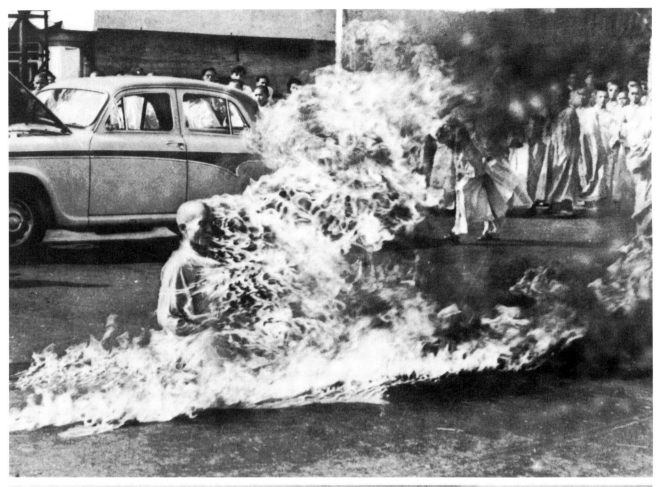

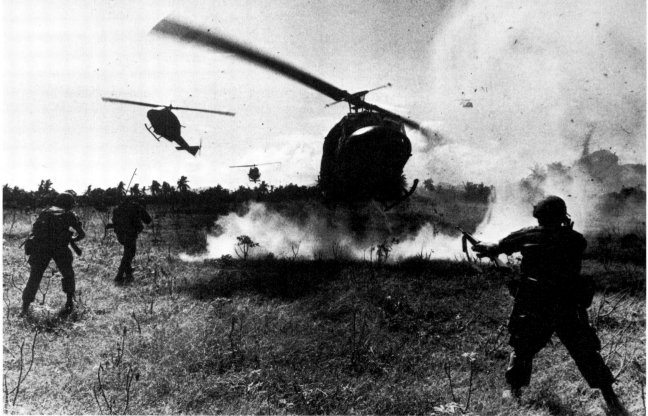

Americans' allies in the south or their enemies in the north – were simply 'gooks', 'dinks', 'slopes', with no more human attributes than a donkey; to the Vietnamese, the Americans were all soft-touch barbarians that one 'conned' but did not invite home. The Americans never did find the key to the Vietnamese mind. They tried very hard indeed at first, but when no signs of any success could be discerned, their approach became more aggressive and desperate. Finally a totally grotesque situation was reached with the US Marines indiscriminately killing friend and foe alike on the pretext of saving them from an evil worse than the napalm bomb. My Lai and other atrocities were the invitable outcome.

The extent of the media coverage of the Vietnam war, both in words and pictures, was unprecedented. Its growth and intensity paralleled what became known as the 'escalation' of war activities. Up to 1960 the American military involvement was quite insignificant, at least in terms of manpower, and very carefully camouflaged. At the time only about 700 US advisers to the Vietnamese army were present, but this number grew rapidly and reached some 17 000 by the end of 1963. This increase again was played down and hardly reported. The first half of 1963 suddenly threw the Vietnamese arena into sharper relief, and the international press immediately took notice. In January the first real battle of the war took place, in Ap Bac, where three Americans were killed. Soon after, Buddhist opposition was highlighted by the dramatic and public immolation of a Buddhist monk, witnessed and photographed by Malcolm Browne of Associated Press. The American build-up of troops, especially helicopter pilots, began in earnest in 1964, and in February the following year, the bombings of Hanoi were ordered by President Johnson. A month later, detachments of Marines were regularly disembarking in Vietnam. Early in 1968 the number of troops reached and exceeded half a million.

In spite of the rapid intensification of the war and the extensive bombings, the Viet Cong staged the famous Tet offensive in February 1968, occupying and holding for a time a number of important points and cities in the South. The capacity of the North Vietnamese to survive all that was rained down on them by the most up-to-date American war methods, and still come back on the offensive, finally convinced the Americans that they were indeed fighting a losing battle. From the end of 1968, despite the additional flare-up of hostilities in Laos and Cambodia in 1970, the curve of American involvement began its downward trend, leading slowly to the January 1973 cease-fire and complete withdrawal.

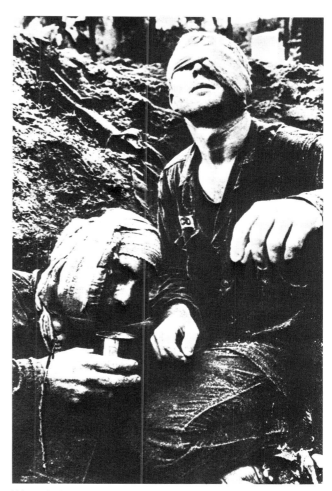

Wounded medic caring for an American soldier, Vietnam, 1966. *Henri Huet.*

The surge and ebb of the American military involvement was reflected in the number of correspondents and photographers in Vietnam. In 1961 there was only a handful of pressmen in the country, and this group remained small and fairly constant until 1963. Between 1963 and 1965 the press corps grew steadily, but it was largely confined to correspondents and photographers on short-term assignments. After 1965 there was a constant increase in the number of permanently resident journalists; by 1968 the reporting community had swelled to 700 people. Then this high-water mark slowly ebbed away – the number was 467 in 1969, 392 in 1970, 350 in 1971, until it fell to only sixty-nine by mid-1974. With the decline of the American war effort, the interest in Vietnam slowly subsided.

What attracted the vast number in the first place, apart from the interest in the war itself, was the freedom of reporting never before experienced and the complete lack of censorship. Whatever other faults the Americans displayed in Vietnam, they did not lack respect for freedom of the press. Correspondents might have been harassed at times, or in some cases not allowed entry visas, but once they were there, their work was never censored. Indeed, what the American authorities

205

attempted *vis-à-vis* the horde of pressmen from all over the world was not to check their copy or their films, but to convert them to the American cause by the most skilful and widespread public relations campaign ever mounted. Not only did they provide lodging, transport, meals, specially conducted tours and presents, but they also employed all kinds of more or less subtle inducements to win favourable copy. Appeals were made to the patriotism and loyalty of the American press representatives, and many smaller papers and some foreign correspondents were even helped financially to travel to Vietnam and report on the war.

But as with the Vietnamese population, where wooing had failed to convert, these methods also foundered in the long run. There were, indeed, a number of correspondents and photographers who took the bait and could not but feel a certain amount of gratitude for such lavish hospitality. Even if no reports were completely biased or falsified, much was concealed and glossed over for a considerable period. For example, the extent of corruption and graft among the US troops, their drug addiction and lax morals, their numerous instances of cruelty and savagery towards foe and allies alike.

The press appreciated their freedom. Accreditation was easy to obtain provided the correspondent or photographer could show that his work would be published and that he had some backing or support from a newspaper or magazine. Simple formalities were all that was needed to acquire a press card. After which the correspondent was free to go virtually wherever he or she pleased. The American servicemen were themselves acutely publicity conscious and would go to almost any lengths to secure a mention or a picture in print.

At no stage of the war was there a well-defined front line. Most of the fighting was sporadic and fairly unpredictable. But whenever there was a newsflash about a skirmish, a battle or planned sortie of either US or South Vietnamese detachments on a 'search and destroy' mission within a reasonable distance of Saigon, all a photographer had to do was go to a taxi rank, mostly of old American vehicles, and hire a cab for the day. This was common during the Tet offensive. Within an hour's taxi ride the photographer could hear the sounds of battle. When the fighting was farther away, he could get a lift in one of the numerous helicopters; there were also daily flights from Saigon to Danang in the northern theatre of operations with up to fifteen places a day reserved for the press corps. Helicopters were on permanent stand-by to fly pressmen virtually anywhere within a 100-mile radius of Saigon, provided that at least three people wanted to go to the same place. As the television crews consisted

Wounded Vietnamese soldier, Vietnam, 1972. *Abbas.*

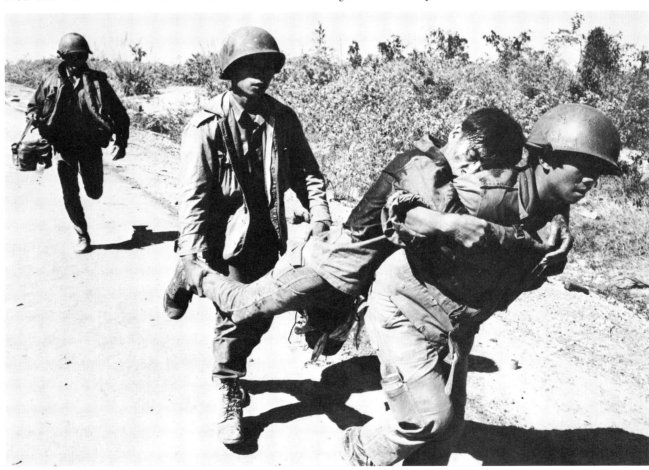

of a minimum of three people, a photographer could join them and find himself in the locality of his choice with relative ease. Such facilities were not just a matter of extravagant generosity on the part of the Americans, for by them they were able to obtain a great deal of publicity at a relatively low cost and also gain additional training for their pilots.

Because of the ease with which they could get to the fighting, writers and particularly photographers were exposed to considerable physical risks. Many died. Forty-five war correspondents were killed in Vietnam, and a further twenty were listed as missing, believed dead. Philip Jones Griffiths dedicated his book, *Vietnam Inc.*, to four close friends who lost their lives in the war: Larry Burrows, Henri Huet, Kyochi Sawada and Keisaburo Shomamoto. The fatalities most frequently occurred on the helicopter flights, but mines and snipers took their toll as well. In May 1968, while driving in a jeep near Cholon, five foreign correspondents encountered a detachment of Viet Cong who ignored the repeated shouts of 'Bao chi' (press) and opened fire with machine guns, according to the one survivor. The news of this cold-blooded killing made a great impression on the reporters; one United Press photographer, Charles Eggleston, armed himself the next day and went alone on a suicidal vendetta. He was never seen again, but apparently he did manage to kill several Viet Cong.

Despite the dangers, many photographers came to the war – lured by the excitement and the prospect of financial rewards. Many came as freelances, paying their own fares, or even hitch-hiked as Tim Page did. The majority found willing employers. Associated Press, one of half a dozen agencies which kept a permanent staff in Saigon, listed eight photographers in Vietnam during 1966, including three Vietnamese – Al Chang, Le Ngoe Cung, and Dan van Phnoe who served them for many years. Another of the AP photographers was Eddie T. Adams, who became famous with his picture of a Viet Cong being shot; Henri Huet, who died with Burrows in 1967, was employed by Associated Press. By 1969 the number of AP photographers had grown to ten, and included a woman, Yvonne Cornu. Their star performer was Horst Faas.

Faas spent eight years in Vietnam working for AP from 1962. He had a permanent base in Saigon and covered all the significant phases of the war. He received the Pulitzer Prize for his war pictures in the early period, as well as the Robert Capa Memorial Award in 1965. With his unemotional approach and totally professional attitude, Faas was an ideal war photographer for the magazines. His operations were always planned in detail. To gain the confidence of the

Father confronts the soldiers with his dead son, Vietnam, *circa* 1968. *Horst Faas.*

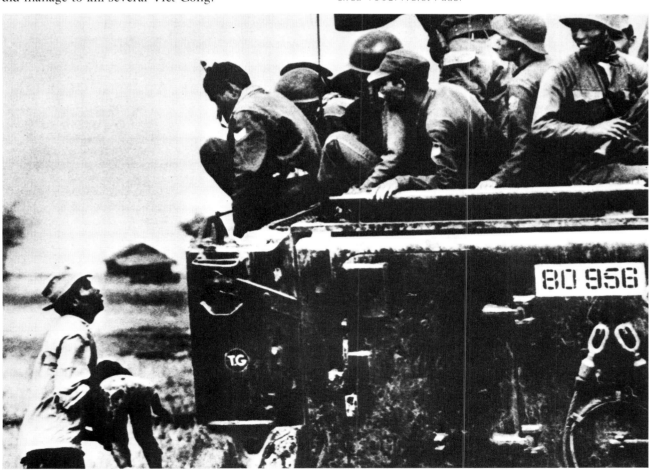

207

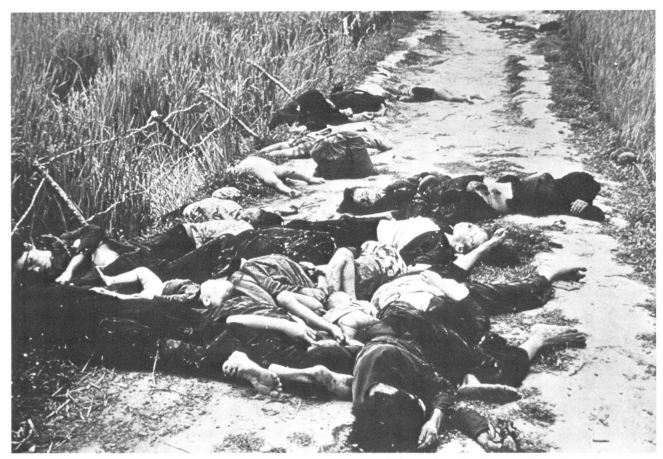

above and right: Victims of the My Lai massacre, Vietnam, 1968. *Ronald Haeberle.*

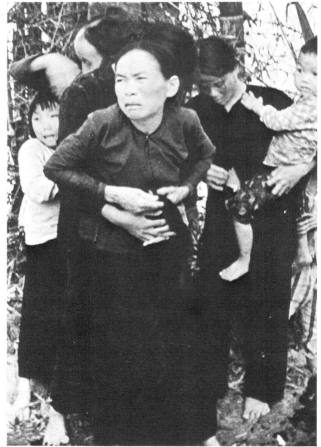

South Vietnamese soldiers and the civilian population, he used to carry a small polaroid camera and distribute instantaneous pictures. His dedication and profession-alism were exemplified by the way in which he would assess the fighting potential of the soldiers he chose to accompany. He invariably refused to go on missions with platoons he considered to be not entirely reliable either due to their lax discipline or slovenly behaviour. He always maintained that he did not mind taking necessary risks, but he never left anything to chance – not even his choice of battle companions. Like Larry Burrows, he designed for himself a special combat out-fit, which included a custom-made aluminium water-proof container for his 35-mm Leicas.

By 1966 Faas was in charge of the whole of the Associated Press outfit in Vietnam. He hired many young photographers as 'stringers', often local Vietnamese, and used them quite ruthlessly. He would buy their pictures, which they had frequently taken at great personal risk, for paltry amounts; the pictures were not even credited to the individual photographers on publication. He developed a depersonalized assembly-line method of picture production. In such a situation a certain amount of exploitation is perhaps inevitable. As, for example, when a negative is bought.

Usually, it is 'clipped' with the adjoining negatives on either side. How is a photographer to know that only the centre negative will be used? Perhaps too protracted a contact with death and danger does change a man. One cannot escape the notion that the brave, tough war photographer, Horst Faas, developed a hardened attitude, especially towards enemy soldiers whom he came to hate and disdain. Whether he was able to maintain a balanced, unprejudiced viewpoint at the same time is debatable.

Such cynicism was prevalent among many of the correspondents, and also among the majority of American soldiers. Philip Knightley quotes John Shaw, a war correspondent: 'Things which shocked you when you first went there six weeks later slide over you.' The process of dehumanizing the enemy reached such an extreme that a 'gook' was no longer a human being but a thing – a big hunt trophy. Knightley quotes many terrifying instances: heads cut off and arranged in decorative patterns, parts of bodies preserved as souvenirs, even lampshades made of skin. Collecting 'interesting' snapshots of dead or dying Viet Cong became a hobby with some G Is. Marines were photographed posing with one foot on the chest of a dead enemy. Killing became a distorted game. Specially printed visiting cards were left on bodies: 'Congratu-

Battlefield near Con Thien, Vietnam, 1967. *David Douglas Duncan.*

lations – you have been killed through courtesy of the 361st' or 'Call us for death and destruction, day or night'. This practice was applied equally to the bodies of women and children.

Not too fine a distinction was made between armed soldiers of the Viet Cong and peasants who might simply have been North Vietnamese sympathizers. Philip Jones Griffiths relates in his book how he went on one of the notorious 'search and destroy' raids with a detachment of inexperienced and rather nervous young soldiers. The moment then saw the figure of a Vietnamese farmer in the distance, they fired and missed. 'The next farmer was not so lucky. Soon he lay dying among the ripening rice in a corner of the paddy field, the back of his skull blown away. He was somewhat conscious, making a whimpering sound and trying to squeeze his eyes more tightly shut. He never spoke and died with the fingers of his left hand clutching his testicles so tightly they could not be undone. "Got him in the balls, knew I hit him," cried the boy from Kansas, until someone took him to one side and explained that they do that to relieve the pain from elsewhere.'

The most publicized example of such wanton, senseless killing was the My Lai massacre. The execution of some 120 civilians, mostly women and children, in the village of My Lai on 16 May 1968 by officers and twenty-four men of C Company, 1st Battalion, 20th Infantry, 11th Brigade, was recorded

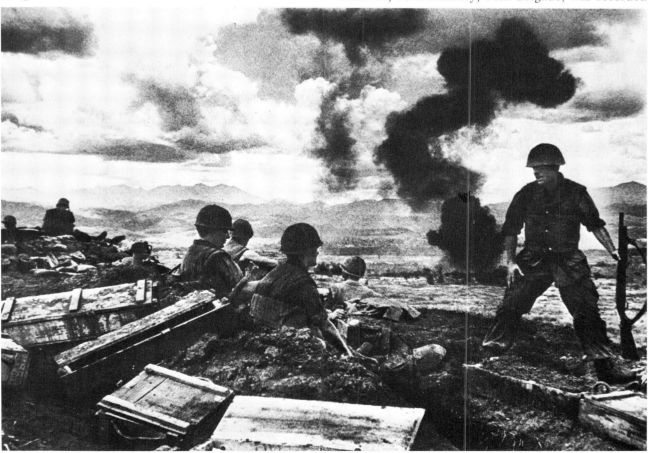

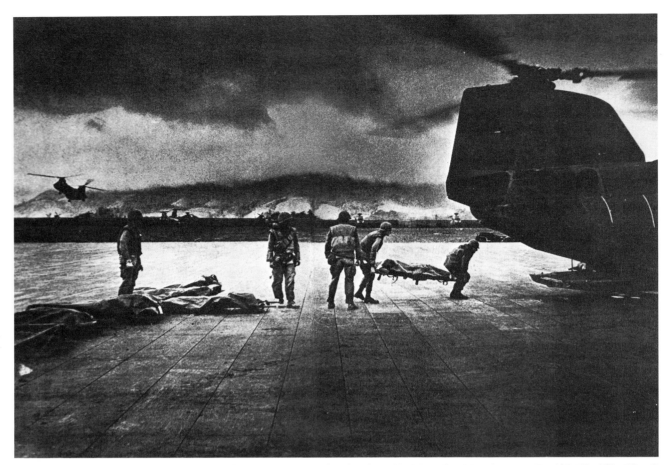

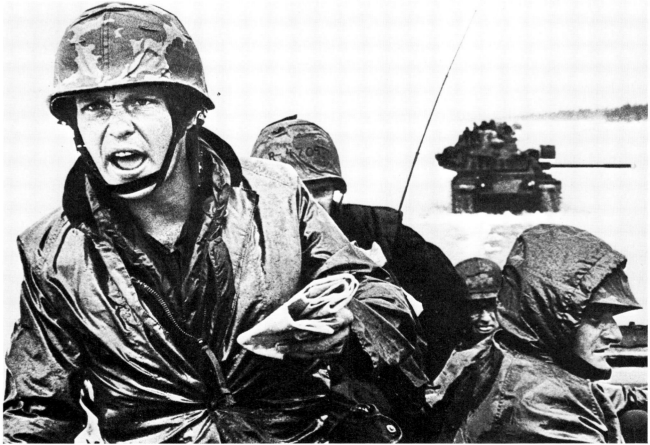

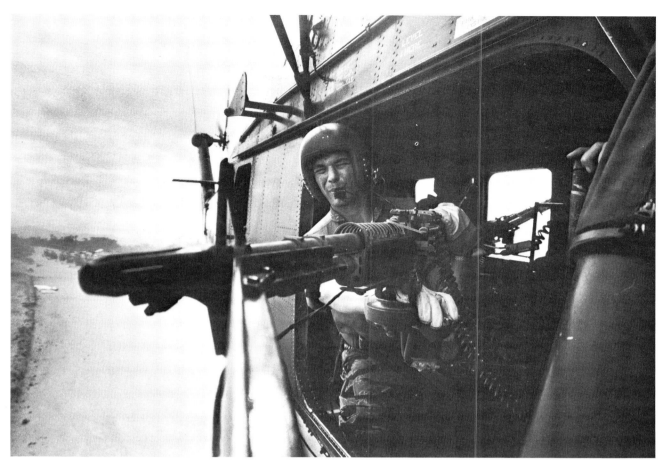

above and right: A ride in the Yankee 13 helicopter. During the flight one of the crew was killed. Vietnam, 1965. *Larry Burrows.*

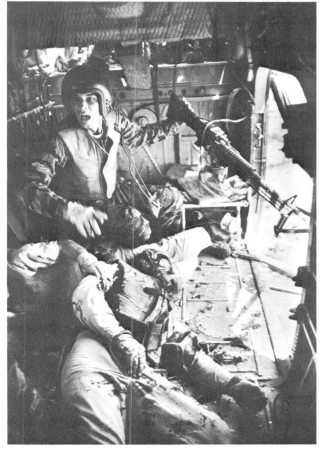

by an army photographer, one Ronald L. Haeberle, of the 31st Public Information Department. On 16 May, Haeberle was carrying three cameras and was using both colour and black and white film. In one of his pictures, a group of terrified women huddle over their children. 'Guys were about to shoot these people,' Haeberle recalled afterwards. 'I yelled "Hold it" and I shot my pictures. M16s opened up and from the corner of my eye I saw bodies falling but I did not turn to look.' The picture shows the group in close up; it is sharply focused and well composed. Another of Haeberle's pictures is of a young boy hugging his wounded younger brother. They both lie in the middle of a path leading into the far distance. The photograph has an aesthetic beauty, a lovely landscape with figures. Minutes after it was taken, as stated by the photographer himself, two G Is approached the boys and each fired a bullet into their heads to finish them off.

It is hard to believe that a group of normal young men from farms in Missouri or offices in Dallas could have behaved in such a way, but we are not concerned

opposite top: Requiem at Khe Sanh; Marines load slain comrades, Vietnam, 1970. *David Douglas Duncan.*

opposite bottom: Marines in action near Khe Sanh, Vietnam, 1970. *David Douglas Duncan.*

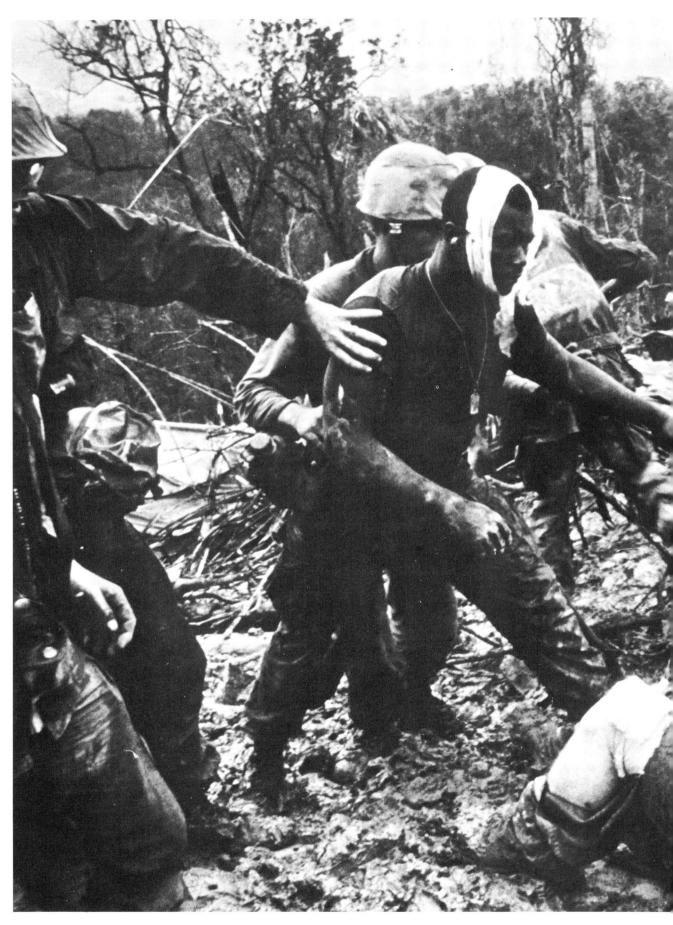

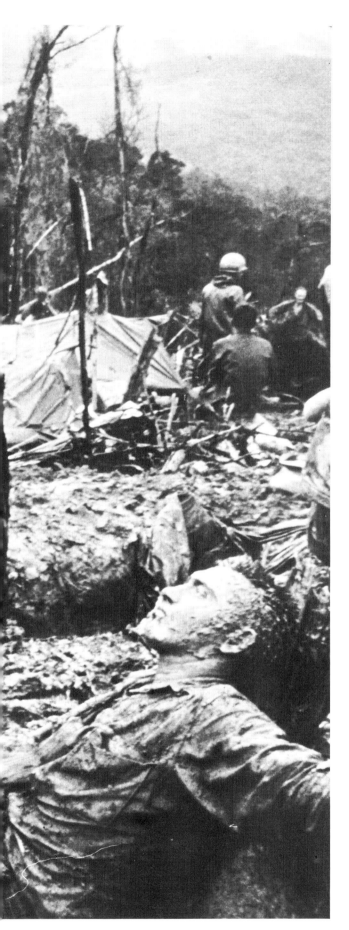

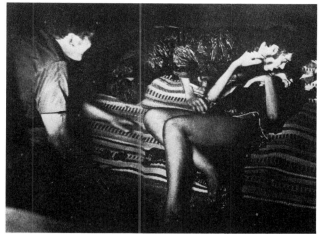

here with the moral issue of soldiers shooting women and children in cold blood. That issue has been aired sufficiently already. What we are concerned with is the extraordinary attitude of the photographer. When we read his story of this devastating half hour and his account of his own reactions while taking the pictures, we find it impossible to comprehend his actions. His pictures are gratuitous. He appears to have taken them purely for the sake of photographing an atrocity, spurred on by the hysteria of the moment. He seems to have had no thought that they could be used as an indictment of the action. On arriving back at base, he simply gave the black and white film to his army unit, and kept the colour shots. They were not made public until a year and a half later, after the details of the massacre itself had come to light.

The events at My Lai were brought to the attention of the authorities by a persistent series of letters to many prominent people in the USA, including the President, from a helicopter gunner who had heard some details of the massacre while still in Vietnam. Most of his letters remained unanswered, but Senator Morris Udall took the matter up with the result that Lieutenant Calley, the commanding officer of C Company, was eventually court-martialled. The whole matter was played down and the papers only published small items about it. The affair might have remained dead and buried, had it not been for another persistent individual, freelance reporter Seymour Hersh (who later wrote a book on the massacre). Due to his patient digging, the scandal was brought into the open and written about in a number of papers in the USA and abroad, but the truth was only completely revealed when Haeberle's pictures were discovered by a reporter from the *Cleveland Plain Dealer*. His photographs were published in the magazine on 20 November 1969 in spite of David Douglas Duncan's pleading with the

213

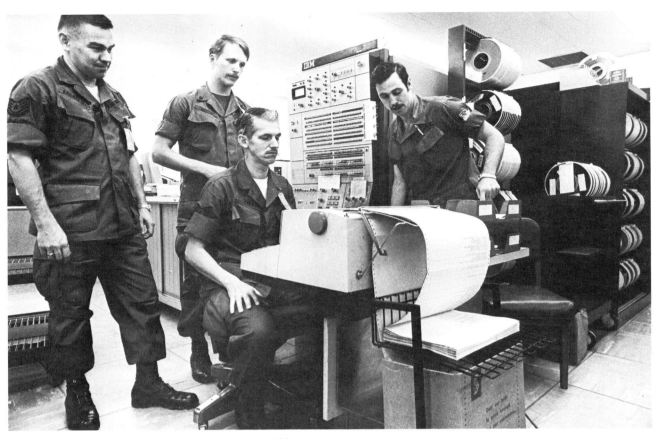

Conducting a war by computer, Vietnam, *circa* 1968.
Philip Jones Griffiths.

editors to withhold them because, so he believed, they were fakes. He also claimed that they would do a great deal of harm to the reputation of the US soldier, as, of course, they did. Later *Life* bought the pictures from Haeberle for $50 000 dollars and printed them in their issue of 19 January 1970.

Like the G Is, Haeberle seems to have undergone, through his experience of war at close quarters, a total distortion of the normal emotional and behavioural responses. The Vietnam War provided an ideal opportunity for studying the reactions of photographers to their work of photographing war. Some of their attitudes have already been discussed in the introduction. Thus, we find a total submergence of moral values in the case of Haeberle which can be compared with the partial and more gradual change that took place in Faas. The deliberate shutting out of unacceptable impressions, almost an emotional cowardice, found in Duncan can be contrasted with Burrows's compassion and distress in perpetual conflict with his loyalty to his public and the country he worked for. Finally, Griffiths displays an uncompromising disgust and revulsion with the inhumanity of men whosoever they may be. Haeberle's action seems to have stemmed from an unreasoning excitement engendered by the situation in which he found himself. Duncan's purpose was quite deliberate: to put the American marine on a pedestal, prompted by a genuine patriotism and love

for his country. Burrows survived to photograph and thereby reveal the insanity of war. Griffiths rises above them all, for he establishes and demonstrates that the evil of war is so great that it can and does deprave and warp even ordinary god-fearing men and transforms gentle boys into monsters.

Duncan, Burrows and Griffiths all produced books wholly or partially about Vietnam, Duncan's *War Without Heroes*, like his earlier *This Is War*, is divided into three acts: Cua Viet – September 1967, Con Thien – September/October 1967, and Khe Sanh – February 1968. The longer one turns the pages of this visual masterpiece, the more one becomes aware of a certain theatricality, as if Duncan were photographing a performance of a play, cut off from the rest of the world. The US marine is seen in close-up going bravely through the motions of making war on an invisible enemy.

Larry Burrows – Compassionate Photographer, which was published posthumously, is only partly devoted to Vietnam. It throbs with life and humanity. It is interesting to see the difference between an early story, 'Yankee Papa 13', which he shot near Danang in 1965 and which, like Duncan's book, is concerned with courage and fortitude (a young marine risking his life for a buddy and crying to see the futility of his actions), and Burrows's later work in Vietnam. His superb colour photographs of the fighting in the Mekong Delta in 1968 are much more pessimistic and grim. Burrows's colour work is outstanding; he achieves a curiously

214

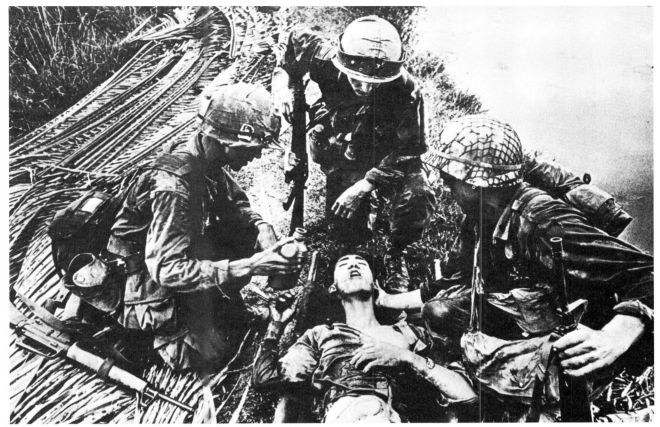

Wounded Viet Cong near Saigon, Vietnam, 1968. *Philip Jones Griffiths.*

deadened tonality of greys and greens, with an occasional vivid splash of red. There are two or three series of pictures in this book which are masterpieces of the métier, unsurpassed by anyone else. The last stories that Burrows shot in Vietnam are suffused with sadness. One is a story about a ten-year-old boy, Nguyen Lau, who had been paralysed from the waist down by a mortar fragment. He had received medical treatment for two years in the States, and his homecoming was photographed by Burrows. His rejection by his family and by his erstwhile playmates led him to leave his native village for good. Burrows's story stands as a symbol of the futility of the American involvement in Vietnam. The last shots Burrows took were of the accidental bombing of South Vietnamese soldiers by US navy planes. A hundred of them were killed – yet another symbol of failure and misunderstanding. Three days later, Burrows himself died, shot down by enemy artillery over Laos.

Many photography critics maintain that Larry Burrows was the greatest of all war photographers. For total commitment and involvement in the subject, as well as for the sheer power and beauty of his images, it would be hard to find his peer. But if we consider the medium of photography to be a supreme witness and recorder of the world and the life we have fashioned upon it, no one has photographed to better or more incisive effect than Philip Jones Griffiths. One of the finest photojournalists today (along with W. Eugene Smith), Griffiths devoted four years of his life to the creation of the definitive book on war. It is not the war which Duncan depicted (the front variety), although there is enough of that in *Vietnam Inc.* to give the book a balanced viewpoint, but a comprehensive, profound image of the totality of war, the way it affects soldier and civilian alike, the way the two become intertwined and together create the environment of a country at war. *Vietnam Inc.* is in the nature of a diary, but also a dissection of war into its various segments. Layer after layer, the facets of the war, the groups of people connected or affected by it, are uncovered and magnified under Griffiths's lens. The country, the village, its inhabitants; the American war machine, its origins, operation, constituent parts, its human element of soldiers and administrators; the interactions and relationships between the cultures of east and west, corruption, graft, drug-taking, prostitution; the degeneration of the soldiers; the misery of the people; the devastation; the slaughter. Griffiths's book has been skilfully assembled – its effect is cumulative; the visual narrative becomes sadder and grimmer as the story progresses. It begins with almost gay pictures of a beautiful, serene Vietnamese village and ends with shattering images of a shattered people, maimed or thrust into insanity by degradation and the constant fear of death. Ultimately the proud and happy Vietnamese become enchained. The book is a great documentary on war in its distressing totality.

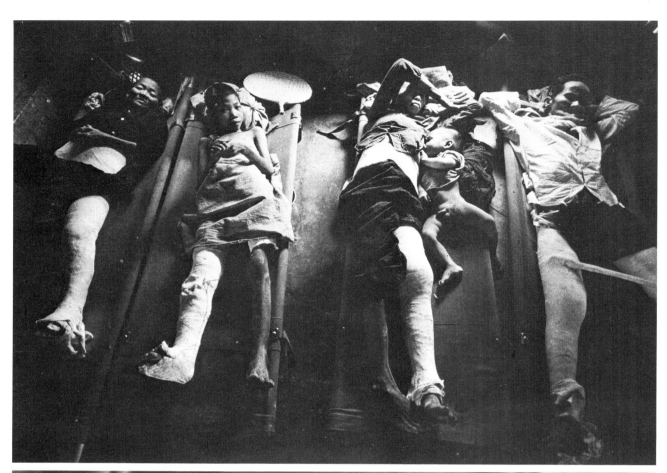

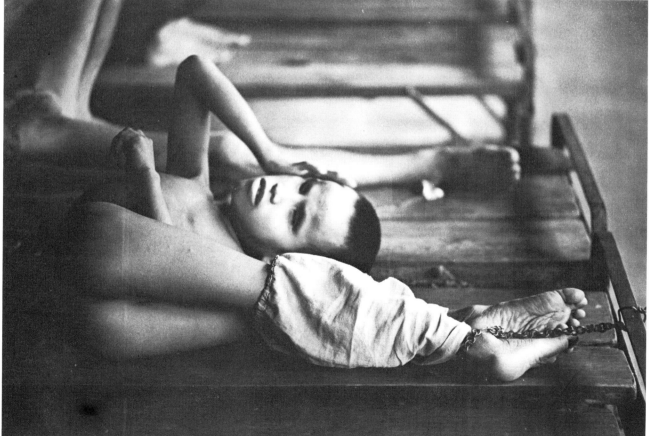

216

opposite: Vietnamese victims of American bombs. Vietnam, 1970. *Philip Jones Griffiths.*

right: Marines assaulting Hill 881, Vietnam, *circa* 1968. *Catherine Leroy.*

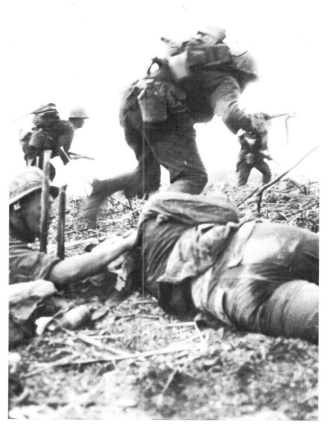

The war in South Vietnam was over-exposed and over-documented. Its effect on the North was hardly revealed. One day, perhaps, a book of pictures or a film taken by a Viet Cong photographer will emerge, but there is little indication that such photographs were taken or preserved. One Western photographer did, however, manage to get a glimpse of the adversary fighting in the South.

During the Tet offensive in 1968, the North Vietnamese for a short time occupied the city of Hue. Unaware that Hue was in enemy hands, Catherine Leroy flew there in the company of a journalist. They arrived in the evening and were able to enter the city where they spent the night in the cathedral. There were some 3000 refugees in Hue at the time and the church was full. The priest was rather taken aback at the presence of two 'whites', but did not object to their staying. They left the safety of the cathedral the following morning and, in spite of carrying a large sign with the words, in Vietnamese, 'French press from Paris', were promptly surrounded and arrested by the 'green men', who tied their hands behind their backs and confiscated their cameras. They were taken to a nearby villa and confined in the servants' quarters. Eventually, a Viet Cong officer arrived who untied them and returned their cameras. He even agreed to an interview and posed for photographs. Leroy and the journalist were later released and allowed to go back to their own side. Leroy's pictures were subsequently reproduced throughout the world.

Very few Western correspondents or photographers were allowed to visit North Vietnam itself. Two who did manage to make the trip were James Cameron and Romano Cagnoni, who thus became the first photographer to visit communist Vietnam for eleven years, since the fall of Dien Bien Phu. They travelled as freelances, paying their own fares. Lengthy negotiations were required before the North Vietnamese authorities agreed to their visit. The decision to admit them may have been influenced by the fact that both Cameron and Cagnoni professed to be ideologically uncommitted. As Cagnoni says, they favoured unification of Vietnam, rather than an American victory. They had applied for visas just after the start of the massive American bombing raids on North Vietnam in February 1965. The visas were granted in the autumn and they arrived in Hanoi in November. They stayed in the North for twenty-six days.

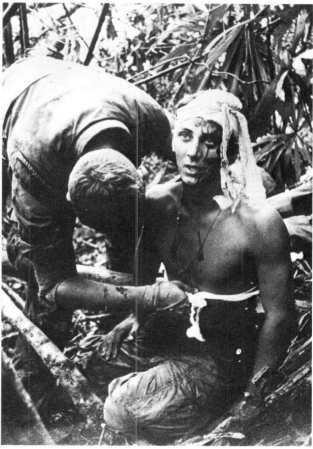

opposite: Final indignity. Mentally disturbed chained in an asylum, Vietnam, *circa* 1970. *Philip Jones Griffiths.*

right: Wounded American soldier, Vietnam, 1968. *Catherine Leroy.*

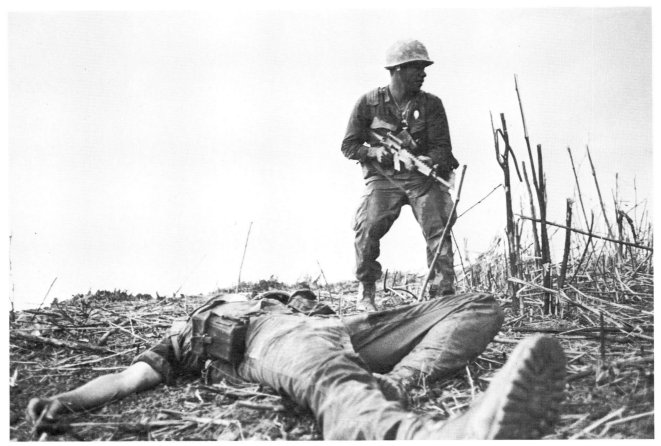

above: Marine scans hilltop for entrenched sniper who killed his comrade, Vietnam, 1968. *Catherine Leroy.*

Their visit was regarded as something of a test case by the North Vietnamese for they were the first non-communist journalists from the West. Although their tour was largely conducted and supervised, they had some freedom of movement, especially in Hanoi. Cagnoni's first ten films were confiscated; they were later returned to him half-ruined by rough processing. However, he was allowed to take the rest of his film out of the country uncensored. He does report that from time to time during his stay a 'large red hand' was raised in front of his camera to prevent him from taking a photograph. Neither Cagnoni nor Cameron were allowed to accompany units on combat missions, but Cagnoni did experience several US bombing raids which he was encouraged to photograph. His pictures were in great demand on his return to the West. *Life*, *Stern* and the *Observer* gave him extensive spreads and an exhibition of his pictures took place in London.

Cagnoni is one of the foremost of the world's photo-journalists. As a war photographer he ranks alongside Duncan, McCullin, Griffiths and Burrows. But where-as Duncan and Burrows have had their pictures prominently and regularly displayed in *Life* and

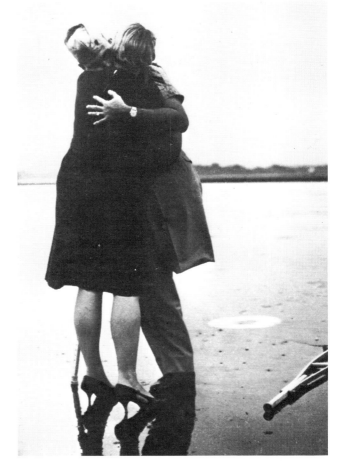

right: Marine who lost a leg in Vietnam returning home, South Dakota, 1966. *Ray Mews.*

218

McCullin in the *Sunday Times*, Cagnoni has always remained a completely independent freelance. Although his pictures have appeared in the leading magazines, including *Life*, *Stern*, *Look* and the British colour supplements, and although he is well known to the world's picture editors, his name is not so familiar to the general public. Hopefully, one day a book of his will appear to demonstrate his stature fully.

After Cameron's and Cagnoni's pioneering visit, a few other Western journalists were also invited to North Vietnam. Among them was Marc Riboud who went to Hanoi in 1968. The photographs that he took on that occasion are published in book form, entitled *Face of North Vietnam*.

The Epilogue – Cambodia

Cambodia remains, for all who visited it before 1970, an image of the Garden of Eden. Philip Jones Griffiths came to visit and photograph the people of Cambodia for the first time in 1967. He took pictures of the enchanted, half-overgrown temples, the colourful dancers, the graceful, naked children clambering on buffaloes and plunging from their backs into the clear

Only one son survived in this family during shelling of Phnom Penh by Khmer Rouge, Cambodia, 1974. *Relyveine.*

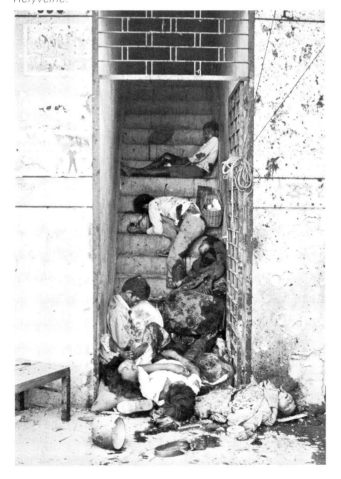

Cambodian streams. Griffiths, a burly, tough campaigner who had photographed the indignities and tragedies of Vietnam, clearly remembers being near to tears when, while framing these idyllic images in his viewfinder, he could hear the bombs falling across the border in Vietnam. One instinctively felt that this paradise was doomed. But no one could have envisaged how total the destruction and annihilation of this dream country would be.

The war in Cambodia was the natural and inevitable extension of the Vietnamese conflict. It provides us with a postscript to the fiasco of Vietnam. A happy, carefree people destroyed almost beyond repair by the uncontrollable contamination of their neighbour. It serves as a final condemnation of war itself, if there still be need for one. But in the history of war photography, it provides a curious footnote, for the photographers remained cocooned in a comfortable and pleasing environment while the war raged about them until it finally engulfed the whole country.

John Swain, a journalist with the *Sunday Times*, commuted between Saigon and Phnom Penh for five years, from 1970 until 1975 when both cities were occupied. He remembers the little colony of pressmen in Phnom Penh with affection. It was a small, closely knit community who lived in the Phnom Hotel. Some, including the photographer Francoise Demulder, were resident there from the beginning of 1973 while the Khmer Rouge roamed the surrounding country, gradually closing the trap around the city. Life in Phnom for the resident and visiting press consisted of peaceful mornings and candlelit evenings, with midday visits to the front, sometimes no more than 15 miles distant, for news and pictures. Francoise acquired a motorbike to roam the countryside within a 15-mile radius of the city. Every year, in the dry season, the Khmer Rouge would mount an offensive, and at these times additional photographers would fly in, either from Vietnam or further afield, to swell the numbers at the friendly Phnom Hotel.

Despite the illusion of comfort and ease, the danger was always present. The mid-day rides in the countryside could end in death and disaster, as many found out. Philip Jones Griffiths recalls an incident, during his third visit to Cambodia at the beginning of 1973, which very nearly cost him his life. He was shooting with some other photographers, including Christine Spengler, a battle for the recapture of a besieged temple on top of a hill less than 20 miles from Phnom Penh. They all knew that they were in a dangerous position. As Griffiths explains, there was 'a possibility of a classical case of ambush'. Through his binoculars he watched a line of government troops with an officer in the lead move down in a triangular formation to try to punch through to the temple.

'I knew,' he recalls, 'that it was sheer madness, but at the same time all the photographers realized that there would be some good pictures if and when we

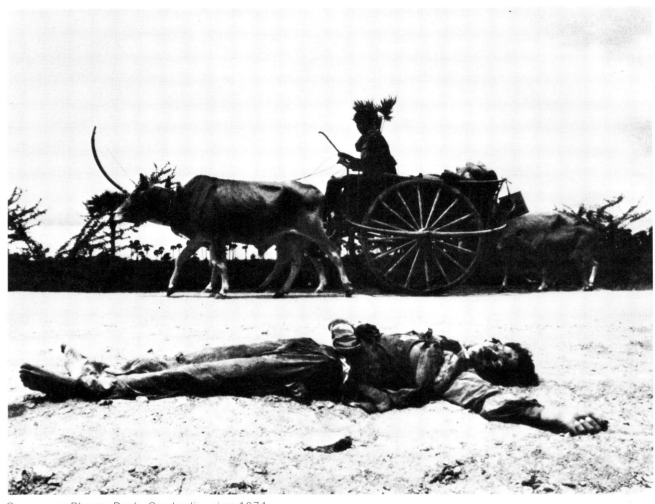

Scene near Phnom Penh, Cambodia, *circa* 1974.
Christine Spengler.

reached the temple. Starving soldiers, there were rumours that they were eating all kinds of animals, locked up for several weeks – it was too good to miss. Studying the layout, I knew that it was crazy, but I had to take a chance. So I jumped down to the road to follow the soldiers. Only one other photographer followed me – John Gemini – the others stayed behind a little.

'I stopped again and noticed that the officer had reached a lonely tree on the side of the road. He stopped for a moment in its shadow to mop up the sweat. The fool. I was in enough wars to know that a lonely tree is just the sort of landmark an artillery officer may zero his mortar into and wait for someone to come. So I stopped 20 yards short and waited; and sure enough it came. The first salvo killed the officer and several soldiers, and then the red gunners started to 'walk' the mortar nearer to us, and a few yards farther each time.

'The ground was already covered with masses of bodies. There was a drainage hole a few feet away and I pushed John and dived for it myself. I got in but he tried to push himself feet first and sat down to do it. In this fraction of a second's exposure he was hit in the back, fortunately not too seriously. To this day I don't know why I wasn't hit.

'We spent some two hours in the hole, thinking and wondering all the time what would happen if the battle failed to go to the right side and we were left there. It was quite serious, because if our soldiers retreated and left us there the Khmer Rouge would come along and pop us one. Then, assuming that our side kept firing all the time, maybe we should be able to crawl out in the night to our lines which were about two kilometres away, in which case, we might easily be shot by our own side. There was a lot of time to think on the various possibilities.

'What finally happened was that a big armoured personnel carrier tried to cross from one side of the paddy fields to the other, where two fields intersected. The Khmer Rouge popped a mortar right into it and blew it up. All these little guys jumped out on fire and screaming; they tried to roll around in the mud of the field to put out the flames, but there was not enough

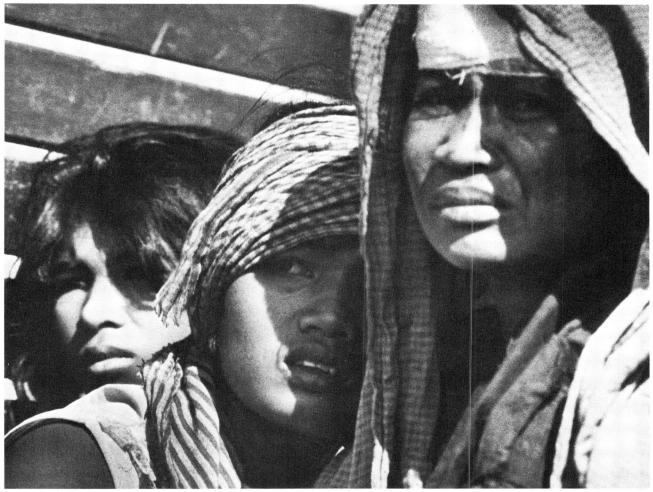

Cambodian family experiences war, Cambodia, 1974.
Romano Cagnoni.

water around. They were screaming their heads off and this had such a demoralizing effect that the order was given to retreat. We simply had to crawl out.

'I shall never know why I am still here. I was deaf from all those bullets passing my ears. I lost all my cameras, of course, and my best roll of film was completely ruined during the crawl back. It got wet, but somehow I got out.'

The roll of film was ultimately lost. In spite of detailed instructions to the French Magnum laboratory, the emulsion was ruined when the film was unrolled in a dry state instead of being soaked apart.

Phnom Penh fell in the second week of April 1975. No photographers were present when the Khmer Rouge occupied the city. The other capital of Indochina, Siagon, fell to the North Vietnamese two weeks later. Francoise Demulder was inside the palace grounds and photographed the North Vietnamese tanks breaking down the gates.

The Indochinese wars were over, at least so far as the West was concerned. Now, as these words are written, the two neighbours, who never loved each other deeply, are themselves at war. Cambodian communists supported by the Chinese fight Vietnamese communists helped by Russia. Their battle cannot be covered by Western photographers.

Conclusion

Crimea, Gettysburg, Afghanistan, Ladysmith, Passchendaele, Spain, Stalingrad, Normandy, Korea, Suez, the Congo, Bangladesh, the Tet offensive, Beirut; wars, campaigns, battles, skirmishes, ambushes; victors, victims, the dead, the mutilated – the constant elements in an unending, ever-changing kaleidoscopic show. The closer to us in time, the more vivid and savage they appear, the My Lai massacre more brutal and pointless than 'The Harvest of Death' at Gettysburg.

Is it only because the American Civil War seems so distant and the Vietnam War so close? Or is it because O'Sullivan only shows us soldiers, whereas over half the pictures from Vietnam make clear the ravages war inflicts upon the civilian population? Brady's own purpose in photographing the Civil War was to make a historical record of the war itself. The pictures taken at that time display no attitude to war, other than acceptance. No anger, outrage, no sense that what they showed could be anything other than what it was – inevitable. They were not taken to have an immediate impact; they had to be redrawn for publication and when they did appear before the public they could only reveal what had already happened in the past, not something that was part of the continuing present. The past, that was over, could not be changed.

Almost all of the Vietnam pictures shown here, however, and many thousands more, were seen by the world within days of their being taken. They were taken to be seen immediately, to have an effect, to make an impact, to move us, stir us, make us feel sickened, to engender in us a sense of outrage. They challenge the inevitability of war. When a man drinking his morning coffee over the breakfast table in his Surrey home looks at the pictures of the wounded and the dying in the most recent battle in Africa or Asia, he knows, if he stops to think about it, that the men and women in the pictures are still suffering, perhaps are still in the process of dying. He knows that he is looking at something which is part of the present, and which carries over to the future.

The photography of war developed with the growth of the illustrated press. It moved away from mere historical record; it became concerned with capturing the action of war, through the visual impact of a picture expressing the impact of war itself on those in combat. With the development of the picture essay in the illustrated magazines, war photography was able to broaden and deepen its frame of reference, concentrating not just on front-line action, but exploring the effects of war on society as a whole. That war photographers were able to widen their field of vision, to sharpen their perceptive scrutiny of the social and moral issues raised by war, has meant that, although

the importance of the illustrated magazine has declined, war photography has continued to develop.

Television has largely replaced the function of the illustrated magazine in documenting what is happening throughout the world. In this aspect, it might have been expected to replace the function of photography, and war photography in particular. This has not happened. On the contrary, war photography has responded to the challenge of television. Freed, as it were, from its former subordinate function, it has concentrated on the affective, expressive qualities of the photographic image and thus has won recognition as a fully independent medium. In this, the power and permanence of the photographic image itself are all important.

The modern still photographer with his 35-mm lightweight camera can surpass the television cameraman through the impact of the image. How many television reportages does one remember vividly in visual terms? They are transitory, seen for a few brief seconds, then gone. But a still photograph has the unique power of permanency, capturing the quintessence of a single moment. It can be returned to, looked at again and again, stored for future viewing. Each of us carries in his memory his own private collection of visual images, to be recalled, evoked by a similar image, by a single word. Some of our own private images will be those provided by the photographer, haunting and persistent pictures which will never leave us. Haunting and persistent, for beyond them what is there left to say? They are self-contained statements, summing the totality of a particular moment, the intensity of an instant held forever within the frame. Capa's 'Moment of Death', his Normandy beaches, Duncan's vacant-eyed GIs in Korea, McCullin's Biafran children, a monk burning in Vietnam, a little girl running naked in terror from a napalm bomb. Once we have seen them, we can never forget them.

As the photography of war has become more penetrating, so we choose to end this book with two selections of pictures reflecting its wider vision, its deeper concerns: pictures of civilians and children amidst the holocaust of war. And as war itself brings changes to our lives, our society, our institutions, these too are reflected in the photographs. Our final group of pictures shows the changing role played by women in war, mirroring the acceleration of their emancipation. And perhaps we can end by asking a question prompted by this change: is the right to fight alongside men in war a worthwhile victory for the feminist cause; or has their new-found freedom to engage in a man's game lost for all of us, men and women, and for our children, the hope of an even greater freedom – the hope that one day we may eventually all be free from the threat of war?

Postscript
Civilians, Children and Women

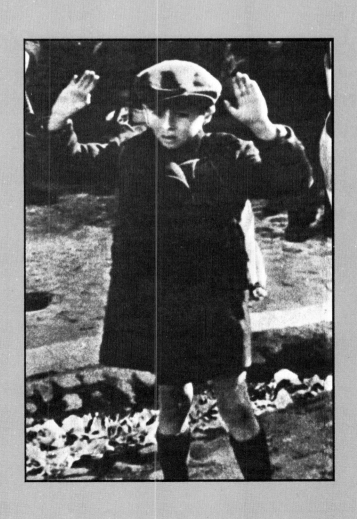

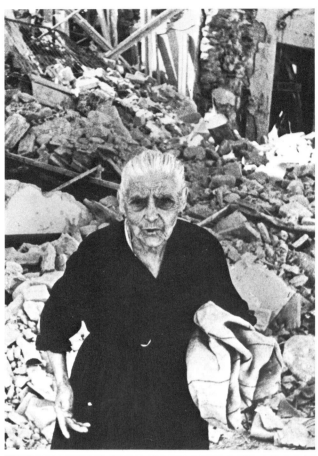

left: The only woman left in the Spanish town of Nules blown up by Franco's troops, Spain, *circa* 1937. *Photographer unknown.*

opposite top: A meal in a ruined house, Russian front, 1943. *Ivan Sagin.*

opposite bottom: A woman collaborator escorted out of town by the jeering inhabitants, France, 1944. *Robert Capa.*

below: A Polish family being taken to concentration camp, Poland, 1940. *Photographer unknown.*

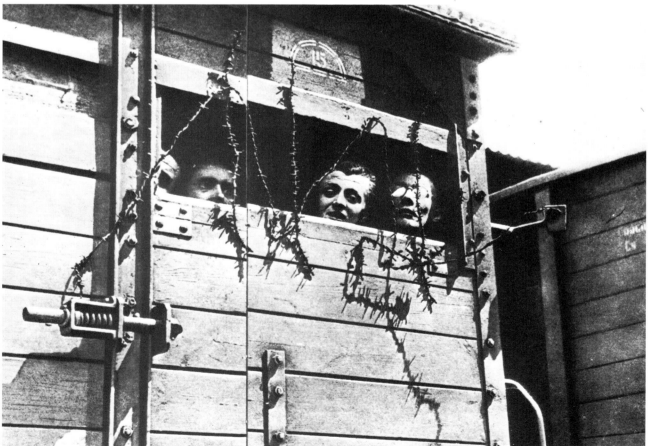

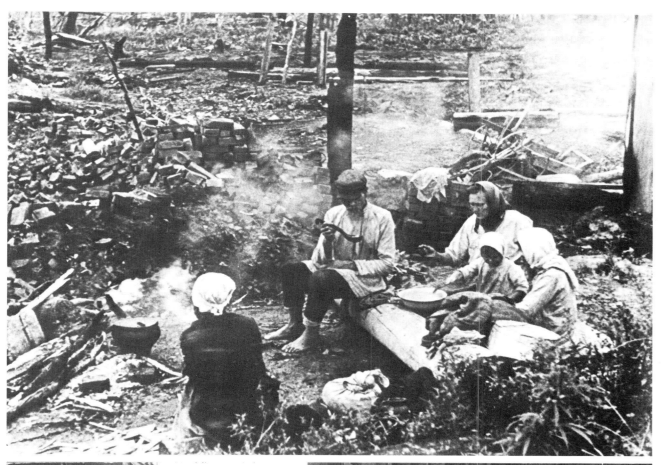

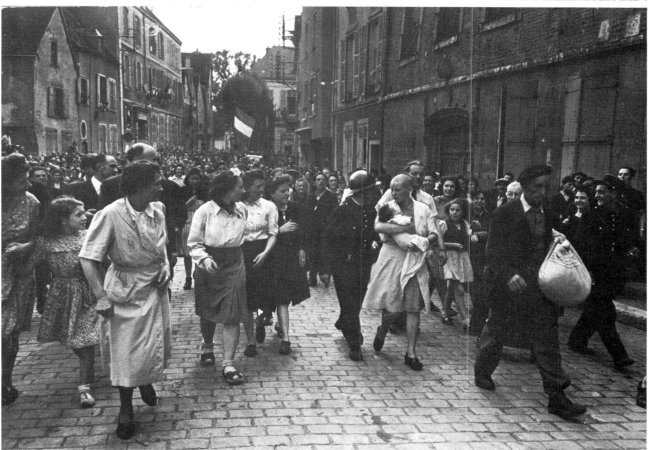

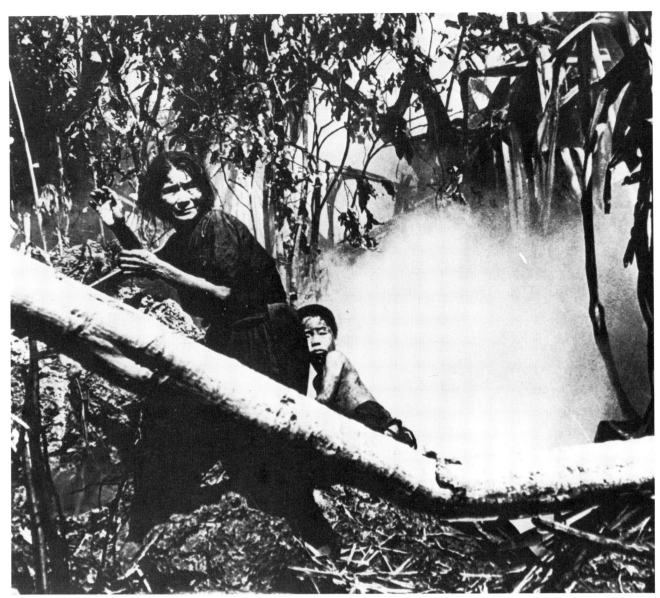

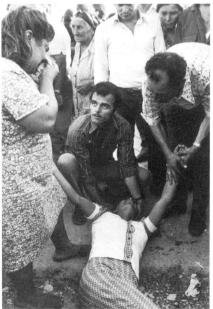

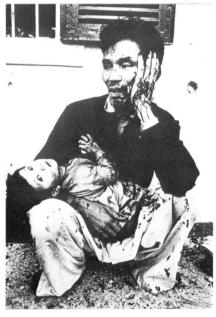

above: Terrified mother and child escape bombardment, Saipan, Pacific, 1944. *W. Eugene Smith.*

far left: Woman in despair after losing her husband, Cyprus, *circa* 1966. *Catherine Leroy.*

left: Father and daughter, Vietnam, *circa* 1968. *Don McCullin.*

opposite: Mother and child, India, *circa* 1973. *Don McCullin.*

226

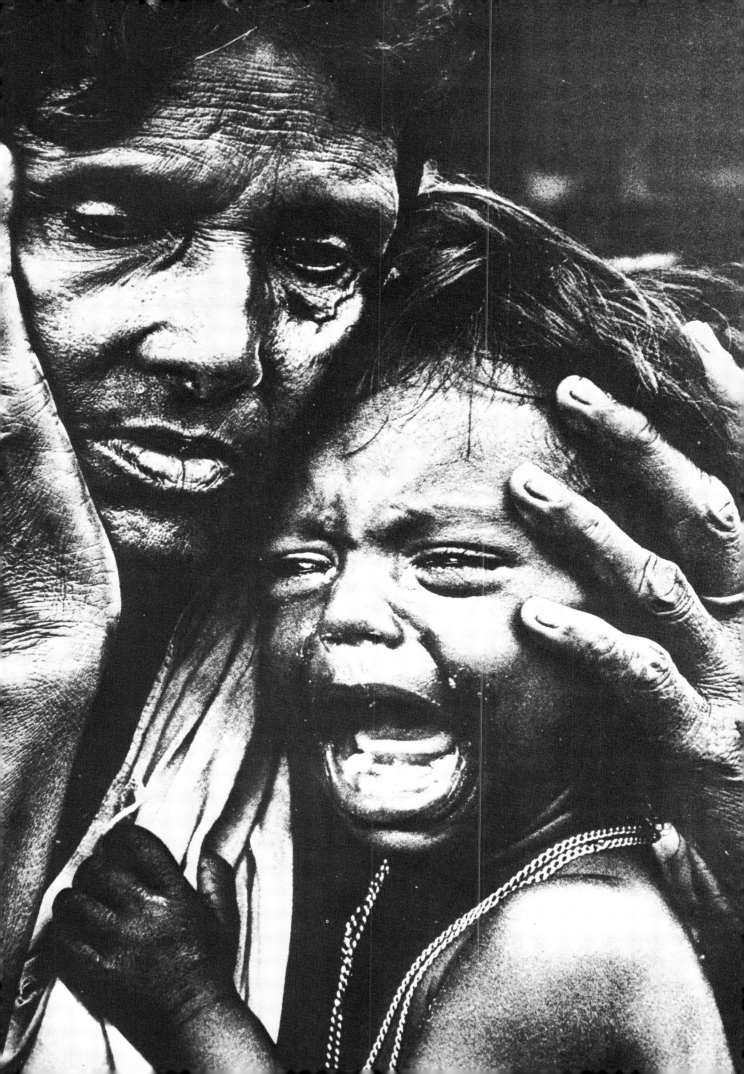

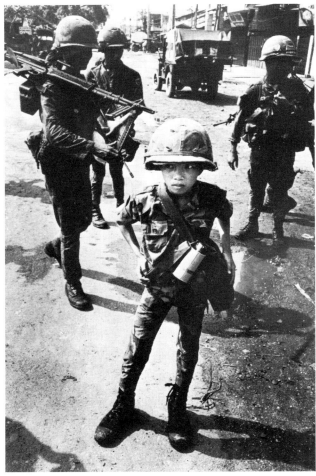

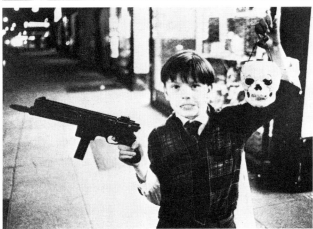

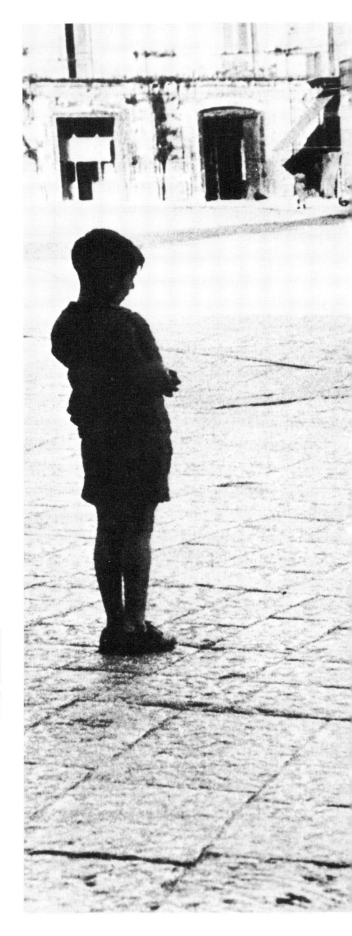

above top: Ten-year-old 'Little Tiger' praised for killing two Viet Cong women – his teacher and his mother, Vietnam, 1968. *Philip Jones Griffiths.*

above: Young Irish boy with a gun and a skull, Belfast, 1970. *Don McCullin.*

right: Children playing soldiers, Naples, 1956. *David 'Chim' Seymour.*

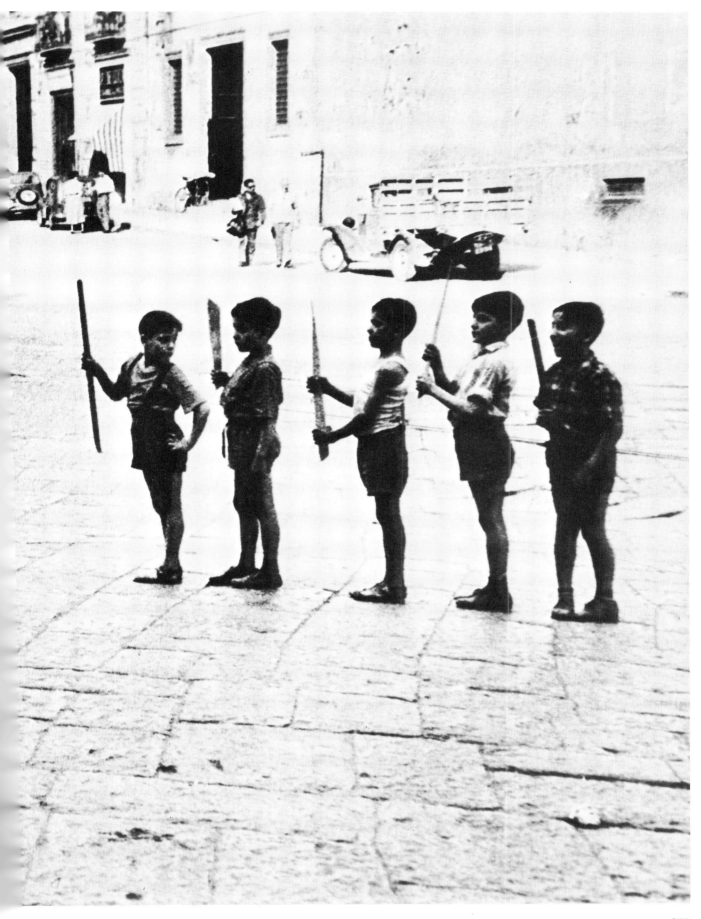

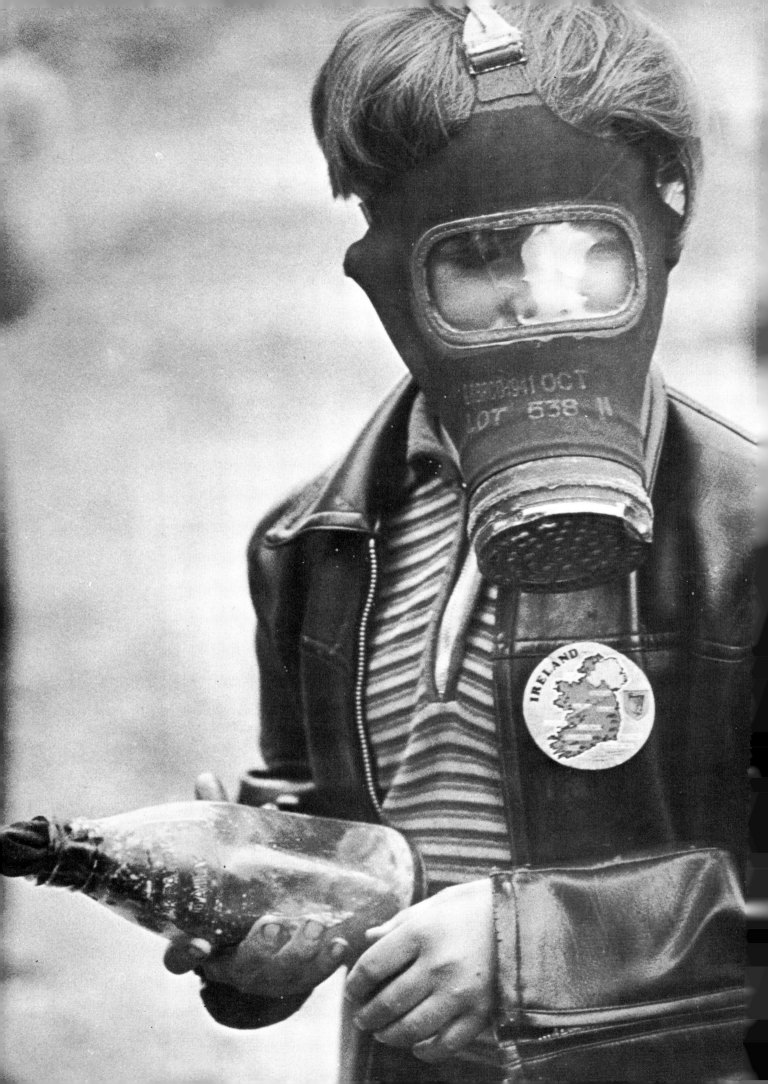

opposite: Young Irish 'bomber', Londonderry, 1969.
Clive Limpkin.

Marching out of Warsaw ghetto to death in concentration camp, Warsaw, 1940. *Photographer unknown.*

Victims of Nazis, Germany, 1945. *Galina Sankova.*

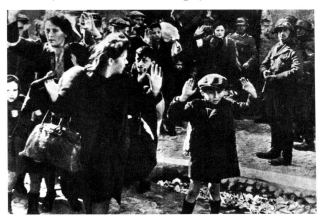

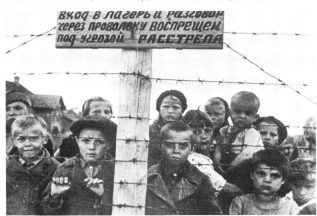

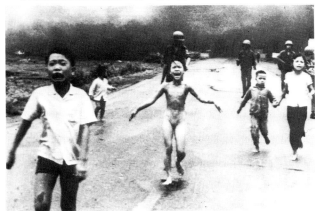

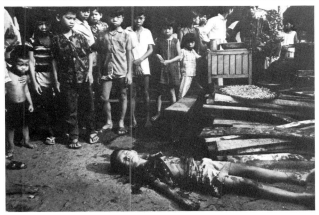

Girl accidentally napalmed by South Vietnamese planes,
Vietnam, 1972. *Nick Ut.*

First sight of death, Vietnam, 1969. *Philip Jones
Griffiths.*

231

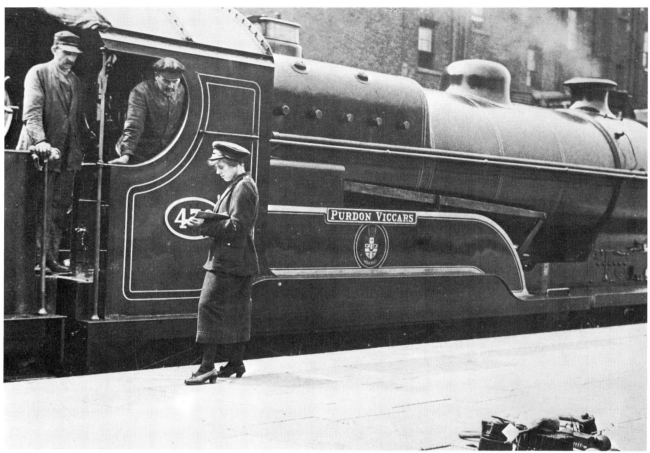

above: Woman railway worker, First World War.
Photographer unknown.

right: Women delivering coal, First World War.
Photographer unknown.

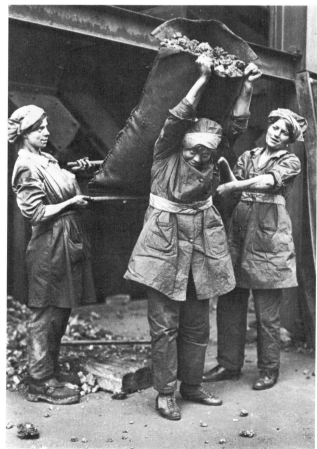

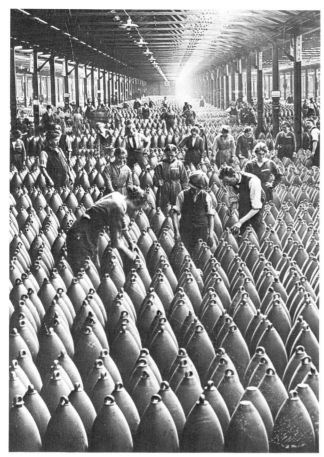

left: Workers in an ammunition factory, First World War. *Photographer unknown.*

below: Group of W A A Cs on parade, First World War. *Photographer unknown.*

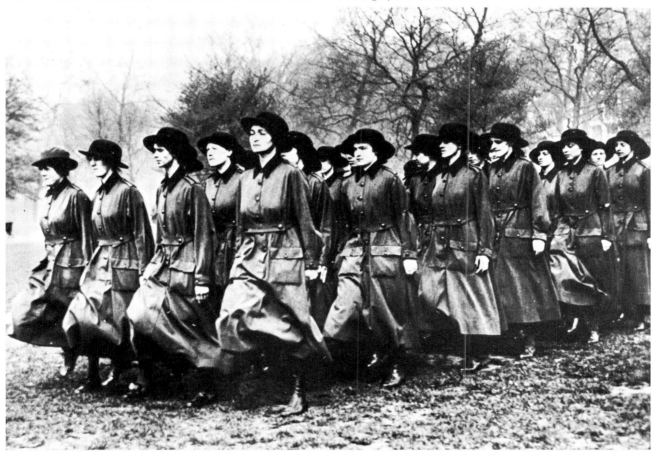

233

Contingent of female soldiers in the Russian Revolution, 1917. *Photographer unknown.*

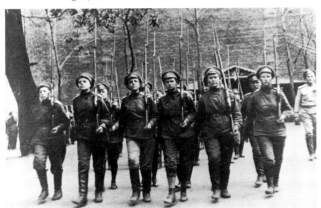

Arab female military unit, Sahara, 1977. *Joseph Filchett.*

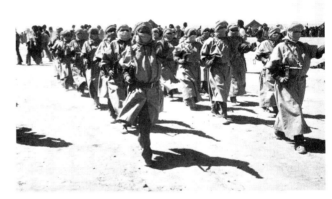

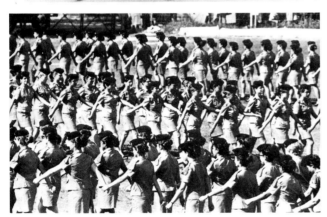

Passing-out parade of Women's Corps, Israel, 1970. *Dave Waterman.*

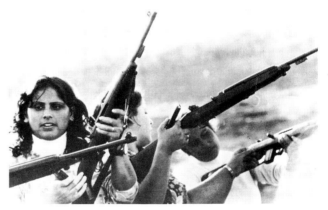

Young Israeli women taking instruction in handling of guns, Israel, 1974. *Roberto Schezen.*

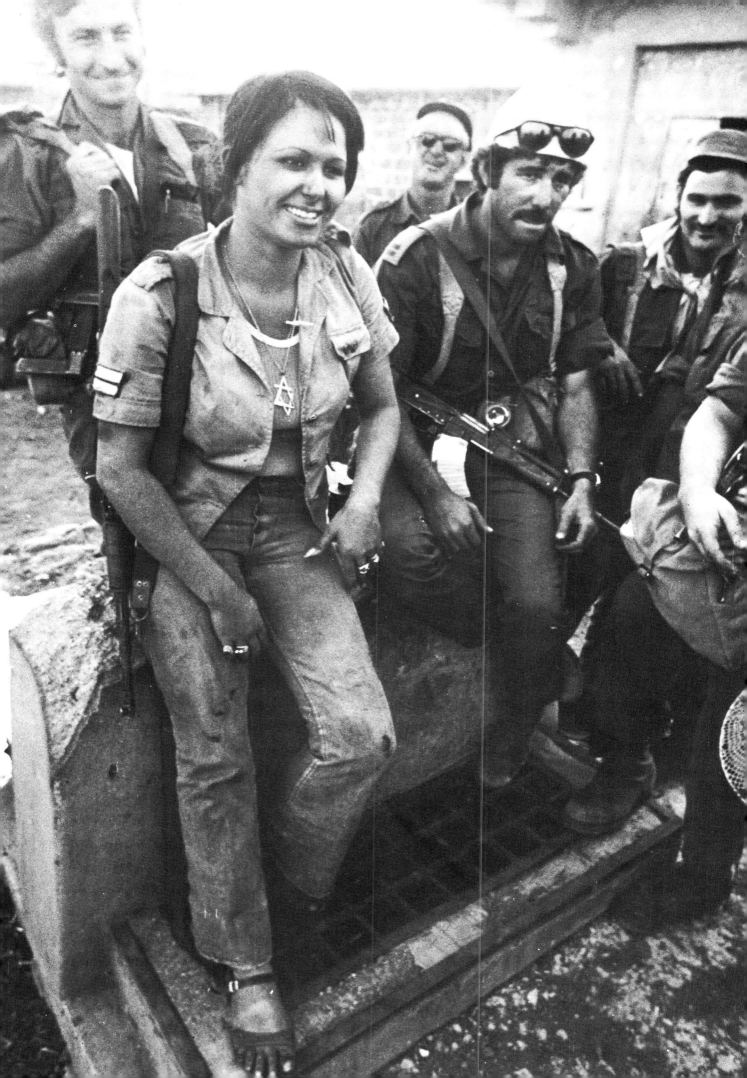

Bibliography

Michel Auer, *The Illustrated History of the Camera*, Fountain Press, 1975.

Hanson Baldwin, *Battles Lost and Won: Great Campaigns of World War II*, Hodder & Stoughton, 1966.

Herbert F. Baldwin, *A War Photographer in Thrace*, Central News Ltd, 1912.

A. J. Barker, *The Civilizing Mission: The Italo-Ethiopian War 1935–6*, Cassell, 1968.

Luigi Barzini, *La Battaglia di Mukden*, Fratelli Treves, 1907.

The Best of Life, Avon, 1975.

Margaret Bourke-White, *Portrait of Myself*, Collins, 1964.

Margaret Bourke-White, *Shooting the Russian War*, Simon & Schuster, 1943.

Leon Bramson and George W. Goethals (eds.), *War: Studies from Psychology, Sociology and Anthropology*, Basic Books, 1964.

Douglas Brown, *Doomsday 1917: The Destruction of Russia's Ruling Class*, Sidgwick & Jackson, 1975.

Larry Burrows – Compassionate Photographer, Time-Life, 1972.

Romano Cagnoni, Italian Institute of Culture, Mexico, 1976.

Robert Capa, *Images of War*, Hamlyn, 1964.

Robert Capa, *Slightly Out of Focus*, Holt, 1947.

Tim Carew, *Korea: The Commonwealth at War*, Cassell, 1967.

Cecil Carnes, *Jimmy Hare – News Photographer*, Macmillan Co., 1940.

500 Fotos de la Guerra, Prologo de Francisco de Cossio, Imprenta Castellana, Valladolid, 1937.

O. Edmund Clubb, *Twentieth Century China*, Columbia University Press, 1964.

Yves Courrière, *La Guerre d'Algerie en Images*, Arthème Fayard, 1972.

Hans Dollinger, *Die Letzten Hundert Tage*, Kurt Desch, 1965.

David Douglas Duncan, *Nomad*, Hamlyn, 1966.

David Douglas Duncan, *This Is War*, Harper, 1951.

David Douglas Duncan, *War Without Heroes*, Harper & Row, 1971.

Mark Arnold Foster, *The World at War*, Collins, 1973.

J. F. C. Fuller, *The Conduct of War: 1789–1961*, Eyre-Methuen, 1972.

Alexander Gardner, *Gardner's Photographic Sketch Book of the Civil War*, Dover, 1959.

Helmut and Alison Gernsheim, *Roger Fenton*, Arno Press, 1973.

Golden Jubilee Book of the Daily Mail – 1896–1946, Associated Newspapers Ltd, 1946.

Robert Goldston, *The Civil War in Spain*, Phoenix House, 1967.

Philip Jones Griffiths, *Vietnam Inc.*, Collier-Macmillan, 1972.

John Hannavy, *Roger Fenton of Crimble Hall*, Gordon Fraser, 1975.

Bert Hardy: Photojournalist, Gordon Fraser, 1975.

Liddell Hart, *History of the Second World War*, Pan, 1970.

Robert Debs Heinl, *Victory at High Tide*, Leo Cooper, 1972.

Robert E. Hood, *Twelve at War*, Putnam, 1967.

Tom Hopkinson (ed.), *Picture Post – 1938–50*, Penguin Books, 1970.

Robert Hunt and Tom Hartman (eds.), *Swastika at War*, Futura, 1975.

Philip Knightley, *The First Casualty*, André Deutsch, 1975.

H. Edward Knoblaugh, *Correspondent in Spain*, Sheed & Ward, 1937.

R. Scot Liddell, *On the Russian Front*, Simpkin, Marshall, Hamilton, Kent, 1916.

Clive Limpkin, *The Battle of Bogside*, Penguin Books, 1972.

Andrew de Lory, Interview with Philip Jones Griffiths, *British Journal of Photography Annual*, 1975.

Don McCullin, *The Destruction Business*, Opengate Books, 1971.

Don McCullin, *Is Anyone Taking Any Notice?*, MIT Press, 1973.

S. L. Mayer (ed.), *Signal – Hitler's Wartime Picture Magazine*, Prentice-Hall, 1976.

Roy Meredith, *Mr Lincoln's Camera Man: M. B. Brady*, Dover, 1976.

Allan A. Michie, *The Invasion of Europe*, Allen & Unwin, 1965.

Boris Mollo, *The British Army from Old Photographs*, Dent, 1976.

Daniela Mrazkova and Vladimir Remes, *Fotografovali Valku*, Odeon, 1975.

Daniela Mrazkova and Vladimir Remes, *The Russian Front: 1941–1945*, Cape, 1978.

Edgar O'Ballance, *The Algerian Insurrection – 1954–62*, Faber & Faber, 1967.

Marc Riboud, *Face of North Vietnam* (text by Philippe Devillers), Holt, Reinhart & Winston, 1970.

George Rodger, *Red Moon Rising*, Cresset Press, 1943.

George Rodger, Introduction by Inge Bondi, Gordon Fraser, 1975.

W. Eugene Smith, Aperture, 1969.

Graham Storey, *Reuter's Century: 1851–1951*, Max Parrish, 1951.

The Great Themes, Time-Life Library of Photography, 1970–72.

John Sweettenham, *Canada and the First World War*, Ryerson Press, 1969.

Robert Taft, *Photography and the American Scene*, Dover, 1964.

P. H. F. Tovey, *Action with a Clic*, Jenkins, 1940.

Wilfrid Pym Trotter, *The Royal Navy in Old Photographs*, Dent, 1975.

Clark Worswick and Ainslie Embree, *The Last Empire: Photographs in British India – 1855–1911*, Gordon Fraser, 1976.

Photographic Acknowledgements

The publisher and the author would like to thank and acknowledge the following sources and institutions:

Alexander Bernfes Collection
Associated Press
Camera Press
The Central Press Photos Limited
Gamma Press
Imperial War Museum
Keystone Press
Library of Congress
Life Picture Service—Colorific
Mauritius Verlag
Magnum Photos
Mansell Collection
The National Photographic Collection of Canada
National Army Museum
Observer Limited
Planet Agency
Paris Match
Popperfoto
Radio Times Hulton Picture Library
Rex Features Limited
The Royal Photographic Society Collection
The Ridge Press Inc.
Sunday Times
Stern/Pix Features

Index

Entries that appear in italics refer directly to photographs.